STUDIES IN THE ANTHROPOLOGY OF PLAY:

PAPERS IN MEMORY OF B. ALLAN TINDALL

****

Proceedings from the Second Annual Meeting of the Association for the Anthropological Study of Play

****

edited by Phillips Stevens, Jr.

Leisure Press
P.O. Box 3
West Point, N.Y. 10996

****

A publication of Leisure Press
P.O. Box 3, West Point, N.Y. 10996

ISBN 0-91843809-8

Cover drawing by David Frederick, supplied by the Audio-Visual Service, Miami University, Oxford, Ohio.

Dedication

Bruce Allan Tindall
1943-1976

"He was born with the gift of laughter,
and a sense that the world is mad."
—Sabatini

The Association for the Anthropological Study of Play was shocked and deeply saddened at the death of its President, Dr. B. Allan Tindall, of cancer, on July 7, 1976. Though fully aware of the severity of his illness, and under heavy medication throughout, he actively presided over the Annual Meeting in Atlanta at which most of the papers in this volume were first presented. His death occurred only three months after that meeting. It is to his memory that all the papers here assembled are respectfully dedicated.

The present structure of the Association bears Allan's stamp. He was elected President-Elect at the Inaugural Meetings in London, Ontario, in April 1974. Shortly thereafter he drafted, single-handed, the Constitution, a comprehensive document which has been only slightly amended since. In

1975 he became President, to serve for two years. Throughout this time he worked tirelessly for the Association. With his colleagues at the State University of New York at Buffalo he had developed a method of observational analysis, and thereafter he dedicated himself to the task of persuading physical educators of the necessity of recognizing the *cultural* factor in sports and in such concepts as "physical fitness", "leisure", and "recreation". Even though heavily burdened by the knowledge and, increasingly, the pain, of his illness, he actively publicized our efforts, represented us at meetings of other professional organizations, and kept a firm hand on the activities of the far-flung members of the Executive Council, all while conducting several research projects simultaneously, writing, teaching a heavy course load at Berkeley, and caring diligently and lovingly for his family. Even right up to his death, his strength, vigor, vitality, and sense of humor were truly inspirational. Those who attended the Atlanta meetings will remember him appearing at one sesson wearing a T-shirt with the legend, "Title IX is Fine". Of him it could truly be said that he knew the meaning of play. He had that rare gift, so lacking in our time, of the ability to *combine* play with earnest. In his opening line of *Scaramouche,* Rafael Sabatini could have been referring to Allan Tindall. He is, and will continue to be, sorely missed. Let the Association be his monument, and let us dedicate ourselves to the ideals for which he stood.

Allan graduated from Mountain View High School in California in 1960. He studied physical education at Brigham Young University and at San Jose State College (B.A., 1968). He received his M.A. in physical education at the University of California at Berkeley in 1969, and his Ph.D. in anthropology and education from that institution in 1973. His dissertation dealt with the cultural premises underlying the game of basketball as played by Utes and Mormons in Utah.

He graduated with Honors and received the Leadership Award from the 7th Army NCO Academy, Bad Toltz, West Germany, in 1962. He was a Deans Scholar at Foothill Junior College where he spent one year before transferring to San Jose State College, where he was also a Deans Scholar. He received Honors in Physical Education at San Jose State in 1968, was named Alternate Fellow at Berkeley, 1968-69, and was awarded an NIMH Predoctoral Fellowship, 1969-72.

He served three years with the Army Corps of Engineers, 1960-63, attaining the rank of sergeant. He was a Research Associate in the Center for Studies of Cultural Transmission, State University of New York at Buffalo, 1972-73, and the next year he became Assistant Professor in the Department of Anthropology. From September 1974 he had been Assistant Professor in the Department of Physical Education at Berkeley.

He was a member of the Council on Anthropology and Education, and served as Secretary-Treasurer of its Committee on Cognitive and Linguistic

Studies, 1974-75. He was an Associate of *Current Anthropology.* He was a Fellow of the American Anthropological Association and the Society for Applied Anthropology.

Between 1970 and 1976 he presented no fewer than 18 papers at professional meetings, perhaps the most notable being his position paper, "Questions about Physical Education, Skill and Life-Time Leisure Sports Participation", written on behalf of TAASP for the UNESCO-sponsored First International Conference of Ministers and Senior Officials Responsible for Physical Education and Sport for Youth, April, 1976. He had organized and was to have presented a paper at a symposium for the Annual Meetings of the American Anthropological Association in November, 1976. Several other projects on which he was working will remain unfinished.

Allan is survived by his wife Gail, and their children, Karen and Brian.

His bibliography of published works, and items in press at the time this volume was being prepared, appears below.

Bibliography of B. Allan Tindall

1970 with C. W. Eckhoff and B. K. Cobb, "Toward an Optimum Articulation between the Anthropological Research Community and Educational Researchers." In Frederick O. Gearing, ed., *Training Anthropologists for Educational Research.* U.S. Office of Education.

1973 with Frederick O. Gearing, "Anthropological Studies of the Educational Process." In B. J. Siegel, ed., *Annual Review of Anthropology.* Palo Alto: Annual Reviews, Inc.

1974a with Wayne D. Hughes, *Annual Report of the Project in Ethnography and Education.* U.S. Office of Education.

1974b *Teaching as a Linguistic Process in Cultural Context.* Report of the National Institute of Education Conference on Studies in Teaching. N.L. Gage, ed.

1974c ed. with Wayne D. Hughes, *Improving Observational Skills for Better Understanding.* SUNY at Buffalo; The Project in Ethnography and Education.

1974d "Understanding a Situation." In Tindall and Hughes, eds.

1974e "Observation as a Continuing Process." In Tindall and Hughes, eds.

1975a "Ethnography and the Hidden Curriculum in Sport." *Behavorial and Social Science Teacher, 2 (2).*

1975b with Frederick O. Gearing, Allen Smith, and Thomas Carroll, "Structures of Censorship, Usually Inadvertent: Studies in a Cultural Theory of Education." Council on Anthropology and Education Quarterly, May.

1975c "The Cultural Transmission Function of Physical Education." *Council on Anthropology and Education Quarterly,* May.

1976a ed., with David F. Lancy, *The Anthropological Study of Play: Problems and Prospects.* Proceedings of the First Annual Meeting of The Association for the Anthropological Study of Play. Cornwall, N.Y.: Leisure Press.

1976b "Theory in the Study of Cultural Transmission." In B.J. Siegel, ed., *Annual Review of Anthropology.* Palo Alto: Annual Reviews, Inc.

n.d. "Organizing Physical Education for Change: an Anthropological Perspective." In M. Marie Hart, ed., *Sport in the Socio-Cultural Process.* 2nd ed. Dubuque: W. C. Brown (in press).

n.d. "The Potential Value in the Anthropological Analysis of Sport." in M. Marie Hart, ed. (in press).

n.d. "A General Cultural Theory of Education." In Frederick O. Gearing and Lucinda Sangree, eds., *Toward a General Cultural Theory of Education.* World Anthropology series. The Hague: Mouton (in press).

Preface

The Association for the Anthropological Study of Play has come a long way in the four years of its existence. Since its founding in 1974 it has regularly published a quarterly Newsletter, and herein we offer our second volume of Proceedings, mostly selected papers presented at the Second Annual Meeting in Atlanta, March 31-April 3, 1976; three of the papers included here appeared first in the Newsletter. The first Proceedings, also published by Leisure Press, appeared in 1976 as *The Anthropological Study of Play: Problems and Prospects,* David F. Lancy and B. Allan Tindall, eds.

This book is divided into five sections of articles, followed by an Appendix containing a comprehensive bibliography very kindly assembled for this volume by Helen Schwartzman. As Editor, I have written brief introductions to three of the sections, those which contain papers volunteered individually for the Meeting. But I have felt a bit uncomfortable doing this, as I do not consider it the Editor's role to abstract papers submitted by others; too often the summary is read instead of the paper itself, and too often the author's main points may have been unintentionally obscured or misrepresented by a biased or careless Editor. Therefore I have kept such "Editor's Introductions" brief and I should, hopefully unnecessarily, advise the reader that they are *not* to be considered as substitutes for the papers themselves! Two of the sections, II and IV, contain papers presented in symposia specially convened for the Meeting, and my job has been made easier by Kendall Blanchard and Brian Sutton-Smith, organizers of these symposia, who provided their own introductions.

This volume is presented as a memorial to Dr. B. Allan Tindall, whose tragic death occurred on July 7, 1977. The foregoing Dedication to Allan offers some general remarks on behalf of the Association; I want to take a brief moment to offer a personal sentiment. I might very possibly not be a member of the Association, most certainly not its President, had it not been for Allan. It was only at his gentle but persuasive insistence—and his offer of transportation—that I attended the Inaugural Meetings at the University of Western Ontario, London, April 1974. And similarly, he paid for more than half the cost of the hotel room we shared in San Francisco during the annual meeting of the American Anthropological Association in 1975, just so that I could afford to attend and participate in a symposium he had organized. It was he who got me fascinated with the study of play, and it was he who helped me to see some neglected areas in this field of study. He was a personal friend, to me and to my wife and children, and we share with his family, Gail, Karen, and Brian, a deep sense of personal loss.

I should include a word about the cover. Its theme, a playful poke at scholarship, is entirely appropriate to a volume compiled in memory of Allan Tindall, principally because it reflects his own unique combination of humor with scholarship. But it is appropriate also because it was designed for the cover of the program of the meeting at which Allan assumed the Presidency of the Association; the combined meetings of TAASP, the American Ethnological Society, and the Central States Anthropological Society, in Detroit, April 1975. The drawing is by David Frederick, and it was freely given to the Association by the Audio-Visual Service of Miami University, Oxford, Ohio; William L. King, Director. It may very well become the Association's logo. We are extremely grateful to the artist and the donors.

The papers in this volume were selected by an *ad hoc* Editorial Board consisting of myself as Chairman, and Maxwell Howell of San Diego State University and Allen Sack of the University of New Haven. I am grateful to them for their great assistance in selecting and suggesting revisions in these papers. I am also grateful to Kendall Blanchard and Brian Sutton-Smith for providing introductions to their sections, and to Helen Schwartzman for providing the Appendix. Finally, heartfelt gratitude is expressed to Dr. James Peterson, Director of the Leisure Press who, sharing my sentiments for Allan Tindall, has ventured to publish these papers.

P.S., Jr.
Buffalo, N.Y.
July, 1977

Contents

Dedication: B. Allan Tindall 3
Preface 7
I. ASPECTS OF SPORTS AND GAMES
Editor's Introduction 11
Goddesses as the Patronesses of Sport Activities in Ancient Mediterranean Mythologies, *George Eisen* 11
Meterological Play-Forms of the Eastern Woodlands, *Michael A. Salter* 16
Anal Linguists, Cry Your "I's" Out: Constructing a Metaphor of Poker, *Susan H. Boyd* 28
Fun and Games in an Urban Setting: Black Children's Games, *Annette Rosenstiel* 34
II. CULTURAL DIMENSIONS OF RECREATION AND LEISURE
Introduction, *Kendall Blanchard* 40
The Cultural Component in Physical Fitness, *Kendall Blanchard* 42
The Cultural Ramifications of Recreation in Belfast, North Ireland, *Mary R. Duncan* 49
From Play to Recreation: The Acceptance of Leisure in the United States, 1880-1930, *Bernard Mergen* 55
A Paleoanthropological Approach to Recreation and Sporting Behaviors, *Steven J. Fox* 65
III. ETHNOLOGICAL STUDIES OF CHILDREN'S PLAY
Editor's Introduction 71
From Javanese to Dani: The Translation of a Game, *Karl G. Heider* 72
Attitudes toward Play among Filipino Children of Negroes Oriental, Philippines, *Janice Ann Beran* 81
Vertigo and Social Structure: Notes on Hausa Children's Play, *Harold Olofson* 88
Some Functions of Aymara Games and Play, *Andrew W. Miracle, Jr.* 98
Research on Children's Play: An Overview, and Some Predictions, *Helen B. Schwartzman* 105
IV. STRUCTURAL APPROACHES TO PLAY
Introduction, *Brian Sutton-Smith* 116
A Proppian Approach to the Analysis of Children's Fantasy Narratives, *Gilbert J. Botvin* 122
The Society and Geography of the Story World, *Daniel H. Mahony* 133
A Developmental Analysis of the Trickster from Folklore, *David Abrams* 145
Structural Parallels in Dreams and Narratives: Development/Sex Differences in Dreams and Stories of Girls and Boys, *M'Lou Caring* . . . 155

Cognitive Structure of Sports Tactics: A Preliminary Investigation, *Thomas R. Stevens* 175

V. THEORETICAL CONSIDERATIONS IN THE STUDY OF PLAY

Editor's Introduction 185

Sport: Play or Work?, *Allen L. Sack* 186

The Development of Play in Childhood: An Application of the Classifications of Piaget and Caillois in Developmental Research, *Elizabeth C. Mouledoux* 196

The Imaginary Playmate and Other Imaginary Figures of Childhood, *Ernestine H. Thompson and Tanya F. Johnson* 210

Towards an Anthropology of Play, *Brian Sutton-Smith* 222

Play as Adaptive Potentiation: A Footnote to the 1976 Keynote Address, *Brian Sutton-Smith* 232

Laying the Groundwork for an Anthropology of Play, *Phillips Stevens, Jr.* 237

APPENDIX

Works on Play: A Bibliography, *Helen B. Schwartzman* 250

I. ASPECTS OF SPORTS AND GAMES

Editor's Introduction

The papers in this section discuss aspects of sports and games in both historic and contemporary settings.

Both George Eisen and Michael Salter discuss supernatural sanctions for sporting and gaming activities. Eisen shows how details in certain Mediterranean mythologies laid the foundations for sports which persist today, while Salter illustrates how, among tribes of the Eastern Woodlands of North America, the main purpose of certain games was to influence the supernatural agencies that controlled the weather.

As an unusual but delightful change of pace, Susan Boyd's contribution offers some interesting insights into a symbolic framework underlying the behavior of poker players.

Annette Rosenstiel, in her analysis of urban black children's games, goes beyond one traditional interpretation, play-as-preparation-for-adult-social-roles, and urges the consideration of specific socio-economic factors as they contribute to and are manifested in game behavior.

GODDESSES AS THE PATRONESSES OF SPORT ACTIVITIES IN ANCIENT MEDITERRANEAN MYTHOLOGIES

George Eisen, University of Maryland

Traditions of sports and competitive games that are alive and flourishing in our day, although often overlaid with modern concepts, are rooted in the ritualistic celebrations of remote times. Brailsford, who studied the Elizabethan period of England, remarked that, "It is not, of course, to argue that the modern forms of games have made dependence on these original sources...The deep, forgotten roots of primitive ritual could still give a strength to later manifestations of the game when reliance on more superficial motives alone might not have been able to sustain it."[1]

The time focus of Brailsford's study, of course, did not permit him to explore in depth this area of investigation. Other scholars have argued likewise for the religious-magical origin of sports and competitive games, but such scholars have merely suggested in general terms that such an association exists. This casual approach to the seminal religious-mythological root of contemporary sports may, in part, explain the tendency of scholars to direct their intellectual energies toward more recent problems.[2]

In the waters of the untapped reservoir of information about the rise and origin of sports, the mythologies of Mediterranean cultures stand out conspicously. Durkheim wrote of mythology that, "The traditions whose memory it perpetuates express the way in which society represents man and the world..."[3] Trencsenyi-Waldpfel supported this notion by stating that, "Although it [mythology] originated within religion, nevertheless mythology generated the first definitions and explanations of the phenomena of nature and society."[4] It is the intent of this paper, therefore, to focus on the mythological background of sports and physical activities, with particular emphasis upon the association of goddesses with sports.

The most familiar examples of such an association are readily at hand in Greek mythology in which goddesses were regarded as inventors of as well as participants in sports. Mythological heroines including Atalanta and others, and of course the fierce Amazons, are remembered as outstanding sportswomen. Greek mythological accounts, however, were not the earliest to attribute sport participation to goddesses. References to mythological physical activities, in Egyptian as well as in Mesopotamian civilizations, predated by millenia the Greek religious legends. Among the deities of Egyptian religion, the lion-goddess Bast was a war goddess in general and was associated intimately with archery. Her relationship to archery was well illustrated by late Greek accounts which compared her to Artemis. Herodotus observed that the Bastian cult was associated also with dancing.[5] Warlike goddesses populated the Eyptian heaven. Neith, for instance, was an ancient goddess of hunting whose cultic sign, a shield and crossed arrows, suggest her association with war and with hunting as well. Sekhet, another divine huntress, was connected with activities of the chase: fowling, fishing, and hunting. Inscriptions found on the murals of Middle Kingdom tombs frequently alluded to her as the "Mistress of Sport."[6]

Proponents of other sport activities were also represented in the divine pantheon of Egyptian religion. For example, swimming was overseen by the goddess Wadjet, and her divine titles included such tributes as "Goddess of Swimming", and "Lady of Power".[7] Dancing and acrobatics were the domain of the fertility goddess Hathor, a universal mother goddess. Greeks have identified her with Aphrodite. In her honor, so Herodotus tell us, dances and acrobatic exercises were presented by priestesses.[8] One should not overlook a subtle consistency that Egyptian beliefs shared with other Mediterranean religions. It was frequently evidenced that several goddesses shared patronage over similar activities in different locations. For instance, the goddess Bast, in addition to being a war goddess, acquired some of the characteristics of other goddesses, serving also as the goddess of joy, music and dancing.

More conspicuous examples are manifested in Babylonian mythology. The Semitic myths were derivative of the religious heritage of the Sumerians; in fact, certain Babylonian myths are quite clearly adaptations, if not simple translations, of Sumerian versions.[9] The discovery of texts in Ras Shamra

(Syria) has provided us with the muths of the fierce warlike goddess Anat. Anat is depicted by the tablets as fighting and massacring warriors, knee-deep in blood as she adds to the pile of heads. Her bellicose nature explains why the victorious Pharoahs of the XIXth Dynasty adopted her as a goddess of Egypt. The Egyptians adopted, too, another Semitic goddess who greatly resembled Anat, the horsewoman Astarte. She, whom we recall from the Old Testament as Astoreth (in plural form—Ashtaroth) or Ishtar, was a goddess of love and fecundity. Notwithstanding her peaceful nature, she was also associated with war and hunting, and Egyptian artifacts often portrayed her naked upon a cantering horse. She served not only as the patroness of horses, but also as the goddess of riding and chariot driving. Her titles included "Strong on the Horse", and "Mistress of Chariots and Horses".[10]

The Minoan civilization of the Aegean, although it did not leave literary references, provided an abundance of hints about the association of the Great Goddess and physical activities. Both Evans and Woody characterized the Cretan Goddess as "Our Lady of Sports".[11]

Sports, in Minoan life occupied an eminent place and were under the patronage of the goddess. Minoan seals, figurines and frescoes illustrate her status, indeed as huntress, archer, toreador, and charioteer. In her capacity as "Mistress of Animals" she was closely associated with hunting.[12] The Goddess' image as huntress was reflected in the numerous artifacts in which she resembles Dyctinna or Artemis, accompanied by wild animals. The acrobats of the bull-ring may have performed their dangerous ceremonial feats in honor of this goddess. All these facts are familiar to contemporary scholars; however, there are some Cretan artifacts which have been overlooked by sport historians and anthropologists. In them, a more obscure feature of the Minoan Goddess is revealed. She is, as Evans identifies her, the "Lady of the Sea".[13] One seal, in fact, shows the goddess floating or swimming on the waves. Several gold signet rings portray the goddess as boating and rowing.[14] The conception of the Minoan goddess as the protectress of swimming and boating was often emphasized in Minoan art, as much of the life of the Minoan revolved around the sea.

The religious ideas of the Minoan civilization may have had some influence upon Greek mythology. There were several goddesses in the Greek culture as well who were considered patronesses of physical pursuits. The case of the goddess Artemis illustrates such an association. She was generally thought to be the goddess of hunting, and often was alluded to by Homer as the "Queen of the Chase".[15] However, there are some less-widely known attributes of this goddess which are significant for scholars. Ancient beliefs indicate that Artemis was also connected with horse-racing, as referred to by the Athenian dramatist Euripides in *Hippolytus:*

Artemis, queen of the ocean main
Queen of the racing-grounds.[16]

This passage has been interpreted by Butler[17] to mean that the best of all courses for horse racing were located on the sea shore, and that Artemis was the patroness of these races. The war-Goddess Athena was also believed to be a protectress of horseback riding. According to legend, she gave the first bridle to the Greek hero Bellerophon, leading to the first use of horses for riding.[18]

Mythology relates Athena to other sport activities as well. (Puzzling as it may seem, Greek mythology related the origin of the sport of wrestling to the goddess Athena.) Her strong links with physical pursuits is well illustrated by Homer. The poet described her manipulations in the *Funeral Games for Patroclus,* when she assisted Diomedes in the chariot race.[19] Odysseus, the hero of Homer, prays for the help of Athena in the foot race:

> Odysseus prayed quick in his heart to blue-eyes Athena:
> "O goddess, hear me, and come put more speed in my feet!"
> Such was his prayer, and Pallas Athena, hearing,
> Lightened his legs and feet and arms.[20]

Female divinities, in general, appear often in ancient art, mounted upon chariots or horseback. Artemis, Aurora, and Selene are represented in this manner. The Amazons, to be sure, are frequently pictured on horseback, riding like warriors. Interestingly, the titles of the fertility goddess Hera alluded to chariot driving. She was venerated at Lebadea as the "Charioteer", and "Holder of the Reins"; names that might have referred to her riding in her golden chariot.[21] The ancient historian, Pausanias' description of the Heraean Festivals, in honor of the goddess Hera, no doubt, is an historical account and therefore goes beyond the scope of this paper.[22] However, the role of Hera as the venerated goddess who oversees the foot races of Greek maidens in quest of fertility should be remembered.

The range of physical pursuits which were connected with mythical heroines would not be complete without mention of the goddess Ino Leucothea and the famous sportswoman Atalanta. Homer informs us that Odysseus, although a strong swimmer, was saved by Ino Leucothea, the sea goddess, who threw her headscarf to the drowning hero.

> Then she gave him the veil and back like a gull she
> plunged in the swollen sea to vanish amid the dark
> waves.[23]

Atalanta was said to excel in sports. Indeed, hunting, running, and wrestling were beloved pastimes of this mythical personage. The legends commemorating her feats in sport activities are too numerous to recount here. However, she never lost a foot race, so the myth testifies, to any man; when finally her future husband beat her in the race, it was accomplished only by the tricky manipulation of Aphrodite.

Greek mythology went as far as to attribute even the discovery of the ball itself to a goddess. It is said that Adrastea, a nymph of Crete to whose care

Rhea had entrusted the child Zeus, made a heavenly ball for him in the Idean cave of Crete.[24] Apparently to ease the boredom of babysitting, the goddess taught the infant Zeus to play with the ball.

In conclusion, one may observe that although in the mythologies of the Mediterranean societies gods and goddesses were equally represented in most areas of life, goddesses were predominant in physical pursuits. It is curious to find that myths such as those described above flourished in a male-oriented society such as that of the Greeks. What is the historical-anthropological significance of this phenomenon?

First, almost all goddesses connected with sport activities were also associated with fertility. This point is perhaps singularly significant, since it seems that the ancient cultures of the Mediterranean, in their early stages, worshipped a universal mother-goddess. This supreme deity, through an evolutionary religious development, assumed various roles including patronesses of physical activities. Moreover, Mediterranean cultures, agricultural in nature, retained traces of an early matriarchal system. This primordial heritage was reflected also in the mythological beliefs of these ancient peoples.

FOOTNOTES

[1]Dennis Brailsford, *Sport and Society, Elisabeth to Anne,* (Toronto: University of Toronto, Press, 1969), p. 58.

[2]Of course one should not fail to mention the important pioneer works of Culin, *Games of the Orient,* (Rutland: Charles E. Tuttle Co., Inc., 1960); R.W. Henderson, *Ball, Bat and Bishop,* (New York: Rockport Press, Inc., 1947); and Uriel Simri, "The Religious Magical Functions of Ball Games in Various Cultures", Ph.D. dissertation, University of West Virginia, 1967.

[3]Emile Durkheim, *The Elementary Forms of the Religious Life,* Trans. by J.W. Swain, (New York: The Free Press, 1965), p. 420.

[4]Imre Trencsenyi-Waldpfel, *Mitologia,* (Budapest, Kossuth Nyomda, 1963), p. 18. (Translated by author)

[5]*Herodotus, The History of,* Trans. B. Perrin, (New York: Appleton, 1893).

[6]Percy Newberry, *Beni Hasan,* (London: Egypt Exploration Fund, 1893-94), vol 2, p. 53; col 1, p. 45.

[7]A.D. Touny and Steffen Wenig, *Sport in Ancient Egypt,* (Leipzig: Offizin Andersen Nexoe, 1969) p. 76; Veronica Ions, *Egyptian Mythology,* (New York: Hamlyn House, 1968)), p. 91.

[8]A.C. Mace, "Hathor Dances," *Journal of Egyptian Archeology,* 6 (1906):297.

[9]van de Walle, B. "Egypt, Syncretism and State Religion," in *World Mythology.* Edited by Pierre Grimal, (New York: Hamlyn House, 1973), p. 63.

[10]Touny, *Sport in Ancient Times,* p. 49, 175; She was worshipped in Egypt from the mid-Eighteenth Dynasty onwards.

[11]Arthur Evans, The Palace of Minos at Knossos, (New York: Biblio & Tannen, 1964), vol 4, pp. 28-35; Thomas Woody, *Life and Education in Early Societies,* (New York: Macmillan, 1949), p. 206.

[12]E.O. James, *The Cult of the Mother Goddess,* (London: Thomas & Hudson, 1959), p. 137.

[13]Evans, *The Palace of Minos...,* vol 4, p. 956.

[14]Ibid. figs. 142, 917, 919, 920, 923, 925, 926.

[15]Homer, *Iliad,* Trans. Ennis Rees, (New York: Random House, 1963), XXI. *The Odyssey,* Trans. Ennis Rees, (New York: Random House, 1960), Vi. pp. 102-106.

[16]Euripides, *Four Plays of,* Trans. A.T. Murray, (Stanford: Stanford University Press, 1930, 215-222; 228-231).

[17]A.J. Butler and D. Litt, *Sport in Classic Times,* (London: Ernest Benn Ltd., 1930), p. 25.
[18]Edith Hamilton, *Mythology,* (New York: Mentor Books, 1969), pp. 134-37.
[19]Homer, *Iliad,* p. 473.
[21]Ibid., p. 486, see also *Odyssey,* pp. 123; 98.
[22]Pausanias, *Description of Greece,* Trans. W.H. Jones, (Cambridge: Harvard University Press, 1966), X. 34:3.
[22]Ibid., VI. xx. 9; V. xvi 1.
[23]Homer, *Odyssey,* p. 89.
[24]Trenscenyi-Waldpfel, *Mitologia,* p. 98.

METEOROLOGICAL PLAY-FORMS OF THE EASTERN WOODLANDS

Michael A. Salter, University of Windsor

This study, historical in nature, focuses on the agrarian-based peoples of North America's Eastern Woodlands.[1] The purpose of the paper is to investigate the relationships that existed between certain games and one aspect of the metaphysical environment—that associated with climatic change.

The natives of this area faced numerous hardships in the course of their day-to-day living. Some, such as sickness and war, could to a limited extent be contained or avoided. Adverse conditions, however, were beyond their direct control. In an aboriginal setting the very survival of an agrarian group was, to a large extent, directly related to the vagaries of the weather. During the summer, frosts and periods of excessive heat or drought always posed a threat to the crops, the products of which even when successful were barely sufficient to sustain a community through the ensuing harsh winter months. Blizzards not only made living unpleasant but, particularly among the more northern tribes, effectively prevented them from foraging for the supplies necessary to supplement their ever meager and always dwindling food reserves.

While it is to be suspected that some individuals, notably the shamans, possessed a certain level of meteorological understanding, the average native attributed the behaviour of the elements to the actions of specific supernatural entities within their respective pantheons. Therefore, it is understandable that as the Indian possessed no direct means of climatic control, he would endeavour to obtain his objectives indirectly by appealing to and appeasing these metaphysical beings. This resulted in a complex of rituals revolving around celestial bodies and elements of the weather.

In most cases the entities involved were believed to be, like their worshippers, extremely fond of games. Indeed, some of them were thought to have acquired their eminent position as a result of, or during the course of a game. A Caddoan myth serves to illustrate: it speaks of two brothers who began to play the hoop and pole game. After several days of competition the younger brother failed to hit the wheel with his missile, whereupon it continued to roll beyond the designated play-area. Following a series of hair-raising adventures, the brothers succeeded in spearing the wheel and ultimately ascended to the sky-world as the spirits, Thunder and Lightning (Dorsey 1905:31-36). As associations of this nature are by no means rare within Indian mythology, it is not surprising to find that some play-forms possessed climatic overtones and served as focal points around which certain meteorological ceremonies revolved.

The peoples of the Six Nations[2] used lacrosse as a means of influencing the elements. They played the game as part of their Thunder Ceremony in order to bring about those climatic conditions necessary to facilitate the growth of their crops. They scheduled the Thunder Ceremony whenever precipitation was required and rarely more than once a year. The most favourable condition for staging the ceremony occurred when the sound of thunder could be heard in the west (Tooker 1970:34)!

The ceremony was scheduled and conducted by the males to implore the Thunderers—seven old men with vast supernatural powers—to bring rain, to control the winds and to continue their warfare against pestilential creatures, both natural and preternatural. The Iroquois referred to the Seven Thunderers as their "Grandfathers" and viewed them as benevolent agents of the Great Spirit. It was believed that in addition to protecting mankind from evil, they were obligated to use the winds and rain to cleanse the earth. For these services, thanksgiving prayers were offered during the Midwinter Festival. However, unlike the Midwinter Festival, the Thunder Ceremony was directed primarily toward the Seven Thunderers.[3]

The ceremony consisted of a tobacco invocation, a dance and a game of lacrosse. As "...lacrosse is the game which supernaturals play in the thunderhead, the lightning bolt their ball" (Eyman 1964:19), the game was considered the principal rite of the Thunder Ceremony. The speaker appointed to direct the proceedings began by offering prayers and tobacco to the Great Spirit and to the Seven Thunderers. The occasion and the import of the game was next explained to the players who were instructed to be in good spirits while playing, to play fairly and to avoid causing unnecessary injury. Naturally malicious sentiments were considered out of place in a game contested for the supernatural.

The athletes, who had undergone a period of fasting prior to the contest, were administered an emetic "to clean them out" just before taking the field. Practices such as these were believed to "purify" the individual and accompanied the majority of those rituals directed towards the more prominent members in their pantheon.

The game was contested by seven old men and a like number of young men selected from opposing moieties. Thus the contest was viewed as being played between the Seven Thunderers and their children. It was characterized by few rules, little violence, and considerable emphasis on skill and speed. Although seven goals were required to win, the outcome was of no significance, at least in terms of the ritual. The ceremonial importance of the game lay in its symbolic representation of the "...conflict between life and death, good and evil, hope and despair", as well as the eternal "...warfare between the thunderers and their enemies, the under-earth deities" (Speck and General 1949: 117). That these dichotomies were reflected in the teams is reinforced by Eyman's (1964:18) observation that the seven older players personified the seven thunder gods—and presumably "life", "good" and "hope".

In another sense the outcome was important, as gambling was commonly associated with the game. Certainly those natives with material items at stake must have displayed more than a passing interest in the result. Although betting was not considered a part of the rite, it "...was never reprobated by their religious teachers, but on the contrary rather encouraged" (Morgan 1954: 281-282). Thus it was not viewed as sacrilegious and hence did not interfere with the ceremony's raison d'etre. Indeed, it was quasi-religious in nature in-so-far as the wagers increased the potency of the rite. It was believed that the more competitive the game the more acceptable it would be to the supernatural. What better way to foster competition than to encourage gambling on the part of the spectators and participants?

It is of interest to note that the number seven, a number sacred to the Iroquois and already mentioned in relation to the number of players on each team and the number of goals required to conclude the game, occurs again in conjunction with the playing field. The field itself varied in length and possessed no side boundaries. At each end of the playing area two posts were set into the ground, seven paces apart. These posts were said to "reach the sky". The distance between the posts and the concept of their height symbolized respectively, the seven deities to whom the game was dedicated, and a physical link between them and those involved in the ritual.

Following the game, the players entered the longhouse singing and dancing, to be joined by any male spectator who so desired. The ceremony was concluded inside with additional dancing, prayers of thanksgiving and the distribution of tobacco and corn mush[4] to the players. That the Iroquois obviously had faith in the ceremony's ability to bring about a desired weather change is apparent from the emphatic statment of a native informant: "...as soon as the lacrosse game is over, rain comes, even if there have been no previous signs of a rainstorm" (Shimony 1961: 164).

Lacrosse was similarly used by other peoples for purposes of environmental control. We have record of the Huron, for example, playing the game on the advice of a shaman, in an attempt to avert adverse weather conditions. Le Mercier (1898: 47) recalls that during May of 1637, just prior to the planting season, the inhabitants of several villages "...tired themselves to death [on the playing field, in the belief that]...the weather depended only upon a game of crosse". Like many of the games employed for mortuary, fertility and medicinal purposes (for further information on these games see Salter (1972, 1973, 1974), the spirit in which this activity was contested was undoubtedly of greater importance in terms of the ritual than was the actual outcome.

Despite the fact that the temperature dropped and some six inches of snow fell several days after this particular contest, the natives remained firm in their conviction that lacrosse was an effective agent of climatic control. This faith indicates that the game had undoubtedly been used for similar purposes in the past and would be so employed again when the need arose. Although the shaman's reputation obviously suffered on this occasion, native belief in the ritual points to a considerable degree of past success on the part of the Huron medicine-men in predicting short-range weather conditions.

Another Iroquois ceremony deserves consideration at this point. This ritual, dedicated to the two major celestial bodies—the moon and the sun[5]—served as an occasion during which the people were able to express gratitude for the warmth emanating from the sun and at the same time to request favourable growing conditions and fine weather for their crops. As such, it was more closely related to certain supplicatory/thanksgiving rites than it was to weather control and will not be fully developed here. What is of interest, however, is that while some tribes such as the Cayuga and the Onondaga scheduled and celebrated the ceremony in the spring by itself, others had absorbed elements of the ritual into their Thunder Ceremony.

One such group was the Seneca who, during times of drought, conducted a rite in honor of the Sun and the Seven Thunderers. This ceremony commenced with a tobacco invocation to the Sun and a plea from the shaman requesting "our old brother, the Sun" (Fenton 1936: 8) not to burn the crops. These preliminaries were followed by a game of hoop and pole (Tooker 1970: 34). The game was contested by two teams made up of players from opposing moieties. It seems likely that as the sun and the moon were believed to compete against each other in the game, and as the moon was also considered responsible for the success of the crops, the teams probably represented these two entities. Thus, on this occasion, the game of hoop and pole may be viewed as a symbolic contest between the two. Certainly, as the moon and sun were believed to derive pleasure from watching the game, it was played in their honor and constituted part of an overall attempt to promote more favourable weather conditions. Although a description of the game as it was played in conjunction with the Seneca Thunder Ceremony is unavailable, it is known that the "Sun" was permitted to roll the hoop first—a roll that had to travel towards the west.[6] If the symbolic association is correct, then it is understandable why victory was considered unimportant, for defeat of the "Moon" by the "Sun" or vice versa, could conceivably jeopardize the ritual. Following the contest, a second tobacco invocation was made, this time to the Thunderers. The ceremony concluded indoors with dancing and a series of individual supplications directed toward the Thunderers and the Sun.

One important element appears to be absent from the Seneca Thunder Ceremony; that element being a rite to produce rain—unless, of course, the post-game invocation and prayers were considered sufficient. Shimony (1961: 163), however, appears to supply the answer when she notes that the Seneca, like the other Iroquoian tribes, always played lacrosse as part of this ritual. Unfortunately, she does not elaborate, nor does she mention the game of hoop and pole. It is questionable, therefore, whether both lacrosse and hoop and pole were contested as part of the one ceremony or in fact constituted the major rites of two separate, but related, ceremonies.

The Arkansas or Quapaw, linguistically related to the tribes of the Huron and Iroquois Confederacies, were split into two major tribal divisions. One division—"the Earth people"—was responsible for the physical well-being of the tribe, while the responsibilities of the other section—"the Sky people"—lay primarily with the supernatural welfare of the populace. Cooperation between the two groups was thus believed to be essential if the society were to survive physically and spiritually.

One of these cooperative ventures revolved around a game somewhat resembling shinny. This game was originally contested between two teams of young men chosen respectively from "the Earth people" and "the Sky people". As in the Seneca hoop and pole game, the players were considered to represent the principal entities involved in the ritual—in this case, the earth and the sky. The contest was formally opened by a representative of the Wind clan—a subdivision of "the Earth people". Even when played socially, the honour of commencing the game was bestowed on any member of this group present. In the ritualistic version of the game, a large circle-enclosed-cross was scratched in centre-field. The ball, having been placed in the centre, was first rolled towards the north along the line drawn to the edge of the circle, and then back on the same line to the centre. This procedure was repeated along the eastern arm of the cross, the southern arm and finally along the western arm, until the ball again rested in the centre of the circle. The individual entrusted with this task next tossed the ball into the air and struck it, to begin the more vigorous part of the rite.

The game was said to have had cosmic significance in reference to the winds and the earth; "...the initial movement of the ball [around the cross] referred to the winds, the bringers of life" (Fletcher and La Flesche 1911: 198), the mid-field circle symbolized the earth. Whether the ritual was also an attempt to promote rain is unclear, although the relationship between wind and rain was an extremely close one within the cosmological framework of many Eastern Woodland tribes. (The Thunderers of the Iroquois, for example, were believed to control both these elements.) The north-south orientation of the field seems to indicate that the sun did not occupy a significant place in the rite. In any event, there is no doubt that the ceremony was used as an attempt to influence the weather.

Shinny was played on social occasions although only by the males; men and boys competing separately. The ritualistic version was exclusively an adult-male game. While large wagers were common when the men played socially, it is not certain that this was the case on other occasions. If gambling were associated with the ceremonial game, then there may have been considerable emphasis on victory. It is more likely, however, that in the same way as the Iroquois were able to separate the materialistic and spiritualistic aspects of their ceremonial lacrosse matches, so too were they separated in this game. On the basis of the tribes previously discussed, it seems probably that in terms of the ritual, these people also placed greater emphasis on the spirit in which shinny was contested than they did on the eventual outcome.

Two other Arkansas pastimes deserve brief mention. It has been observed that whip-tops were only played with during the winter months. The climatic association is interesting, although whether it resulted from seasonal taboos, as was the case with the ring and pin, and stick games of the Delaware, or the simple fact that ice served as an ideal base upon which to spin these toys, is questionable. The second activity is in many ways remarkably similar to contemporary Hallowe'en practices. Masked boys circulated throughout the community issuing a "trick or treat" ultimatum to selected elders. Although Fletcher and La Flesche (1911: 370) refer to this as a "sport", it seems to be ritualistic in character, particularly as the practice only occurred "in the spring, after the thunder had sounded..." The fact, too, that lightning and thunder were symbolized both in the apparel and behavior of the youngsters, seems to support this. Whatever ceremonial connections there may have been are lost; however, the amusement does appear to have had climatic overtones.

Before proceeding, it should be emphasized that the societies previously referred to—the Huron, Iroquois, Caddo, and Arkansas—were all linguistically related. On the other hand, the tribal group to be discussed below was a member of a different linguistic phylum, a fact that bears remembering when considering the underlying rationale and believed outcomes of these climatic rites.

On the basis of existing evidence, only two Delaware games appear to have had climatic associations. One of these was a pastime that closely resembled the Caucasian game of pick-up sticks. A player dropped some sixty-five grass straws onto a blanket and, using a hooked quill, attempted to remove as many as possible from the cluster without disturbing the others. Each separated straw contributed, according to its individual value, to the contestant's point-total. The game was terminated when one of the players had achieved the total previously agreed upon. The game of "scattering straws" was played by men and women, either together or separately, and usually involved gambling (Speck 1937: 104-6). Like this game, the game of ring and pin was also an adult indoor gambling game. The principal item employed consisted of a number of hollow animal bones attached by a piece of string to a sharpened stick or bone. The object of the game was to swing the bones through the air and impale as many as possible on the stick. As in the game of straws, the contest concluded when a predetermined point-total had been reached by one of the competitors (Brinton 1890: 186).

The interesting thing about these two games is that both could only be played during the winter months and participation in them was restricted to those individuals who had been born during that season (Flannery 1939: 88). It was commonly thought that a breach of these conditions would bring about bad luck, assumedly in the form of sickness. However, the climatic association went further than this as the Delaware believed that blizzard conditions would automatically follow the playing of each game. Despite this belief, these games continued to be played. The question as to why the Delaware participated in activities that were thought to create unpleasant conditions is perplexing. However, if one adopts the belief that there is only so much inclement weather that one can be subjected to in an agricultural year, this practice then becomes understandable; for by playing these games during the winter months, the chances of adverse weather occurring during spring (planting season) and summer (growing season) may be decreased. In any event, it would appear that the games were vestiges of earlier rituals conducted in honour of those believed to control the elements. The resultant storms were thus regarded as the means by which these entities acknowledged the ceremony and the ensuing harsh weather was viewed more as a spiritual blessing than as an undesirable event.

Thus, the games of the Delaware differed in several respects from those of the other tribes viewed in this paper. In the first place, the Huron, Iroquois, and Arkansas employed vigorous team games in a standardized ceremonial setting, as devices to influence or control the weather.[7] The Delaware games, on the other hand, individualistic and sedentary in nature, do not appear at the time of their recording to have been conducted as part of a standard ritual. Further, while the games of the other cultures were used to produce positive results by averting inclement weather and/or by promoting favourable climatic conditions, the Delaware believed that the playing of certain games would inevitably result in adverse weather. These differences have a direct linguistic relationship. This would seem to suggest that although cultural artifacts may transgress linguistic boundaries basically unchanged,[8] the ideologies associated with the artifacts, particularly if they relate to the metaphysical, may not diffuse as readily.

In summary, it is apparent that the survival of any agrarian-based society is largely dependent upon the whims of the elements. This was certainly the case with the basically sedentary peoples of eastern North American who relied solely on their summer harvest and the available local game to tide them over the winter months. As extended periods of heat and drought, snap frosts, violent storms and the like, could rapidly decimate the economic base of a tribe, it is little wonder that the natives did all in their power to prevent such disasters.

Knowing the elements to be beyond the control of mere mortals, these Indians sought to exert some degree of influence through a variety of rituals directed toward the supernatural. Among the Iroquois, Huron and Arkansas, games frequently served as the principle rites in these ceremonies. Some, like the bowl game, were employed in conjunction with major annual ceremonies such as the Midwinter Festival (Blau 1967: 35-36). While possessing climatic overtones, they were, however, more in the nature of thanksgiving rites than agents of change. Any effects stemming from these rituals were of the long-term variety. On the other hand, the play-forms previously discussed, when contested under certain conditions, were all believed capable of promoting rapid environmental change. The accompanying Table and Figure attempt to outline, in a diagramatic fashion, the interrelationships among these games, the supernatural, and climatic change. Thus, such activities as hoop and pole, lacrosse and shinny were played on a needs basis in honour of the thunder, the lightning, the moon, the sun and/or the wind, on the assumption that positive weather changes would result. Failure of these changes to materialize was attributed to incorrect ritualistic procedure and could be rectified by conducting the ceremony again. Other activities, such as the ring and pin and straw games of the Delaware, and possibly the whip-top contests of the Arkansas, were associated with the negative weather conditions. More specifically, these six games were believed: 1) to promote rain; 2) to temper the winds; 3) to avert inclement weather; 4) to terminate periods of excessive heat, and/or 5) to result in adverse weather. Native faith in this cause-effect relationship suggests a considerable degree of meteorological knowledge and predictive skill on the part of the shamans—knowledge that was essential if the expected change were to eventuate and the shamans retain their authority and status within the community.

METEOROLOGICAL PLAY-FORMS OF THE EASTERN WOODLANDS

Society	Game	Contestant	Season Played	Spirit(s) Involved	Result of Contest	Remarks
Huron	Lacrosse	Men v men (Intervillage)	Spring	?	Harsh Weather Averted	
Iroquois	1. Lacrosse	1. Men v men (Intermoiety)	1. Summer -drought	1. Thunderers Great Spirit	1a. Rain b. Favourable Winds	1. Gambling. Pre-game preparation
	2. Hoop and Pole	2. Men v men (Intermoiety)	2. Summer -drought and extreme temperatures	2. Sun, Moon Thunderers	2a. Cooler weather b. rain?	
Arkansas	1. Shinny	1. Men v men (Intermoiety)	1. Summer	1. Winds	1a. Favourable winds b. Rain?	1. Gambling. Pre-game preparation
	2. Whip-tops	2. Boys v boys	2. Winter	2. ?	2. ?	
Caddo	Hoop and Pole	Men v men	Summer	Thunder and Lightning	Rain?	
Delaware	1. Straw Game	1. Men and Women	1. Winter	1. Winter Spirit	1. Blizzard conditions	1. Gambling
	2. Ring and Pin Game	2. Men and Women	2. Winter	2. Winter Spirit	2. Blizzard conditions	2. Gambling

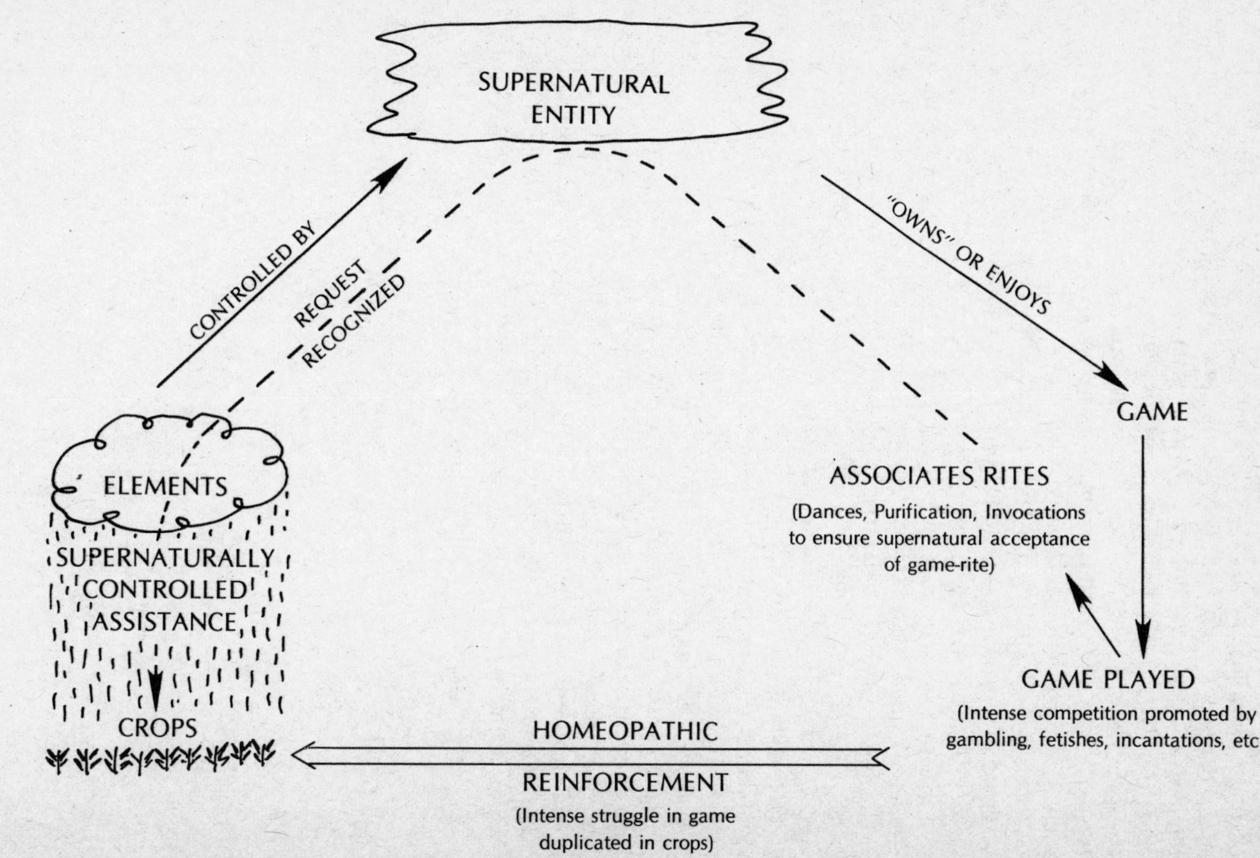
SUPERNATURAL ENTITY
CONTROLLED BY
REQUEST
RECOGNIZED
"OWNS" OR ENJOYS
GAME
ELEMENTS
SUPERNATURALLY CONTROLLED ASSISTANCE
CROPS
ASSOCIATES RITES
(Dances, Purification, Invocations to ensure supernatural acceptance of game-rite)
GAME PLAYED
(Intense competition promoted by gambling, fetishes, incantations, etc.)
HOMEOPATHIC
REINFORCEMENT
(Intense struggle in game duplicated in crops)

through; these articles are temporary enclosures. *Bullet, nail, peg,* and *gun* imply projectiles. *Plow, rake* and *whipsaw* are extensions of the hand for cutting or dividing.

In Diagram 1, motion-action words connote containment, equilibrium, diminution, augmentation, and flight. The interesting idea to note is that there is only one motion-action word for flight. Organic referents indicate the main characters of the poker game as well as the characters' anatomy. Natural states refer to tactile sensations that connote uncomfortable physiological and psychological states.

The main symbolic action and intimidation theme of bulls at play are outlined in Diagram 2. *Nuts* and *balls* refer to gonads. *Wiring, locking,* and *nailing* illustrate symbolic means to intimidate an opponent's balls. However, there are overt ways to *lock someone's nuts* and covert ways to *nail someone's nuts.* These symbolic actions are designed to *scare* a player and make him *shy;* the intimidated player will have three options— *chasing cards, running,* or *folding.* The frightened player is forced to play catch-up ball.

In Diagram 2, manipulation and intimidation of a player's balls are coupled with affective domains of castration and gore. The symbolic actions by overt and covert competitors continue containment, diminution, augmentation, and equilibrium as game strategies. Furthermore, players in tandem can force opponents out of the action by *whipsawing* and *The Big Squeeze.* For example, two players will gang up on an opponent as the first player sandbags, while the second player will plow in large raises. If the middleman wants to stay with the action, he must match the second player's raises. Often the first player holds the winning hand. At the level of symbolic action, sexual and intimidation themes of bulls at play enter the poker arena.

FOOTNOTES

[1]The Eastern Woodlands extend from slightly north of the St. Lawrence River to the Gulf of Mexico, and from the Atlantic Ocean to just west of the Ohio River in the north and the Mississippi River in the south. They include part of Ontario and Quebec, all New York, southern New England, the middle Atlantic states, and the southern states as far west as Louisiana. When the Europeans first entered the region it housed more than one hundred and twenty different tribal groups. Although they spoke a variety of languages and dialects, they all fell into one of five linguistic families—families that were affiliated with either the Macro-Siouan or Macro-Algonquian Phyla. This study focuses on ten of these groups belonging to the Iroquoian, Caddoan and Siouan Families of the Macro-Siouan Phylum and the Algonquian Family of the Macro-Algonquian Phylum.

[2]The Six Nations or the League of the Iroquois, hereafter referred to as the "Iroquois", consisted of the following tribes: Cayuga, Mohawk, Oneida, Seneca, Tuscarora and Onondaga.

[3]The Midwinter Festival was the highlight of the Iroquoian ceremonial calendar. Held in late January or early February, its rites of personal well-being, supplication and thanksgiving were directed toward the entire agricultural and cosmic hierarchy of the Iroquois.

[4]The corn mush appears to symbolize the seventh Thunderer, who as an earthling, was crushed by the other six Thunderers in a corn mortar in order to change his shape and thus facilitate his ascendancy into the spirit world. The Cayuga referred to the game, when played on this occasion as "beating the mush".

[5]In point of fact, the Moon Ceremony and the Sun Ceremony were two separate and distinct rituals; however, as their aims were similar, most Iroquian tribes conducted them in conjunction with each other.

[6]An east-west orientation was common to most activities that involved the sun.

[7]An exception here was the whip-top contests of the Arkansas. It is possible that beliefs and taboos, similar to those held by the Delaware, may also have been associated with this activity.

[8]Generally speaking, the playforms of the Macro-Algonquian peoples, as represented by the Delaware, are remarkably similar to those found within such Macro-Siouan societies as the Huron, Iorquois, Caddo, and Arkansas.

REFERENCES CITED

Blau, Harold, 1967 Notes on the Onondaga Bowl Game. In, *Iroquois Culture, History and Prehistory*. Proceedings of the 1965 Conference on Iroquois Research, pp. 35-49. Albany. The State University of New York.

Brinton, Daniel G., 1890 *Essays of an Americanist.* Philadelphia. Porter and Coates.

Dorsey, George A., 1905 *Traditions of the Caddo.* Washington. Carnegie Institution.

Eyman, Frances, 1964 Lacrosse and the Cayuga Thunder Rite. *Expedition* 6, No. 4 (Summer): 14-19.

Fenton, William N., 1936 An Outline of Seneca Ceremonies at Cold Spring Longhouse. *Yale University Publications in Anthropology,* No. 9, pp. 1-23. New Haven. Yale University.

Flannery, Regina, 1939 *An Analysis of Coastal Algonquian Culture.* Anthropological Series, No. 7. Washington. The Catholic University of America.

Fletcher, Alice C. and Francis La Flesche, 1911 The Omaha Tribe. *Twenty-Seventh Annual Report of the Bureau of American Ethnology to the Secretary of the Smithsonian Institution, 1905-1906.* Washington. Government Printing Office.

Le Mercier, Francois Joseph, 1898 Le Jeunes Relation, 1637. *The Jesuit Relations and Allied Documents* 14. Edited by Reuben Gold Thwaites. Cleveland. the Burrows Brothers Company.

Morgan, Lewis Henry, 1954 *League of the Ho-De-No Sau-Nee or Iroquois* 1. New Haven. Human Relations Area Files.

Salter, Michael A., 1972 Mortuary Games of the Eastern Culture Area. *Proceedings of the Second Canadian Symposium on the History of Sport and Physical Education,* pp. 160-197. Ottawa. Department of National Health and Welfare.

1973 Medicinal Game-Rites of the Iroquoian Linguistic Family. *Proceedings of the North American Society for Sport History,* pp. 30-1. University Park. Pennsylvania State University.

1974 An Analysis of the Role of Games in the Fertility Rituals of the Native North American. *Anthropos: International Review of Ethnology and Linguistics* 69, Nos. 3-4: 494-504.

Shimony, Annemarie Anrod, 1961 Conservatism Among the Iroquois at the Six Nations Reserve. *Yale University Publications in Anthropology,* No. 65. New Haven. Yale University.

Speck, Frank Gouldsmith, 1937 Oklahoma Delaware Ceremonies, Feasts and Dances. In, *Memoirs of the American Philosophical Society,* 7, pp. 99-106. Philadelphia. The American Philosophical Society.

________ and Alexander General, 1949 *Midwinter Rites of the Cayuga Long House.* Philadelphia. The University of Pennsylvania Press.

Tooker, Elisabeth, 1970 *The Iroquois Ceremonial of Midwinter.* Syracuse. Syracuse University Press.

ANAL LINGUISTICS, CRY YOUR "I's" OUT: CONSTRUCTING A METAPHOR OF POKER

Susan H. Boyd, University of Montana

This paper explores the lexical referents of poker players in order to construct a metaphor of the game. The data were gathered during my thesis research of commercial poker games in Missoula, Montana. The main themes of the game metaphor are: making money, intimidation, lying, and sexual identity. Since the original study stressed a dramaturgical model, poetic and dramatic motives in play are "explained" by the game metaphor, bulls at play.

The playful element of poker is the manipulation of verbal symbols by gamesmen, i.e., the drama and poetry of bulls at play. With clever manipulation of the drama and language, a poker player attempts: to control his image, to deceive his opponents, and to intimidate potential winners by "bulling them off the pot." Although players state that their reason for playing poker is to make money, word play is an essential feature of the games. Suggested techniques for studying word play and a game metaphor are:

1) *Compilation of a particular game's language and symbols* that describe and explain the game. What is said and how often it is said are important, especially during crucial moments of the game. A cross-check of the vocabulary list can be done with flashcards. Use interviewing techniques from Berlin, Breedlove, and Raven; use at least two game environments that are fairly well-defined, sociometric groupings (Berlin, Breedlove, Raven 1970). Note variation between game environments. Discover what is said.

2) *Analyzation of associational linkages* among verbal symbols that players discuss. Note the players' elaborations of the game metaphor, especially during victories or defeats. Discover why it is said.

3) *Explanation of connotations* during game action. Observe key themes

and connotations of the game metaphor within a model of dramaturgical interaction. Note the symbols that are controlled and manipulated for impression management. Discover what is dramatically accomplished.

4) *Exploration of language games* within the play environment. Note the novel shifts in concepts and expressions—puns, substitutions, and deletions.

Discover elements of expressive play for expression management.

This paper has three main sections:

1) Symbolic Articles and Symbolic Actions—what poker players say and do symbolically.

2) Dramatic Action of the Poker Game—how the players manipulate symbolism of the game metaphor, and

3) The Poetic Motive in Poker Play—how the players manipulate expressive, verbal behavior in game management.

For the discussion of symbolism, I assume that symbols are multireferential and economical, i.e., key aspects of poker play are condensed in a single, symbolic article. Furthermore, I assume that symbols have sensory cues and that symbols are unified by associational linkages in the game metaphor (cf. Turner 1962 and 1967). The dominant symbol of the game of the poker metaphor is *bull,* since it combines the main sensory and conceptual *significata* in action and thought during the gaming encounter (Turner 1967: 28-32). The associational linkages are connotations of symbolic articles and actions, i.e., connotations are concepts that symbols convey (cf. Turner 1962, Burke 1962, and Langer 1958). Symbolic articles are signposts of cognitive structure, whereas symbolic actions imply social relations in play.

Symbolic Articles and Symbolic Actions

There are four main groupings of symbolic articles that are found in a poker player's repertoire: mechanical, motion-action, organic, and natural states (Diagram 1). These symbolic articles describe both the contents of poker hands and game strategy. For example, a player might say:

> He had the bullet. No wonder he was plowing. If I had a cinch
> like that, I'd probably flash my door card to tap off my opponent.
> That's a good way to sandbag and to put a lock on his nuts.

Bullet is an ace. *Plowing* refers to boosting the pot with large raises. A *cinch* is a winning hand. The strategy of *flashing* a *door card* suckers another player, i.e., the player believes that the *door card* is the only power card you hold. By *tapping off* a player, one can bring more money into the pot. *Sandbagging* is simply *slow betting,* which suckers more players into the pot.

Even at the level of symbolic articles, one may assign connotations. For example, in Diagram 1, the mechanical list (cinch, lock, nuts, etc.) can be analyzed with the connotation of containment, i.e., fasteners and enclosures. *Door, window,* and *tap* (Spigot) have connotations of seeing or going

DIAGRAM 1

Symbolic Articles of Cognitive Structure

mechanical

cinch	door	bullet	wheel	plow
fence	window	nail	ball	rake
hook	tap	peg		whipsaw
lock				
nuts				
screws				
wire				
catch				
(sandbag)				
(pot)				

motion-action

catch	balance	bust	build	ran
cinch	center	fold	bump	
lock	check	cut	plow	
nail	straddle	jacked off	raise	
pull in	hung-up	raking	kick(er)	
squeeze	sandbag	shaving		
crimp	rotate	tapping		
	pat(stand)	whipsawing		

organic

bug	bull	fish	gut	horns
			ass	nuts
			hole	balls
				hind

natural states

blind	freeze	heat	heavy
		cold	sharp
			rough

DIAGRAM 2

Symbolic Actions of The Poker Game

Action	Overt Means	Covert Means		
wiring				
locking				
nailing				
cinching				
squeezing	raising	checking		
screwing	plowing	straddling		
catching	bumping	balancing		
shaving	building	sandbagging		
jacking off		pulling in one's horns		
whipsawing			NUTS	
busting			BALLS	To:
folding				scare
tapping				shy
pegging				chase
				run
				freeze out

Dramatic Action of The Poker Game

Another main theme of the poker encounter is lying. In a dramaturgical model of impression management, there is a very real sense of plotting and performing. In Diagram 3, lying and plotting continue to convey containment, augmentation, diminution, and "guised" equilibrium. In a dramatic sense, the cast includes bulls, bugs and fish. The bull is "the heavy." The bug is joker and the only wild card used in these poker games. The bug is capable of effective, surreptitious action; it is small and annoying like a gnat's sting. When removed from their restricted environment, the hapless fish (suckers) are immobilized. Fish are easily out of their element, whereas bulls and bugs have more adaptability. Beyond this, there are reproductive connotations of bugs versus fish and the reproductive largesse of a bull.

The connotations of containment, diminution, augmentation, and equilibrium are put in play behind the foil of the poker game, the blind. In the argot of poker players, covert and overt manipulations of the blind are called *bulling the game.* For example, door or window cards are flashed to sucker opponents. A competitor may plow in to bump his opponents. Chattering, bull shitting, and talking loose can conceal a very controlled approach to card strategy. Self-effacement is another ploy!

> The last time I got a pat hand was when my mother laid
> hers to my backside.

Social relations in poker play at the dramatic level of analysis imply a cast, a plot, script, tension, and a climax.

DIAGRAM 3

Dramatic Action

Cast:	Bulls (large, aggressive, imposing *personae*)	
	Bugs (small, surreptitious, mobile *personae*)	
	Fish (small, surreptitious, restricted *personae*)	
Plot:	Lying and deceit to intimidate and manipulate the fish.	
	Bulls plot from behind the blind by:	bumping
		plowing
		flashing
		sabotaging
		chattering
		screwballing
		sandbagging
		cold-decking
		bull shitting
		talking loose
	These tactics are designed to scare fish.	
Script:	Normal versus Verbal Stylization	
Tension:	Threats of symbolic castration, gore and undesirable, tactile sensations.	
Climax:	Demise of the fish and victory of the bulls.	

The Poetic Motive in Poker Play

With regards to a poker script, there are particular styles of language associated with *bulling the game*. The connotations of containment and augmentation are acted upon by two types of poker players:

1) A Tight Ass refers to a player who uses a very controlled, statistical approach to card play. A Tightie does not believe in luck.

2) A Loose Ass player uses an aggressive show of force and money. A Loosey believes in luck (Boyd 1975)

In a speech situation of the poker game, The Tightie represents the player most likely to use a nominal speech style. The Loosey, however, uses a verbal style. A verbal style shortens the number of letters and syllables, uses fewer clauses, and decreases a distinct sentence pattern (Wells 1960: 215-217). The verbal style interjects more of the speaker's personality, especially when the speaker uses the imperative form (Wells 1960:215-217).

DIAGRAM 4

Nominal and Verbal Stylization

1) CUT THE CARDS

Tightie	Loosey
"Cut the cards."	"Cut 'em!"
"Cut the deck."	"Cut 'em up!"
"Will you cut the cards."	"Whack 'em!"

2) PUT A DOLLAR IN THE DARK

Tightie	Loosey
"Put a dollar in the dark."	"Behind the gun, dollar in."
"Put a dollar in."	"Darken it!"
"Dollar in the dark."	

3) PRONOMINALIZATION

There is a condensation:

Cards = Them = 'Em

In Diagram 4, there are two styles of speech for requesting a cut of the cards. Paralinguistic activity is in accord with a nominal or verbal stylization. For example, a Tightie might tap the table with a couple of fingers to indicate, "Cut the cards." A Loosey will indicate his pleasure with a bravado wave of the hand or by thumping his hand loudly on the table. In Diagram 4, the second example occurs during a loball hand. When you place *a dollar in the dark,* it means that a player must open the loball hand blindly. This opening player must ante without rejecting his unseen hand. The player seated to his left may *straddle* (the fence) by placing another *dollar in the dark.* the straddler buys the option to pass, while all remaining players must *bet, check,* or *raise.* In a dramatic sense, *straddling* and *checking* a bet are "guised equilibrium," i.e., the remaining players are forced to commit themselves to a strategy. *Put a dollar in the dark* may refer to either the blind opener or the straddler.

In a poetic motive of play, the condensation of symbols and speech in a verbal stylization contrasts with the nominalization of subjects and objects—a quasi prose style. For example in Diagram 4, "Whack 'em," "Darken it," and "Behind the gun," convey connotations beyond the deck of cards; the verbal style creates more sound and fury in the poker encounter. The increased use of pronominalization (cards = them = 'em) create the ambiguity of *'em.* By inference and punning logic a player substitutes *balls* for *cards.* Some players deliberately choose a verbal style as a deceptive device. House dealers may speed up the rhythm of play by switching to a verbal stylization. A verbal style heightens competition, since the main themes are punned upon, enacted and recalled by a Loosey's game chatter. With the poetic motive of play, poker games become contests of one-upsmanship and punning. For example, the epitome of chaos in poker game action is a *screwball*—a trickster who chatters and louses up the game with an unsystematic deployment of his hand. This real-life joker figuratively *screws someone's balls* by stealing verbal and card action. *Bull shitting* and *talking loose* give more energy, tension, and dramatic flair to the poker game.

In conclusion the associational linkages of bulls at play contain desirable sensory attributes of natural bulls—sheer, brute strength, vitality and reproductive largesse. On the other hand, bulls are harnessed competitors who embody masculine values of entrepeneurial activity in a socio-cultural sense—bulls of the stock market. There is a dance between the desirable and obligatory attributes of natural and social bulls; the game metaphor conjoins promises and threats in competitive action. Harnessing brute force creates a more cerebral approach to *bulling the game. Locking someone's nuts* is a social and economic besting of an opponent's productive potential.

Poker players rarely say, "We play like bulls." More often, gamesmen are bulls in the arena of dramatic and poetic play. There is a conscious attempt to construct impressions and expressions when a player bulls the game. When asked why participants played poker, the most frequent response was, "To make money, of course." The economic theme of the poker game is translated into stylized threats against a player's sexual prowess. The game metaphor illustrates thematic form and content of poker as well as culturologically valued goals of American entrepreneurs. Through ritual and poetic play of the poker game, emotional and social relationships reiterate ties and conflicts among competitors.

BIBLIOGRAPHY

Berlin, Brent, Dennis Breedlove and Peter Raven, 1970 Covert categories of folk taxonomies

In Man makes sense. Eugene Hammel and William Simmons, eds. Boston, Little Brown and Co.
Boyd, Susan, H., 1975 Poker Playing as a dramaturgical event: bull power, meaning and commitment for efficacious gamesmanship. Unpublished Master's Thesis University of Montana, Missoula.
Burke, Kenneth, 1962 What are the signs of what? Anthropological Linguistics 4(6): 1-23.
Langer, S., 1968 Philosophy in a new key. New York, Mentor Books.
Turner, Victor, 1962 Chihamba, the white spirit. Rhodes-Livingston Papers: 33. New York, Humanities Press.
1967 The forest of symbols. Ithaca, New York, Cornell University Press.
Wells, Rulon, 1960 Nominal and verbal styles. *In* Styles in language. Thomas Sebeok, ed. New York, Wiley.

FUN AND GAMES IN AN URBAN SETTING: BLACK CHILDREN'S GAMES

Annette Rosenstiel, William Paterson College of N.J.

A careful analysis of children's games reveals that they serve several very important social functions. They are pre-adaptive; i.e., they provide models for adult activity, although they do not necessarily condition the participant to transfer precise response patterns in adult life. To a certain extent, therefore, they provide guidelines for the performance of certain adult activities. However, their significance extends beyond this (Loizos 1967: 238). From a structural point of view, they recreate in microcosm certain adult activities. Recent theoreticians of play (e.g. Stevens 1976) suggest a blending of the earlier structuralist approach, which concerned itself mainly with the overt aspects of play, with the developing functionalist approach, which considers the cover aspects of play through an analysis of the ways in which play contributes to the adaptive potential of the individual.

The anthropological study of play is concerned with both the overt manifestations and the covert significance of play and games. This paper deals with forms of play and games manifested in a specific socioeconomic setting. Examining the factors affecting the forms of play, it compares the conclusions reached by this observer with those expressed by other students of play and its social significance.

The games described here are played by black urban children between the ages of six and sixteen, approximately the years when the children are expected to attend school. Some games, in fact, are school-related. Others are played within the black community itself. The games as discussed here are played by black children in an urban low-income housing development, and have been observed *in situ,* and/or recreated in simulated form on videotape as part of a course on Educational Anthropology given by the author. Some games were recorded and brought to class for discussion by participant-observers; later, some of these, and others, were presented by black students to the class and were videotaped live.

The games represent a wide spectrum of the play activities of children in urban inner city areas. They fall into a number of the categories identified by Sutton-Smith and Rosenberg (1961). Some are played in and around schools; some are street games; others are social games played at home or out-of-doors. The games described in this paper fall into eight of these categories: leader games, chasing games, kissing games, card games, singing games, guessing games, games of skill, and role reversal games. Since the games were observed by girls, most of the games recorded are girls' games. A description of some of these games follows.

Seven Ups is a guessing game played in ghetto classrooms, by children in grades 2 to 6. To start the game, the teacher selects seven students, usually those who were the best in the class that day. These students line up in front of the class, while the rest of the students put their heads down on their desks, close their eyes, and put their thumbs up. The seven then walk around the class and each one touches the thumb of one student. They try to pick someone they feel is not peeking.

When a thumb is tapped, the child keeps it down so that no one else will touch it. When the teacher sees that the seven have returned to the front of the class, she says, "Heads up, Seven up!" At this time, the seven who were tapped stand up and try to guess, one at a time, who picked them. If they guess correctly, they replace the person who had selected them as one of the seven up. The game is repeated until a few minutes before the dismissal bell.

Hide and Go Git It, a variant of Hide and Seek, is a clandestine chasing game, usually played by children ranging from eight to twelve years of age, though the age range is flexible. The children are generally at the age where they can recognize the difference between male and female, and begin to explore sexual difference. The girls run and hide, usually in a place where they can be found, but try to give the impression that they do not want to be caught.

When a little girl is caught by a little boy, he has the right to have sex (called "Pussy") with the girl. The game is usually played in the bushes or behind a house or garage. It is very seldom that they have actual intercourse, but they simulate copulation. The boys often pull their pants down, and the girls lift their skirts up, sometimes standing, sometimes lying down. Since there are times when simulation is replaced by actual intercourse, there are social sanctions against playing the game, but it persists nevertheless.

Spin the Bottle is a popular black children's game. It is played by a group of children ranging in age from six to sixteen. A large circle is formed. A bottle is placed in the center of the circle and is spun. When the bottle points to a person of the opposite sex, that person must kiss the spinner. Both players are then eliminated, and a new person spins the bottle. The game is repeated until everyone has had an opportunity to spin the bottle and to be kissed.

Pig is a card game played by girls from the age of eight or nine years, and up. It combines elements of card playing, running, touch tag, and role reversal, as well as forfeits.

The players sit at a table. A plastic hair curler is placed in the center of the table. The cards are shuffled, and the dealer distributes a card to each player. The dealer continues to deal the cards, one at a time. The goal is to obtain four cards of a kind. The players pass on to the player at their left any card they receive that they do not need or want.

The first girl to have four cards of a kind yells "Pig!", throws the hair curler to the other side of the room and runs to retrieve it. The other girls try to get it and tag her before she gets back to her seat. If she is tagged before she gets back to the table, she is P. The game continues until one girl is "pig."

The game occasions much hilarity and shrieking, and cries of "get her!" "I got it!" "Look out!" "You got pig!" is the taunt of the other players, as a forfeit is imposed on the winner, who now becomes the loser. Forfeits, decided on by the other three girls, may include kissing a boy, acting like a "fag," acting "like a ninety-five year old man," talking to a stranger, "kissing every boy you see on the street," or other similar acts, including stealing something from a store.

Jumping Rope is a game in which two girls turn the rope and chant, while the third jumps. At the end of the chant, the speed of turning increases, as the turners count at an increasingly rapid pace, until the jumper loses her footing. The chant that accompanies this game is "Postman, postman, do your duty...," inserting the name of each jumper in turn in the second line, as follows:

Postman, postman, do your duty
Here comes Jane, the American beauty.
She can wiggle, she can waggle,
She can do the split.
But she can't wear her skirt above her hip.
First comes love,
Then comes marriage,
Then comes Janie with a baby carriage.
1-2-3-4-5-6-7-8-9-10, etc.

Uncle Remus is a children's singing game, played by an indeterminate number of children. A circle is formed. One child struts around it, while the others sing and clap their hands, singing:

Here comes Uncle Remus
Walking down the street

With the Boogie-Woogie
Right at his feet.
You got to shake it, shake it,
Shake that thing.

When the song nears its end, the child who is strutting around the circle goes into the middle of the circle and dances in front of another child. They then exchange places, and the same song and action are repeated, replacing the name "Uncle Remus" with the name of the new player.

A variant of this game is *Tutti Frutti,* sung as follows:

Here comes Trudy (or another girl's name)
My Tutti Frutti
And we all love her
So very truly.
She makes my heart go
Boompety-boom
Boompety-boom
Boompety-boom.

Stone Teacher is a leader game played by children of elementary school age. It is usually played in a hallway or another place where steps are available. One child elects himself "teacher," and stands in front as the rest of the children sit on the first step. The "teacher" offers one of the children the choice between two closed hands, one of which contains a stone. If the child guesses correctly, he can move up to the next higher step. The "teacher" then puts his hands behind his back, and may either change the stone to the other hand, or keep it in the same hand. He then puts his hands in front of him, and asks the next child to guess. The game continues, taking each child in turn until one child has reached the top step.

Jacks is a very popular game among black girls. It can be played with any number of girls, and requires ten jacks and a ball. A girl puts all ten jacks in one hand, and then tosses them on a flat surface, usually the floor. Then she throws the ball up with one hand, and picks up one jack with the other hand, catching the ball at the same time. The goal is to pick up all ten jacks. If the player misses, the next girl tries. When a player's turn to play arrives, she announces her goal as, "This is my twosy," "This is my tensy," starting with the number she missed the previous time. Sometimes, in playgrounds, there are tournaments to determine the "Jack Queen."

Playing House. It was impossible to observe a game of "playing house" *in situ,* so a group of black girls offered to "play house" and several other games for the benefit of the entire class. A videotape machine was secured, and two other students recorded the session live.

Each girl chose her own role; and age levels selected were between seven played cards, got food from the imaginary refrigerator, and held a conversation on the level of seven and nine-year-olds, even to threatening what "mommy" would do when she returned to find "such a mess," thus illustrating the "rigid imitation of parental power" described by Sutton-Smith (in Herron and Sutton-Smith 1971).

One unexpected result of the videotaping was a heightened awareness of the need for actual observation to supplement description, since in some instances written or oral descriptions were not identical with performance, and analysis of the observed games showed the difference to be due to linguistic differences rather than observational inadequacies.

Conclusion

In spite of its universality, play is affected by the socioeconomic context in which it is performed. Variant forms of particular games reflect specific factors such as sex, socioeconomic level, language, intelligence, racial differences, materials available for play, and the locale where the play takes place (Herron and Sutton-Smith, 1971, p. 16).

A study of the games presented in this paper has borne out many of the theories that have been advanced by analysts of play and its social meaning. The games presented here, and the manner of their presentation, show an extraordinary adaptability, and the ability of young adults to simulate early childhood and to recall vividly the games in which they had participated as young children. It also indicates that in some instances, particular play patterns of childhood persist into young adulthood.

Although this particular study was made on a necessarily limited scale, it would be valuable to extend its scope to include a wider range of games played in the inner city, for a fuller understanding of patterns of interaction as manifested in play.

NOTE

I am indebted to the members of my class in Educational Anthropology who participated in this project, and especially to Cynthia Davis, whose initial research and organization of the videotaped play session helped to make our study of black children's play more meaningful.

REFERENCES

Herron, R.E. and Brian Sutton-Smith, *Child's Play*. New York: John Wiley & Sons, Inc., 1971.

Huizinga, J., Homo Ludens: *A Study of the play element in culture*. London: Routledge and Kegan Pul, Ltd., 1949.

Loizos, Caroline, "Play Behavior in higher primates: A Review," *In,* Desmond Morris, ed., *Primate Ethology*. Chicago: Aldine (Garden City, N.Y.: Doubleday & Co., Anchor Books, 1969).

Stevens, Phillips, Jr., "Laying the groundwork for an anthropology of play,: *In,* TAASP Newsletter, 3 (2): 2-14, Summer, 1976.

Stone, G.P., "The Play of little children," *Quest,* 1965, Monograph IV, 23-31. Reprinted in *Child's Play,* Eds., R.E. Herron and Brian Sutton-Smith. New York: John Wiley & Sons, Inc., 1971, pp. 4-17.

Sutton-Smith, Brian and B.G. Rosenberg, "Sixty Years of historical change in the game preferences of American children," *Journal of American Folklore,* 1961, 64: 17-46. Reprinted in *Child's Play,* Eds., R.E. Herron and Brian Sutton-Smith. New York: John Wiley & Sons, Inc., 1971, pp. 18-50.

and nine. Patterns of family interaction emerged in the role playing, and personality differences showed clearly in the simulation. One girl refused to play. Another said, "You gotta play. I'm older'n you, and I say you gotta play." "Well," answered the first girl, "I'm seven." The second one replied, "Nine's older'n seven. I'm nine, and I say you gotta play."

They had planned to use the instructor's desk as the kitchen table around which they would play, but they soon found the table was uncomfortable. So, they scrounged for materials. From another classroom which is used as a daycare center, they borrowed two square tables, which proved too low, so they put one on top of the other, to make a play surface. This caused considerable hilarity when periodically, in their excitement, they tilted the tables, sometimes ruining a game, but having a hilarious time setting things to rights again. They took food from an imaginary refrigerator, which they called "the frig," chided each other for talking too much, or dropping things on the floor, at which point one of the girls announced dictatorially, "You'll catch it from mommy for being so messy." From time to time, in their simulation of "playing house," they interspersed other games, which were variants of the games described earlier. These games were played spontaneously, and had not been planned in advance. The playing continued until one "child" announced petulantly, "I don't wanna play no more. Let's watch TV." "OK," responded the other three, and the game was over.

Comment

Stone (1965) has said that child's play as drama involves role taking, and gives the child a different view of himself. Similarly, it requires a clearly defined space (Huizinga, 1949). Stone further emphasizes the fact that it demands "the assembly and arrangement and control of space, props, equipment, clothing and bodies, as well as other elements." (Stone, op. cit., p. 12.)

These factors were clearly illustrated by the students who played the games in class. In order to play the Uncle Remus and Jumping Rope games, they needed more space than was normally available, so they good-naturedly rearranged the chairs to make more room. There was no rope available, so they played with an "imaginary" rope.

In playing in that part of the game that required running after the hair roller, they enjoyed themselves immensely, running around the chairs, sometimes slipping and falling, but always with great good humor. Questioning by other members of the class elicited the information that playing PIG does not stop after elementary or even high school. "We play it in the dorm, too," they announced.

But the greatest test of ingenuity came in the simulated game of "playing house," where the entire setting, other than the tables, was imaginary. They

II. Cultural Dimensions of Recreation and Leisure

Introduction

by Kendall Blanchard, Middle Tennessee State University

One of the persistent themes in Allan Tindall's work in recent years has been his frequent reminder that many of the basic concepts employed by sociologists, anthropologists, and physical educators (e.g., sport, play, leisure, physical education, recreation) have never been adequately defined. In a significant position paper prepared for UNESCO on behalf of TAASP, Tindall (1976:3) pointed to the weaknesses implicit in the normal usages of two of these concepts.

> It is highly unlikely that the terms "sport" or the term "physical education" occur in in direct parallel in languages of a non-European origin...
>
> In the literature with which I am familiar "sport" has no definitive meaning or referent. Many disparate types of activities are labeled "sport." Professional and amateur athletic competition as well as hunting and fishing activities are all labeled sport.
>
> Similarly, while "physical education" is viewed a bit more precisely, no consistent meaning for the term can be found. Physical education programs occur at the primary, secondary, and collegiate levels of education, and include such diverse activities as tennis, ping pong, bowling, fly fishing, backpacking, canoeing, basketball, handball, track and field, judo, karate, aikido, yoga...A further complication arises when we consider that many programs offer instructional as well as competitive opportunities.

Tindall has also argued that many of these so-called "sport" activities are defined in different ways in different cultural contexts. For example, in his work with the Utes, he discovered that the basketball they played was distinct from that played by their Anglo-Mormon counterparts. In fact, he argued that basketball was "functional in both the Ute and Anglo-Mormon communities as an agent for the maintenance of these two community cultures" rather than being of any acculturative significance (Tindall, 1975:10).

Tindall's work has inspired others to look for the uniquely cultural dimensions of more general sport behavior. For example, Blanchard (1974:12) has looked at the form of basketball played by the Ramah Navajos in comparison to that played by their Anglo-Mormon neighbors and concluded that basketball in those situations is of little culture-change significance. The Navajos have "simply borrowed a new form of play and molded its essentials to fit ongoing needs and values" so that it is possible to talk about a unique activity which can be labeled "Navajo basketball."

The idea for the symposium for which these papers were written was born out of several conversations between Tindall and myself, the persons eventually responsible for its organization. It was felt that it would be of great value to look at the broad phenomena of recreation and leisure from as many possible disciplinary perspectives as possible, to first see them in terms of their diversity as they are manifested in and defined by particular cultural/historical settings. Secondly, it was deemed important that questions regarding the general, cross-cultural meaning of these phenomena be raised.

The articles themselves reflect the desired diversity: Blanchard as a cultural anthropologist, Fox as an archeologist, Duncan as a recreationist, and Mergen as a historian. Each in his or her particular context has looked at the meaning of recreation and leisure and the ways in which these activities are constricted and defined by specific cultural contexts.

Blanchard describes a physical fitness program recently conducted among the Mississippi Choctaw, notes its failures, treats Choctaw notions of fitness and health, and suggests ultimately that the program failed precisely because of the attempt to impose a Western model of physical fitness completely foreign to the Choctaw experience. Physical fitness is thus seen as having an important, initial cultural dimension.

Fox looks at the recreation and leisure phenomena and suggests that while little data relevant to the problem has been collected and recorded by archeologists to date, such information is not beyond possible retrieval. For him, general definitions are important at this stage because it is only as they are developed that archeologists can begin formulating appropriate questions prior to excavation and analysis.

Duncan, as a recreation specialist, looks at the phenomena here under scrutiny as they occur among the people of Belfast, Ireland, where she has done extensive field work in recent years. As a result of her analysis of the play patterns and games of local children, it is obvious that these events are defined ultimately by current social and political realtities in strife-torn Belfast.

Mergen, the historian, considers the prevelant emphasis on work in late 19th and early 20th century America, and analyzes the forces that led to the eventual creation of a leisure ethic by the end of the 1920's. Throughout the article, the situational variability plaguing definitions of words like "play," "leisure," and "recreation" are evident. In the final analysis, the reader is left with the impression that the most one can say about these activities, as they are defined by scholars and laymen alike in early 20th century America, is that they are not work. Whatever they are, however, they only have meaning as they are understood within a particular sociocultural milieu.

While these presentations do not resolve the general conceptual problems, they do illustrate quite clearly the difficulties one encounters in attempting to deal with the recreation and leisure experiences from a transcultural perspective. They also illustrate once again, that, as Tindall (1976:1) has suggested, if meaningful research is to proceed, "considerable time must be devoted to establishing an operational meaning for the terms," and developing models of cross-cultural validity for these activities.

REFERENCES CITED

Blanchard, Kendall A. 1974 Basketball and the culture-change process: the Rimrock Navajo case. Council on Anthropology and Education Quarterly, V(4):8-13.

Tindall, B. Allan 1975 The perceptual and cultural meaning of basketball. Unpublished paper presented at the American Anthropological Association meetings, San Francisco (December).

________. 1976 Questions about physical education, skill and life-time leisure sports participation. Position paper presented to UNESCO on behalf of the Association for the Anthropological Study of Play, for the First International Conference of Ministers and Senior Officials Responsible for Physical Education and Sport for Youth (April).

The Cultural Component in Physical Fitness

Kendall Blanchard, Middle Tennessee State University

The meaning of "physical fitness," like that of the broader concept of "health," is a culture-bound category (Firth, 1959:142; Maclachlan, 1958:94), and as such is a legitimate problem for medical anthropology.[1] The intracultural analysis of physical fitness as a dimension of personal health provides a unique perspective for doing ethnomedicine and a means for aiding, ultimately, in the maintenance of community health among specific groups, especially those caught up in the debilitating process of culture change.

In this paper I describe a physical fitness program conducted recently among the Mississippi Choctaw and discuss its shortcomings within the context of local conceptions of health and physical fitness. Defining "fitness" from a uniquely Choctaw perspective, I suggest ways in which such programs might be more effective.

Background

In the summer of 1975 I worked as a consultant to the recreation program of the Mississippi Band of Choctaws in the Pearl River community. One activity I suggested and helped to implement was a physical fitness program. It was felt that such a program would be valuable, and the tribal leadership and health personnel agreed. The Choctaw are subject to many medical difficulties, the negative effects of which can either be completely avoided or at least alleviated by proper exercise. For example, while hypertension and heart disease are not abnormally prevalent, overweight, stress, and a variety of circulatory problems are common to the population. Also, diabetes mellitus inflicts a high percentage of Choctaw, and without proper exercise the victim may face the necessity of limb amputation in later life.[2] On a more general level, it was assumed that fitness was a desirable state in any society.

After several weeks of advance publicity and response from interested members of the community, the program was initiated on the afternoon of June 1. From that point, sessions were conducted daily using the track, exercise machines, sauna, and locker rooms at Choctaw Central High School. Every weekday afternoon for the next ten weeks, beginning at five, participants went through approximately 15 minutes of group warm-up calisthenics, ran, jogged, or walked a minimum of one mile, worked out individually in the weight room and sat in the sauna. For the conscientious, this usually meant a total of five hours of strenuous exercise each week. Also, throughout the summer instruction on nutrition and dieting was offered, performance records were maintained, and in conjunction with Dr. James Smith, then director of the Choctaw Agency Indian Health Service Hospital, the activities of persons with known medical problems were closely monitored.

Altogether, 114 persons enrolled for the program. Of that number, 99 were Choctaw (64 female; 35 male). In addition, many others took part in an occasional daily routine without formal enrollment. On the basis of the vital statistics actually collected, the average Choctaw male participating in the program was 27.8 years old, weighed 207 pounds, was 5′8″ tall, and was approximately 30 pounds overweight. His female counterpart was 25.9 years of age, 159 pounds, 5′3″, and about 20 pounds overweight.[3]

During the early stages of the program, daily turn-outs were impressive and reflected a general enthusiasm that had been generated in the community relative to the new activity. Most participants expressed a desire to lose weight, though occasionally those with less obvious problems of disproportion talked in terms of increasing their general track-and-field skills, and even bad weather failed to discourage the budding fitness buffs.

By late June, however, excitement began to wane. Participants complained of a failure to see any significant weight loss, many actually contending that the exercise had merely increased their appetites and thus gross poundage. The new principal at the high school charged that the facilities were being abused and attempted to close them to all tribal activities. A sauna bench collapsed under the combined weight of several of the heftier perspirers. Late afternoon thundershowers, high heat, and oppressive humidity increased as the summer progressed. All of these factors contributed to the subsiding enthusiasm, so that by mid-July, daily attendance had dwindled to an average of about ten persons, in most cases self-confessed, hard-core fitness addicts who had little need for the motivation provided by an organized program.

In appraising the overall effects of the 1975 Choctaw physical fitness program, significant, positive results are difficult to isolate. In many cases, endurance and stamina levels increased, as reflected in distance running performance. Participants also appeared to have enjoyed the interaction and usual festive mood of the large group activities. On the other hand, however, nutritional and diet suggestions were largely ignored, weight loss was minimal, and few if any of the exercisers were motivated to initiate a year-round, personal fitness schedule as a result of the program. It must be admitted that from several perspectives this phase of the recreation calendar was a failure. The obvious question is "Why?".

The meaning of health and physical fitness

The understanding of fitness employed by most physical educators in this country suggests that it is an ideal state toward which one should continually strive even though it can never actually be achieved. For example, Clarke (1967:14) defines physical fitness as "the ability to carry out daily tasks with vigor and alertness, without undue fatigue, and with ample energy to enjoy leisure time pursuits and to meet unforseen emergencies." Fitness is thus not a static reality; no matter how "fit" you are in this context, there is always room for improvement. In turn, this improvement is defined in terms of four variables: 1) strength 2) muscular endurance, 3) cardio-vascular endurance, and 4) flexibility (Hockey 1973:16).

This same dynamic quality is also basic to most universal understandings of "health." For example, the World Health Organization (1946) defines the concept in its constitution as "a state of complete physical, mental and social well-being and not merely the absence of disease or infirmity." Firth (1959:142-145) has observed the existence of a plethora of definitions for "health," and has taken special issue with that contained in the WHO constitution. He suggests that objectives will vary in different times and situations. He also questions the significance and quantifiability of well-being, in particular, social well-being (see Bates, 1959:59, for a similar critique of the attempt at a universal definition of "health"). The difficulties involved in dealing with the term at trans-cultural levels is illustrated by the existence among many groups of conditions considered normative that Westerners would perceive as pathological (Lieban, 1973:1044). Indeed, the literature is replete with various understandings of health that are relative only to specific cultural contexts (Polgar, 1968; Parsons, 1958; Read, 1966).

I would suggest that the concept of physical fitness is subject to the same variability and must be defined only within particular sociocultural settings.

Little general information and no specific data on traditional Choctaw ethnomedicine is available in published form. It is apparent that the Choctaw have long placed a premium on health maintenance, the development of physical skills, stamina, strength, and endurance, and the utilization of many curing techniques (see Swanton 1931:212-241). Typical of many Native American groups, Choctaw dealt with the matter of personal health within the broader framework of ideological and social realities.

Among the Choctaw today, there is still a sense in which the concept of health has obvious spiritual and social dimensions. However, increasingly it is being influenced by the semantic categories of English.

The Choctaw word for health is *achukma,* a term basic in the response to the greeting *Halito! Chimachukma?* (Hello! Are you fine?). To be fine is to be healthy, and one can wish no better state for a friend or kinsman.

The notion of "physical fitness" has no immediate translation in Choctaw but is treated much the same way as it is among English speakers. Detailed analysis, however, suggests some significant semantic differentials.

In the attempt to elicit and isolate an emic model of Choctaw physical fitness, I developed two projective techniques, in one case using a list of words, in the other a battery of pictures.

The first of these two devices, a "word association check list," was composed of two sections. The first asked informants to respond to a list of 31 adjectives as these applied to what a healthy person should *be* (big, fat, happy, old, thin); the second, 13 verbs, to what a healthy person should *do* (ache, sleep, work, sweat). Results from this schedule were generally inconclusive, but the responses by the Choctaws suggest that they are more concerned with process and ability than form. For example, being fat is not desirable because there are many things a fat person cannot do (run, play ball), not because obesity is disproportioned, unsightly, or difficult to clothe.

The visual projective technique proved to be more valuable. Utilizing the nine drawings of female somatotypes from Sheldon's *The Varieties of Human Physique* (1940:291-299), removed the figure enumeration, had them copied individually, and asked a sample of Choctaw informants to place the drawings (nude, front and side view) in sequential order, from best to worse, in terms of the way they perceived the ideal female body. Next I went back through the pictures with each respondent and asked him or her to comment critically on each one. Both ranking and comments were recorded. Later I repeated this process with a sample of Anglo residents in Murfreesboro, Tennessee, of similar age and educational background (see Table 1).

TABLE 1:
Response to female somatotypes:
Choctaw and Anglo ranking[a]

Ranking	Choctaw (Average)	Anglo (Average)
1	136 (1.90)	136 (1.93)
2	117 (2.00)	127 (2.07)
3	127 (2.15)	117 (3.23)
4	172 (4.71)	172 (4.43)
5	362 (5.00)	171 (4.47)
6	171 (5.33)	362 (5.17)
7	632 (6.86)	632 (6.83)
8	731 (8.48)	731 (8.63)
9	711 (8.52)	711 (8.37)
	n = 21	n = 30

	(males: 12)	(males:24)
	(females: 9)	(females: 6)
	(ave. age: 24.9)	(ave. age: 23.7)

[a]The data have been cross-checked to test for possible sex bias, but male/female differences have proved to be of no significant consequence.

When the numerical rankings were totaled, averaged, and compared, differences between Choctaw and Anglo perceptions were judged to be of no significance (see Table 1). However, when the comments were grouped and analyzed according to positive, neutral, and negative on one plane, and linearity, muscularity, and curvilinearity on another, several interesting patterns were revealed.

In the first place, Choctaw respondents were more likely to perceive linearity (e.g., thin, skinny, bony) than their Anglo counterparts, and in most of these cases assigned a negative value to the quality (see Table 2).

TABLE 2:
Somatotype responses:
valuation relative to linearity

	Choctaw	Anglo	Total
Negative	24	7	31
Positive	6	7	13
Total	30	14	44

Chi-square: 4.127 at 1 degree of freedom

On the other hand, the Choctaw observers were less likely than the Anglos to comment negatively on curvilinearity (far, overweight, gross, heavy), in many cases actually assigning a positive value (see Table 3).

TABLE 3:
Somatotype responses:
valuation relative to curvilinearity

	Choctaw	Anglo	Total
Negative	71	102	172
Positive	26	4	30
Total	97	106	203

Chi-square: 21.331 at 1 degree of freedom

Even more interesting, perhaps, are the responses of the two groups to the quality of muscularity. Less than 25 percent of the Choctaw group expressed any awareness of the muscularity (muscular, masculine, butchy, stocky) evident in somatotypes 171, 172, and 362. On the other hand, over 50 percent of the Anglos noted this element. Also, when Choctaws did respond to this quality, it was generally in favorable terms. This is reversed in the white sample (see Table 4).

TABLE 4:
Somatotype responses:
valuations relative to muscularity

	Choctaw	Anglo	Total
Negative	1	27	28
Positive	6	7	13
Total	7	34	41

Chi-square: 11.370 at 1 degree of freedom

From another perspective, when the total responses to the most obviously muscular of the drawings (171 and 172) are analyzed, Choctaw comments are found to be significantly less negative (see Table 5).

TABLE 5:
Somatotype responses:
total valuations relative to 171 and 172

	Choctaw	Anglo	Total
Negative	21	35	56
Positive	17	3	20
Total	38	38	76

Chi-square: 13.300 at one degree of freedom

Based on projective test analysis, information gathered from the literature and informant discussion, as well as intensive observation, the following can be suggested relative to the Mississippi Choctaw perception of physical fitness:

1. The quality of being healthy and/or fit is an extremely desirable state.
2. Physical fitness is a more static quality than it is for most Western physical educators and is approached with a slighter degree of seriousness. Apparently it is a noble goal, but if one pursues it too intently, the original recreational purpose of the process is violated.
3. Among the Choctaws, fitness is rarely correlated with being "thin" or "lean." Conversely, being overweight does not necessarily mean "unhealthy" or "unfit."
4. The Choctaws, as opposed to urbanized Southern whites, are less likely to correlate fitness and masculinity. The "male athlete" model is less viable in this context.
5. Muscularity is not a negative quality in females, from the perspectives of both Choctaw men and women. Men find the quality sexually attractive, though often apparent only at unconscious levels, while women view it as a desirable trait. Several female informants have argued that physical strength is an important feminine characteristic. It is seen as functional in hard work as well as in the process of "taking care of your man."[4]
6. Induced sweating for the Choctaws is an active element in the maintenance of general health, while for Anglos it is a more passive process

of temporary weight reduction. Sweating has long had a medical significance for the Choctaw people (Swanton, 1931:230-236), and this penchant for perspiring was manifested in the 1975 fitness program as sauna-centered activities became the main attraction of the sessions for the majority of the participants.

7. Physical fitness is essentially a social process to be pursued as community recreation rather than individually. With reference again to the program herein described, those persons consistently attending the afternoon exercise routines by themselves were rare. Most participants came only if they were accompanied by a contingent of kinsmen and neighbors. Many confessed to this as a necessary prerequisite to their attendance.

Conclusions

While the 1975 Choctaw Tribal Recreation physical fitness program failed for many reasons, I would suggest that the most obvious weakness in the experiment was its short-sighted attempt to impose a Western model on a Choctaw situation.

In light of what is now known about the Choctaw definition and perception of physical fitness, the following suggestions are offered relative to improving the possibility of future program success in this situation:

1. Physical fitness goals, if they are to effectively motivate community adults toward meaningful participation, must be defined in terms of generally accepted health values; feeling good, being happy, having a good time.

2. Activities should be scheduled to facilitate the broadest possible community participation and at times not unduly punishing because of temperature extremes.

3. As much as possible, program activities should be designed without the imposition of artificial sexual distinctions (i.e., male versus female). Sex and age group segregation tends to limit the positive effect group psychology as a motivation technique.

4. Exercise should be geared to balance intermittent periods of exertion and relaxation as opposed to enforcing continuous strain. The "interval training" techniques of Fox and Mathews (1974) could easily be adapted to the Choctaw situation.

5. Weight loss and body definition should be defined as secondary goals of the fitness program.

6. Activities should include as much diversity as possible.

In general, physical fitness is a culturally conditioned concept, and such programs, if they are to contribute effectively to community health, must reject universal models and operate within the constraints imposed by specific socio-cultural settings.

NOTES

[1]The earlier material in the medical anthropology literature appears to have dealt more adequately with cultural definitions of health (Caudill, 1953), while recent work tends to focus almost entirely on disease and illness (see Fabrega, 1971; Lieban, 1973; Colson and Selby, 1974).

[2]Estimates by Indian Health Service officials suggest that as many as one out of every five Mississippi Choctaws will contract the condition during the course of his or her lifetime.

[3]The ideal weights were calculated from Metropolitan Life Insurance Company charts (Hockey, 1973: 72-73). In most cases, individuals were evaluated as having "large frames," so that while these figures are of questionable specificity in light of an apparent high Choctaw body density factor, ideal weight-loss estimates were minimized. It is of note that in most cases, the ideal weights extracted from the MLI charts were consistent with ideal weights participants selected for themselves.

[4]This helps to explain why, during the summer program, so many women insisted on working out with heavy weights doing exercises designed to strengthen the upper arms and chest despite my instructions to the contrary.

REFERENCES CITED

Bates, Marston. 1959 The ecology of health. In, Iago Galdston (ed.) Medicine and Anthropology. New York: International Libraries Press, pp. 56-77.

Caudill, William. 1953 Applied anthropology in medicine. In, A. L. Kroeber (ed.) Anthropology Today. Chicago: University of Chicago, pp. 771-806.

Clarke, H. Harrison. 1967 Application of Measurement to Health and Physical Education. Englewood Cliffs, N.J.: Prentice-Hall.

Colson, Anthony C. and Karen F. Selby. 1974 Medical anthropology. In, Bernard J. Siegel (ed.) Annual Review of Anthropology. Palo Alto, pp. 245-262.

Fabrega, Horacio, Jr. 1971 Medical anthropology. In Bernard J. Siegel (ed.) Biennial Review of Anthropology. Stanford, pp. 167-229.

Firth, Raymond. 1959 Acculturation in relation to concepts of health and disease. In, Iago Galdston (ed.) Medicine and Anthropology. New York: International Libraries Press, pp. 129-165.

Fox, Edward L. and Donald K. Mathews. 1974 Interval Training. Philadelphia: W. B. Saunders.

Lieban, Richard W. 1973 Medical anthropology. In, John Honigman (ed.) Handbook of Social and Cultural Anthropology. Chicago: Rand McNally, pp. 1031-72.

Maclachlan, John M. 1958 Cultural factors in health and disease. In, E. Gartly Jaco (ed.) Patients, Physicians and Illness. Glencoe, Ill.: Free Press, pp. 94-105.

Parsons, Talcott. 1958 Definitions of health and illness in light of American values and social structure. In, E. Gartly Jaco (ed.) Patients, Physicians and Illness. Glencoe, Ill.: Free Press, pp. 165-187.

Polgar, Steven. 1968 Health. Encyclopedia of the Social Sciences, 6:330-336.

Read, Margaret. 1966 Culture, Health and Disease. London: Tavistock.

Sheldon, W. H. 1940 The Varieties of Human Physique. New York: Hafner.

Swanton, John R. 1931 Source Material for the Social and Ceremonial Life of the Choctaw Indians. Bulletin, BAE 53. Washington.

The Cultural Ramifications of Recreation in Belfast, Northern Ireland

Mary R. Duncan, San Diego State University

Children adapting their play-forms to shifting socio-political environments

is not a new phenomenon. During the Eoka Campaign in Cypress between 1955 and 1959, children were actively recruited and used in the front lines. One guerilla leader noted that young children love danger; they must take risks to prove their worth. These risks, though dangerous, are seen as games by the children. (Whale 1973:3) Likewise, children's recreation and play-forms in Belfast, Northern Ireland appear to reflect their country's cultural and socio-political conflict.

This paper will deal specifically with the cultural aspects of recreation in Belfast and how recreation has possibly contributed to the present conflict in Northern Ireland. All data were secured from personal interviews, participant-observation, publications and cultural informants. Two types of interviews were utilized. Formal interviews were conducted with recreation agency personnel and other community leaders. The second type was less formal and occurred as this researcher shopped, waited for buses and socialized at local pubs. In addition, data were collected and analyzed from private and governmental agencies. (Duncan 1975: 46-60).

Background

Belfast is frequently described as a culturally segregated city. Housing, schools, employment and recreation activities are divided into two categories—Irish Catholic and British Protestant.

> The result of this has been the creation of a deep division...so deep and all-pervasive... that it affects all classes and occupations. What friends you make...what games you play...what societies you join...are determined by whether you are Protestant or Catholic. (Hanson 1973:15).

This cultural spirit was magnified when thousands of English and Scottish Protestants migrated to Ireland during the 1500's. The ensuing conflict between the indigenous Catholic Irish and the newly-arrived Protestants resulted in a Protestant victory. Since then, this 1690 victory has been celebrated each year on July 12 by large crowds of boisterous British Protestants.

The current conflict in Northern Ireland flared up in 1969, following a July 12 celebration, when Protestant mobs burned and gutted approximately 200 Catholic homes. The British Army quelled the 1969 riots but violence still flares as the minority Catholic population struggles to gain economic and political parity with the Protestant majority.

Britain's 1971 internment policy, jail without trial, provided hundreds of recruits for the Catholic supported Irish Republican Army (IRA), since ninety percent of those jailed were Irish Catholic. Protestants responded to the IRA threat by joining the Ulster Defense Association (UDA), a Protestant urban guerrilla group. In addition to their underground activities, both groups sponsor numerous recreation and sporting events for children and adults.

History of Irish Sports

Through sports and recreation this conflict can be traced back to 200 A.D. when the legendary Irish hero, Finn McCool, used a hurling stick to settle a lovers' quarrel. Hurling is a game similar to field hockey. Hurling, gaelic football, road bowling and handball have all been banned by the British at various times since 1550. During those years the Irish had secret hurling matches between parishes, with as many as two hundred men on each side.

In the late 1880's, following the potato famine, there was a revival of Gaelic games which helped to rekindle Irish pride and nationalism. All "foreign" games, meaning non-Gaelic, were then scorned by the Irish sporting associations and even today, the Anglo sports of soccer, rugby and cricket are secondary in popularity to Gaelic football and hurling. (Uris 1975:51)

It appears that this cultural division in sports and recreation is reinforced by the schools and churches.

Schools, Churches and Recreation

During Bernadette Devlin's school days, she often skip-roped to this song:

> St. Patrick's Day will be jolly and gay,
> and we'll kick all the Protestants out of the way.
> If that won't do, we'll cut them in two,
> and send them to hell with their red, white and blue.

Protestant children countered with:

> If I had a penny, do you know what I'd do?
> I would buy a rope and hang the Pope
> and let King Billy through. (Starling 1972:13)

This latter rhyme referred to the 1690 battle when William of Orange defeated James II. Since then generations of Catholic and Protestant children have been raised to hate one another.

The influence of the churches is best illustrated by the different ways in which Catholics and Protestants recreate. Protestant churches in Northern Ireland are noted for their "puritanical" attitudes characterized by their strong opposition to gambling, drinking and dancing. As recently as 1974, Protestant churches objected to the Sunday opening of public swimming pools and the usage of children's swings in city parks. Gambling and drinking among Catholics is more socially acceptable plus they frequently hold their major sporting events on Sunday afternoons. Many Protestant ministers preached that, "too much merriment was evil, and we must be careful not to emulate the Catholic barbarians."

Schools intensify the cultural and religious split by discouraging extra-curricular activities between Catholic and Protestant teams. This lack of sectarian contact is compounded when one realizes that no Catholic school in Northern Ireland officially plays rugby or cricket; traditional Catholic games like Gaelic football and hurling are not played in state schools.

(Darby 1973:9)

The absurdity of this situation was discussed by Bernadette Devlin. She recalled that her Catholic school produced a champion netball team that could have beaten any team in Northern Ireland, but the nuns wouldn't let them play Protestant schools for fear that the girls would be required to sing "The Queen's Song", salute the British flag or stand for the British national anthem, (Devlin 1969:62).

The schools and churches still promote cultural and religious holidays, which frequently erupt into major sectarian riots. Such an event ignited the present conflict in Northern Ireland.

Current Forms of Recreation 1969-1975

Since the Protestants still celebrate part of their heritage through the July 12 parades, the Catholics respond with two similar events—one religious and one political.

The Feast of the Assumption, celebrated on the 15th of August, is in memory of Mary, the Mother of Christ. According to Catholic theology she rose to heaven on that date. Extracts from *Call My Brother Back* (McLaverty 1939:9) provided this description:

> If the Orangemen celebrated the Twelfth of July, the Catholics celebrated the Feast of the Assumption...they marched with green sashes, drank porter, talked about Home Rule for Ireland. Boys came around with bin-lids and circled the fire like wild Indians, rattling, shouting, and yelling...Then suddenly all the commotion stopped; policemen came up the streets an chased the crowd for singing rebel songs. "It's a bloody shame!" said a woman from the shelter of her doorway. "Sure they're doing no harm. It's well see yiv little else to do!" "They wouldn't chase the Prods when they had their bonfire on the 12th of July," said another. The police took no notice as the woman jeered at them. One by one the crowd stole back to the bonfire and Alec produced his melodeon and played Irish dances, many doing reels at the edge of the flames. All through the night they sang and danced, and only when the stars were fading from the sky did they leave the warmth of the fire for bed.

Another holiday emerged in the Catholic communities, but the Ninth of August was not festive. At the time of this study (1974-75), memories were still fresh, hatred ran deep, and families still suffered from the injustices and hardships caused by internment. On August 9, 1971, 342 people were arrested and interned without charges under the Special Powers Act—virtually all of them Catholic.

Thus, a new holiday was born, but the merriment was low-keyed. Bonfires were built, people drank, children banged their bin-lids or trash can lids and blew shrill whistles. Historically, the banging of bin-lids or trash can lids and whistles were used to warn Catholic men that the British were coming. The song, "We Shall Overcome," in addition to Irish songs, was sung around the bonfires, as relatives wept and remembered loved ones injured or killed in recent times, or still interned.

In spite of the strong emotional overtones, this holiday was preceded by eager anticipation, the fun of gathering burnable refuse and children making colorful political banners.

Current forms of recreation are reflected in these holidays as well as the songs and games the children play and the organizations they join. One youth worker stated:

> Youth on both sides of the sectarian divide are very much caught up in the acting out of political opinions, with attitudes condoned by a whole history and tradition. Until 1969, such behavior was largely ritualized and therefore controlled through parades and festivities. Now that political agitation has moved on from parades, the youth—especially Catholic teenagers caught up in civil rights have found more adventurous things to do...The parents will defend, even support, the youth as soon as authorities move against them. (Overy 1972:10)

A favorite pastime for both Protestant and Catholic children was to antagonize the British soldiers with rocks and obscene slogans to incite the soldiers to shoot their rubber bullets. These large rubber bullets were then sold by the children to researchers and journalists for souvenirs; this is indicative of how the kids get their pocket money. Other enterprising youngsters earn money by serving as guides through bombed-out sections of Belfast.

"Street-fighting" was a common game in Belfast, with the "Irish" and "British" players identified by armbands. They play with bottles, chains, old boards, and simulate injuries by smearing ketchup on their faces. British soldiers have commented that the children play with amazing realism—all learned by watching real battles.

Simulated street fighting soon escalates into real street battles between residents and British soldiers. The legendary street battles gave rise to many absurd situations. One took place during the spring of 1972 when both sides called a truce so everyone could go home and watch the World Cup Soccer championship on television. It was not uncommon for both sides to call a truce for tea and then resume their battle until the evening news came on.

One such situation happened to this researcher. I had spent the night recording rebel songs and I commented in a joking manner that what I really wanted to record was a bomb explosion. Later that morning I walked back to Queen's University where I had a room. While napping a bomb woke me up. Since that was not an unusual occurrence, I got up, ate, and walked back to my informant's apartment. As I entered the apartment, one of the young men said to me, "Where were you this afternoon? We came by but the college girls said you weren't there." Then, in a half-disgusted way, he asked, "Did you hear the bomb go off at four o'clock?" "Yeah, it woke me up, so what else is new?" "Too bad," he shrugged, "that was for you and your tape recorder." To them, this type of activity was an acceptable way of life, but I was deeply dismayed and felt shocked by their obviously sincere effort to please me. It was obvious that this bombing had been done as a lark—it had been their recreation for that afternoon.

Handling explosives and other types of guerrilla activities are frequently learned when youngsters join Fianna, a junior IRA club, or one of its Protestant counterparts. It has been said that puberty rites in Belfast consist of learning how to hijack cars, make bombs, conduct surveillance on British patrols and run messages for guerrilla commanders. This problem was reinforced by a recreation leader who said:

> So long as the fighting continues at such a pitch, I see very little indeed that can "be done" in terms of redirecting this activity. For what can compare to this excitement, sense of purpose and comradeship? But, if approached sensitively, the potential for eventual creative action is tremendous. The vitality and seriousness of these young people is very special.

Graffiti had become a common art form and vividly illustrated the cultural conflict as well as identified the political climate of each neighborhood. The following are examples of slogans commonly seen on Belfast war-torn buildings: "End Internment," "Join Fianna," "Prod Ulster not for Rebel Bastards" (a reference to the IRA), "One hope, one Crown, No Pope in Our Town," "Informers will be shot," "Touts Beware" (informers), "IRA Forever," "UDA Rules."

Playing in ruins and creating toys from war debris or building forts from other war materials, participation in demonstrations or joining a childrens' choral group which teaches rebel songs or posing for a researcher's camera—all are common forms of recreation in Belfast.

Conclusion

The future appears bleak when one considers that schools and housing are still segregated, Protestant and Catholic children learn different sports and even celebrate different holidays. Positive efforts are being made, through recreation, to bridge the gap between these two cultures, but these attempts are meeting with limited success.

The words on a Belfast City Truck best depict the conflict in Belfast. Written on the truck was "Department of Parks & Cemeteries." It's quite ironic that in Belfast, the same department is in charge of play and death. Perhaps this best summarizes the suggested conclusion, that in Belfast, violence has become recreation and recreation has been a divisive rather than a unifying factor between the Irish Catholic and British Protestant cultures.

BIBLIOGRAPHY

Darby, John, "Divisiveness in Education," *Northern Teacher,* Winter, 1973.

Devlin, Bernadette. *The Price of My Soul.* London: Pan Books, Ltd., 1969.

Duncan, Mary Hackett. The Effects of Social Conflict on Recreation Patterns in Belfast, Northern Ireland. Dissertation, United States International University, San Diego, California, 1975.

Hanson, Richard. "Politics and the Pulpit," Community Forum, III, No. 3, 1973, 15.

McLaverty, Michael. *Call My Brother Back.* Dublin: Allen Figgis & Co., Ltd., 1939.

Overy, Rush. "Children's Play," Community Forum, II, No. 10, 1972, 10.
Starling, Susan J. "Play in Belfast," Community Forum, II, No. 1, 1972, 13.
Uris, Jill & Leon. *Ireland—a Terrible Beauty.* Doubleday & Co., Inc., New York, 1975.
Whale, John. "Modern Guerrilla Movements," Community Forum III, No. 2, 1973, 3.

From Play to Recreation: The Acceptance of Leisure in the United States, 1890-1930

Bernard Mergen, George Washington University

From Work to Play

Perhaps the Gospel of Work was always a myth, an ideal which a few men held in order to justify their extraordinary success and the accumulation of wealth far beyond their immediate needs. Perhaps, as Alasdair Clayre has recently argued, the belief in the spiritual nature of work was held only by writers who were, in fact, creative, spontaneous, and psychologically fulfilled by their work.[1] Clearly, the so-called work ethic was never as monolithic as history text books sometimes make it seem. Nevertheless, work superseded religion in two significant ways in the 19th century: (1) as an escape from death; and (2) as a way of establishing an individual identity within a community.[2]

Where religion had held out the hope of salvation of the soul, work held out the promise of unlimited success and a kind of immortality gained by social recognition and family legacy. Where church membership and spiritual well-being had once defined a person's place in society, work offered occupational solidarity and peer group esteem. These characteristics, plus the industrial discipline necessary for factory work make up what I am calling the *work ethic.*[3]. What I find most interesting is that the attack on the work ethic, when it comes in the early 20th century, is highly articulate and massively organized. From the rhetoric of the disciples of leisure, one would expect a much more awesome opponent. My own theory is that the advocates of play, leisure, and recreation in the early 20th century were responding to much more fundamental changes in American society than the 8-hour day or the lack of play space in the slums. Play, and later recreation and leisure, were symbols for a whole complex of values and attitudes about opportunity, creativity, and self-fulfillment.

A good example of this is Henry Curtis' comments on Edwin Markham's poem, "The Man with the Hoe," in *The Playground,* December 1912. The poem, which describes the bowed, broken toiler of Millet's painting in both Darwinian and Marxian terms, was first printed in William Randolph Hearst's San Francisco *Examiner* in 1899, and then widely reprinted during the next decade. It was one of Samuel Gompers' favorite poems, appearing frequently in the pages of the *American Federationist.* It is one of the poems which influences the radical Mary French in Dos Passos' novel, *The Big Money*. In short, "The Man with the Hoe" summed up an attitude toward the exploitation of labor shared by a whole generation. Quoting the lines:

> How will you ever straighten up this shape;
> Touch it again with immortality;
> Give back the upward looking and the light;
> Rebuild in it the music and the dream...

Curtis comments that Markham is describing a man without play. Give him the leisure and the opportunity to play and you can restore "the music and the dream."[4]

This is also essentially the message of writers such as Alexander Chamberlain in *The Child: A Study in the Evolution of Man,* in 1900, and Temple Scott in his book, *The Uses of Leisure,* in 1913. "Play in childhood," Chamberlain summarized, "is concerned with everything; emotions, feelings, acts, thoughts, imaginings, speech, all begin their career under its subtle, shaping influence, and the really genial among adults never lose in science, art, literature, the 'play,' which makes it a joy to be alive and to use life."[5] Scott mocked the work ethic and justified a leisure ethic by reference to the Declaration of Independence. "We are machines that are run down each evening," he wrote, "to be cranked up again each morning. And we are actually glad thus to labor...leisure is the first requisite for making possible for us the pursuit of happiness."[6] The assault on the work ethic was seldom direct, however, but took the form of a new emphasis on play.

The relation of the play movement to adult recreation in threefold: (1) in its belief in the restorative power of nature, (2) in its insistence on establishing a separate area for recreation, (3) in its attempt to remove the corrupting influence of commercial amusements. First in origin is what has been called the "back to nature" impulse.[7] As early as 1836, Emerson wrote in his essay, "Nature:" "In the woods, too, a man casts off his years, as the snake his slough, and at what period soever of life, is always a child. In the woods is perpetual youth." The association of nature-youth-play was carried on by that cohort of early outdoor enthusiasts who made the Adirondacks synonymous with wilderness recreation. Joel T. Hadley, author of *The Adirondack; or Life in the Woods* (1849) developed Emerson's theme:

> In the woods, the mask that society compels one to wear is cast aside, and the restraints which the thousand eyes and reckless tongues about him fasten on the heart, are thrown off, and the soul rejoices in its liberty and again becomes a child in action. The ludicrous incident, the careless joke, the thrilling story, the eager chase, are all in place in the forest, and as harmless as the sports of the deer.[8]

Twenty years later, William H. H. Murray described a delightful scene in which he and several companions, inspired by the beauty of their surroundings and the freedom of their situation, began turning somersaults and dancing.[9] And the novelist Charles Dudley Warner observed that "All this virginal freshness invites the primitive instincts of play and disorder."[10]

While the upper-middle class continued to play in the forests and mountains, they became increasingly concerned about providing similar experiences for future generations and for the immigrant, urban poor. The national park and playground movements went forward together from the 1880's on, part of a larger concern for the conservation of resources, both natural and human. The close relationship between forest conservation, city planning, and social work was made clear in a special issue of the *Annals of the American Academy of Political and Social Science* on "Public Recreation Facilities," in 1910. Under the editorship of John Nolen, the landscape architect, the issue contains articles on national, state, and city parks and forests, and on the social significance of parks and playgrounds for immigrants and children.[11] In his introduction, Nolen asserts that "It is time to preach the gospel of relaxation," and Howard Braucher, Secretary of the Playground Association of America, carried the idea forward by proclaiming that, "Philosophers have now agreed that play is as much a part of life as work—that each day, if complete in itself, is made up of work, play and rest; that life without play is incomplete; that play is not a preparation for more work, but is itself life."[12]

Defining Play and Leisure

Although the concern for children's play was dominant at first, because it was assumed that good play habits had to be learned early in life, adult behavior both at work and at play was potentially more disruptive and the focus of the reformers shifted accordingly. This is nowhere better revealed than in the name changes of the Playground Association itself. Organized in 1906, it began publishing a journal, *The Playground,* in 1907. In 1911, the members voted to change the name of the organization to Playground and Recreation Association of America. The journal became *Playground and Recreation* in 1929, and *Recreation* only in 1931. The Association had become the National Recreation Association in 1930. The evolution of this organization was partly the result of the accomplishment of its primary goals, the establishment of supervised playgrounds in every city in the United States, and partly a response to the demands of business and industry that its work force be better disciplined to correct the problems of absenteeism and high labor turnover. Surveys were taken to determine what people actually did with their spare time and the results showed that they spent most of their time "doing nothing" or "just fooling around." Very often this meant drinking, gambling, or attending commercial amusements such as the burlesque or movies.[13]

As early as 1891, Stewart Culin had described gambling games of boys in Brooklyn, N.Y.,[14] but few Progressive reformers were willing to acknowledge gambling as an integral part of play. Prohibition was the only answer to gambling and drinking, but regulation was a possible solution to the problem of pool rooms and nickelodeons. John Collier, who would later become Franklin Roosevelt's Commissioner of Indian Affairs, began in 1910 to control the content and environment of motion pictures in New York City.[15] Writing on "Motion Pictures: Their Function and Proper Regulation," in *The Playground* in 1910, Collier emphasized the opportunity for social workers to influence local exhibitors to show educational and uplifting films. He also urged the use of movies to attract children and adults to playgrounds and community centers. The close connection between movies and play, especially fantasy, was understood by the reformers. Orrin Cocks, in the *National Municipal Review* in 1914, described

> ...fathers and mothers gather[ed] with their children before the motion picture screen to quaff deep draughts of life. Tired muscles and weary nerves are recreated. The powerful actions and motives of life pass before them. They dream their dreams and see their visions as the skillful artist depicts the thrilling situations of other lives. While the interest is sustained, minds are busy. Interest brings enlightment. Who can tell how the spirit of a man grows! Certainly this new form of art takes its place as a great spiritual force.[16]

The appeal of motion pictures was confirmed by a remarkable survey taken by George E. Bevans in 1912, and published the following year as a Columbia doctoral dissertation under the title *How the Workingmen Spend Their Spare Time.*[17] Using investigators paid by the Home Mission Board of the Presbyterian Church, Bevans collected 1,070 questionnaires, from workers in New York and a few other cities, containing information on the use of spare time in relation to hours worked per day, occupation, marital status, age, nationality, and income. The results showed that the largest percentage of time of all working men was spent with family or friends, or reading the newspaper, but of the commercial amusements, motion pictures led the list for workers who put in nine or more hours a day on the job. Bevans' tables are interesting for what they reveal about the definition of "spare time."

The basic list of the ways in which spare time was used included: labor unions, clubs or lodges, church or synagogue, public lectures, art galleries, library, private study, night school, motion pictures, theater, dance, saloon, pool, cards, family, newspaper, magazine, books, and friends. Obviously there were many activities omitted from the list because their percentages were too small to be significant, or because they were not preceived as spare time activities by the respondents or the investigators. The bias of the investigators is suggested by the distinctions made among public lectures, private study, and night school. Workers who enjoyed an 8-9 hour day reported a preference for public lectures, while those who toiled eleven hours and more spent almost as much of their spare time in night school as the 8-9 hour group. Similarly, by distinguishing between book and newspaper reading, Bevans could show that book reading increased as the hours of work declined. In another table, which showed the percentage of time devoted to various activities (1) from supper to bed time, (2) on Saturday afternoons, (3) on Sundays, (4) on holidays, and (5) the "most profitable ways to spend time," the choices included: work, friends, home, reading, studying, saloon, church or synagogue, meetings, theater, indoor pleasures, athletic games, excursions, and walking. Thus Bevans could show the deprivation of the men who worked over eleven hours a day—men who had little time for Saturday afternoon athletic games or holiday excursions. Clearly, spare time did not mean idleness, but it did include the simple pleasures of "excursions" and walking.

Bevans' statistics were a strong argument for the eight-hour day and the five-day week, despite the fear expressed by some that free time would be spent at spectator sports, which in turn might unleash violent emotions in the crowd.[18] Increasingly, the nature of work and play was seen in psychological rather than sociological terms. Where the work and play ethics of 1890 had been defined by their relation to group solidarity and the social system, they were now seen more as individual attitudes which varied from person to person. Wilbur P. Bowen summarized the new concept nicely in an article for *Hygiene and Physical Education* in 1909. "Work," wrote Bowen,

> may be defined as doing something for the sake of certain results that we hope to accomplish...Play...may be defined as doing something for the sake of the satisfaction received in the doing...The determining factor is the mental attitude of the doer toward the things he is doing, while he is doing it; and since the mental attitudes change, not only from week to week but from moment to moment, the same occupation may be play, work, and drudgery in turn to the same individual in the same hour.[19]

Industrial Recreation

The challenge and potential of this perspective was obvious. If work could be made stimulating, it could become play, and if play were boring, it would become work of the worst kind. The challenge was picked up in the new personnel management movement, defined and promoted by Meyer Bloomfield from about 1915 on.[20] Personnel management, or employment management as it was called then, is the crucial link between what was going on in business and industry and what was developing in social work and the play movement, because key features of employment management were psychological testing, to find the right job for the worker, and the provision of services such as sanitary lunch rooms and recreational facilities. On the eve of World War I a few companies were experimenting with Industrial Recreation, the name given to a wide range of leisure time activities for workers sponsored by their employers.

Writing in *Industrial Management* in 1917, C. B. Lord of the Wagner Electric Manufacturing Company of St. Louis, and Mary Barnett Gilson, Employment Manager of the Clothcraft Shops of the Joseph and Feiss Company of Cleveland, extolled the virtues of company sponsored athletics as a means of improving the health of the employees and of building company spirit.[21] The growth of certain war industries, notably shipbuilding, stimulated both personnel management and industrial recreation. At Hog Island near Philadelphia, for example, the Emergency Fleet Corporation of the United States Shipping Board built the world's largest shipyard and employed 30,000 workers between November 1917 and November 1918. Among the provisions for that facility were a baseball stadium seating 5000, a club house with a basketball gym, tennis courts and bowling alleys, and two YMCA's, one for white and one for black workers.[22] Just after the war the Bureau of Labor Statistics of the United States Department of Labor surveyed the welfare work of several thousand industrial establishments and found most of them providing club rooms for reading, cards, checkers, and similar games, and a few equipped with billiard rooms, bowling alleys, gymnasiums, swimming pools, tennis courts, baseball and football fields, and golf courses.[23]

Although it is difficult to determine exactly how widespread the industrial recreation movement was, or to what extend workers actually participated in the activities offered, a picture does emerge in the writings of recreation directors and in an occasional response by a representative of labor. A. H. Wyman, Welfare Director of Carnegie Steel, described the full range of sports offered at Carnegie's plants in 1919, but admitted that the number taking part varied from 1% at the Waverly Warehouse to 30% at Mingo, with an average of 12% for the units reporting.[24] The *American Physical Education Review* devoted most of its January 1924, issue to the subject of industrial recreation. L. C. Gardner summarized the emerging attitude toward this phase of industrial relations:

> Industrial community recreation is not a cure-all...While incomplete as a happiness program it is more than a pastime, more than entertainment and more than a device for heading off labor troubles...A sane, moderate program of recreation that aims to give everybody something to do in his leisure is one way an employer can insure his workers coming to work refreshed and alert and in a happy frame of mind.[25]

All the authors mention football, soccer, bowling, boxing, baseball, and basketball as activities popular with the male workers, but Ruth Stone of the Hawthorne Works of the Western Electric Company in Chicago is more revealing about the discrepancies between the company's ideas of recreation and the worker's.

> A suggestion for golf lessons which came from the office girls met with some objection by the girls in the factory, but their prejudice was overcome and it is now a popular sport...A class in gymnastics last year did not prove a success. This was probably due to our lack of equipment and proper facilities, and we question the advisability of offering it another year...A curious bit of psychology was encountered with horseback riding. While the shop girls considered golf outside the realm of activities, they embraced horseback riding with an astonishing amount of enthusiasm. At first it was impossible to secure enough horses to supply the demand...

Finally, she noted the unexpected popularity of rifle shooting.[26] Interpretation of these observations is difficult, but they suggest patterns of play and attitudes toward recreation that have generally been ignored. The girls in the shop may have chosen horseback riding and shooting because they came from rural backgrounds, or because they represented values and styles which they sought to imitate. Obviously few felt as G. J. W. Patrick that golf was "the perfect ideal sport."

> It has all the needed recreational elements. It has a restorative power excelling all therapeutic arts. It represents a reversion to the natural outdoor life. We range over the hills in the open, using the muscles of the legs, arms, and trunk. We carry a club and strike viciously at a ball. We search for the ball in the grass as our ancestors searched for their arrows. There is a goal and the spirit of rivalry and a chance for self-expression. The nerve currents course through ancient channels. We return to our work refreshed and rejuvenated. Golf, to be sure requires fine adjustments of eye and hand at the moment of striking but there is no continuous strain upon them and skill of this kind is a proper element in play. It is unfortunate that the opportunities for golf are now limited to the few. Nothing better could happen to our nation than a wide extension to our people of the opportunities to play golf.[27]

Professor Patrick's middle-class, middle-aged enthusiasm may be pardoned, I think, but the point should be clear that *most concepts of work and play are rooted in beliefs which are inappropriate to a theory of play.* By focusing narrowly on what is defined as work or play by a few individuals, we may miss the complex interrelation between the two. Nor is play only a mental attitude as Bowen maintains. Play is a cultural process which may be glimpsed in brief encounters and fleeting moments of many activities. Frances Donovan, an educated woman who wrote of her experiences in several occupations in the 1920's described one of the ways in which a waitress combined her work and play.

> Tipping is the gambling factor in the life of the waitress. It redeems her work from dull routine and drudgery and puts into it the problematical. It is the same thing that makes the man shake the dice for his cigars instead of paying outright for them. To get a tip is, as William I. Thomas says, 'like winning a game. It involves the same uncertainty. It has in it the element of chance, of luck; it is the getting something for nothing, the legitimate satisfaction of the gaming instinct, which is no more dormant in the female than in the male.'[28]

To their credit many recreation professionals did attempt to learn what the working class wanted to play, and to provide opportunities for them to play it. *The Playground* reported efforts to provide recreation for striking miners and for farm workers in the hop fields of Oregon.[29] They rejoiced in every opportunity to report interest in recreation by the American Federation of Labor, but those occasions were rare.[30] When a representative of labor did write on leisure it was usually to deplore the paternalism of industrial recreation, or to urge that workers devote their spare time to education and the arts in order to improve their social and economic position. Increasingly it appears that labor and the recreation movement were working at cross purposes. Above a certain income and in certain jobs, men and women wanted more opportunity to play, below that level they were often willing to sacrifice enjoyment for upward mobility. Moreover, leisure time spent in the pursuit of pleasure weakened the labor movement itself. P. J. Conlon editorialized in the *Machinists' Monthly* in 1930: "In bygone years [Labor Day] was devoted to organizing speeches, but since the automobile and radio have become so popular, it is now used as a three-day vacation period at the end of the vacation season, and is not so generally observed by Organized Labor as in the days when outdoor picnics were the order of the day..."[31] There is, of course, considerable irony in Conlon's complaint, for Samuel Gompers had argued that the 8-hour day would make the wage earner a better consumer. "He goes to and from work at a time when well-dressed people are on the streets. He really has time and opportunity for making comparisons and forming desires. He has longer time to stay at home, see other homes better furnished, and consequently wants a better home for himself. He wants books, pictures, friends, entertainment."[32]

Leisure: The Unfinished Revolution

By the end of the decade of the 1920's the advocates of recreation and play had succeeded in establishing a leisure ethic, but they were plagued by doubts. The October 1929 issue of *Playground and Recreation* featured an article entitled, "Are We Carrying the Play Idea Too Far?" which assured its readers that

> We, no more than you, are in favor of a pleasure mad community or nation...Because it is our business to emphasize this side of life, the importance of a reasonable amount of play and recreation, it must not be assumed that the Playground and Recreation Association of America, its members, its board members or its staff, does not wholeheartedly also believe in work, both because we need work to produce things which we need and also because work itself carried out under proper conditions is a fine, wholesome, character-building activity.[33]

With the nation entering into a long economic depression and with unemployment rising, it was inevitable that the concepts of work and leisure would be modified and redefined again. If Americans were no longer distrustful of leisure, they were still unconvinced of its potential for increasing social cohesion, nor were they prepared for further increases in free time.

In 1934, Morris S. Viteles, in his management text, *The Science of Work,* concluded that "the permanence of a social system—of a civilization—is determined by its ability to maintain and direct to its desired ends the will-to-work."[34] Work, not play, was still the basis of civilization. At the same time, Marion Flad interviewed 418 of her colleagues at the University of Southern California to find out what they did with their leisure time. Assuming with her professor, Emory Bogardus, that "If 'work makes the worker,' then leisure makes the rest of the personality," she was horrified to discover that, "There is common report that no real thought had been given to the use of leisure time."[35] If students, professors, and social workers couldn't use their leisure time constructively, what hope was there for the rest of the country? Perhaps the answer came in a popular movie of this same year, 1934, *Stand Up and Cheer.* Hollywood's answer to the Depression in this film was the creation of a Secretary of Amusement, who put Shirley Temple, Stepin Fetchit, and the rest of America to singing and dancing their time away.

Conclusion

This paper has sketched some of the outlines of the subject of changing concepts of work and play in the first three decades of this country. Its purpose has been to show that there are temporal as well as cultural dimensions to the study of recreation and leisure. Men have always played, in the sense that play is a voluntary elaboration of patterns of behavior, but their reasons for doing so have varied.[36] Just as the Ute and Anglo-Mormon high school students studied by Allan Tindall could play the same basketball game and maintain separate cultural orientations,[37] generations of Americans have taken walks, played baseball, or gone to movies for reasons varying from personal pleasure to social improvement. The attempt to redefine play and to organize it into socially acceptable activities resulted in the narrowing of the range of sports and games available to most American adults in the 1920's. Advocates of the "leisure ethic" hoped that organized recreation would result in a unified and improved national culture. Forty years later, we are just beginning to understand the reasons for their failure.[38]

FOOTNOTES

[1]Alasdair Clayre, *Work and Play: Ideas and Experience of Work and Leisure,* N.Y.: Harper and Row, 1974.

[2]This is an idea suggested by Daniel Bell, *Work and Its Discontents,* Boston: Beacon Press, 1956, p. 56.

[3]For other reviews of the work ethic, see E. P. Thompson, *The Making of the English Working Class,* N.Y.: Vintage Books, 1966; and Herbert Gutman, "Work, Culture and Society in Industrializing America, 1815-1919," *The American Historical Review* 78, 3, June, 1973, pp. 531-588. Gutman's concept of culture is borrowed from Eric Wolf, Sidney Mintz, and Clifford Geertz, but is not quite appropriate for his data.

[4]*The Playground* 6, 9, December 1912, pp. 310-311.

[5]Alexander F. Chamberlain, *The Child: A Study in the Evolution of Man,* second ed., N.Y.: Scribner's, 1907, p. 27.

[6]Temple Scott, *The Uses of Leisure,* N.Y.: B. W. Huebsch, 1913, pp. 12 and 37.

[7]Bernard Mergen, "The Discovery of Children's Play," *American Quarterly* 27, 4, October 1975, pp. 399-420.

[8]Joel T. Hadley, *The Adirondack; or Life in the Woods* (1849) pp. ii-iii. For this and the following two references I am indebted to my student, Philip Terrie.

[9]William H. H. Murray, *Adventures in the Wilderness, or Camplife in the Adirondacks* (1869), pp. 88-100.

[10]Charles Dudley Warner, *In the Wilderness* (1878), p. 130.

[11]*Annals of the American Academy of Political and Social Science,* 35, 2, March 1910.

[12]*Ibid.,* p. 113.

[13]See, for example, George E. Johnson, *Education Through Recreation,* Cleveland: The Survey Committee of the Cleveland Foundation, 1916, p. 49. For a good survey of the history of the National Recreation Association, see Richard F. Knapp, *Play for America: The National Recreation Association, 1906-1950,* Ph.D. dissertation, Duke University, 1971, and a series of articles in *Parks and Recreation,* 1972-1975.

[14]Stewart Culin, "Street Games of Boys in Brooklyn, N.Y.," *Journal of American Folklore* 4, July-September 1891, p. 234. For biographical information on Culin, see *Who Was Who in America,* vol. I, Chicago: Marquis, 1966, p. 283, and Alyce Cheska, "Stewart Culin: An Early Ethnologist of Games," *Newsletter: The Association for the Anthropological Study of Play* 2, 3, Fall 1975, 4-13.

[15]John Collier, "Motion Pictures as a Factor in Municipal Life," *National Municipal Review* 3, 4, October 1914, pp. 708-712.

[17]George E. Bevans, *How Workingmen Spend Their Spare Time,* N.Y., 1913, pp. 20 and 46.

[18]J. L. Gillan, "The Sociology of Recreation," *American Journal of Sociology,* 19, 6, May 1914, pp. 825-834.

[19]W. P. Bowen, "The Meaning of Work and Play," *Hygiene and Physical Education* 1, 5, July 1909, pp. 408-410.

[20]Meyer Bloomfield, "The New Profession of Handling Men," *Annals of the American Academy of Political and Social Science* 61, September 1915, p. 121-126.

[21]C. B. Lord, "Athletics for the Working Force," *Industrial Management* 54 October 1917, pp. 44-47; Mary B. Gilson, "Recreation of the Working Force," *ibid.,* pp. 52-58.

[22]*Hog Island News* 1, 17, June 15, 1918, p. 1. The files of the United States Shipping Board (Record Group 32), the National Archives, contain much information on recreation in the government shipyards.

[23]United States Department of Labor, Bureau of Labor Statistics, *Welfare Work for Employees in Industrial Establishments in the U.S.,* Bulletin 250, U.S.G.P.O., 1919.

[24]A. H. Wyman, "Recreation in Industrial Communities," *American Physical Education Review* 24, 9, December 1919, pp. 473-480.

[25]L. C. Gardner, "Community Athletic Recreation for the Employees and Their Families," *American Physical Education Review* 29, 1, January 1924, pp. 4-5.

[26]Ruth I. Stone, "Recreational Activities for Women Employees," *ibid.,* p. 8.

[27]G. J. W. Patrick, "The Play of a Nation," *Scientific Monthly* 13, 4, October 1921, p. 354.

[28]Frances Donovan, *The Woman Who Waits,* Boston: Richard G. Badger, The Gorham Press, 1920, p. 202.

[29]"Recreation for Miners on Strike," *The Playground* 17, 7, October 1923, p. 386; "Recreation in the Oregon Hop Fields," *ibid.,* 17, 12, March 1924, pp. 645-646, 670.

[30]"Organized Labor and Recreation," *The Playground* 18, 2, May 1924, pp. 124-126.

[31]*The Machinists' Monthly* 42, October, 1930, pp. 583-584. See also Al Towers, "Recreation and Industry," *The Playground* 18, 6, September 1924, pp. 335-336, 370; Matthew Woll, "Leisure and Labor," *ibid.,* 19, 6, September 1925, pp. 322-323; James H. Maurer, "Leisure and Labor," *ibid.,* 20, 12 March 1927, pp. 649-655; William Green, "The Five Day Week," *North American Review* 1926, pp. 566-574.

[32]Samuel Gompers, "The Shorter Workday—Its Philosophy," in *Words That Made American History: Since the Civil War,* edited by Richard Current and John Garraty, Boston: Little, Brown, 1965, p. 428.

[33]"Are We Carrying the Play Idea Too Far?" *The Playground* 23, 7, October 1929, pp. 445-446.

[34]Morris S. Viteles, *The Science of Work,* N.Y.: Norton, 1934, p. 414.

[35]Marion Flad, "Leisure Time Activities of Four Hundred Persons," *Sociology and Social Research* 18, January-February 1934, p. 274.

[36]Stephen Miller, "Ends, Means, and Galumphing: Some Leitmotifs of Play," *American Anthropologist,* 75, February 1973, pp. 87-98.

[37]B. Allan Tindall, "The Perceptual and Cultural Meaning of Basketball," paper presented at the 7th Annual Meeting of the American Anthropological Association, San Francisco, California, 1975.

[38]David E. Gray and Seymour Greben, "Future Perspectives," paper presented to The National Congress of the National Recreation and Park Association, October 3, 1973.

A Paleoanthropological Approach to Recreation and Sporting Behaviors

Steven J. Fox, Middle Tennessee State University

Introduction

Unlike more direct techniques employed in the study of cultural phenomena, archaeology relies almost exclusively upon analyses of physical remains of culture, the residues of human behavior. Among the more frequently encountered data are: artifacts, the actual tools, weapons, and other material fragments of culture; artistic depictions in various media; and special task areas present within each locus of prehistoric activity that the archaeologist investigates.

Traditionally, archaeology has focused upon descriptions of economic and ritual aspects of culture, as these are represented disproportionately in the data observed and collected during field studies. Consequently, interpretations of prehistoric cultural behaviors have been limited in focus. Over the past two decades there has been a gradual shift in orientation on the part of many American archaeologists away from the traditional descriptive approach to prehistory toward more comprehensive, explanatory models of extinct cultural process systems. The advocates of these new perspectives maintain that, theoretically, each archaeological site contains all necessary information for complete reconstruction, interpretation, and explanation of the multitude of cultural behaviors purveyed by its former inhabitants, and that these data need only be properly collected and analyzed (Binford 1962, 1968; Deetz 1967; Watson, LeBlanc, and Redman 1971). The implications for the utility of the new explanatory approach to archaeological data for the study of sport and recreation are readily apparent.

All sociocultural systems, extinct as well as extant, are, generally speaking, organizationally and operationally analogous. Much expository knowledge may be gained through the responsible application of ethnographic analogies (Ascher 1961; Heider 1967), particularly when these are used in conjunction with a well formulated research problem (Binford 1964). Hence, any attempt to elicit information on the relative importance of sport and recreation in prehistoric sociocultural systems is dependent upon the recognition of extinct cultures as once dynamic behavioral networks, and upon the utilization of a formal design for collecting the necessary data.

The Archaeological Record

At the present time there are few direct references to sport and recreation behaviors in the archaeological literature. Several explanations may be offered for this situation. First, few archaeologists appear to be willing to confront these as cultural phenomena worthy of scholarly investigation. Second, those individuals who have acknowledged the respective roles of sport and recreation in prehistory have often used these as part of a larger framework for classifying data that cannot be readily inserted into more conventional categories of cultural behavior. The net result of the latter situation is that anomalous artifacts frequently become known by such classificatory references as "gaming objects," even though this may not actually represent a cultural reality. Third, a converse of the above, is the misrepresentation of material evidences of sporting and other forms of recreation as manifestations of economic, ritual, or other cultural behaviors. Finally, the archaeologist is confronted with the very real problem of actually gathering the material data of sporting and recreation activities, which are, for the most part, few. Unfortunately, the latter situation more accurately represents the present state of knowledge than do any of the other aforementioned alternatives.

The paucity of information on sporting and recreational behaviors contained in the archaeological record, particularly from sites representing non-centralized sociocultural systems, is in itself significant; realizing, of course, that only the most durable fragments of cultural will be preserved for the archaeologist. This negative evidence for recreational activities is extremely important, especially when viewed in its broader cultural context. As it is highly improbable that the artifacts attributable to sporting and other recreational activities were always fashioned from perishable materials, or that no artifacts for such activities were ever manufactured at all, alternative hypotheses explaining the roles of sport and recreation in prehistoric cultures must be formulated.

Predictive Cultural Models

The archaeological remains of culture are, above all, manifestations of the interactions between a technology and a physical environment. As technologies, hence economies, become increasingly efficient, greater time will become available to members of a society for engaging in more formalized, institutional, non-economic cultural activities. Moreover, there is a marked tendency for these non-economic sociocultural behaviors to display increasingly complex forms relative to improved productive efficiency within the techno-economic sector (Steward 1949, 1955; White 1959). Therefore, it is imperative that at least the material manifestations of all non-economic sociocultural phenomena, including sport and recreation, be viewed against this background.

It is predicted that the least elaboration of sporting and recreational activities will be present among cultural groups with an hunting-and-collecting mode of techno-environmental adaptation, as this is the least efficient of all adaptive strategies. The archaeological evidence, or lack of it, bears out this assumption. Correspondingly, mechanisms of sociocultural integration are rarely formalized among groups of this stage.

At the other end of the cultural evolutionary continuum, those groups with an highly efficient economic base should manifest the most intricate social structures, and engage in rather formal sporting and recreational activities. Again, the archaeological evidence supports the hypothesis.

Cultural systems with an exploitative hunting-and-collecting, economic base will tend to lack the necessary free time on a predictable, regular basis to develop and maintain structured, institutionalized, sporting and recreational pastimes. The bulk of the archaeological evidence for these pursuits is confined, at least from Western North America, to text descriptions of artifacts designated "game counters" (Dick 1965; Jennings 1957), "gaming sticks" (Aikens 1970; Jennings 1957), and "dice" (McGregor 1965). "Chunkey stones" have been reported from prehistoric sites in Eastern North America (Fowler 1973; Lewis and Kneberg 1946); these artifacts are so designated because of their general similarity to stones used in the chunkey game as played by certain Historic Period groups of this region. Yet, the facts of the situation are such that, beyond classification, the actual significance of these items to their associated cultural behaviors is left largely to conjecture.

More important, however, is the probability that most of the evidence for sport and recreation among peoples at this stage of adaptation has gone, and will continue to go, undetected. The reason for this is that a considerable proportion of these activities are individual-oriented and concerned with the development, and/or improvement of skills that will also be of value in economic endeavors. The artifacts of sport and recreation are quite often also those of food procuring, and their dual function is almost certain to escape even the most careful scrutiny by the archaeologist. The absence of special recreation areas within most archaeological sites also inhibits the recovery of these data. Emphasis upon individual performance is understandable in the context of exploitative adaptive strategies, especially when it is acknowledged that early acquisition and effective implementation of specific skills are necessary for the economic well-being of the individual and, at the very least, his familial unit.
and, at the very least, his familial unit.

At the opposite end of the developmental spectrum, among populations manifesting an advanced level of sociocultural integration, formalized sport and recreational activities appear almost exclusively in situations where there exists a more-or-less reliable economic base emphasizing acquisition of subsistence resources through production rather than exploitation. Correspondingly, cultures at such a level of adaptive efficiency also manifest rather complex social structures, often including an extensive division of labor with specialists in government, religion, warfare, and, not infrequently, specialists in competitive sport. In the case of New World Archaic States, such as the Aztec and Maya, the cultural data exists in relative abundance both in the archaeological and ethnohistorical records, particularly with respect to the highly competitive "ball game." Not only are the ball courts themselves present in many archaeological sites, generally major urban and ceremonial centers (Hardoy 1973; Thompson 1970; Weaver 1972; Willey and Bullard 1965); but descriptions of the game being played have survived reasonably intact in the ethnohistorical texts (Soustelle 1962; Tozzer 1941). Less structured forms of sport and recreation presumably existed also; however, material evidences of these have not been reported in the archaeological literature.

The important distinction that should be made here is, in contrast to the sporting and recreational pursuits of peoples with uncentralized sociopolitical systems, the fact that these endeavors have far transcended the individual and become incorporated into the institutional frameworks of the societies. They are collective, formally structured activities of societal importance. Furthermore, these sporting activities are often initiated in conjunction with specific political and/or religious events. Sport becomes, in these contexts, integral to the state as a mechanism for promoting and maintaining social solidarity. Thus, sport is a specialized form of ritual behavior that functions in association with the secular forces of the larger social order. When sport and recreation become ritualistic behaviors they are also subject to investigation and analysis by the archaeologist. Ritual behaviors are structured, and to a large extent, predictable, thus providing a measure of security to the participants as well as the observers. These behaviors tend to occur at more-or-less regular intervals and at special locations; in the case of ritualized sport, the fields of competition, objects (artifacts) of competition, and ornamental adornments of the participants are all familiar to the members of the culture and potentially recoverable by the archaeologist.

Further accompanying the institutionalization of sport and recreation in complex sociocultural settings is the ritualization of sport beyond simple competition, and beyond the acquisition and improvement of physical skills, although, presumably, these were also important.

The archaeologist must, at this juncture, also rely upon sources of information for behavioral reconstruction and explanation that cannot be wholly attained through examination of material culture remains alone;

most valuable in this regard are the uses of ethnographic analogy and ethnohistoric texts when such are available. Furthermore, he must attempt to generalize to accomodate all aspects of sporting behavior in all socio-cultural contexts, at least as such represent a "category" of human cultural behavior, and so as to accomodate potentially divergent, culture-specific conceptions of sport and recreation.

Summary and Conclusions

As noted in the first part of this paper, archaeology possesses the techniques necessary for collecting the material data of sport and recreation as integral cultural phenomena. These methods become increasingly valuable when used in conjunction with other anthropological models of behavioral explanation. Fundamental to the contemporary archaeological focus it the emphasis upon the exposition of the dynamics of extinct cultural systems.

The problems confronting the archaeologist interested in investigating the place of sport and recreation in prehistoric cultural settings are, for the most part: lack of previously conducted research into these behaviors; and absence of a model of cultural behavior that integrates sport and recreation with other components of cultural process systems.

Therefore, the archaeologist must seek to formulate his own explanatory framework if he is to effectively pursue this avenue of cultural analysis. Given the rather specific nature of the problem at hand, and the complexities involved in isolating these data, it is highly probable that special techniques will have to be devised for the extraction of the desired information. These will, as should all archaeological research, have to be incorporated into formal, problem-oriented research designs if they are to be of use in explaining as well as reconstructing prehistoric cultural patterns of sport and recreation.

LITERATURE CITED

Aikens, C. Melvin 1970 Hogup Cave. *University of Utah Anthropological Papers,* No. 93. Department of Anthropology, University of Utah.

Ascher, Robert 1961 Analogy in Archaeological Interpretation. *Southwestern Journal of Anthropology.* Vol. 17. 317-325.

Binford, Lewis R. 1962 Archaeology as Anthropology. *American Antiquity.* Vol. 28. 217-225.

1964 A Consideration of Archaeological Research Design. *American Antiquity.* Vol. 29. 425-441.

1968 Archaeological Perspectives, in *New Perspectives in Archaeology.* Sally R. Binford and Lewis R. Binford, eds. Chicago: Aldine Publishing Company. 5-32.

Deetz, James 1967 *Invitation to Archaeology.* New York: Natural History Press.

Dick, Herbert W. 1965 Bat Cave. *The School of American Research, Monograph* No. 27. Santa Fe, New Mexico.

Fowler, Melvin L. 1973 The Cahokia Site, in Explorations into Cahokia Archaeology, revised edition. Melvin L. Fowler, ed. *Illinois Archaeological Survey Bulletin,* No. 7. University of Illinois. 1-30.

Hardoy, Jorge E. 1973 *Pre-Columbian Cities.* New York: Walker and Company.

Heider, Karl G. 1967 Archaeological Assumption and Ethnographic Facts: A Cautionary Tale from New Guinea. *Southwestern Journal of Anthropology.* Vol. 23. 52-64.

Jennings, Jesse D. 1957 Danger Cave. *University of Utah Anthropological Papers,* No. 27. Department of Anthropology, University of Utah.

Lewis, Thomas M. N. and Madeline Kneberg 1946 *Hiwassee Island: An Archaeological Account of Four Tennessee Indian Peoples.* Knoxville: University of Tennessee Press.

McGregor, John C. 1965 *Southwestern Archaeology.* Second Edition. Urbana: University of Illinois Press.

Soustelle, Jacques 1962 *Daily Life of the Aztecs.* New York: Macmillan Company.

Steward, Julian H. 1949 Cultural Causality and Law: A Trial Formulation of the Development of Early Civilizations. *American Anthropologist.* Vol. 51. 1-27.

1955 *Theory of Culture Change: The Methodology of Multilinear Evolution.* Urbana: University of Illinois Press.

Thompson, J. E. S. 1970 *Maya History and Religion.* Norman: University of Oklahoma Press.

Tozzer, Alfred M. 1941 Landa's Relacion de las Cosas de Yucatan. *Peabody Museum of Archaeology and Ethnology, Papers.* Vol. 18. Harvard University.

Weaver, Muriel Porter 1972 *The Aztecs, Maya, and their Predecessors: Archaeology of Mesoamerica.* New York: Seminar Press.

White, Leslie A. 1959 *The Evolution of Culture.* New York: McGraw-Hill Book Company.

Willey, Gordon R. and William R. Bullard 1965 Prehistoric Settlement Patterns in the Maya Lowlands, in *Handbook of Middle American Indians, Vol. 2,* Robert Wauchope, General editor. Austin: University of Texas Press. 360-377.

III. ETHNOLOGICAL STUDIES OF CHILDREN'S PLAY

Editor's Introduction

The papers in this section represent aspects of what has really been *the* principal focus of social scientists interested in human play. But, as I think these papers demonstrate, the introduction of an anthropological perspective offers some fresh insights into what was in danger of becoming a rather hackneyed field of investigation.

Karl Heider discusses a case of misunderstanding in planned culture change; the Indonesian Government aimed to acculturate the Dani of highland New Guinea, partly through the introduction of a Javanese game. But, in his words, "instead of the game transforming the Dani into Javanese, the Dani translated the game into Dani." Heider's general message is a strong statement of a theme echoed in many other papers in this volume, and which is explicitly stated in Kendall Blanchard's Introduction to Section II: that the "rules" of a game, or any other play-form, correspond to the "rules" of the culture in which it is played; hence the game cannot be studied divorced from its cultural context.

Janice Beran's paper is also a study of play in the context of culture change. In her study of children's games in the Philippines an attempt is made to show correlations between attitudes toward play and degrees, or levels, of modernization. Correlations do not necessarily show cause, but Beran, using a "semantic differential technique," concludes that a measurement of the degree and rapidity of social change can be found in analyzing attitudes of children toward their play-forms. It might be profitable to compare her findings with those of Mary Duncan in Belfast, Northern Ireland, as presented in Section II.

The focus shifts to a different level of interpretation in Harold Olofson's criticisms of Roger Caillois' assertions about vertigo and competition. Again, Olofson demonstrates that the cultural context must be considered. In games played by Hausa youth in Zaria, Nigeria, according to Olofson's convincing data, vertigo *can* occur in a competitive context, indeed, it is a central element in this context; but its presence is recognized as a necessary obstacle, a thing introduced solely for the purpose of being overcome. The overcoming, or controlling, of this artificially-induced vertigo, then, is one of the principal objectives of the game, and one of the hallmarks of success in the context of play-as-socialization.

Andrew Miracle, too, analyzes the socialization function of play, comparing games and other play forms of Aymara children of the *altiplano,* or high plateau, of Bolivia, with the behavioral patterns of adults. The Aymara subsistence technology enforces a work ethic, and a superficial overview would support a current hypothesis that in societies in which children are regarded as economic assets, play is severely limited. But Miracle suggests that, for the Aymara at least, this hypothesis is misleading; Aymara children do play, and they play quite a lot—although well away from the elders—and their play serves several important socializing functions.

In the concluding chapter of this section, Helen Schwartzman offers a detailed and critical overview of research into children's play. She indicates that most research has focused on text and has ignored *context,* and much has ignored both, and she suggests that any comprehensive theory of play must account for both. She criticizes aspects of the many enculturation- and socialization-function approaches to children's play; and she sees as one stumbling-block hindering *all* approaches, the lack of accord among researchers as to the meaning and applicability of certain terms, labels, and categories under which children's play forms have, often arbitrarily, been placed. She also discusses, as I have from another angle in the final chapter in this book, the widely-ignored problem of *communicating the play message.* Following this discussion, the ethologists' "child-as-monkey" view is criticized; and she concludes with a brief look at the phenomenon from the perspective of developmental psychology. As she discusses each category of investigations into play, she offers some thoughtful predictions as to future directions of that particular area of research. Of great value is her comprehensive bibliographic coverage, which is supplemented by her lengthy bibliography in the Appendix.

Aspects of certain of the theoretical premises discussed and conclusions drawn by the authors in this section are discussed more fully by Brian Sutton-Smith in his chapter, "Towards an Anthropology of Play."

From Javanese to Dani: The Translation of a Game[1]

Karl G. Heider, University of South Carolina

Introduction

This paper deals with the interrelationship between play and the rest of culture. It is an account of what happened to a game which was introduced into the culture of the Grand Valley Dani, a group of New Guinea highland Papuans who live in the Indonesian province of Irian Jaya. The game came from Java, and was part of a concerted program of culture change being carried out by the Indonesian government. The goal of the program was to change the Dani into proper Indonesians. The introduction of the game was not a success. Although the Dani children avidly adopted the game, they also adapted it. Instead of the game transforming the Dani into Javanese, the Dani translated the game into Dani.

We begin with the assumption that play is a basic part of culture. The trivial implication of this for anthropology is that therefore play, and games in particular, should be recorded, described, and catalogued. So we have countless publications on cat's cradles and the like. Too often these are merely descriptive lists, giving no idea of the circumstances and cultural context of the game.

But there is also a non-trivial implication: that games can be studied holistically, as functional elements in a socio-cultural system. Cross-cultural studies show that the different sorts of cultures and the different sorts of games are not randomly associated, but rather, some sorts of games tend to be associated with some sorts of cultures. If, then, games co-vary with other cultural traits, we are led to the important question of Why?, and What is the process of this co-variance?

John Roberts and his associates have done much work along these lines. With Sutton-Smith, he has written about the "conflict-enculturation" hypothesis (Roberts and Sutton-Smith 1962). From their work comes the suggestion that childhood conflicts lead to games and other "expressive models" which result in the assuaging of that conflict.

What they show, in fact, is that cultures tend to display 1) certain kinds of culture-specific conflicts (or problems or frustrations) and 2) certain types of games. They assume that the conflicts result from peculiarities of the specific socio-cultural system, and that in some way or another the people in that system will choose or develop means to ameliorate the conflict. And they call these means "expressive models."

Underlying all this is a dynamic assumption, an assumption of process, or selection, or problem-solving devices on the part of the culture. Roberts and his colleagues do not explore this, for their studies are concerned with showing that there is a general pattern. And in fact, they state quite explicitly that

> although the importance of acculturation in the study of games was recognized, recently introduced games were excluded from consideration.
>
> (Roberts and Sutton-Smith 1962:169)

But the very valuable work of Roberts and his colleagues points the way to the next step, which is the investigation of the dynamics of the process. We can move beyond the static model of culture, and use a dynamic model to deal with the idea that as problems arise, solutions are worked out.

The simplest of these dynamic models would be a kind of cafeteria-line concept: when cultures are faced with a wide range of possibilities, they choose to adopt those traits (in this case, games) which fit their needs. A variation of this model would see culture as changing, and in the course of this change, accepting or rejecting games according to the changing needs of the culture. For examples of such studies, there is Sutton-Smith's paper on Maori games (1951) and Kuschel's (1975) account of games on Bellona, a Polynesian outlier in the Solomon Islands.

I call these simple models because although they may allow for changes in the culture as a whole, they tend to treat the games themselves as immutable static traits to be ingested or expelled from the culture.

In the Dani case which I shall describe here, it was the culture which remained virtually constant, and the game which was plastic. It is clear that the model should be complex, allowing for the possibility that both culture and game can change, presumably in the direction of greater mutual consistency. The value of this model is to focus attention on the change in the game as well as the culture. A good example of this is a paper in which Maccoby and his colleagues describe the relationship between "Games and Social Character in a Mexican Village" (1964). This is the account of a cultural experiment—they introduced a new sort of game, apparently in the attempt to help children of the village alter their social character. (They were particularly concerned with the submissive attitude towards authority which they saw expressed in games as well as in the culture as a whole.) This attempt at culture change failed. The children quickly distorted the game to conform with other games and even then seem to have stopped playing it after the experimenter withdrew.

The Dani

The Grand Valley Dani are a Papuan culture living in the central highlands of West New Guinea (now the Indonesian province of Irian Jaya). They are best known through Robert Gardner's film, *Dead Birds* (1963). My own research began in association with Gardner, and I have made four trips to the Dani, staying for a total of about two and a half years between 1961 and 1970.

In many respects the Grand Valley Dani are a typical New Guinea Highland Papuan culture: they practice sweet potato horticulture and raise pigs; until the mid 1960s they used mainly stone axes and adzes, and warfare with bows and arrows and spears was endemic. (For a general ethnography, see Heider 1970). On the other hand, they are particularly unusual in having a general pattern of low psychic energy, manifested as little interest in sexuality, intellectualty, and peak experiences of all sorts, a pattern which I have described elsewhere (Heider 1976; n.d.) But here the main feature of interest is the nature of Dani play.

Roberts and his colleagues have made a useful definition of games which specifies one part of the total realm of play: they define games as

> recreational activity characterized by
> 1) organized play
> 2) competition
> 3) two or more sides
> 4) criteria for determining the winner, and
> 5) agreed-upon rules
>
> (Roberts, Arth and Bush 1959:597)

They point out that play is pan-cultural and that nearly all societies know games of some sort:

> ...games are found in most tribal and national cultures, but in some interesting cultures they are either absent or very restricted in kind and number.
>
> (Roberts and Sutton-Smith 1962:167)

The Dani are one of those interesting cultures which have no games. Previously, in describing Dani play, I had remarked that "there is almost complete lack of competition in play" and "there are no games in which score is kept or in which there is even a winner." (1970:193)

In terms of crucial criteria of the Roberts definition, the Dani lacked games.

Then, about 1969, a true game was introduced to the Dani, and in 1970 I frequently saw it played. (Also, I made two 20-minute videotape records of it, and one of which I have had printed out on 16mm film for purpses of close analysis.[2])

But according to our definition of games, what I saw was play and no longer a true game. It was the feeble shadow of a formerly-robust Asian game which the Dani children had already managed to strip of most of its game-attributes.

I call the game Flip-The-Stick. (I could discover no Dani name for it in 1970.) It is fairly simple, although at first glance it does seem complex. There are two sides, a batter and one or two outfielders. The batter stands at the goal (a small depression in the ground, made by rotating a heel in the soft earth) and uses a two-foot long reed bat to flip or hit a short reed stick towards the outfield. The outfielder catches the stick or, if he has missed it, picks it up and throws it back, trying to do something which will allow him to take over as a batter. The batter tries to stay at bat, racking up points. There are three different ways to hit and score, which the batter goes through in turn and, if not put out, begins again. (The next section describes the game in detail.)

That is the way the game should be played, and the way it is played elsewhere. The game is known from Pakistan to Korea (according to various people from South and East Asia who have seen the Dani film and recognized the game) and east into the Pacific as far as the Gilberts, [according to Kuschel's Bellonese informants, who said that their version "originally came from the Gilbert Islands" (1975:55)].

Apparently the game was introduced to the Dani schoolchildren as a recess game by one or more Javanese schoolteachers. But I have no data on what took place at the moment of introduction. [It is clear from the Maccoby et. al. (1964) account of introducing a game to a Mexican village how important such data are.] At any rate, I did not see it played by Dani in 1968 or between 1961 and 1963. So it is possible to say with fair confidence that the game was introduced about 1969 by Indonesian (and probably Javanese) schoolteachers; that the Dani children took it up and transformed it; and that in 1970 it was being played spontaneously by Dani boys and girls both at school (during recess) and at home.[3]

Unfortunately, I have no first-hand account of the details of the Asian form of the game. But I make certain assumptions about that form based on comments by Asians who have seen the Dani film and drawn by logical inference from the structure of the game as played by the Dani. For example, when the batter measures out a distance with the bat and shouts out Indonesian number words (otherwise the game is carried on in the Dani language) I conclude that in Java this was to reckon the score.

The Rules of the Game: A formal description

The goal of this paper is to examine the changes which the Dani made on a Javanese game, and to describe how, in important ways, the game was made Dani. But here, in this section, I shall describe the basic rules or procedure of the game which can be discovered from watching the Dani children play it. This formal description of the game is more elegant than the behavioral description on which this paper is based, and of course, much more elegant than the complex activity which I observed and filmed in the Grand Valley. Although the formal description is in some respects and for some purposes adequate, it is obviously a stripped-down account, and it totally neglects those behavioral aspects of the game which figure in this analysis. [And, incidentally, it is quite different from what Sutton-Smith (1959) calls "formal analysis."] Now, if we had comparable conventional formal descriptions of the game from Java and elsewhere (and it is certainly a major defect of this study that we do not) I assume that they would be very similar to what I shall present below. The methodological implications of this are important: these formal descriptions would not identify the various important differences in the way the game is played, and so would not allow the sort of cultural analysis which I attempt here.

The formal description, then, of an unnamed game observed and recorded on videotape among the Grand Valley Dani of Irian Jaya, Indonesia in 1970, is as follows:

Players: One batter; one or two (rarely more) fielders; played by boys and girls, ages about 6 to 14, usually with children of their own sex.

Equipment: One reed, about 1 cm in diameter, and about a meter long ("the bat"); one shorter reed, about 10 cm. long ("the stick").

Place: A reasonably level field extending out at least 10 or 15 meters from the goal; a shallow depression ("the goal") a few centimeters deep, dug out by rotating a heel in the earth; there are no boundaries—the goal is the only ground mark.

Rules: The game proceeds through each of three variations and then begins again until a fielder is able to replace the batter. In each variation, the batter sends the stick to the outfield; the fielder tries to catch it in the air and if successful, becomes the batter.

Variation 1
the hit: the short stick rests across the goal depression, perpendicular to the batter-fielder axis. The batter puts the end of the bat under the stick and flips it out towards the outfield.
the return: if the outfielder fails to catch the stick, he picks it up and throws it at the bat, which the batter either holds upright in the goal, or lays across the goal (these alternatives are apparently in free variation.) If the fielder hits the bat with the stick, he takes over as batter; if not, they proceed to
Variation 2
the hit: the batter holds the stick upright in the goal with one hand and, wielding the bat in the other, hits the stick towards the outfield.
the return: if the outfielder fails to catch the stick, he picks it up and throws it as close to the goal as possible. The batter now defending the goal with his bat, tries to hit the stick away.

From wherever the stick lands, whether hit away by the batter or not, the batter measures out the distance to the goal in bat lengths, shouting out the numbers as he goes. If the distance is less than one bat length, they exchange positions; if not, they proceed to
Variation 3
the hit: The stick now rests with one end protruding out over the goal depression. The batter hits that end with his bat to send the stick spinning up into the air, and then hits the air-borne stick towards the outfield.

If he succeeds in both, and if the stick is not caught in the air by the outfielder, the batter measures the distance from the stick to the goal, again in bat lengths shouting out numbers. If the distance is more than one bat length, they proceed to
Variation 1 and so forth.

The Translation

The basic assumption of this paper has been that play is a part of culture, consistent with the rest. Without taking the assumption of consistency to a ridiculous extreme, it does make sense that a game which was totally inconsistent with a culture would have a hard time. If it did not actually alter the culture, it would be rejected or itself altered.

The game came to the Dani as part of a whole program of schooling introduced by the Indonesian government, which is intended to educate—that is, to transform—the Dani children. We have some evidence that in its early years, at least, the program was not at all successful. The schoolrooms were in the hands of the teachers, who could maintain the appearance, at least, of Indonesian structure. On the other hand, this game, Flip-The-Stick, is a much more sensitive test to what really was happening. It had been turned over to the children, with no external controls or corrective forces, and they had a free hand to make it Dani.

The game is still recognizable, but in terms of several major aspects it has undergone change. In each of these aspects the game was brought closer to other Dani play forms and to Dani culture in general.

Competition

An important criterion in the definition of games quoted above is "competition."

In Dani life as a whole there is strikingly little competition. An obvious place to look for competition would be in the maneuvering for various statuses, or ranks, in a society. But Dani society is quite egalitarian. There are leaders, of course, but they are Big Men who lead by consensus, rather than Chiefs who rule by virtue of coercive authority. And, although there are some differences in wealth, these differences are not displayed. Houses, attire, and even the sizes of pig herds are not overt signs of importance. (cf. Heider, 1970:88).

Also, the Dani engage in little competitive confrontation in their interpersonal relations within the group.

The Javanese game, on the other hand, is quite competitive, with two sides, with scores tallied and a winner determined. The Dani version of the game does retain the two sides. And one might say that when one player replaces the other at bat, a winner of sorts has been determined. But the idea of counting an overall score and ending up with the winner of the game has been lost. The play is relaxed and non-competitive.

Quantification

Dani culture has little concern with quantification. (Heider 1970:170). The scorekeeping, which is so essential to the form of the original game, has been dropped from the Dani version. And that scorekeeping was, of course, not merely competition, but it was quantified competition, and so it was inconsistent with Dani culture on two counts.

Interestingly enough, the Dani children retain a vestige of scorekeeping in their version of the game. Although when playing they speak their own language, at the appropriate moments they do shout out Indonesian number words (there are no Dani number words beyond three or four). However, these number words are not being used for counting and, indeed, are not always spoken in the same order.

Casualness

The Dani children show a remarkable degree of casualness in the playing of the game. Several games go on simultaneously in overlapping spaces with only the slightest signs of defense of space. Sometimes a single player will be an outfielder for two games at once. There clearly are rules as described in the formal account above, but they are not strictly observed. There is a great deal of what I would call fudging or even cheating. For example, outfielders, instead of playing the stick from where it has landed, would usually kick it forward into a more advantageous position. And only rarely, in the most blatant situations, does one child challenge another for breaking a rule.

This casualness, or flexibility, has often been mentioned in accounts of New Guinea Highland societies and the Dani are no exception. Elsewhere I have discussed how difficult it can be to use such terms to characterize an entire culture (1970:5-7). But on the whole, Dani behavior does often seem to exhibit casualness. And this play, which is so far from the strict insistence on rules and procedures, is a good example.

Discussion

Not only do the Dani lack true games, but certainly as late as 1970 their traditional culture was strong enough to resist games by altering one introduced game into a more compatible form of play. This is a strong conclusion which raises questions about the nature of a society which lacks and even rejects games. But before pursuing this, we should take a look at the definition of "game."

One might hold that the five criteria quoted above are absolute attributes, present or absent, according to which we can say that the Dani are one of the few cultures in the world which lack games. However, it seems more realistic to treat the boundary which marks games off from the rest of play as a fuzzy one, or rather, a zone of transition, and the criteria as relative, not absolute. Then we can accurately say that when the Dani play Flip-The-Stick, they have tremendously de-emphasized competition, winning, and score keeping, thus moving the game away from that end of the play spectrum in which are found true games.

Elsewhere I have interpreted the general Grand Valley Dani resistance to change in terms of their basic conservatism (Heider 1975). The game of Flip-The-Stick provides a partial exception to this resistance to change, in the sense that it is one of the few traits which the Dani did accept from the outside; but because of the changes which it underwent, it supports the general principle of Dani conservatism.

The functional approach to the study of games (in contrast to mere description or historical/diffusionist studies) focuses on the ways in which the games fulfill certain basic needs, whether they be practice at skills which are important in the culture ["the psychoanalytic notion that games are exercises in mastery" (Roberts, Arth and Bush 1959:604)] or working out of cultural conflicts arising from the socialization process (Roberts and Sutton-Smith 1962). Since the Dani do not have games to perform these functions, they presumably have other means. Certainly many of the less formal amusements of the children are means of learning and practicing skills (see Heider 1970:193-199).

But there is a final, tantalizing suggestion: if, following Roberts and Sutton-Smith's line of thought, we suggest that games function to resolve various sorts of conflicts; and further, if games are in some respects especially good ways of resolving some kinds of conflicts and preparing children for adult life; then, might it not be that one would expect to find an absence of games in those cultures with relatively low conflict? This is all very speculative. But elsewhere I have developed the case that the Dani culture is resistant to change in part at least because of its remarkably low level of stress (Heider 1975) and that there is in general little conflict in Dani society (Heider n.d.). So the Grand Valley Dani do present a single case of association between low conflict and absence of games. This I present as suggestion, not as conclusion.

NOTES

[1]This paper is based on fieldwork carried out in Indonesia in 1970 under a grant from the Foundations' Fund for Research in Psychiatry. It was first presented, in somewhat different form, at the Council on Anthropology and Education Symposium held in conjunction with the American Anthropological Association meetings in San Francisco, December 7, 1975. This paper will appear, again in somewhat different form, as a chapter in a forthcoming book on Dani Thought and Personality.

It is particularly appropriate that this paper appears in a volume which honors the memory of Allan Tindall, for the writing of it was done only after months of his gentle insistence and under his strong encouragement.

[2]One of the two 20-minute videotapes which I made of this game at Wakawaka in 1970 has been printed out on 16 mm film (black and white, with synchronous sound) through the good offices of Professor Henry Breitrose of the Department of Communication, Stanford University. I have used this film to in two ways: 1) to give Introductory Anthropology classes a chance, in 20 minutes, to do some "fieldwork" by studying the film and trying to work out the rules of the game in relation to the behavior which appears on the screen; and 2) to give classes in Nonverbal Behavior a common resource for a wide range of micro-analyses. Despite the relatively poor resolution of the images, fairly fine details can be studied. I hope to be able to make this film available through a distributor in the near future.

[3]Interestingly, around the school at Jibika only girls played it; but at the Wakawaka school, an easy hour's walk away, where I made the video-tape records, it was played by both boys and girls.

BIBLIOGRAPHY

Gardner, Robert 1963 *Dead Birds.* A film produced by the Film Study Center, Peabody Museum, Harvard University. Dist: McGraw-Hill Contemporary Films, New York.

Heider, Karl G. 1970 *The Dugum Dani. A Papuan culture in the highlands of West New Guinea.* Chicago: Aldine.

1975 Societal intensification and cultural stress as determining factors in the innovation and conservatism of two Dani cultures. *Oceania* 46, 1:53-67.

1976 Dani sexuality. A low energy system, *Man,* N.S. II, 2:188-201.

n.d. *Dani Thought and Personality.* unpublished manuscript.

Kuschel, Rolf 1975 Games on a Polynesian outlier island: a case study of the implications of cultural change. *Journal of the Polynesian Society* 84.1:25-66.

Maccoby, Michael, Nancy Modiana and Patricia Lander 1964 Games and social character in a Mexican village. *Psychiatry* 27:150-162.

Roberts, John M., Malcolm J. Arth and Robert R. Bush 1959 Games in culture. *American Anthropologist* 61, 4:597-605.

Roberts, John M. and Brian Sutton-Smith 1962 Child training and game involvement. *Ethnology* 2:166-185.

Sutton-Smith, Brian 1951 The meeting of Maori and European cultures and its effect upon organized games of Maori children. *Journal of the Polynesian Society* 60, 2, 3:93-107.
1959 A formal analysis of game meaning. *Western Folklore* 18:13-24.

Attitudes Toward Play among Filipino Children of Negros Oriental, Philippines

Janice Ann Beran, Iowa State University

This paper is a portion of a study to attempt to identify the effects of modernization upon children's play. It was hypothesized that the degree of modernization experienced might correlate with attitudes toward certain aspects of play. It has been shown by previous researchers (Roberts and colleagues 1959, 1963; Nydegger and Nydegger 1966; Seagor 1971; Lancy 1975) that play and games are recognized as systematic cultural patterns. As such, they fulfill an important function in the learning and maintaining of behavior patterns. They play an important role in the social interaction process. Within this context children learn through play to relate to their peers and assess their own rights and responsibilities. Thus, attitudes shown by children in and through play may be indicative of the amount of modernization experienced. In this study, the play of children in one developing country, the Republic of the Philippines, was studied as it is a reflection and a parameter of social changes attendant upon modernization in the south central province of Negros Oriental.

A search of the available literature showed there was no suitable instrument to measure children's attitudes toward play. The initial purpose became to develop an instrument that would measure children's attitudes toward play and to study the influence of modernization. An instrument, based on the semantic differential technique developed by Osgood, Suci, and Tannenbaum (1967) was developed. The semantic differential is a technique of measuring the meaning of concepts by bipolar adjectival scales. There is not one standard test for this technique and an instrument must be constructed for each particular situation. This technique has been used in numerous studies, including cross-cultural, and has been shown to provide rather precise meanings of concepts as judged by individual subjects.

Methodology

Instrument. For this study concepts related to play in the Philippines were used and it was these concepts upon which the subjects made their interpretations. Concepts chosen were based on attributes related to Philippine social values, the structure of play, and specific games. The concepts were based on previous studies by the investigator (Beran, 1973a,

1973b,) review of pertinent literature (Osgood, 1969, 1974b,) as well as expert opinion.[1] They are shown in Table 1.

Table 1: Concepts

1. My Play
2. Losing at Play
3. Joining the Game after It Has Started
4. Playing with Relatives
5. Native Playthings Made of Bamboo, Leaves, Wood, and Clay
6. Native Games Like Dama and Sungka
7. Fiesta
8. Playing in the Forest
9. Comics, Radio, Television, and Movies
10. Cheating at Play
11. Chess and Checkers
12. Modern Dances
13. Winning at Play
14. Leaving before It Is Finished
15. Playing with Neighbors
16. Imported Playthings Like Dolls and Battery Operated Toys
17. Native Games Like Piko, Tubig-Tubig, Kayukok, and Sipa
18. Playing with Foreigners
19. Gambling during Play, Taking a Chance
20. Playing with Animals
21. Games Like Soccer, Basketball, Volleyball, and Karate
22. Native Dances
23. Quitting a Game Because You Can't Catch Anyone—Hiya
24. Playing Even Though Someone Is Cheating—Pakikisama
25. Showing Respect for Other's Wishes—Galang
26. Use of Third Person to Settle an Argument—Lakad
27. Giving in to Wishes of the Group—Pakikisama

Each concept was numbered and underlined with the 20 scales below it, so that the subjects would work on one concept at a time. The same 20 scales, alternated in polarity, direction, and numerical order, were used for each concept to prevent biases of response order. The adjectival scales (Cebuano-Visayan translation) are shown in Table 2. The evaluative factor, as developed by Osgood, Suci, and Tannenbaum (1957), was given particular emphasis on the 20 scales used.

For each of the 27 concepts, the respondent had to decide upon her evaluation of the concept. For instance, concept 13 (Winning at play) as seen in Table 1 required that the subject evaluated the concept on the 20 bipolar scales. In the first adjectival response scale, if the subject considered winning to be very important, she would encircle five; if she considered it somewhat important, she would encircle four; if the subject was uncertain or had no opinion, she encircled three; if she considered winning a play to be somewhat unimportant she encircled two; and if she considered it very unimportant, she encircled one.

Table 2
Sample Concept with Adjectival Scales
kun makadaug ako sa dula (Winning at play)

dili importante (unimportant)	1	2	3	4	5	*importante* (important)
maayo (good)	1	2	3	4	5	*dili maayo* (bad)
may bili (valuable)	1	2	3	4	5	*walay bili* (worthless)
makaguol (sad)	1	2	3	4	5	*makalipay* (happy)
makadalagkulba (frightening)	1	2	3	4	5	*dili makadalagkulba* (not frightening)
alisto sa huna-huna (wise)	1	2	3	4	5	*dili alisto sa huna-huna* (foolish)
walay kinahanglan (unnecessary)	1	2	3	4	5	*gikinahanglan* (necessary)
gipugos (required)	1	2	3	4	5	*kagustohan* (voluntary)
matinabangon (cooperative)	1	2	3	4	5	*iya-iya* (competitive)
makiangayon (friendly)	1	2	3	4	5	*dili makiangayon* (unfriendly)
kanunay (usual)	1	2	3	4	5	*dili kanunay* (unusual)
dili maki-amigo (lonely)	1	2	3	4	5	*maki-amigohon* (companionable)
makatabang (beneficial)	1	2	3	4	5	*makadaut* (harmful)
makakulba (tense)	1	2	3	4	5	*dili makakulba* (relaxed)
dili husto (improper)	1	2	3	4	5	*husto* (proper)
lisod (hard)	1	2	3	4	5	*sayon* (easy)
manggiloy-on (compassionate)	1	2	3	4	5	*salbahe* (cruel)
walay rason (unreasonable)	1	2	3	4	5	*may rason* (reasonable)
ma-apilon (inclusive)	1	2	3	4	5	*walay apil* (exclusive)
pinili (preferable)	1	2	3	4	5	*biya* (not preferable)

Examples of instruments are presented in the Cebuano-Visayan dialect.

The instrument was written initially in English and then translated in Cebuano-Visayan, the language of people in Negros Oriental, with the assistance of the person who had been investigator's language tutor[2] for five years.

Subjects. Two-hundred and seventy one 11 year old girls and boys participated in the study. This age was chosen because they were able to read and write, could work for extended periods of time, and were not yet playing the highly organized sports. The cluster method of sampling was utilized because it was a naturally occurring sample and was economical in terms of time.

Three categories of study communities were chosen, representing three levels of modernization. Dumaguete City, the administrative, educational, trade, and service center of the Province of Negros Oriental was chosen as a coastal urban technologically developed area. Among the 121 children enrolled in this study in two public and private schools in the city, 91% had been born in Dumaguete City and 5% had been born in other technologically developed communities giving an overall sample of which 91% were at least one generation removed from technologically undeveloped communities. The geographical representation of subjects is shown in Table 3.

Table 3. Geographical representation of subjects included in the study

	Type		Sex	
Category	Public	Private	Female	Male
Schools in an urban community				
North Central Elementary	X		16	14
City Central Elementary	X		16	15
Silliman University Elementary		X	16	14
St. Paul's Elementary		X	15	15
Schools in intermediate communities				
Sagrada Elementary	X		17	13
Bong-ao	X		16	14
Tagbino	X		14	9
Schools in an interior rural community				
Lambdas Elementary	X		17	13
Cangguhob Elementary	X		17	13
Ban-ban Elementary	X		4	3
Grand total	8	2	148	123

Three communities were selected as representing the intermediate stages of technological development. All were located in rural agricultural towns with vehicular transportation to Dumaguete City. All of these intermediate communities were in the process of technological development which included use of mechanized equipment.

The third type of community were those located in relatively remote interior mountain areas, reached only by three or five hour bus rides from the nearest technologically developed cities, followed by up to two hours of hiking. People lived by subsistence farming using human and animal power. The major introductions from outside the community included the public elementary schools and the chapels visited only occasionally by clergy from other communities.

Observations of study areas

The instrument was designed to be completed in approximately two 45 minute sittings. In the urban schools, particularly the private schools, children completed the instrument in 45 minutes. All the children in the urban schools were in the upper grades and could read and easily follow directions; they were likewise familiar with printed tests. The intermediate children, most of whom were in third and fourth grades, were very interested and cooperative and worked very diligently to please both the teachers and the investigator. The rural children were, for the most part, in the lower grades. This was their first experience with a printed individualized instrument. They took a longer time to complete the instrument and a few needed assistance.

The investigator was accompanied on all the trips out of the city by her eleven year old son. He was proficient in Cebuano-Visayan and familiar with the play activities of the children. This as well as the investigator's personal acquaintance with the teachers and general familiarity with the area greatly facilitated the study. The actual field work, including making arrangements through proper school officials, took five weeks.

Results

Reliability of the instrument. The Cronbach Coefficient Alpha, a test of internal reliability, yielded reliability coefficients on the 27 concepts between .951 and .721 with an acceptable mean of .841 on a scale of 0-1. The positive observations made during the actual survey, the coherent responses of the children on the instrument, and the internal reliability of the attitudes seemed to indicate that the instrument was reliable in assessing attitudes toward play at varying levels of modernization.

Factor Analysis. Principal factor analysis with varimax orthogonal rotation was performed for all concepts. Nine principal factors accounted for 80.05% of the total variance. The factors and contributing concepts are shown on Table 4.

Effect of type of community on children's attitude toward play. Mean scores were calculated for the nine factors by locations of schools. Differences were tested by analysis of variance. Significant differences at the 0.01 level were found on all nine factors according to locations of schools. Pairwise *t* tests were then used to assess the significance of the differences among attitudes of children in the four location sites for each of the nine factors. These results are shown in Table 5.

Table 4. Group factors with principal contributing concepts

Factor I. Everyday or commonplace things

1. My play
2. Losing at play
3. Joining the game after it has started
4. Playing with relatives.

Factor II. Anxiety situations

8. Play in the forest
10. Cheating at play
14. Leaving the game before it is finished
19. Gambling during play/taking a chance

Factor III. Desirable activities

9. Comics, television, radio, and movies
12. Modern dances
13. Winning at play
15. Playing with neighbors
17. Native games like piko and tubig-tubig
21. Soccer, baseball, volleyball, and basketball

Factor IV. Unfamiliar or foreign

16. Imported playthings like battery operated toys and dolls
18. Playing with foreigners.

Factor V. Avoiding conflict
24. Playing even though someone is cheating—pakikisama
26. Use of a third person to settle an argument—lakad
27. Givin in to the wishes of the group—pakikisama

Factor VI. Filipino or indigenous activities
5. Homemade playthings
6. Native games like dama and sungka
7. Fiesta

Factor VII. Foreign table games requiring strategy
11. Chess and checkers

Factor VIII. Maintaining smooth interpersonal relations (SIR)
23. Quitting a game when you can't catch someone—experiencing hiya.
25. Showing respect for someone's wishes—lack of appropriate galang

Factor IX. Playing with animals
20. Playing with animals

Table 5. Difference in attitudes of children in public and private schools in communities at three stages of technological development[a]

Factor	School			
Everyday things (Factor I)	IRUR[b]	UPUB[b]	UPRI[b]	INTER[b]
	3.26	3.48	3.52	3.85
Anxiety situations (Factor II)	UPRI	UPUB	IRUR	INTER
	2.73	3.04	3.07	3.57
Desirable activities (Factor III)	IRUR	UPRI	UPUB	INTER
	3.30	3.45	3.46	3.82
Unfamiliar or foreign (Factor IV)	IRUR	UPRI	UPUB	INTER
	2.86	3.38	3.39	3.80
Avoiding conflict (Factor V)	IRUR	UPRI	UPUB	INTER
	3.17	3.28	3.33	3.73
Filipino or indigenous activities (Factor VI)	IRUR	UPRI	UPUB	INTER
	3.22	3.47	3.56	3.90
Games requiring strategy (Factor VII)	IRUR	UPRI	UPUB	INTER
	2.97	3.29	3.44	3.68
Disrupting smooth interpersonal relations	UPRI	UPUB	IRUR	INTER
(Factor VIII)	2.69	2.93	2.95	3.23
Play with animals (Factor IX)	IRUR	UPRI	UPUB	INTER
	3.19	3.21	3.26	3.65

[a]Those means not underscored were significantly different from each other.

[b]IRUR (interior rural), UPUB (urban public), UPRI (urban private), INTER (intermediate).

Analyses showed great similarity between children in the urban private and public schools. It was only in attitudes toward anxiety situations that the private school children reflected the greater effects of social modernization as they were influenced by formal education instruction and home environment.

The children of the intermediate communities showed significantly more positive attitudes as reflected in their highest ranking of all nine factors as shown in Table 5. Their more positive evaluations indicated an openness to introduced innovations as well as a tendency to uphold traditional Philippine values. They were significantly different from the children in technologically developed areas and interior rural areas.

The significant differences between the attitudes of children in technologically developed urban schools and interior rural schools brought out several important characteristics. The interior rural children differed significantly (0.01 level) from the urban children in attitudes toward everyday things (Factor I), desirable activities (Factor III), unfamiliar or foreign (Factor IV), and Filipino or indigenous activities (Factor VI). Additionally, the rural children differed significantly from the urban private school children in attitudes toward anxiety situations (Factor II) and from the urban public school children on foreign table games requiring strategy (Factor VII).

The rural interior children generally scored all factors lower particularly the unfamiliar or foreign and the foreign table games requiring strategy, indicating lack of exposure and uncertainty toward these factors. They viewed their everyday things with less enthusiasm and joy than did the children of any of the other communities, reflecting the stoic acceptance of life which generally characterized their parents.

The experience of play which evoked a response of pleasure and positiveness among all other children did not do so to the same extent with the rural children. Perhaps this was a reflection of the adult emphasis on working to accomplish the absorbing task of producing enough for the family to subsist. The lack of enthusiasm appeared to be an important impediment to development of change from within or to adoption of change from outside the community.

The intermediate children were affected by the influence of teachers who were upwardly mobile in orientation and by the rapid social change in which they were immediate participants. The urban children living in the technologically developed environment were familiar with urbanization and had not personally experienced transition from rural to urban life.

Summary

Findings through the use of the semantic differential technique indicate that exposure to urban technologically developed areas did significantly affect attitudes children held toward various facets of their play. The conclusion was thus reached that the degree of modernization experienced did affect attitudes and that play was indeed a parameter of social change attendant upon development in Negros Oriental.

NOTES

[1]Lorna P. Makil, Philippine sociologist; Verna M. Alih, Philippine anthropologist; and Pascual Kapili, Philippine educator.

[2]Mrs. Epifania Ebarle.

REFERENCES

Beran, Janice A. 1973a Characteristics of children's play in the southern Philippines. *Silliman Journal* 20 (1st Qtr.): 100-113.

1973b Some elements of power in Filipino children's play. *Silliman Journal.* 20 (2nd Qtr.): 194-207.

Lancy, David F. 1975 The role of games in the enculturation of children. Paper presented at 74th annual meeting of the American Anthropological Association. San Francisco.

Nydegger, William F. and C. Nydegger. 1966 Tarong: an Illocos barrio in the Philippines. Pp. 687-693. In Beatrice Whiting ed. *Six Cultures Series.* Vol. 6. John Wiley, New York.

Osgood, Charles E. 1969 Semantic Differential Technique in the Comparative study of culture. Pages 303-334. in James G. Snider and Charles E. Osgood eds. *Semantic Differential Technique.* Aldine Publishing Company, Chicago.

Osgood, Charles A., Suci, George J., and Tannenbaum, Percy H. 1957. *The Measurement of meaning.* University of Illinois Press, Urbana, Illinois.

Roberts, J.M.; Arth, J.J. and Bush R.R. 1959 Games in culture. *American Anthropologist,* 61:597-605.

Roberts, J.J. and Brian Sutton-Smith. 1962 Child Training and game involvement. *Ethnology* 2, 166-185.

Seagoe, May V. 1971 A comparison of children's play in six modern cultures. *Journal of School Psychology* 9:61:72.

Vertigo and Social Structure: Notes on Hausa Children's Play

Harold Olofson, Rochester, Michigan

Introduction

Roger Caillois, in his discussion of the elements of play that go to make up games, defined vertigo as an "attempt to momentarily destroy the stability of perception and inflict a kind of voluptuous panic upon an otherwise lucid mind...[a] surrendering to a kind of spasm, seizure, or shock which destroys reality with sovereign brusqueness." (1961:23). He claimed that "there is a vertigo of a moral order, a transport that suddenly seizes the individual. This vertigo is readily linked to the desire for disorder and destruction, a drive which is normally repressed" (1961:24). Because this means loss of self-control, vertigo destroys the conditions, the rules, upon which another play-element is based, namely, competition; thus, the combination of competition and vertigo in games is "unnatural" and "inconceivable" and is probably excluded from the universe of play (1961:72-73).

It is doubtful that there is a biogenetically based drive toward disorder or vertigo, as Caillois implies; rather the times and places where vertigo is purposefully experienced by human beings are likely to be determined by cultural learning and to have cultural patterning. The more fascinating product of Caillois' analysis is the opposition which is implied between vertigo and all levels of normative, rule-determined social order ranging from social interaction and social structure to moral order. A systematic study of the role of vertigo in human societies, both within and without the play-frame, has not been taken up. Such an endeavor could conceivably be an example of how a concept developed in the study of play was found applicable to the study of societies and cultures as integrated wholes.

The condition of vertigo is essentially one of disorientation which if extended in time becomes physically uncomfortable, indicative of physical disorder, and, indeed, a threat to ongoing social order. Disorientation has both physical and social implications. For these reasons, we would expect to find it limited to structurally specific times and places within a societal program and even within the typical life-history of individuals within a culture. In addition, we would expect it to take on symbolic meaning within these limited segments. For example, it is likely that physical, bodily disorientation and imbalance can become symbolic of social disorientation and instability. It is probable, then, that the distribution of vertigo cross-culturally is to a significant extent coterminous with those "betwixt-and-between" ritual states which Victor Turner has termed "liminal" (Turner: 1969). Thus disorientation may be found to occur extensively in the central stages of rites of passage or rituals of rebellion. In addition to occurring in rites of individual and group transition and change, the vertiginous effects of disorientation might also be seen to arise in other socially interstitial conditions, thinking here particularly of those symbolic and spatial interfaces between cultures, ethnic groups, classes, and castes. Data on shamanism and spirit mediumship cults suggest that vertigo is common in the change-over between natural and supernatural planes. Vertigo may also be useful as a factor of socialization through implicit metacommunication within the context of structured play, by pointing up the necessity of self-control to attain desired ends and by symbolizing the opposite of what is socially desirable. It is this latter point which I wish to enlarge upon here through some examples of rough games engaged in by young male children among the Hausa of northern Nigeria.

It is important at the outset to note the role of vertigo in the background against which the play takes place. It appears that there is an opposition between vertigo and the moral and communicational orders of Hausa society. Much of this opposition rests on a complex of norms of face-work which emphasize, all told, balance and self-control in public. First of all, there is *kunya,* a sense of shame, embarassment, or modesty, which is perhaps the most frequent norm invoked in conversation. *Kunya* is closely intertwined with *girmamawa,* the showing of respect for others and especially for parents, elders, and important people. Standing in contrast to this is *fara'a*, an even, cheerful demeanor. When *fara'a* becomes overflowing the individual threatens to make a boisterous public display of himself, in which case he might be considered to lack *kunya* or *girmamawa.* These norms of behavior must be kept in balance. In addition there is *hak'uri* or patience, an attitude very frequently stressed in the socialization of young people. *Mutunci* is a sense of respect for others which also implies a sense of respect for one's own personality and self. *Fulanintaka* is a behavioral norm which emphasizes bashfulness, reticence, self-denial, and lack of emotional response to pain in public.[1] Based on this complex, the Hausa character has a distinct distaste for disorientation, especially in public. For an adult to stumble accidentally and fall in the street is a matter of great shame to him, if witnessed, for there is in it the hint of an inability to physically control himself publicly that just might have implications for other aspects of his social personality. Drunkenness, particularly when displayed before elders, is not only contrary to Islam, but shameless in the sense that the drunken individual has lost self-control. Witch attack, which works with great suddenness in Hausa culture, leads to the victim experiencing dizziness, loss of interaction tonus, and collapse, perhaps even cataplexy. "The body becomes slack," the Hausa say, as a result of the witch's shameless, anti-social inability to control his own innate addiction for human souls and flesh. I see this as a total "loss of face" for ongoing communication on the part of the victim. In public displays of the *bori* spirit-possession cult, which some Hausa see as shameless behavior, the devotees frequently make the transit into a trance state where they engage in mimicry of the spirits, by falling flat on the ground with a rigid or slack bodily tonus. The devotee is said to experience *juwa* or *jiri,* "dizziness, giddiness," and the eyes turn up into the head (*juya idanu*); after the transition the individual is said not to know what he does. Here vertigo marks a liminal period between two social orders, the one of real life, and the one of the spirit pantheon, and for the individual, between two personalities, the one of being himself, and the one of not being himself. I look upon this as "substitution of face." The possession becomes an excuse for his behaving publicly in a way which attracts attention to him, when that display can be attributed as coming not from his everyday self but from the spirit which "rides" (*hau*) him. Finally, we can mention madness (*hauka*) frequently curable only by entering the *bori* cult. The madman indicates that he has lost all sense of shame by going about covered with dirt and wearing insufficient clothing. His social disorientation is frequently symbolized by a propensity to wander seemingly without aim in garbage heaps, in the wilderness, or down the middle of highways where he becomes a hazard to traffic.

With this background in mind, we can proceed to an analysis of play.

Data[2]

Hausa boys' games have been described for the Hausa of Zamfara by Kurt Krieger (1954). The games described below are ones described for me by a young adult male native of the walled city of Zaria, and represent his experiences and observations of them as a boy growing up in that town. The games are given in the order in which he remembered them, and they represent the play of boys (segregated from the play of girls) between the ages of approximately five to fifteen.

1. *Shagaregare.* A group of boys, holding hands, move rapidly in a circle counter-clockwise. A boy on the outside shouts *Shagaregare!* and is answered by the others in chorus with the insult *Shege! Shege!* ("Bastard! Bastard!") He attempts to pull one from within the circle to the outside so that he can take his place, but in so doing he may be hit in the stomach or lose some teeth. *Shagaregare* was translated by my informant as "Hang on and go 'round and 'round." But it is interesting to note that the caller could be using the the verb-adverb combination of *sha,* "to drink," and *gara,* "dazed, stupified," i.e. "drink blows." There is also *gara,* "to hasten," "to skim along a surface" (Bargery 1934).

2. *Allambaku-allamkarb'e.* The morpheme *allam-* is related to the noun *alla,* "writing board." Again, a single boy shouting *Allambaku!* "Keep track of being given!" starts against a group responding *Allamkarb'e!* "Keep track of receiving!" This refers to keeping in mind the placement of individuals, as the game in progress could get confusing. The outsider attempts to enter the crowd and capture one of its members to begin forming his own group, but if he attempts to grab a stronger boy, he may be lifted up and thrown to the ground. Thus one "knows who is strong and who isn't," said my informant. As the second group forms, members of the first group may attempt to recapture individuals back into their ranks. The last one left from any group will begin again, and the game may conclude when the remaining outsider is not strong enough to catch any of the others to make his own team; these are likely to be older than he.

3. *Na yi k'olin-k'oli.* The game begins when a boy moves counter-clockwise within a circle of boys. From within the circle another boy takes the role of singer, and the repartee goes as follows:

Circler:	*Na yi k'olin-k'oli* "I make the highest of the high."
Chorus:	*Jemage!* "Bats!"
Singer:	*Yaro, dubi sa'anka!* "Boy, look for your contemporary!" (i.e. "Don't look for a boy older or stronger than you!")
Chorus:	*Jemage!*
Singer:	*Karka fad'a ubanka!* "Don't quarrel with your father!" (i.e. "Don't fight with someone older than you, he may be your father!")

The circler suddenly throws his legs around the waist of a victim and hangs backward like a bat, touching the ground with his hands if he is not too tall. The recipient does nothing except let the other take his place, and begins moving around himself, but if he has been replaced by someone much younger than himself, he can eventually get his revenge by hanging on him, and "the littler boy will suffer" as he will not have the strength to stand the weight.

4. *Kulli-kurciya-kulli.* This is "weaving in and out like the dove swooping down and flying up." Again, boys stand in a circle holding each others' hands; one of them leaves his position and weaves in and out around the circle back to his place. If he forgets where it is, the others join in giving him a good beating. Then the one next to him goes outside, and the game ends casually when everyone tires. The patter is designed to confuse the "dove":

Singer: *Kulli-kurciya!*
Chorus: *Kulli!*
Singer: *Kowwa ya b'ata gida?* "Who has lost his house?"
Chorus: *Kulli, ya sha duka!* "The one going in and out, he shall be thoroughly beaten."
Singer: *Ya sha duka har da tokari, har da tsunguli!* "He will be beaten severely with kicking and punching!"

5. *Wasan hula.* The cap-game: Boys stand in a circle holding their hands in readiness to receive the cap of one running behind their backs, but they cannot follow him with their eyes. Upon receiving it, a boy turns to his right and begins beating the boy next to him with the cap. Both the victim and his tormentor run around the circle back to their positions, the one trying to outdistance the other. The cap is then returned to its owner, who has been waiting to receive it and who will continue in his role. The participants have removed their shirts, presumably so that the caps will sting more. Should a boy being chased make the mistake of falling down or muddle-headedly forgetting his position he will continue to receive blows until he gets himself clear and back to his position.[3]

6. *Yak'in samari.* The traditional "war of the youths" of the Hausa towns is an interesting, though less vicious, counterpart of the gang wars of urban boys in our own large settlements. My informant took part in about four of these, around the ages of eight to twelve. In Zaria, the war used to take place in its most striking form annually within the walled town on the naming day of the Prophet Mohammed, on the grounds call *Albarkawa,* "People of blessings." It could not take place on the Prophet's birthday as on that day the boys had to be free to carry out obligatory visits to relatives. The grounds were situated in an uninhabited field separating two populous sections of the town. This area was visited early in the day by the Emir of Zazzau Zaria and other dignitaries to read about the life of the Prophet; when they dispersed the fight would begin.

The struggle was between boys from the opposite sides of the field, the *'Yan Hayi,* "Children of the High-ground," and the *'Yan Bakin Kasuwa* or "Children from Around the Market." The *'Yan Hayi* were, in their turn, comprised or rivalrous neighborhoods joining together for the event. Thus it is interesting to note the segmentary model of complementary opposition at work here. The fission and fusion of the subgroups took place on the same day. Earlier in the day the neighborhoods or wards of the *'Yan Hayi* were divided into two opposing sets of allies: (1) *'Yan Unguwan Zagezegi,* "Those from the Ward of the Zaria People" (my informant was one of these); *'Yan Kwarbai,* "The Sons of the Ward of Raiders"; *'Yan Unguwan Doya,* "The Children of the Ward of Yam (sellers)"; and *'Yan Unguwan Mad'aka,* "Those of the Ward of Pounders," versus (2) *'Yan Unguwan Magajiya,* "Children of the Head Courtesan's Ward"; together with the *'Yan Unguwan Lalle,* "Sons of the Henna Ward"; and *'Yan Unguwan Kahu,* "Those of the Ward of Kahu (padded cloth)-makers." These two fought each other on *Titin Magajiya,* "Magajiya's Street," but later coalesced against the *'Yan Bakin Kasuwa.* My informant did not have knowledge of segmentation among the latter, but knew that in earlier years they had fought with the *'Yan Albarkawa,* "Children of the People of Blessings" (located adjacent to the field of battle), but that they had joined together because the *'Yan Albarkawa* had too few numbers.

At the field each side assembled on opposite sides and charged. Weapons included thorn-sticks just previously gathered from the bush, and sling-shots (*roban harbi,* "shooting-rubbers"). Significantly, the eldest boys, aged 13 to 15, preceded the youngest, aged 6 to 7. The fighting would move back and forth across the open space and if one side turned tail they could seek shelter in the nearest compounds of the citizens. Bloody head and arm injuries were common. Two confrontations would occur, probably spontaneously and without leadership, before individuals got tired and went home. For about three days afterwards the "High-grounders" would risk being beaten if they attempted, individually, to go to market.[4]

The *yak'in samari* had in 1971 been stopped by the local police for some years as a result of parental complaint about injuries. On the usual day guards were posted at strategic points on both sides of the field, and other police patrolled the neighborhood of *Titin Magajiya.*

Interpretation

According to Caillois vertigo and competition do not appear together. In terms of testing strength, however, these games suggest the presence of a combative or competitive spirit, in combination with the vertigo that comes from the roughness of the play and which must be controlled. If so, Caillois' assertion is quite wrong.[5] Let us look at the games more closely for the vertigo elements. In *shagaregare,* depending on one's etymological interpretation of this word, the *shege* "drinks blows" to the point of becoming dazed, or the members of the circling group "hang on and go 'round and 'round." In *allambaku-allamkarb'e* the outsider attempting to get himself into the circle may be up-ended. In *na yi k'olin-k'oli* the circler hangs on his victim in dizzying upside-down fashion like a bat and may himself suffer eventually from the pain and disorientation likely to result from a larger, older boy hanging on him. In *kulli-kurciya-kulli* a boy running about the circle may, as a result of the vertigo this causes in combination with the movement of the circle and the threats portended in the chanting of the group, become disoriented, lose his place, and suffer further distraction through being beaten for his loss of self-control. This theme is repeated in *wasan hula*. *Yak'in samari* I take to be a less highly structured though more grandiose variation of rough play, one which could lead to serious injuries and vertigo resulting from blows to the head.

Now, the function of the vertigo described in these games would seem to arise from the symbolic use made of it in the structure of the play. I suggest that we can picture vertigo here as providing a series of implicit metacommunications which may have significance for the socialization of the children involved, in terms of their relationship to three levels of social order: (1) membership in Hausa society generally; (2) their positioning within the social structure of that society; and (3) their participation in society on the interactional or communicational level.

First, in terms of the relation of the child to the society as a whole, the circle games particularly reveal an interesting structure. Within the play-group there is, in addition to an implicit boundary separating the play from the rest of the world, a more interior boundary which distinguishes symbolically between the inside and the outside of the society. The child who is "it" is on the outside, has been moved there through some arbitrary signal such as the sting of a cap, or by being painfully forced out, and must make the attempt to overcome vertigo and pass it on to another in order to get reinstated into the group. At times any one participant is opposed to the larger circle, and at other times he is reabsorbed into the group, which is symbolic of society at large, by his own efforts. The outside position of the person who is "it" is especially emphasized in the game *shagaregare* where he may be called a "bastard" (*shege*). This insult as used in other contexts in Hausaland and implies here that a liminally disoriented individual is illegitimate or parentless, indeed, has no proper standing in society; thus the insult received may act as a stimulus for re-entry. Another notion of the outsider, in the game *kulli-kurciya-kulli,* is that of the individual who has "lost his house (or home)." In Hausaland stable family life at home is considered superior to the somewhat despised life of loose and shameless wandering as an individual entirely on one's own and beholden to no one (see Olofson 1976). Vertigo here is symbolic of these states of "outsiderhood", and the outsiders' movements are perceived as movements of non-human beings such as free-wheeling doves and bats that defy gravity and proper upright orientation. The general meta-message appears to be "Belong to society as it is properly conceived." For example, kin relations are to be seen as valuable.

The rivalry element is clearly there when it is seen that in order to get in, an individual must put another into the disadvantaged position.

Secondly, in terms of the status of the child within Hausa social structure, we note first that any one instance of these games is likely to involve children of different ages. In the game *na yi k'olin'k'oli,* this is symbolized in warnings made by the singer to the circler that he should jump on those of his own age, his contemporaries or *sa'a,* rather than on his "father" or *uba,* which symbolizes a child older than he. A child is still likely, however, to test his strength against those older than he, and, sooner or later, to come out the worse for wear. I suggest that the vertigo experienced here is symbolic of *placement* within a system of social status. I like the word "placement" because of the implication of an object forcibly being put in its place. The child begins to be aware, through his dealing out as well as reception of vertiginous feelings, of a significant dimension of Hausa status. The status system within the game involves the reinforcement of a distribution of respect according to age and strength, which in the play-frame is symbolic of that distribution in everyday life. While testing his abilities, the child simultaneously learns the metacommunication, "know the strength of age." At this early age, it most likely becomes apparent that older boys are also the stronger and the smarter, and, as in the case of *yak'in samari,* they precede the younger into battle, thereby protect them, and thus should be respected. I suspect that these correlations made at an early age carry on over into adult respect for the old, even if the old have grown relatively weak physically. This dimension of the games points up the typically African theme of the use of age as a principle of social differentiation which must be learned.[6]

Thirdly, in terms of the child's participation in ongoing interaction, which comprises the stuff from which social organization is built up and sustained, I suspect that, though my informant did not give direct evidence of this, future research in Hausa children's rough play will show it to be instrumental in teaching the child a sense of emotional self-control and poise in public and in the face of pain and disorientation, i.e. what we noted above as *ulanintaka.* Thus a hurt child will likely get up and continue on. In addition, respectful behavior for others—especially for the older—is taught not by going *through* the paces of respectful behavior *(girmamawa)* but by going *against* respectful norms experimentally in the laboratory of play and seeing what happens to one.

Concluding Remark

The data for Hausa play have indicated that vertigo can occur together with competition, but in the Hausa context it is used *against itself.* In other words, vertigo is allowed in play so that it can be overcome as an undesirable state of affairs. Except in special instances, as in boxing or spirit possession, adult Hausa try to avoid disorientation in favor of the constant cultivation of social graces. Moreover, they think of children's play such as described here as something not to be taken seriously and sometimes, as in the case of *yak'in samari* in Zaria, not to be tolerated. Thus it is unlikely that Hausa adult males, who even refuse to tell folk tales to children, leaving that up to the youngest wife, have ever allowed themselves to become enough interested in children's play or in vertigo to have constructed games of vertigo for them. It is probable that these games were devised primarily by adolescent and pre-adolescent boys for use as self-socializing reinforcement mechanisms which they interposed between their wider experiences of society—experiences which guided them in game construction—and their future roles in that society. If so, there is a likelihood that the adult Hausa attitude toward vertigo which sees it as distasteful comes to them in a significant degree from the play-symbolics of Hausa children—of themselves when children. The uses of vertigo in Hausa play, as instituted therein by Hausa children, may well contribute to the integration of society as a whole.

NOTES

[1]This is also *fillanci* or *fillako* (see LeVine 1973:26-27).

[2]The data for this paper were gathered while the author was engaged in research in two areas, Hausa presentation of self, and Hausa urbanization, in Zaria and Funtua, northern Nigeria, 1969-71. The early phase of rough play for boys described herein is followed by an adolescent phase which is typified for some by annual participation in the Hausa youth festival *(kalankuwa)*. The socializing function of this activity is described in a forthcoming paper.

[3]Other Hausa boys' games are more "intellectually" oriented, such as *dakunku-dakunku,* "your choice-your choice," which is similar to our own "twenty questions." One boy, a quizzer, sits apart from the group and communicates with them through a messenger. The messenger approaches him and the quizzer whispers to him, perhaps, *kad'anya,* "shea-butter tree." The messenger returns to the boys and says:

Messenger: *Dakunku-dakunku!*
First boy: *A cikin me?* "From within what (category)?"
Messenger: *A cikin itatuwan garin nan.* "From within the trees of this town."
First boy: *Mangwaro.* "Mango."
Second boy (after approached by the messenger): *Goruba.* "Dum-palm."

The messenger turns away if no one can answer, saying to them *kad'anya ta wuceku fuu!,* "The *kad'anya* passed you at high speed!" The one who gets the answer goes to sit with the quizzer. When one boy remains after a series of "your choices," and he is unable to guess a correct answer for three questions (three being symbolic to the Hausa of separation), all of the others approach him, touch their fingers to their lips, dab saliva on him, and then cover him with dirt as if he were feces, saying *leb'u tukunyar kashi!* "Lips-shit pot!" Probably a younger, less knowledgeable boy, he is treated as if he were distinctly outside the pale of social respect.

[4]The rivalry between these two areas continued in different form one week after the fasting of *Ramadan,* when adult boxers (also usually butchers by profession) of *Hayi* had a week-long match with those from the area of the market, an occasion replete with drummer, praise-singers, and magicians.

The girls of Zaria were said to be generally behind the boys of their wards, but did not show themselves on the war-grounds. However, they did have their own ongoing feud with the girls of *Tudun Wada,* a suburb outside of the walls populated by Hausa originally not native to the walled town. This erupted into stone-throwing on the festival of *Jafi,* the day of the parade of the District Heads before the Emir, when the outside girls came into the town to see the festivities. My informant thinks that they may have had a war of their own at the wall itself. The Zaria girls also paid praise-singers to sing songs of abuse (*zagi*) about the girls of the other side.

There are data to suggest that versions of the youths' war are widespread in Hausaland. In Funtua, Katsina Province, it is called *wowo,* "the throwing of fired guinea-corn stalks," taking place on *Id-el-Maulud* at night (for the fireworks effect) on the site of the old market, and involving a traditional rivalry between two groups of two neighborhoods each. For the ward of *Zangon Barebari* in Kano City, Usman, Bichi, and Perchonock (n.d.:11) report that the youth sometimes fought those of *Gabari* and *Darma,* "but when faced with a more distant foe like *Koki,* for example, [these] ally together to fight. The fighting, according to the [wardhead] was organized just like a miniature battle with Sarki and all the other titles...it was considered improper if an older person took part." Thanks are due to Usman *et al* for a copy of their work. In the city of Katsina each town gate has a settlement connected with it, whether originally to guard each entrance to the city, or having come about in the manner of the traders settling in the faubourgs of Mediaeval European cities (though in Katsina inside the walls rather than outside), I am not certain. I was told by one who grew up in one of these wards, *Unguwan K'ofar Durbi,* that when its boys went out of the walls and into the bush to look for animal feed, they might have an unfortunate meeting at *any* time of the year with the boys from a neighboring gate, *Unguwan K'ofar Bai,* and upon their return, rumours would fly and war would begin. Fights also took place between them on the occasion of the "youth festival" of either neighborhood. For Soumarana in Niger, Raynaut (1972:134) describes how the youth of the two moieties of the village frequently quarrel over winning the favors of the girls, particularly when a boy attempts to acquire the good graces of a girl from the opposite moiety. Battles over such incidents—with the members of a moiety apparently backing up their own member in the rivalry—are enacted in a central place in the village called *hilin yak'i,* "the hill of war," and frequently lead to wounds from flying sticks and stones. Equilibrium is restored, traditionally, when the father of the boy who has been the aggressor goes to the house of the mistreated youth taking powdered antimony, used as a restorative, and offering his blessings.

[5]Indeed, it seems to me that there is an element of vertigo in all competitions that involve tension arising out of either violence, a race against the clock, or both. One need think only of boxing, skiing, and chess.

[6]See LeVine (1970:284-288) for a discussion of this in the African context, and Smith (1955:14) for its use specifically among the Hausa.

REFERENCES CITED

Bargery, Rev. G.P. 1934. *A Hausa-English Dictionary and English-Hausa Vocabulary.* London, Oxford University Press.

Caillois, Roger. 1961. *Man, Play, and Games.* New York, Free Press of Glencoe.

Krieger, Kurt. 1954. 'Knabenspiele der Hausa,' *Baessler-Archiv* n.f. 3: 225-232.

LeVine, Robert A. 1970. 'Personality and Change,' in J. Paden and E. Soja (eds.) *The African Experience,* Vol. I, pp. 276-303. Evanston, Northwestern University Press.

——— 1973. *Culture, Behavior, and Personality.* Chicago, Aldine.

'*Yawon Dandi:* A Hausa Category of Migration,' *Africa* 46, 1, 66-79.

— 1976b 'Playing a Kingdom: A Hausa Meta-Society in the Walled City of Zaria, Nigeria.' In David F. Lancy and B. Allan Tindall, eds., *The Anthropological Study of Play: Problems and Prospects,* pp. 156-164. Cornwall, N.Y., The Leisure Press.

Raynaut, Claude. 1972 *Structures normatives et relations electives.*

Smith, M.G. 1955. *The Economy of the Hausa Communities of Zaria.* London, Her Majesty's Stationery Office.

Turner, Victor. 1969. The Ritual Process. Chicago, Aldine.

Usman, Shamsuddeen, Kassim Musa Ahmed Bichi, and Norma Perchonock. n.d. 'Oral Traditions Concerning the History of the Wards in the Area of Kurmi Market, Kano City.' Offprint.

Some Functions of Aymara Games and Play

Andrew W. Miracle, Jr., Texas Christian University

The purpose of this paper is to view the relationship between the socialization process evidenced in the games and play of Aymara children and the patterns and processes of adult members of Aymara Society.

There are about three million Aymara today, with the majority living in Bolivia and the rest in Peru and Chile. Along with their language, the Aymara have preserved much of their traditional agricultural practices, religious beliefs, political institutions and other cultural trappings. Most Aymara live on the *altiplano,* a high plateau situated at 12,000 to 14,000 feet above sea level. Agriculture is a difficult means of livelihood on the altiplano, but for most it is the only means available. (In some communities, fishing, mining, or a cottage industry, such as weaving, provide a supplement to agriculture). Due to shortages of arable land and machinery, and owing to the types of crops which can be grown, farming is necessarily intensive, demanding long days of hard work in exchange for subsistence-level harvests. Low levels of average production are compounded by almost annual losses to frost, hail, drought or flooding.

The agricultural patterns of the Aymara depend upon cooperative labor. There are a variety of traditional forms of cooperation, but the most important form of cooperative aid is *ayni.*[1] *Ayni* includes reciprocal labor, especially for planting and harvesting, and lending and borrowing, especially in connection with fiestas. *Ayni* involves long term, perhaps lifelong relationships of reciprocity. Careful records are kept by memory so that it is known how much one owes and how much one is owed. Allowances are made for inflation or devaluation of the national currency.

It would appear that change in the economic sphere has been related to the development and growth of the market system which is tied to the increased use of cash, the introduction of consumer goods in rural areas, and a continually improving system of transportation. The marketing of produce is extremely important for the Aymara; it also consumes much time and energy. While most Aymara families rely upon marketing specialists, at one time or another almost everyone participates in marketing.

Some Factors Affecting Play Habits and Opportunities

There are six age grades in Aymara. Babies are called *wawa* for the first two years of life. Prepubescent children are either *imilla* (girl) or *yuqallo* (boy). After puberty, youths are known as *q'axu,* or called *tawaqu* (young woman) or *wayna* (young man). An adult is a *jaqi*. An elder is called *chuymani* (a person of age). The final stage of life is that of the dead.

The adult-nonadult distinction, however, is primary for the Armara. One becomes an adult only through marriage. The term for adult, *jaqi*, also means human being or person. Thus, an unmarried individual is somehow incomplete, not quite a full person. This relates to the fact that the family is the basic social unit. Only a husband-wife unit can participate fully in the economic, political and ceremonial life of the community. The sphere of children, with its concommitant roles and responsibilities, is clearly distinguishable from that of adults.

Children begin contributing to the economic welfare of the family at an early age. Often two- to three-year-old children tag along with older siblings as they go about chores, the younger ones carrying a handful of fodder or helping out as best they can. Four- and five-year-old children may be left alone to watch the sheep graze. Young children also help their parents in the fields, pulling weeds, breaking clods or hoeing. As they grow older children assume more and more responsibilities. Children of 10 or 12 may have a small plot or a row in a larger field which is theirs to tend and from which they gather the rewards at harvest time. If it is feasible, children may attend school, but then their chores must be done before and after school hours.

The number of rural communities with a school has increased dramatically since the revolution of 1952 in Bolivia. However, many communities, especially in the more remote regions, are still without a school. In those communities where there are schools, the school may serve as a focal point for community activities. School children also engage in play before school, after school and during recess. While school teams participate in soccer contests with teams from other schools, such events will not be considered in detail in this brief paper. Neither will events of a ceremonial nature, such as fiesta dances, intercommunity rivalries, bullfights, or modern folk-game contests, be discussed. The focus here in on the games and play of children. The discussion begins with a look at the stated ideals and sanctions affecting such activity.

One should play only after finishing all work. Better still, one should do something useful while playing, such as carrying feed or caring for animals. One Aymara woman I interviewed recalled that as a young girl there was no end to work. Always she and her friends would want to play and they would make plans to play, but then they would be unable to finish all their chores so that they could play. "Never was it possible to find time to play," she said. Once she had been left at home to do the cooking. She got involved in playing and let the corn burn. She said that she learned not to do that. Another time, because she was playing, her pigs got into the potato field. Her mother was so angry that the girl had to flee to her grandmother's.

Children are not free to play at home in the house. It is felt to be bad for parents to allow their children to play because this will result in the children growing up to become rebellious, and to be lazy. Children can play in front of their parents only if there is no work for the children to do. Even when there is no work to be done and the children are allowed to play, the parents will tell the children to go further away (out of their sight) and to play away from the conversation of the parents so as not to disturb them. The parental sanction against playing is strong. In the lakeside community of Qumpi, a man told me that when he was young his father would sometimes catch him playing with other children. He would then have to run away and hide.

Children often play while watching the sheep. If there are no crops where the sheep are being grazed, then they do not require much supervision and the children are free to play. However, often there are crops in the same general area and then the children must watch the sheep constantly to see that they do not jump the stone wall to prevent them from getting too close to crops, or else they will run over and chase the sheep away. Another place where children do much of their playing is at school.

An Inventory of Games and Play from a Single Community

In order to explore the function of games and play more fully, an attempt was made to inventory the recreational activities of children in Chukinapi, a small farming community on the shore of Lake Titicaca. In addition to observations, a list of the children's games known and played in the community was elicited from youths in the community. Though undoubtedly there may be some omissions, the inventory serves as a starting point.

Mud dolls. Children make various figures from mud and clay and then play with them.

Totora boats. Boats are made of *totora* reeds. These are models of the traditional boats used on the lake. Children make them just to play with them.

Houses of stones. In areas where sheep are pastured I have seen houses, even whole villages, made of rocks up to 10 inches square or more.

Tinqana or marbles. Marbles are sometimes made of mud, which is then allowed to dry. Small fruits and round seeds are also used for marble games. Sometimes store-bought marbles are used.

Playing market. Sometimes children will pretend to sell "oranges." "I am going to the Yungas,"[2] one will cry. Then the inedible orange berries of a particular shrub will be picked and used in the play. Sometimes these "oranges" will be bartered. Other times leaves will be used as money to buy and sell them.

Slingshot. It is considered a diversion to walk around with a homemade *flecha* or slingshot. Many youths, about 9-15, carry slingshots, which are sometimes used in herding. On one occasion, I saw a boy of 12 hit a bird from a distance of seven or eight meters. The bird was sitting in a tree about four meters off the ground. The shot decapitated the bird. While some birds (e.g., coots) can be hunted for food with slingshots, oftentimes, as in this case, birds are killed simply for sport. The boy I observed had no intentions of using the bird he shot.

Hunting nests. Children like to hunt for birds' nests, looking for baby birds and bird eggs. The eggs are not collected for food; children just look at them out of curiosity. Semantically, this is considered a game.

Hunting honey. Children and youths sometimes hunt the nests of wild bees. The bees native to the region do not build large nests and there is never much honey to be found in any given nest. Often the hunters are bitten, but they will continue their search.

Imanaq"asina or hide-and-seek. This game is also called by the Spanish *oculto carlo.*

T"unk"una or hopscotch. This is said to be the most popular game in Chukinapi. This game can be played almost anywhere; in the field while watching sheep for instance, where grids can be drawn in the dirt. Both boys and girls play it, from about ages six or seven to fifteen or more. Like most games of skill it is better if those playing are about the same age. If there is an older one and a younger one it is not fair and not much fun because the older one almost always wins. This game is sometimes played by older males for money.

Once in Chukinapi I was walking with two young married men (25-30 years old). We came across a place in the mountains where sheep were pastured where the lines of a *t"unk"una* game were still visible. The two were going to make a wager and play the game, but they could not agree on the amount of the wager. They said they had not played since they were "boys."

Wik"u wallpa or blindman's bluff. In Spanish this game is called *gallinita ciega* or blind little hen. This is the same name as the Aymara.

Katun katuna or tag. The Spanish name of the game is *pesca pesca.* The number of bases varies with the number of players, and there is a player on each base. Another player tries to catch one of the others as they run from base to base.

Futbol or soccer. Girls do not play much *futbol;* this is about the only game with a sex bias. All the others are enjoyed by both boys and girls; and the two sexes play them together, not just separately. Sometimes the boys will make the girls play soccer with them. It is said that because the girls do not know how to play well they are made the goal keepers. Girls are afraid to play *futbol* with the boys since they do not know how to play well. It may be that the boys get girls to be goal keepers when there are not enough boys to make a good game. Once in a while the teachers will try to organize a game of *futbol* for the girls at school in order to teach them how to play.

Wiskitu past-ayita or pasado a barquitos. In this game the players try to pass some object secretly while one tries to find the object being passed among the others.

Other Play Forms

In areas other than Chukinapi I have observed additional types of play and other games. Moreover, the literature contains descriptions of various games reportedly known by the Aymara of other regions.[3]

Marbles, tops, *aros* (hoops), cards, and above all *futbol* seem to be popular in all of the towns and villages. Soccer fields are everywhere. Where there are three or four houses, there is likely to be a playing field. I have seen shepherds playing cards in the fields while caring for their sheep. Cards are played by both sexes from about ages 10 to 20. I have seen boys six to twelve years old playing with tops, marbles, and *aros,* even in the fields. Tossing stones or pitching pennies also are popular, and older boys often wager on such games.

Pets are also kept by children. In Qumpi I observed two girls about nine years old playing with their pet lamb or *chijita.* This term is used only for lambs, and only when they are kept as pets.

Aymara children also engage themselves in many other types of play. For example, on several occasions I observed young children (under 12) swinging on low eucalyptus branches, as one would on a vine. Also, I have seen friendly games of chase develop between a girl and a boy of the same age. This involved prepubescent children, five to ten years old. Usually the play starts when the boy feigns to hit the girl or pretends that he is going to chase her and hit her. The girl would respond equally. Then they would chase each other in turn, with no sex role differentiation. Even though this example involves very young children, this pattern is the same as that of traditional courtship, whereby teenage boys and girls hit and chase each other as part of the courting ritual.

Origins and Functions of Some Games and Play Forms

It is impossible to fix with confidence the historical origins of games such as those listed in the Chukinapi inventory. Most seem to be indigenous or have probable indigenous antecedents reinforced by either analogous or homologous Hispanic games. For example, the top, marbles, hopscotch, and even *futbol* and dice have historical counterparts in both traditional Aymara and Hispanic cultures. Few strictly Aymara games remain. Pitching games and board games are reported for some areas which may represent pre-Colombian Amerindian games.

For activities such as *aros,* kites, *wiskitu past'ayita,* the slingshot, *imanaq"asina,* and *wik"u wallpa,* the historical roots can only be guessed. The literature, however, does not suggest indigenous origins. Some of the games and play known by the Aymara seem to be prevalent in various cultures. Only a few of the games now played by the Aymara are definite

Hispanic imports. Among these would be card games, and *futbol,* as it is now played. However, there is strong evidence that some form of team ball game was played by the Amerinds of this area prior to the arrival of the *hispanos.*

Almost all of the games played by the young people of Chukinapi stress skill. None are totally dependent upon luck or chance. If this is compared with the emphasis on luck (or the capriciousness of nature) in Aymara stories, the combination might imply that one needs skill in addition to luck if success is to be realized. In addition, the games involve little group strategy. This might reflect the Aymara reticence to manipulate others within the community, though no such disinclination is shown for outsiders nor the Hispanic system.

Aymara juvenile recreation tends to be individualistic or involve only one or two others. Most games require no props or elaborate devices. The activities are congruent with the time and space grids of Aymara young people. The events are designed for the normal routines of watching the animals, going to school, and to the calendar of daily chores.

Games and play are vehicles for socialization. Aymara youngsters learn agricultural skills, basic marketing practices, animal husbandry, and boat-building skills from various play activities. They also imitate the construction of stone buildings and altars.

They learn of man in nature. They ready themselves for marriage and learn musical skills necessary for fiestas. They practice the roles and responsibilities of adults. And they learn about relations with other communities through *futbol* and other contests.

As has been noted, the majority of play and games cited may involve more than one person, but need not do so. The number playing is flexible and dictated by the number present more than by the rules of the game. The places where play occurs and the times also dictate who will be playing together. Those shepherding together, walking to and from school together, and performing chores together are likely to be siblings or close kin. There are no sanctions regarding the choice of playmates, but it seems that children most often play with relatives because they are the ones most often around at the times and places where play usually occurs. The most notable exceptions would be play that occurs at school.

An analysis of play and games by age levels provides some interesting insight. Babies or *wawa* usually have no special toys, though they may pick up a stick, a rock, or anything handy with which to amuse themselves. This is the stage in life of the most tactile contact, and in a sense *wawa* play with people, mother or older sibling for example, and not with things. Older children entertain themselves as well as the younger children. Children up to five or six have the most time to play and are allowed to play the most. It is difficult for older children to find time or permission to play. Most play of older children occurs at school or in the fields while shepherding. Older children seem to play organized games to a greater extent than younger children who are more often engaged in chase or other less structured activities. Adolescents have little time for games and play. Their recreation is found in school, courtship, conversation, music and dancing, and travel, especially travel to the city.

It has been suggested that in cultures where children are an economic asset that there is not much play (Sutton-Smith 1974:13). According to previous reports (e.g., Carter 1971:132) this might have been held as valid for the Aymara. I would suggest that these may have been somewhat misleading, since Aymara children do engage in quite a bit of play. The view of these earlier reports may be due to the adult perspectives of the researchers, or to the perceptions of the children involved. Perhaps the observers saw little play occuring around the home or in the fields when parents were present. Or, perhaps the children did not play in front of the observers due to the fact that the observers were identified as adults as well as strangers and this inhibited the children's play activities.

Conclusions

Three functions of childrens' play and games among the Aymara are evident. First, play reinforces the adult nonadult dichotomy. Nonceremonial play and participation in games is confined largely to the sphere of children. The economic activities of adults which consume most of their time prohibit or severely restrict the opportunities for games and play. Activities such as fiesta dancing which provide entertainment for adults are not considered as play.

Secondly, play and games teach children some skills necessary for adult life, and childrens' socialization includes the internalization of the idea that a high premium is to be placed on work. Children may play, but they learn that work is more highly valued.

According to the Aymara concept, play is considered to be nonproductive economically. Hunting coots for food or searching for birds' nests to rob would constitute different categories than shooting a slingshot just for fun and inspecting nests out of curiosity. Not a single informant ever mentioned hunting as a recreational activity.

Owing to the difficulties imposed by the environment and the patterns of subsistence agriculture which prevail, a strong emphasis on the value of work is a prerequisite for cultural survival. Adults chastise chilren who do not work hard and express negative views towards the games and play of children. These negative sanctions serve to reinforce the belief in a work ethic.

Finally, much of the play and many of the games of children teach cooperation and provide for patterned interaction among peers. This interaction in play helps form the basis for future relationships. This is necessary to prepare children for participation in adult roles, especially with regard to *ayni* (cooperative aid). Before the advent of schools in the *campo* this was probably an essential function of games and play. Nowadays, interaction at schools also may serve this function.

NOTES

[1]All Aymara words used in this paper are written with the alphabet developed by Mr. Juan de Dios Yapita at the *Institute de Estudios Linguisticos* in La Paz. Mr. Yapita is also director of the *Instituto de Lengua y Cultura Aymara* in Bolivia. In this alphabet aspiration is represented by /"/. A glottal stop is indicated by /'/. The /q/ is a uvular occlusive. The /x/ is a uvular fricative. The /j/ is a glottal fricative. Other consonants approximate the Spanish equivalent. There are, however, only three vowels in Aymara: /a/, /i/ and /u/.

[2]The Yungas are steep subtropical valleys on the eastern slopes of the Andes. The Yungas are about a half-day driven from the city of La Paz.

[3]For other examinations of Aymara games and play see Buechler and Buechler 1971; LaBarre 1948; Paredes 1966; Rowe 1946; and Tschopik 1946 and 1951.

BIBLIOGRAPHY

Buechler, Hans C. and Judith-Maria Buechler 1971 *The Bolivian Aymara.* New York: Holt, Rinehart & Winston.

Carter, William E. 1971 *Bolivia: A Profile.* New York: Praeger.

La Barre, Weston 1948 *The Aymara Indians of the Lake Titicaca Plateau, Bolivia.* American Anthropological Association Memoir 68.

Miracle, Andrew W., Jr. 1976 *The Effects of Cultural Perception on Aymara Schooling.* Ph.D. dissertation, University of Florida.

Paredes Candia, Antonio 1966 *Juegos, Juguetes y Divertimientos de Folklore de Bolivia.* La Paz, Bolivia: Ediciones ISLA.

Rowe, John Howland 1946 Inca Culture at the Time of the Spanish Conquest. *In Handbook of South American Indians.* Julian H. Steward, Ed. Washington, D.C.: Smithsonian Institution, Bureau of American Ethnology Bulletin 143. Vol. 2: 183-330.

Sutton-Smith, Brian 1974 Towards an Anthropology of Play. The Association for the Anthropological Study of Play *Newsletter* 1, 2:8-15.

Tschopik, Harry, Jr. 1946 The Aymara. *In Handbook of South American Indians.* Julian H. Steward, Ed. Washington, D.C.: Smithsonian Institution, Bureau of American Ethnology Bulletin 143. Vol. 2:501-574.

1951 *The Aymara of Chucuito, Peru.* Anthropological Papers Vol. 44, Part 2. New York: American Museum of Natural History.

Research on Children's Play: An Overview, and Some Predictions

Helen B. Schwartzman, Institute for Juvenile Research, Chicago

In this paper a brief examination of anthropological, sociological, and psychological studies of children's play is presented. Specific topical areas within each disciplinary orientation are noted and evaluated here, and predictions as to research trends to be expected in the future are made.

Collectors and Classifiers

The urge to collect, categorize, and preserve texts of children's play and games began in the late 19th century. Gomme's two-volume work *The Traditional Games of England and Scotland* (1894, 1898), Newell's *Games and Songs of American Children* (1883) and Culin's numerous studies (e.g., 1891, 1907) are examples of this approach as practiced by English and American folklorists and ethnologists. The more recent investigations of Brewster (e.g., 1945, 1952), Howard (e.g., 1958, 1959), I. and P. Opie (1959, 1969) and Abrahams (1969) continue in the tradition of the antiquarian. As Sutton-Smith (1974) has suggested, this approach to the investigation of children's play may be characterized by its emphasis on the collection of play texts (i.e., descriptions of the play or game event itself) to the exclusion of discussion or analysis of play contexts (i.e., the social, psychological, or environmental correlates of the event).

Following also in the tradition of the collector are recent structural analyses of children's play and games as advocated by Dundes (1964), Redl, Gump and Sutton-Smith (1971); Sutton-Smith (1972a); Parott (1972) and Von Glascoe (1976). Dundes (1964:276-277) argues, for example, that certain ordered units of action, or *motifemes,* may be isolated as the "minimum structural units" of both games and folktales. Here he follows the work of the Russion folklorist Propp (1958) who analyzes the distribution of functions among the *dramatis personae* of folktales (e.g., villany, struggle and pursuit, relate to the action sphere of the villain). In order to illustrate this approach, Dundes analyzes a variety of children's games (e.g., Hare and Hounds, Hide and Seek, Mother May I?) in terms of the functions, or motifemes, evident in the games.

Parrott (1972), on the other hand, chooses to use an emic (as opposed to etic) framework for analysis of children's play and in this way focuses on a description of significant features and categories of games as perceived by the players themselves. On the basis of interviews and observations with a group of American second-grade boys, Parrott states that her informants classify their own play activities in three different ways: 1) as games (e.g., Kick the Can); 2) as "goofing around", (e.g., sucking icicles;) and 3) as "tricks" (e.g., tripping someone). She then proceeds to outline and diagram the significant features of each of these three play categories as reported to her by the players.

Structural analyses of children's play focus on the collection and categorization of play texts, again with little attention paid to the play context. Unlike the antiquarians, however, structuralists do not interpret play in reference to diffusionist or survivalist theories. Instead linguistic theories and models are employed. It is my suggestion that instead of continuing to employ linguistic models for analysis of play texts what is needed is the development of theories of play which account for both the texts and contexts of this behavior. Following this model, it will then be important to utilize it for the study of children's linguistic play as currently there are only a few such reports available (e.g., Haas 1964: Dundes, Leach and Oskok, 1972; I. & P. Opie 1959, and Chukovsky 1968).

Comparisons

The 1959 study of Roberts, Arth and Bush entitled "Games in Culture" led to a re-opening of interest in play and game research for anthropologists, psychologists, and educators. In this article the authors attempt to explain both the function and geographical distribution of games. A number of studies are characteristic of this approach: Roberts and Sutton-Smith's (1962) "conflict-enculturation hypothesis"; Sutton-Smith and Roberts', "Studies of an Elementary Game of Strategy" (1967); Roberts, Sutton-Smith and Kendon's (1963) "Strategy in Games and Folktales", etc. This approach was also used to provide a format for the reporting and interpretation of information on children's play and games in the child socialization study known as the *Six Cultures* project (B. Whiting 1963). Other studies of cross-cultural and intra-cultural variation in children's play employing a statistical methodology have been made more recently by Seagoe (1971a, 1971b) and Seagoe and Murakami (1961). Here children's play in England, Norway, Spain, Greece, Egypt, the United States, Japan, and in three American subcultures (e.g., White, Mexican-American, and Black) has been investigated. Differences in play reports associated with age, sex, type of schooling, cultural and ethnic factors are examined.

Sutton-Smith (1974:11) has recently offered his own criticism of this research by suggesting that these are studies of play *contexts* (i.e., "asserted relationships about psychogenic and sociogenic correlates of games") without much reference to play texts. This criticism is certainly applicable to the majority of large-scale cross-cultural and intra-cultural quantitative studies currently being pursued. However, an alternate view can also be proposed. That is, that these studies tend to ignore not only text but also context. This research school may be characterized by its use of a "search and seize" methodology in which games are pulled from their original socio-cultural systems and placed in artificially constructed contexts for analysis (i.e., those set up by statistical design). In these instances it would seem that both play text and play context are ignored.

Imitation and Imagination

There are two issues of importance currently being raised by investigations of children's role play. The first topic concerns the relationship existing between play and imitation or play and enculturation. The most common interpretation of children's play, according to Loizos (1969), is to view it as practice for adult activity. The frequent utilization of this interpretation by ethnographers has recently been described and criticized by Schwartzman and Barbera (1976), and it was criticized even earlier by Fortes

(1938) in his description of Tallensi children's play. Lancy (1974, 1975, 1976) has also noted that the idea that play functions to enculturate children is very common, but it has rarely been tested. In order to explore its validity he has used a variety of techniques (e.g., participant observation, interviews and experiments) in studies of African (Kpelle) and more recently American children (1976). Most specifically an attempt is made here to draw relationships between the socio-dramatic play of children and the learning of work or occupational roles in a culture.

Children's play has also begun to be investigated as a vehicle for the learning and practicing of culturally appropriate sex roles. Lever's recent studies (1974, 1975) of sex differences in children's play and game behavior are important examples to consider. An attempt is made in these works to test whether boys' games are more complex than girls' games. Complexity is defined here in terms of role differentiation, interdependence between players, size of play group, degree of competition, explicitness of goals, etc. Lever reports that the results of her investigation indicate that in fact, boys' games are more complex, in the above terms, and she suggests that these games may therefore better prepare males "for successful performance in a wide range of work settings in modern complex societies." (1975:3).

Another approach taken toward the study of game roles is Sutton-Smith's (1972b, 1974) recent investigation of role reversals and inversions apparent within the structure of certain children's games. He calls these the "games of order and disorder" and states that examples of such games are: Ring-Around the Rosy, Poor Pussy, Queen of Sheba. According to Sutton-Smith, these types of games are particularly important for researchers to consider because they suggest that play may not always serve a socializing function as it may, at times, seek to challenge or reverse the social order. This is so because "these games often model the social system only to destroy it" (1974:12) (e.g., everyone acts in concert and then collapses), and they also often mock conventional power roles by providing unconventional access to such roles (e.g., everyone gets a turn). It is my suggestion that in searching for ways to understand the learning of occupational and sex roles, which I predict will be one of the trends in future role studies of children's play, it may be useful to consider the role inversions and role mocking behavior said to be characteristic of the "games of order and disorder". Perhaps, in these games, children have always been questioning and/or mocking culturally stereotyped sex roles, and our urge to view play as primarily a socializing force has made it difficult to perceive the satirical and critical nature of this activity.

The second major issue of interest to students of role play is the investigation of relationships between imaginative sociodramatic play and culture. Smilansky's (1968) studies bear on this topic as she suggests that based on her research in Israel certain groups of children appear to have less facility for imaginative role play than others. In her work, children of North African and Middle Eastern parents are said to engage in this type of play with much less frequency and with less ability than children of European parents. Sutton-Smith (1972) has utilized these studies to suggest that there may, in fact, be "two cultures of games:" ascriptive and achievement game cultures. In the former, Sutton-Smith states that there is more interest in imitative and nonimaginative play activities, while in the latter imaginative play is quite frequent. Singer in *The Child's World of Make-Believe: Experimental Studies of Imaginative Play* (1973) continues in the fashion of Sutton-Smith and Smilansky, by presenting a discussion of techniques for measuring "imaginative predispositions" in children as well as descriptions of experimental play interventions. For example Freyberg, in that volume, discusses changes in the imaginative behavior of American urban "disadvantaged" kindergarten children exposed to a specific training program in make-believe.

I predict that research on differences in children's imaginative and sociodramatic play behavior correlated with differences in the children's sociocultural backgrounds will continue to be conducted in the future. This research will also be utilized to justify the institution of "training programs" such as that described by Freyberg. In evaluating these studies, however, it is important to maintain a critical perspective. Smilansky's studies have, for example, recently been challenged by Eifermann's (1971) recent investigations of Israeli children's play. Most significantly, Eifermann reports that the "culturally deprived" children in her sample not only develop the ability to engage in symbolic play, but "they do so at a significantly higher rate than do their 'advantaged peers' " (1971:290) Another factor of importance to bear in mind in evaluating the work of Smilansky, Sutton-Smith, Singer and Freyberg is the problem of definition of terms. In the literature on play there are many, often conflicting, views as to what constitutes "imaginative", "make-believe", "symbolic", or "sociodramatic" play behavior. I believe that the first priority of researchers should be on the clarification of these terms. Finally, it is very likely that different children display their imaginative or make-believe abilities in various ways. All of these various expressions of imagination must be investigated before researchers declare a group of children to be "imaginatively disadvantaged."

Communication

According to Bateson (1955, 1956) play can only occur among animals able to meta-communicate. In his terms, meta-communication requires the ability to distinguish messages of differing logical types. These messages then act as "frames" (or contexts) providing information about how another message should be interpreted. In Bateson's argument, in order to understand an action, as play it must be framed by the message "this is play". However, this message is by nature confusing because it generates a paradox of the Russellian or Epimenides type wherein a negative statement contains an implicit negative meta-statement (1954:180). The simplistic translation for such a message in a play fight would be, "this bite is not a bite". As can be seen, in Bateson's terms, the texts and contexts of play are intimately related to one another and cannot be studied independently and in isolation from one another. Other researchers who have suggested the importance of considering the systematic relation of play texts to play contexts are Geertz (1972); Goffman (1961, 1974); Miller (1973); Schwartzman (1973, 1976) and Sutton-Smith (1971, 1974).

One interesting experimental study of children's play communication is reported by Garvey and Berndt (1975). In this study, the investigators were particularly interested in how children communicate "pretending." Pretend play is defined in this report as an action involving "some transformation of the Here and Now in which the child is actually situated" (1975:1). It is suggested that there are, at least, five types of pretend communication: 1) *negation of pretend* involving a transformation back to the "here and now" from an ongoing pretend state [e.g., "I'm not the dragon anymore" (p. 4)]; 2) *enactment communication* relates to actions, gestures, attitudes, etc. engaged in by the play in order to signify a pretend identity; 3) *play signals* are markers of a play orientation such as giggling, grinning, winking, etc.; 4) *procedural* or *preparatory behaviors* are also necessary so that objects are apportioned correctly (e.g., "This is my telephone") and that rights are clarified (e.g., "I didn't get a turn") (p. 5); and 5) *explicit verbal mention of pretend transformations* is said to occur in a variety of ways (e.g., the child may mention a partner's role, "Are you going to be a bride?"; or his/her own role, "I'm a work lady at work", and so forth) (p. 7). The investigators suggest that these verbal transformations are important to study particularly because for children of this age, "the saying is the playing" (p. 9). The importance of this observation, in my opinion, is the researcher's recognition of the intimate relation existing between play texts and play contexts.

Behavioral Definitions

Ethological studies of non-human primate play have been made by a number of investigators (see Loizos 1969 for a useful review). This approach has recently been utilized for the study of children's behavior (e.g., Blurton-Jones 1969, 1972) and the specific study of children's play (e.g., Smith and Connoley 1972). The ethologist's emphasis on the observation and description of anatomically defined items of behavior has led to an interest in the development of a behavioral definition of play, one capable of use for making interspecies comparisons (see Loizos 1969 for such a definition). I predict that the approach of the ethologist will be used to generate a number of studies of children's play in the near future. And it is for this reason that a specific examination and critique of the general research orientation of the child ethologist is in order.

Advocates (e.g., Barsamian and Clapp 1974) of the child ethology method argue that it will produce more rigorous analyses of child behavior and also allow for more valid and reliable comparisons of human primate behavior with that of non-human primate activity. Adopting this approach, the child ethologist assumes that the behavior of children is directly equivalent to the behavior of monkeys, chimpanzees, gorillas, etc. This assumption of equivalence is reflected by the fact that behaviors which the investigator wishes to study are, whenever possible, defined in anatomical terms, (e.g., smile—corner of mouth turned upward). These definitions are used in order to allow for inter-species behavioral comparisons. The child's use of language is generally defined as "talk" (i.e., the occurence of word utterances). What the child "says" is often presented only in terms of the frequency of the "talk" and only rarely is the content of what is "said" considered. This attempt to study children "as if" they are monkeys disregards a basic part of the child's social context (i.e., what the child says about what he/she does) and appears to be in direct contradiction to the ethologist's desire to study behavior in naturally occurring contexts.

In order to study "the child as monkey" from what is construed to be a more "objective" vantage point, the child ethologist must also adopt a metaphor for conceptualizing his/her own investigative or exploratory activity. It is my suggestion that this approach requires the ethologist to assume a "quiet as a mouse" presence in the research situation. In order to foster this image, the investigator is encouraged to respond "passively" to the approaches of children and, if possible, to avoid talking at all to the children involved in the study (see particularly Blurton-Jones 1969). If the ethologist successfully adopts this stance, it is hoped and expected that his/her presence will soon become likened to the presence of a totally insignificant being (i.e., "a mouse not a man"). Once this metaphorical transformation has occurred, it is felt that the researcher will be free to observe and record the children's behavior in a detached and therefore "objective" manner. This approach to the achievement of objectivity in research situations appears to be in direct contrast to the anthropologist's desire to both *participate* and *observe* in research contexts.

This critique of child ethology is offered not in an attempt to revive the "man is unique" argument. Instead, it is presented as a suggestion to practitioners of child ethology to re-examine the orienting metaphors guiding their research with the assumption that more appropriate metaphors are available for use in conceptualizing the activities of both children and anthropologists (see Schwartzman 1976). I would also argue that if this re-examination does not occur then it will be impossible for ethological researchers to understand the phenomenon of children's play (i.e., "the saying and the playing"). And finally I would suggest that this approach is utlimately in danger of eliminating itself for it will be hard to continually justify the use of a method which is guided by two metaphors which relegate both children and researchers to silence.

Affect, Intellect and Development

Psychological studies of children's play have been most significantly influenced by Freud and Piaget. Freud's interpretations of children's play are by now well-known and generally center around the idea that children act out and repeat problematic situations in play in order to master them (e.g., 1905, 1920). The utilization of Freudian theories of play is today most apparent in the widespread use of this activity for diagnostic, therapeutic (e.g., Klein 1955, Axline 1969) and research (e.g., Levin and Wardwell 1971) purposes. In all these instances, however, play *texts* are used as a *context* for the diagnosis and treatment, or research investigation, of children's non-play behavior.

For Piaget (1962) play has primacy over the process of accommodation (i.e. the child modifies his/her mental set in response to external demands). The ontogeny of play, in Piaget's terms, must be viewed in relation to the development of intelligence in the child. Therefore, each cognitive stage which is discussed exhibits a characteristic type of play activity. Piaget relates the three major types of play (e.g., sensory motor play, symbolic play, and games-with-rules) which he has outlined to specific cognitive stages and he argues that over time play becomes "more and more adequately adapted to reality" characterized less by "the deformation and subordination of reality to the desires of the self" (1971:229). Sutton-Smith (1971b) has recently taken issue with this approach in his presentation of a critique of what he refers to as Piaget's "copyist epistemology", and his desire to reduce play to a cognitive process.

There are many recent studies of children's play which explore the affective, cognitive and developmental dimensions of this behavior (e.g., see particularly Bruner 1972, 1975, and Sutton-Smith 1971c, 1975). A currently fashionable trend in psychological research is to combine Freudian and Piagetian theories. Gould's (1972) analysis of a series of children's "spontaneous play fantasy productions", collected for her by teachers in an American middle-class nursery school, is an example of this approach. In her interpretation of these fantasy or play texts, she draws on the work of both Piaget and Freud to relate these events to the cognitive and affective developmental level of the individual children in the nursery school. This approach to the *use* of play for the development of an understanding of a child's non-play behavior is likely to continue in the future. However, because play itself is not the subject of investigation, such studies continue to be of dubious value to the student of play.

Conclusions

On the basis of this review a number of anthropological studies of children's play are suggested. Most importantly, anthropologists should begin to produce "ethnographies of children's play" which report both the texts and contexts of this activity. As there are few such studies available now virtually all theorizing about play has been done on the basis of investigations of Western children's play (or non-human primate play in the case of the ethologists). Clearly this bias cannot continue in the future. Research studies must also begin to examine not only how play contexts affect texts, but also how texts may influence contexts (see particularly the "games of order and disorder"). Relationships between play and enculturation and imagination and culture must also continue to be investigated. And, finally, cross-cultural studies focusing on affective, cognitive, and developmental issues must be conducted to put Freud and Piaget's theories to the ethnographic test. I am really suggesting that what is needed today in anthropology is a six, or better yet, a sixteen, cultures of play project.

NOTE

This paper summarizes an article entitled, "The Anthropological Study of Children's Play" which appears in the 1976 *Annual Review of Anthropology,* Bernard J. Siegel et al, eds. Vol. 5, Palo Alto: Annual Reviews, Inc.

REFERENCES CITED

Abrahams, R. D. (ed.) 1969 *Jump Rope Rhymes: A Dictionary.* Austin, Texas, University of Texas Press.

Axline, V. M. 1969 *Play Therapy.* New York: Ballantine.

Barsamian, G., B. Clapp 1974 Child Ethology: Turning TV on The Kids. Paper presented at Annual Meeting of the Central States Anthropological Society, Chicago, Illinois, March 27-30.

Bateson, R. 1955 A theory of Play and Fantasy. *Psychiatric Research Reports.* December.

1956 The Message "This is Play". In *Group Processes: Transactions of the Second Conference.* New York: Josiah Macy Foundation, pp. 145-151.

Blurton-Jones, N. 1969 An Ethological Study of Some Aspects of Social Behavior of Children in Nursery School. In *Primate Ethology,* D. Morris Ed. Garden City, New York Do, Doubleday, pp. 437-463.

1972 *Ethological Studies of Child Behavior.* Cambridge: Cambridge University Press.

Brewster, P. G. 1945 "Johnny on the Pony, A New York State Game". *New York Folklore Quarterly* 1:239-240.

1952 Children's Games and Rhymes. *The Frank C. Brown Collection of North Carolina Folklore,* 1:32-319, Durham, N.C., University Press.

Chukovsky, K. 1968 *From Two to Five.* Berkeley: University of California Press.

Culin, S. 1891 Street Games of Boys in Brooklyn. *Journal of American Folklore* 4:221-237.

1907 *Games of North American Indians.* 24th Annual Report, Bureau American Ethnology, Washington, D.C.

Dundes, A. 1964 On Game Morphology: A Study of the Structure of Non-Verbal Folklore. *New York Folklore Quarterly,* 20:276-288.

Dundes, A., J. Leach, B. Ozkok 1972 Strategy of Turkish Boys' Verbal Dueling Rhymes. *Journal of American Folklore* 83:325-349.

Eifermann, R. 1971 Social Play in Childhood. In *Child's Play.* R. Herron and B. Sutton-Smith Eds. New York: John Wiley pp. 270-297.

Fortes, M. 1938 Social and Psychological Aspects of Education in Taleland. *Africa,* Supplement to Volume II.

Freud, S. 1905 *Jokes and Their Relation to the Unconscious.* New York; W. W. Norton (1963 edition).
1920 *Beyond the Pleasure Principle.* New York: Bantam Books, (1959 edition).

Garvey, C., R. Berndt 1975 The Organization of Pretend Play. Paper presented at Annual Meeting of the American Psychological Association, Chicago, Illinois, September.

Geertz, G. 1972 Deep Play: Notes on the Balinese Cockfight. *Daedalus* 1-37.

Goffman, E. 1961 *Encounters.* Indianapolis: Bobbs-Merrill.
1974 *Frame Analysis,* New York: Harper and Row.

Gomme, A. B. 1894 *The Traditional Games of England, Scotland and Ireland,* Vol. 1, London: David Nutt.

Gould R. 1972 *Child Studies Through Fantasy.* New York: Quadrangle.

Haas, M. 1964 *Thai Word Games.* In Language in Culture and Society: A reader in Linguistics and Anthropology. D. Hymes, Ed. New York: Harper and Row pp. 301-303.

Howard D. 1958 Australian "Hoppy" Hopscotch. *Western Folklore* 17: 163-175.
1959 Ball Bouncing Customs and Rhymes in Australia. *Midwest Folklore* 9:77-87.

Klein, M. 1955 The Psychoanalytic Play Technique. *American Journal of Orthopsychiatry* 25: 223-237.

Lancy, D. F. 1974 *Work, Play, and Learning in a Kpelle Town.* Ph.D. thesis, University of Pittsburgh.
1975 The Role of Games in the Enculturation of Children. Paper presented at the 74th Annual Meeting of the American Anthropological Association, San Francisco, California, December 2-6.
1976 The Play Behavior of Kpelle Children during Rapid Cultural Change. In *The Anthropological Study of Play: Problems and Prospects.* David F. Lancy and B. Allan Tindall, eds. Cornwall, N.Y.: The Leisure Press.

Lever, J. 1974 *Games Children Play: Sex Differences and the Development of Role Skills.* Ph.D. Thesis, Yale University, New Haven.
1975 Sex-Role Socialization and Social Structure: The Place of Complexity in Children's Games. Paper presented at the Annual Meeting of the Pacific Sociological Association, Victoria, B.C.

Levin, H., E. Wardwell 1971 The Research Uses of Doll Play. In *Child's Play,* R. Herron and B. Sutton-Smith, Eds., New York: John Wiley, pp. 145-184.

Loizos, C. 1969 Play Behavior in Higher Primates: A Review. In *Primate Ethology.* D. Morris Ed., Garden City, N.Y.: Doubleday pp. 226-282.

Miller, S. 1973 Ends, Means, and Galumphing: Some Leitmotifs of Play. *American Anthropologist* 75:87-98.

Newell, W.W. 1883 *Games and Songs of American Children.* New York: Harper Bros.

Opie, I., and P. Opie 1959 *The Lore and Language of School Children.* New York: Oxford University Press.
1969 *Children's Games in Street and Playground.* Oxford: Clarendon Press.

Parrott, S. 1972 Games Children Play: Ethnograpy of a Second-Grade Recess. In *The Cultural Experience,* J. Spradley; D. McCurdy, Eds. Chicago: Science Research Associates, pp.207-219.

Piaget, J. 1962 *Play, Dreams and Imitation in Childhood.* New York: W. W. Norton.
1971 Response to Brian Sutton-Smith. In *Child's Play.* R. Herron and B. Sutton-Smith Eds. New York: John Wiley pp. 326-336.

Propp, V. 1958 Morphology of the Folktale. *International Journal of American Linguistics,* Part III. Vol. 24.

Redl, F., Gump, P., B. Sutton-Smith 1971 The Dimensions of Games. In *Child's Play.* R. Herron and B. Sutton-Smith, Eds. New York: John Wiley pp. 408-418.

Roberts, J. M., M. J. Arth, R. R. Bush 1959 Games in Culture. *American Anthropologist* 61:597-605.

Roberts, J. M., B. Sutton-Smith 1962 Child Training and Game Involvement. *Ethnology* 2:166-185.

Roberts, J. M., B. Sutton-Smith, A. Kendon, 1963 Strategy in Games and Folktales. *Journal of Social Psychology* 61:185-189.

Schwartzman, H. B. 1973 *Real Pretending: An Ethnography of Symbolic Play Communication.* Ph.D. Thesis, Northwestern University, Evanston. (Helen E. Beale)

1976a Children's Play: A Sideways Glance at Make-Believe. In *The Anthropological Study of Play: Problems and Prospects.* David F. Lancy and B. Allan Tindall, eds., Cornwall, N.Y.: The Leisure Press.

1976b Metaphors for Children and Models of Development in Anthropology. Paper presented at the joint meeting of the Central States Anthropological Society and the Society for Applied Anthropology, St. Louis, Missouri, March 17-21.

Schwartzman, H. L., and L. Barbera 1976 Children's Play in Africa and Latin America: A Review of the Ethnographic Literature. In *The Anthropological Study of Play: Problems and Prospects.* David F. Lancy and B. Allan Tindall, eds. Cornwall, N.Y.: The Leisure Press.

Seagoe, M. V. 1971a A comparison of Children's Play in Six Modern Cultures, *Journal of School Psych.* 9:61-72.

1971b Children's Play in Three American Subcultures. *Journal of School Psych.* 9:167-172.

Seagoe, M. V., K. A. Murakami 1961 A Comparative Study of Children's Play in America and Japan. *California Journal of Educational Research 11:124-130.*

Singer, J. L. 1973 *The Child's World of Make-Believe; Experimental Studies of Imaginative Play.* New York: Academic Press.

Smith, P. K., K. Connolly 1972 Patterns of Play and Social Interaction in Pre-school Children. In *Ethological Studies of Child Behavior.* N. Blurton-Jones, Ed. Cambridge: Cambridge University Press. pp. 65-95.

Sutton-Smith, B. 1971a Boundaries. In *Child's Play.* B. Herron and B. Sutton-Smith Eds. New York: John Wiley, pp. 103-106.

1971b Piaget on Play: A Critique. In *Child's Play.* R. Herron and B. Sutton-Smith Eds. New York: John Wiley, pp. 326-336.

1971c The Role of Play in Cognitive Development. In *Child's Play.* R. Herron and B. Sutton-Smith, Eds. New York: John Wiley, pp. 252-260.

1972a A Formal Analysis of Game Meaning. In *The Folkgames of Children.* B. Sutton-Smith, Austin, Texas: University of Texas Press, pp. 491-505.

1972b Games of Order and Disorder. Paper presented at Annual Meeting American Anthropological Association, Toronto, Canada, December.

1972c The Two Cultures of Games. In *Folkgames of Children.* B. Sutton-Smith, Austin, Texas: University of Texas Press. pp. 295-311.

1974 Toward an Anthropology of Play. The Association for the Anthropological Study of Play *Newsletter,* 1:8-15.

Sutton-Smith, B., J. M. Roberts, et al 1967 *Studies in an Elementary Game of Strategy.* Genetic Psychology Monograph 75:3-42.

Von Glascoe, C. 1976 The Patterning of Game Preferences in the Yucatan. In *The Anthropological Study of Play: Problems and Prospects.* David F. Lancy and B. Allan Tindall, eds. Cornwall, N.Y., The Leisure Press.

Whiting, B. B. (ed.) 1963 *Six Cultures: Studies of Child Rearing.* New York: John Wiley.

IV. Structural Approaches to Play

Introduction

by Brian Sutton-Smith, Teachers College, Columbia University

(Editor's note: Dr. Sutton-Smith's introduction is adapted from an article authored by himself and Daniel Mahony, which appeared as "A Research Programme in Play and the Arts" in the Ontario Psychologist, *and is reproduced here by permission of the Editor of the* Ontario Psychologist.*)*

This introduction to the papers that follow will focus on the research programme developed by my students and myself at Teachers College during the past three years, much of which is as yet unpublished. Some of the issues with which we are concerned are as follows:

The Definition of Play and Games

In a number of papers we have offered definitions of play and an examination of current research and theory in this area (Sutton-Smith, 1975a). In particular we have concentrated on the power tactics children use upon each other prior to play (Sutton-Smith & Savasta, 1972), and on the types of play to be found in the pre-school period (Sutton-Smith, 1971). We have also studied games in historical, anthropological and psychological perspective (Sutton-Smith, 1972). More recently we have begun to examine the interrelationships between play and the arts (Sutton-Smith, Abrams, Botvin, Caring, Gildesgame, Stevens, 1975). As most of this material has been published it will not be detailed here.

Play Function as Preadaptive

In most of the animal literature it continues to be assumed that play prepares the animal for his subsequent adaptations in the adult state. Animals that have more to learn are said to play more (Bruner, 1972; Reynolds, 1972). Those that play more are said to need strength and skill in subsequent life (Aldis, 1975). It has always been difficult to see any direct connection between the play of human children and adult adaptation. However, a series of recent studies of a correlational and experimental nature, showing relationships between play and creativity would seem to imply that play is preadaptive rather than directly preparatory (Wallach & Kogan, 1965; Lieberman, 1965; Sutton-Smith, 1968; Feitelson & Ross, 1973; Dansky & Silverman, 1973). It could be argued that on the basis of these studies that play potentiates responses which have a probablistic rather than a necessary relationship to subsequent adaptation. Such a notion of *adaptive potentation* would be consistent with the wide range of responses from the most repetitive to the most ingenious, from the serendipitous to the ridiculous which have been described as included within the definition of play. The freedom from constraint which is the essential feature in most descriptions of play (Huizinga, 1949; Erikson, 1972; Csikszentmihalyi, 1974) could be seen as providing the necessary condition for this wide range of responses, response permutations and response combinations, only some of which ever bear fruit in everyday adaptation.

If it could be shown that some of these free play responses of players are of a higher cognitive level than their responses in more constrained circumstances, such a preadaptive line of reasoning would gain considerable support. There are several studies which support this line of reasoning (Nicolich, 1975; Overton & Jackson, 1973), and in two doctoral theses of our own we have found support for this point of view (Tucker, 1975; Peterson, 1976). Most pertinent is the study by Peterson (1976) in which children asked to tell stories under various conditions of constraint told stories of the highest cognitive level under the freest conditions. When simply "make me up a story" was compared with making a story response to a T.A.T. card or a Rorschach card, the former condition achieved the highest cognitive response. The measure of cognitive level used in this experiment was the product of a series of studies of children's creation of plot structure in stories (Sutton-Smith, Botvin and Mahony, in press), but in its final form was the work of Daniel Mahony (1976). It deals with the variables of character, interaction, plot, subplot, space-time and genre.

We have assumed in this project that art, like play, is also a preadaptive. This has been the view taken by various art theorists such as McLuhan (1965) and Peckham (1967) and can be said to be supported by the work of Overton and Jackson (1973) as well as Peterson's (1976) work on narratives, above. That is, if one interprets narrative as art rather than fantasy play. We have assumed that art makes use of the organizational abstractions (Vygotsky, 1967) or prototypes of play (Fein, 1975) but involves the additional awareness of the need to objectify these through a public media of symbolic forms understood by significant others (Gardner, 1973).

Structural Developments in the Arts

In our current studies we are attempting to identify the basic forms of structure involved in various kinds of expressive media as a first step to the further analysis of the role of adaptive potentiation in child development. In a doctoral thesis, Cornelia Brunner, dealing with children's perception of visual works of art, found that they justified their aesthetic judgments on changing bases with age. From the youngest (seven years) to the adult respondents there was a shift in concepts from those which might be labelled "realism" through "moralism", structuralism", communication" to "empathy". Each "stage" in development parallels one of the classic theories of aesthetics (Brunner, 1975). In more recent studies we have focused on the common mental organization to be found at any given age level to underly such diverse expressive media as dreams, story telling, play with toys, games, songs and musical compositions, drawings, dance and film-making. Briefly, we see children as advancing through five major stages of mental organization as these registered in expressive structures. The stages are:

(a) figure-ground organization (1-3 years)
(b) part-whole articulation (4-5 years)
(c) space-time reversals (6-7 years)
(d) space-time and interactional reversals (8-9 years)
(e) manipulation of genre (10)

At age 2-3, for example, children focus their attention upon asymetrical figure ground organizations in which the figure is given a disproportionate importance in expression over against the ground. We find these polarized identities in children's toy play, in the central characters of their first stories, and in the "primordial" circles of their art. At this age their expression has its own kind of "pivot" grammar parallel with such tendencies in their language. From 4-5 years, children become concerned to co-ordinate their expressive behaviours with a greater sense of articulation within the whole. We have shown that within their dreams and stories children now no longer concentrate only on the central character but include also interactions, amongst central characters (Mahony, 1976). Pilot studies on drawings by Daniel Gildesgame have shown that the same co-ordination occurs within the human figure and its various parts. In games we have shown that the same co-ordination occurs between central characters (Punchinello, Farmer in the Dell) and the peripheral members of the dancing circle [Sutton-Smith, 1972 (a) (b)]. Marylouise Caring has shown that dreams follow a similar path to stories (1976) although in some cases we have discovered that the dream is on a much higher level of cognitive organization than any other expressive media that the child uses. While we are uncertain as yet concerning the conditions that promote the reporting of these very advanced dreams, the theoretical importance of this finding is great insofar as the dream would appear to constitute the most unconstrained example of play life. Preliminary investigations suggest that there is an experimenter effect in our study group, with male rather than female students instigating higher level fantasy stories from both girls and boys (Peterson, 1976). If dreams can be educed under certain favourable conditions so that they show higher levels of complexity, their value for prognosis of subsequent cognitive adaptation becomes suggestive.

At about the age of five we have observed parallels between the way in which children use a palindromic (ABA) organization in the stories, games and songs that they make up. In the latter case for example, up until the age of about four, children show no need for a resolution in the songs they compose nor in their interpretation of whether music played for them is resolved or not. But around five years, the songs they create terminate by returning to the first verse after an intervening and different verse. At that age, they also demand similar resolution in the music that they hear. Songs return to base just as players in games of tag do and as picaresque characters in children's stories do. We have dealt in most detail with the structure of children's stories, based on a system derived by Gilbert Botvin (1976) from the writings of the Russian folklorist, Vladimir Propp (1958). Using a seven stage system, Botvin has shown significant shifts with age from the concatenated stories of five years to the multiple subplots of eleven years. As in language a lengthwise co-ordination of dyadic units (chase-escape; attack-defend, etc.) precedes the embedding of subplots within the general structure. In a partial correlational analysis, Botvin has demonstrated that story length is a product of the acquisition of these new structural competences rather than age alone. In a parallel study David Abrams has focussed on the character of the trickster motif as found in the content of the children's stories or in the cartoons that they watch (1976). The earlier stories of children up until about eight years of age have the regressive "trickster" characteristics spoken of by Radin (1956), whereas the tales of older children have the higher level shrewdness and cognitive reversibility mentioned by Levi-Strauss (1963). In the cartoons they watch, children generally prefer trickster characteristics several levels ahead of those they are capable of producing.

In the studies of Frank Eadie and others on children's film-making (1976), the most remarkable feature in the films of 11 to 13 year olds is their willingness to explore and manipulate the formal properties of the media itself. Children of these ages are not as satisfied as younger children with hero tales simply told. They quickly become enamoured of their capacity to pixillate, and cut in order to produce a great variety of magical effects. While we find some of the same effects in story telling at this age, they are nowhere so pronounced as in this particular expressive form. Nor does such flexibility seem so apparent in our current studies of adolescents' usage of tactics in sports (Stevens, 1976). In another pilot study Sara Zarem and Daniel Mahony have found that the more sophisticated film techniques are used most frequently in the older parts of the plot structure. That is children seem to reserve their experimentation for the parts of their stories with which they have the greatest familiarity, such as the central characters and the central locations.

Conclusion

I have mentioned here only a sampling of our current research but this will at least give a flavour of our attempts to establish the major organizational levels which the child reaches in each particular expressive media. If our conceptual systems are adequate to the expressive forms we are currently investigating then we should soon be able to assess the levels of a child's development in any expressive media. We acknowledge, of course, that the assessment of such levels is not the same as the assessment of aesthetic value. However, we would contend that questions of aesthetic value cannot even be approached until some understanding of the child's current level of cognitive organization is available. A child can only be expressive within the limits of the structure available to him, and the appreciation of his "aesthetic" can only be done by outsiders in terms of those limits, even though they may often be seen as caricatures of the real thing [Sutton-Smith, 1975 (b) (c)].

If expressive structures are anticipatory, as we believe them to be, then their assessment becomes of great importance to social science because of their predictive value. The child's complexity and organization in his dreams, play and art give an indication of what he may be getting "ready" for in his more constrained forms of adaptation. How one bridges the gap from such potentiated responses to more realistic forms of accommodation and how often this gap is bridged are important problems that follow, though at present they have hardly even been envisaged let alone studied. They are clearly critical for any adequate theory of prediction. It follows also that if play and the arts are the true growth centres of the human mind then their importance to education is much increased. When opportunities for their development are not provided, as is typically the case, then children's own capacity for innovative responses must be curtailed. From the present point of view the imagination is the centre of the child's responsive education. He may learn conforming responses by many other techniques. But he will not learn to regularly transform responses in innovative ways unless his imagination is put at the centre of the educational process. Perhaps we are arriving at that point in the development of our civilization where the measure of our future survival is not the amount of early stimulation we give children but the respect which we pay to the opportunities for each child's imaginative reconstruction of events.

BIBLIOGRAPHY

Abrams, D. A. A developmental analysis of the "Trickster" in children's narratives. Paper delivered to The Association for the Anthropological Study of Play (TAASP), Atlanta, 1976.

Aldis, O. *Play Fighting.* New York, Academic Press, 1975.

Botvin, G. A Proppian-Structural Analysis of Children's Fantasy Narratives. Paper delivered to T.A.A.S.P., Atlanta, 1975.

Bruner, J. Nature and uses of immaturity. *American Psychologist,* 1972, 27, 1-22.

Brunner, C. Aesthetic Judgment: Criteria used to evaluate representational art at different ages. Ph.D. dissertation, Columbia University, 1975.

Caring, M. Structural parallels between dreams and narratives. Paper delivered to T.A.A.S.P., Atlanta, 1976.

Csikszentmihalyi, M. *Flow: Studies of Enjoyment.* P.H.S. Report, University of Chicago, 1974.

Dansky, J. L. & Silverman, I. W. Effects of play on associative fluency in preschool children. *Developmental Psychology,* 1973, 9, 38-43.

Eadie, F. A developmental analysis of children's film making. In preparation, 1976. Co-workers include Susan Spielberg, Lily Shohat, Karen Hansen, Pete Lazzaro, Joy Dryer, Sara Paternak Sara Zarem.

Erikson, E. H. *Childhood and Society.* New York: Norton Books, 1972.

Fein, G. A transformational analysis of pretending. *Developmental Psychology,* 1975, *11,* 297-303.

Feitelson, D. & Ross, G. S. The neglected factor: play. *Human Development,* 1973, *16,* 202-223.

Gardner, H. *The Arts and Human Development.* New York: Wiley, 1973.

Huizinga, J. *Homo Ludens: A Study of the Play Element in Culture.* London: Routledge and Kegan Paul, Ltd., 1949.

Lieberman, J. N. Playfulness and divergent thinking: An investigation of their relationship at the kindergarten level. *Journal of Genetic Psychology,* 1965, *107,* 219-224.

Levi-Strauss, C. *Structural Anthropology.* New York: Basic Books, 1963.

Mahony, D. The Society and Geography of the Story World. Paper delivered to T.A.A.S.P., Atlanta, 1976.

McLuhan, M. *Understanding Media: The Extensions of Man.* New York: McGraw-Hill, 1965.

Nicolich, L. M. A longitudinal study of representational play in relation to spontaneous imitation and development of multiword utterances. Final Report, *National Institute of Education,* Rutgers, New Jersey, 1975.

Overton, W. F. & Jackson, J. P. The representation of imagined objects in action sequences: A developmental study. *Child Development,* 1973, *44,* 309-314.

Peckham, M. *Man's Rage for Chaos, Biology, Behavior and the Arts.* New York: Schocken Books, 1967.

Peterson, L. Constraining the child's story-telling situation: does it make a difference? Ph.D. dissertation, Columbia University, 1976.

Propp, V. Morphology of the Folktale. *International Journal of Linguistics,* 1958, *24,* 1-134.

Radin, P. *The Trickster.* New York: Schocken, 1956.

Reynolds, P. Play, language and human evolution. Paper presented to A.A.A.S., *Washington, D.C.,* December, 1972. (Author's address, Australian University, Canberra).

Stevens, T. Cognitive Structures in Sports Tactics. Paper delivered to T.A.A.S.P., Atlanta, 1976.

Sutton-Smith, B. Novel responses to toys. *Merrill-Palmer Quarterly,* 1968, *14,* 151-158.

Sutton-Smith, B. Children at Play. *National History,* 1971, pp. 54-59, (a).

Sutton-Smith, B. The expressive profile. *Journal of American Folklore,* 1971, *84,* 80-92, (b).

Sutton-Smith, B. *The Folkgames of Children.* Austin: University of Texas Press, 1972 (a).

Sutton-Smith, B. Games of order and disorder. Annual Meeting of *The American Anthropological Association.* Toronto, November, 1972 (b).

Sutton-Smith, B. Current Research and Theory on Play, Games and Sports. Paper presented to *American Medical Association.* Annual Meeting, Atlantic City, 1975, (a).

Sutton-Smith, B. Initial Education as Caricature. Paper delivered to the *Conference on Aesthetic Education,* Lehigh University, 1975, (b).

Sutton-Smith, B. & Savasta, M. Sex differences in play and power. Paper presented at the Annual Meeting of the *Eastern Psychological Association.* Boston, April, 1972.

Sutton-Smith, B., Abrams, D., Botvin, D., Caring, M., Gildesgame, D. and Stevens, T. The Importance of the Storytaker: An investigation of the imaginative life. *Urban Review,* 1975, *8,* 82-95.

Sutton-Smith, B., Botvin, G., and Mahony, D. Structures in fantasy narratives. *Human Development,* in press.

Sutton-Smith, B. A developmental structural account of riddles. In B. Babcock Abrahams (Ed.) *Symbolic Inversion.* University of Pennsylvania Press, in press.

Tucker, J. The role of fantasy in cognitive-affective functioning, *Ph.D. Thesis, Teachers College, Columbia University,* 1975.

Vygotsky, L. S. Play and its role in the mental development of the child. *Soviet Psychology,* 1967, *5,* 6-18.

Wallach, M. A. & Kogan, N. *Modes of Thinking in Young Children.* New York: Holt, Rinehart & Winston, 1965.

A Proppian Approach to the Analysis of Children's Fantasy Narratives

Gilbert J. Botvin, Teachers College, Columbia University

According to Piaget (1951) the rudiments of fantasy play emerge in children between 12 and 13 months of age. While fantasy takes the form of play in young children, it generally manifests itself as dramatic role playing and storytelling in older children (Pulaski, 1973). Children begin formulating primitive stories as early as two years of age, yet Piaget (1955) observed that it is not until the age of seven or eight that they are capable of organizing a story into a coherent whole. Prior to this age children "tend to break up the whole into a series of fragmentary and incoherent statements" (Piaget, 1955, p. 130). Related facts and events are connected by means of the conjunction "and then" with little or no regard for temporal, causal, or logical order.

Little is known of the process through which children develop the requisite skill to construct a well-organized and coherent narrative. Although chldren's ability to *recall* or *reconstruct* an ordered series of events may be dependent on the acquisition of specific cognitive skills (e.g., reversibility) or particular elementary concepts (e.g., causality or spatio-temporal relations), the ability to construct a coherent fantasy narrative would seem to be primarily dependent on the development of narrative competence, i.e., the acquisition of a rule system or grammar for organizing and presenting fantasy material in narrative form. While the developmental acquisition of a rule system or grammar has been amply documented in the areas of play (e.g., Sutton-Smith, 1975) and linguistics (Brown, 1973), there has been little attempt to study similar development in the area of children's fantasy narratives. One possibility for the paucity of research in this area may be the lack of an adequate methodology for analyzing children's narratives from a cognitive-developmental perspective. Previous studies of children's fantasy narratives have generally been conducted within a psychoanalytic framework and have employed various types of content analysis. However, such approaches appear to be neither methodologically adequate nor logically appropriate for the study of narrative development.

Proppian Analysis

Recently, Sutton-Smith, Botvin, and Mahony (in press) stated that the acquisition of narrative competence is a learning of increasingly structured performances and suggested an analytic approach to the study of children's fantasy narratives similar to that developed by the Russian folklorist Vladimir Propp. In *The Morphology of the Folktale* (1928) Propp analyzed a corpus of 100 Russian fairy tales and compared them according to their structural components. Propp observed that fairy tales could be decomposed into motifs which could be further decomposed to yield action elements or "functions."

A function represents an *action* or *event* and is generally expressed as a verbal noun (e.g., interdiction, flight, interrogation, violation, departure, pursuit, etc.). In Propp's terms a function is understood as "an act of a character, defined from the point of view of its significance for the course of action" (p. 21). Moreover, functions are defined independent of the character performing them. For example, in the case of abduction it is not important whether the character abducted is the tsar's daughter or the daughter of the court jester; what is important is the act of abduction. For Propp, functions served as the basic units of analysis, the building blocks of the folktale. Once tales have been analyzed into their components parts they may be compared on the basis of these structural components. According to Propp, "the result will be a morphology (i.e., a description of the tale according to its component parts and the relationship of these components to each other and to the whole)" (p. 19). Propp's method, therefore, was to abstract the sequence of predication or action occurring in each tale, symbolize it, and combine these symbols together thus yielding an abstract formulation of each folktale. As a result of his analysis, Propp concluded that for the fairy tale the number of basic elements (functions) are limited and these elements always appear in the same order.

Similarly, children's fantasy narratives may be viewed as the concatenation of a series of actions or events in a more or less lawful and predictable way (Sutton-Smith, 1974). Like Propp's functions, these actions or events may be regarded as the basic unit of analysis. Thus, children's narratives, like folktales, may be decomposed into an aggregate of structural components. These components, when abstracted from a narrative, symbolized, and strung together according to the narrative's chronology, yield the *plot* of the narrative. For example, if narrative *N* is composed of the event sequence A + B + C + D, the analysis would focus on the organization of events A, B, C, and D. Therefore, the narrative is analyzed in terms of the event sequence characterizing that particular narrative. Thus, any given narrative may be reduced to a positional string of symbols which represent the chronology of the events occurring in that narrative. This type of analysis is specific and precise, and facilitates the discovery of narrative syntax, i.e., the rules by which the elements of a narrative are organized.

Development of Structural Complexity

According to Werner, development "proceeds from a state of relative globality and lack of differentiation to a state of increasing differentiation, articulation, and hierarchic integration" (1957, p. 126). That is, development is viewed as a unitary progression toward increasingly complex hierarchic organization. Psycholinguistic studies offer evidence of the validity of Werner's orthogenic principle, at least in terms of the relative complexity of certain linguistic structures and their developmental order of acquisition.

For example, children progress from (1) a series of single word utterances, to (2) a series of simple sentences, to (3) the coordination and conjunction of simple sentences, to (4) embedded sentences (Brown, 1973). Therefore, following general developmental principles such as those stated by Werner and implications from psycholinguistic research, we might expect similar increases in the structural complexity of children's fantasy narratives as they grow older.

One potential advantage of a Proppian approach to children's fantasy narratives is that it may provide a technique for determining structural complexity. In an earlier paper Sutton-Smith et al. (1975) noted that children's narratives may be divided into two broad categories similar to those found by Propp: (1) those developing out of villainy and (2) those developing out of lack (state of insufficiency). Moreover, children's narrative, like the tales of the North American Indians studied by Dundes (1964), appear to be constructed around a nuclear dyad of something lacking (or villainous action) and then a response in which the lack is liquidated (or the villainy is nullified). In this context, the minimum requirement for a tale is the presence of a nuclear dyad (either lack/lack-liquidated, or villainy/villainy nullified). As tales increase in complexity additional elements are interposed between the lack (or villainy) and the lack-liquidated (or villainy nullified). The nuclear dyad serves to delineate the boundaries of a story or episode within a story. Several nuclear dyads may be strung together in a series forming episodes, or a primary dyad may contain one or more intervening nuclear dyads forming subordinate plots or subplots. Thus, through the application of Propp's methodology and Dundes's notion of nuclear dyadic structure, children's narratives may be analyzed in terms of their structural complexity.

Levels of Structural Complexity

Based on the general developmental course suggested by Werner (1957) and the order of acquisition of linguistic structures indicated by psycholinguistic research, we have formulated seven levels of structural complexity for children's fantasy narratives. In each case the basic unit of analysis is an action or event and the basic structure is the dyad. Increasing structural complexity has been conceived in terms of the articulation and hierarchical organization of nuclear dyads as well as the integration of intermediary elements between the initial and final terms of the nuclear dyad.

Level 1. Narratives at this level lack coherence and structural unity. Prior to this children's narratives are the result of juxtaposing several proper nouns with only the implication of action. However, while narratives at this level do contain a series of events, they are merely the result of a more or less random concatenation.

Example: Pirates found a treasure full of diamonds (Fortuitous Discovery).

A police boat saw the pirates (Reconnaissance Fulfilled). The pirates won (Victory).

Level 2. Narratives at this level are short but structurally symmetrical. They are characterized by the presence of one nuclear dyad. Although these

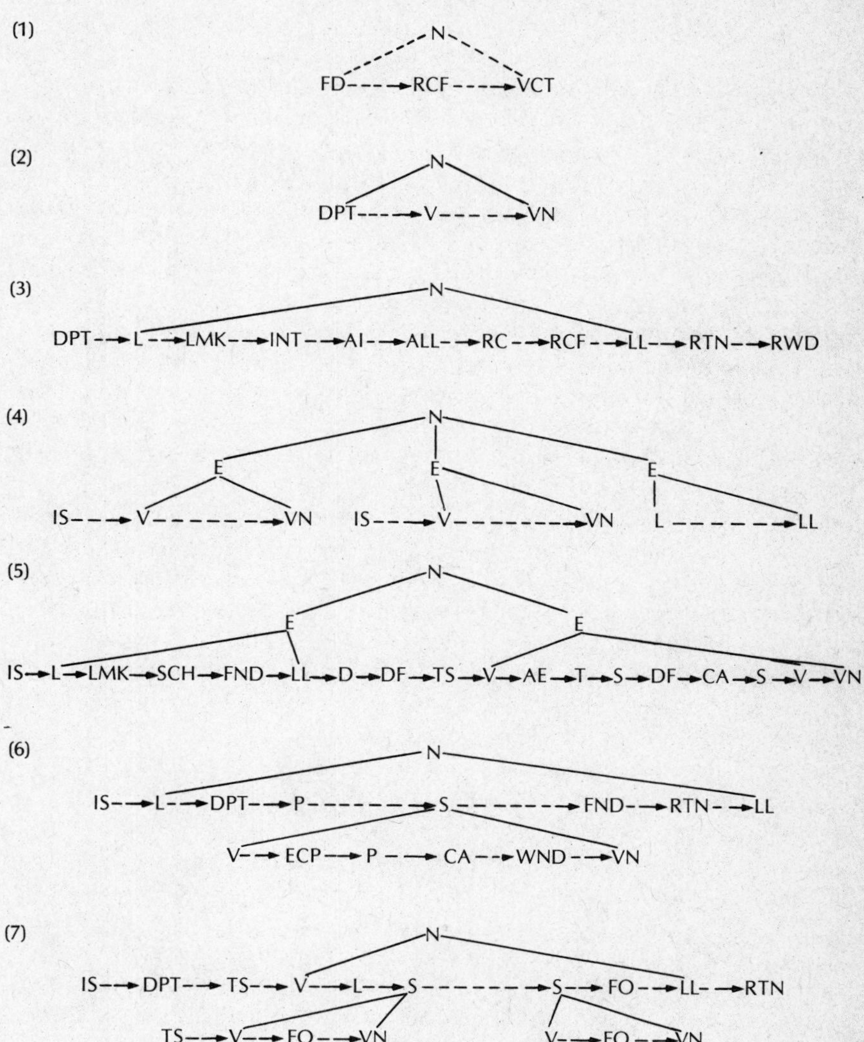

Figure 1. Sample Analysis of the Levels of Structural Complexity
Where N is narrative, E is episode, S is subplot, and the other letters stand for elements in the nuclear dyads referred to in the text.

narratives may have action elements either before (preparatory) or after (consequential) the nuclear dyad, no elements may occur between the initial and final terms of the dyad.

Example: An astronaut went into space (Departure). He was attacked by a monster (Villainy). The astronaut got in his spaceship and flew away (Villainy Nullified).

Level 3. This level is characterized by the internal expansion of the narrative through the use of intermediate action elements. Narrative at this level are differentiated from those of level 1 by the elaboration of action through the interposing of elements between the initial and final terms of the nuclear dyad.

Example: Once there was a little. She went walking in the woods (Departure) and soon it was dark. It was so dark she couldn't find her way back home (Lack). She cried and cried (Lack Made Known). An owl heard her and asked if she was lost (Interrogation). She said yes (Acquisition of Information). The owl said he would help her find her way home (Alliance). He flew up in the air and looked around (Reconnaissance). After finding out which way to go (Reconnaissance Fulfilled), he said, "Okay follow me." Then he led the girl out of the woods and showed her the way home (Lack-liquidated). When she got back home she was so happy (Return). She gave the friendly owl a kiss and thanked him (Reward), and told her parents she would never go walking in the woods by herself again. The end.

Level 4. These narratives are characterized by the conjunction of two or more action sequences (primitive episodes). That is, these stories are the result of the concatenation of elementary dyadic structures. Moreover, there is the loss of the intervening elements of level 3 and a regression to level 2 constructions, while there is an attempt to expand the boundaries of the tale through repetition. Increases along one dimension result in a decrease along another dimension.

Example: There was this friendly lion in Asia (Initial Situation), but he was captured (Villainy) and brought to a zoo. Then the lion escaped (Villainy Nullified). He was walking down the road (Initial Situation) and a truck tried to run him over (Villainy), but he managed to get out of the way (Villainy Nullified). He began to get hungry (Lack) so he ate a rabbit (Lack-liquidated). The end.

Level 5. This level is characterized by the conjunction and coordination of elementary dyadic structures as well as the internal expansion of intermediate action elements. Narratives at this level, therefore, are composed of two or more well-developed episodes.

Example: Once Batman and Robin were in a haunted house (Initial Situation). Robin fell through a trap door in the floor and landed in an underground river (Lack). Robin pressed his magic watch to signal Batman for help (Lack Made Known). Batman heard the signal and looked all over the house for Robin (Search). Then he saw the trap door (Find). He lowered a rope from his Bat-belt and pulled Robin out of the water (Lack-liquidated). Then they heard a scream (Deception). They thought it was a girl, but it was Spiderman (Deception Fulfilled). They looked around and the screams seemed to come from the attic. Batman and Robin ran up to the attic to save the girl but Spiderman was hiding behind the door waiting for them (Threatening Situation). When they came in Spiderman threw an extra strong spider-net over them (Villainy). They tried to get out but they couldn't (Attempted Escape). "I've got you now," he said. "I'm going to kill you, and Wonderwoman and I are going to take your Batmobile and live in your Bat Cave" (Threat). But Batman told him that he had a special key for the Batmobile and Bat Cave (Deception). And when Spiderman came over to get the key (Deception Fulfilled) Batman hit him right in the face and knocked him down (Counterattack). Then Batman and Robin got out of the net and beat up Spiderman (Struggle, Victory) and then put him in jail (Villainy Nullified) so he wouldn't bother them anymore. The end.

Level 6. This level is characterized by the single embedding of one dyadic structure within another, i.e., the subordination and hierarchical organization of nuclear dyads. The main action of the narrative is interrupted by a subsequence of action. In other words, this is the beginning of the use of subplots.

Example: A man named Mr. Dirt lived in the country all by himself and owns a farm (Initial Situation). One calf got away went into the wood and headed for the mountains (Lack). So Mr. Dirt went up the mountain after the calf (Departure, Pursuit). On the way a bear came after Mr. Dirt (Villainy). He ran up a tree (Escape) and the bear climbed up the tree after him (Pursuit). Mr. Dirt threw his ax at the bear (Counter-attack) and hit the bear in the head. Blood poured out of his head (Wound) and the bear fell down and died (Villainy Nullified). A few minutes later the calf ran over to Mr. Dirt (Find) and they went back to the farm (Return, Lack-liquidated).

Level 7. This level is similar to level 6, but is characterized by the multiple embedding of dyadic structures. The main action sequence is interrupted by two or more subsequences. There is the subordination of plots within plots.

Example: Once upon a time there was a little fish named Josh (Initial Situation) and he was going to a fish fair (Departure) and there were fishers over the fish fair (Threatening Situation) and the fishermen caught everyone including Josh (Villainy). Then they put all the fish in the fishers hole (Lack) and there were sharks and sting rays (Threatening Situation) and a sting ray was going after Josh (Villainy) and then a shark chased the sting ray because he wanted to eat the sting ray (Fortuitous Occurrence).

So the sting ray stopped chasing Josh (Villainy Nullified) and ran away from the shark. So the shark and the sting ray got into a big fight. But then another shark was going after Josh (Villainy), but then instead the shark gobbled up his mother (Josh's mother), and Josh's dad, and Josh's sister (Fortuitous Occurrence). And then he left (Villainy Nullified). And then the boat was sailing and sailing and sailing. There was a big storm that night. And it hit against the rocks and made a big hole in the fishes hole (Fortuitous Occurrence) and Josh escaped (Lack-liquidated) and went back to his house (Return) and he stayed there until he was big.

Experimental Application

In order to test the validity of our seven levels of structural complexity and the hypothetical order of acquisition, the fantasy narratives of 80 children randomly selected from a larger sample of 150 New York City public school children were analyzed and scored for their structural complexity. With the exception of the youngest group which was composed of four 3-year-olds and six 4-year-olds, there were 10 children from each of the following age groups: 5-, 6-, 7-, 8-, 9-, 10-, and 12-year-olds. In addition, each group contained an equal number of males and females. A total of 80 spontaneously-told fantasy narratives were collected by graduate students, decomposed into their component action elements and analyzed in terms of the organization and integration of nuclear dyads and medial action elements. Narratives were then scored according to our seven levels of structural complexity.

Table 1
Distribution of Ss by Age and Level of Structural Complexity
(N = 10 per Age Group)

	Levels of Structural Complexity						
Age	I	II	III	IV	V	VI	VII
3 - 4	9	1	—	—	—	—	—
5	1	2	6	1	—	—	—
6	—	1	6	2	1	—	—
7	—	—	2	5	2	—	1
8	—	—	2	2	5	1	—
9	—	—	2	1	5	—	2
10	—	—	1	—	8	—	1
12	—	—	—	1	4	4	1

p .001

Table 1 provides a summary of the main findings of this investigation. The high correlation between structural complexity and chronological age (r(78) = .70, p .001) would seem to be strong evidence for the empirical validity of our seven levels of structural complexity and their hypothetical order of acquisition. Inspection of the total number of subjects in each of the seven structural categories indicates that 31.25% of the fantasy narratives in our sample were well-developed episodes (level 5) and 16.25% were primitive episodes (level 4). Thus, the most frequently used general structure was episodic (47.5%). Only 12.5% of the subjects in our sample told narratives more complex than level 5.

In general, the order of acquisition of narrative structures appears to be similar to that of analogous linguistic structures. Children under the age of three tend to concatenate a series of proper nouns without any statement of action, but merely use the *implication* of action when constructing a narrative. Our data show that at around the ages of three or four children begin to explicitly state events and action, yet these narratives are incoherent and fragmented. Primitive structures emerge around the age of five. At this age children seem to have learned that actions are organized into a whole and move from some initial state *A* to some final state *B*. Children around the age of six begin to elaborate and expand narratives of this elementary dyadic type and rather than a direct movement from *A* to *B* the fundamental action (plot) is mediated with a number of events that connect *A* and *B* together, giving the narratives more interest and coherence.

The conjunction and coordination of multiple action sequences (episodes) marks a major developmental acquisition. While narrative length (total number of action elements) progressively increases with added structural complexity ($r(78) = .72$, p .001), the most dramatic shift occurs once children learn to form simple episodes through the repetition of the basic dyadic structure, i.e., the shift from level 3 to level 4 structures. As Sutton-Smith et al. (1975) recently noted, narrative complexity may at first be manifested as repetition. In some cases this may be the result of the simple repetition of the first nuclear dyad (e.g., lack + lack-liquidated; lack + lack-liquidated) or it might involve the use of a different nuclear dyad in the subsequent episode (e.g., lack + lack- liquidated; villainy + villainy-nullified).

At first glance, the number of elements used by children in their fantasy narratives appears to be a function of chronological age. However, despite the significant correlation between narrative length and age ($r(78) = .75$, p .001), the present findings clearly indicate that it is structural complexity which, in large part, accounts for the length of children's fantasy narratives. In particular, it is the ability to chain together action sequences constructed around nuclear dyads that permits the use of additional elements. Structure, then, tends to constrain narrative length.

Moreover, while children begin to use embedded dyadic structures at around the age of nine, the use of multiple embedded structures does not become a frequently used structure until after the age of 12. As we mentioned above only 12.5% of the children in our sample told fantasy

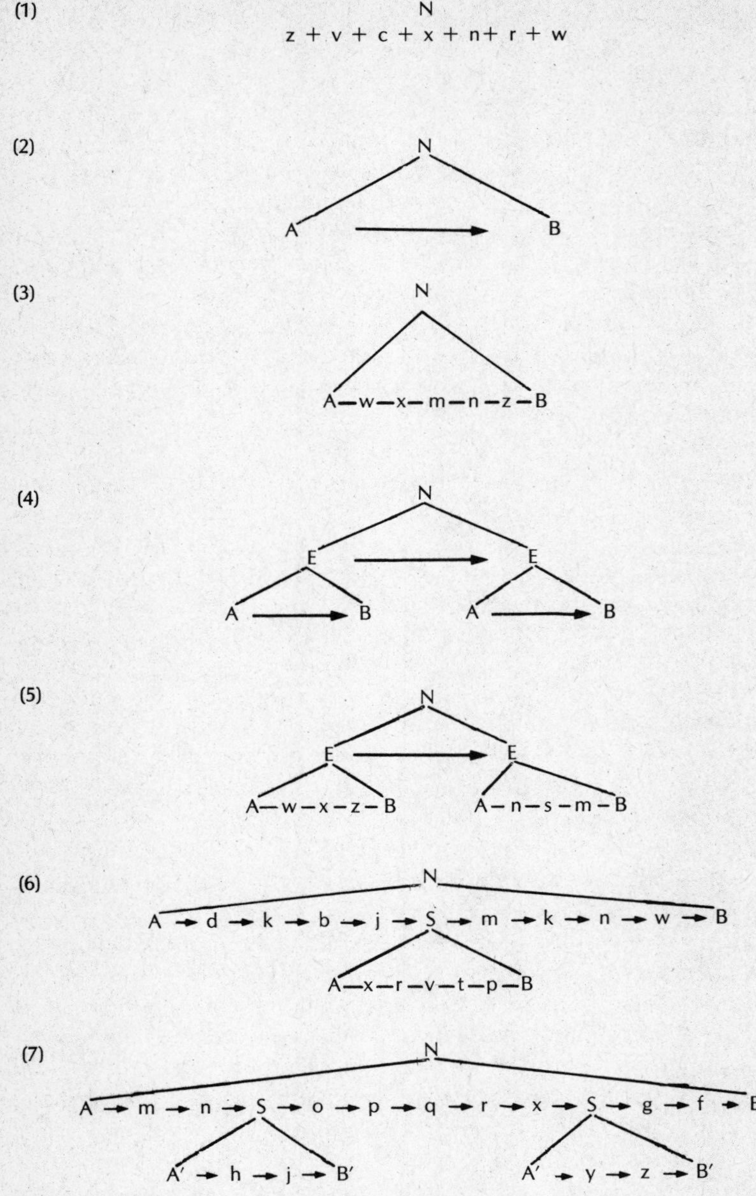

Figure 2. Schematization of Levels of Structural Complexity
Where narrative N is composed of primary (upper case) and secondary (lower case) plot units which may be coordinated as episodes (E) or hierarchized into plot and subplot (S).

narratives with subplots. The most common general structural type involved the coordination and conjunction of action sequences (47.5%). This suggests that there is a general decrease in the rate of development of structural complexity between the ages of nine and ten. At these ages children continue to employ level 5 structures, primarily telling narratives of an episodic character. One possible explanation is that children at this age typically do not possess the cognitive competence to use more complex structures. While episodic fantasy narratives involve the conjunction of additional action sequences, narratives with one or more subplots require considerably more cognitive skill. In composing level 6 and level 7 narratives, it is necessary to form an internal representation of the general structure before actually beginning the narrative. For example, if narrative N is moving from state *A* to state *B* through events w, x, y, z, and these events are interrupted by subplot *S* which moves from state *A′* to *B′* through events m, n, o, p, it is necessary to remember state *B* as well as the events w, x, y, z, while one is elaborating the action sequence which leads from *A′* to *B′*. This is analogous to what happens in linguistic development. The complexity of a grammatical sequence increases as the number of intervening subsequences increases. In more technical terms, center embedded relative-clause sentences are more difificult than left or right branching sentences and the difficulty increases with the number of embedded clauses (Bever, 1970). Moreover, coordination and conjunction is less difficult than embedding. Fantasy narratives with level 4 and level 5 structures are analogous to compound sentences where simple sentences are linked together by conjunctions. On the other hand, fantasy narratives with level 6 and level 7 structures are analogous to center-embedded sentences. As Bever (1970) pointed out, one of the main cognitive constraints on language development and the use of more complex structures is memory. Immediate memory constrains the use of embedded structures and limits the length of intervening sequences. Like center-embedded sentences level 6 and level 7 narratives involve the interruption of the main action sequence (plot) by an intervening action subsequence (subplot), therefore, they are more difficult than either level 4 or level 5 narratives. And, finally, level 7 narratives are more difficult than level 6 narratives because of the increased number of intervening subsequences.

Summary and Conclusions

In this paper we have suggested the application of a Proppian approach to the analysis of children's fantasy narratives as an alternative to the content-oriented approaches of earlier research. In an attempt to demonstrate the efficacy of such an approach, Propp's methodology and Dundes's notion of dyadic structure were used to define six types of narrative structure. Following general developmental principles and implications from psycholinguistic research, these structural types were ordered into a hypothetical developmental sequence forming levels of structural complexity. Analysis of 80 spontaneously-told fantasy narratives composed by children ranging from three to twelve years of age validated these hypothetical levels of structural complexity, indicating that the order of acquisition of narrative structures is similar to that of analogous linguistic structures.

In general, a Proppian approach (i.e., syntagmatic approach) would seem to be a valuable methodology for investigating children's fantasy narratives from a cognitive-developmental perspective. Once these narratives have been decomposed into their structural components, they may be compared along a number of dimensions. Such an analysis would seem to have great potential for highlighting the differential effects of sex and age on the composition of fantasy narratives. For example, the frequency of occurrence of specific elements, pairs, or groups of elements, as well as the precise order in which they occur, would facilitate discovery of the *syntax* or *rules of composition* operative for particular sex and age groups. Thus, a Proppian approach to children's fantasy narratives could potentially provide considerable information about the development of narrative competence.

REFERENCES

Bever, T.G. The cognitive basis for linguistic structures. In J.R. Hayes (Ed.), *Cognition and the development of language.* N.Y.: Wiley, 1970.

Brown, R. *A first language.* Cambridge, Mass.: Harvard University Press, 1973.

Dundes, A. *The morphology of North American Indian folktales.* Helsinki, Finland: FF Communications, #195, 1964.

Piaget, J. *Play, dreams, and imitation.* New York: Norton, 1951.

Piaget, J. *The language and thought of the child.* New York: World Publishing, 1955.

Propp, V. *The morphology of the folktale.* International Journal of American Linguistics, 1958, 24, #4.

Pulaski, M.A. Toys and imaginative play. In J. Singer, *The child's world of make-believe.* New York: Academic Press, 1973, 74-103.

Sutton-Smith, B. Children's narrative competence: the underbelly of mythology. Paper presented to the annual meeting of the American Folklore Society, Oregon, November, 1974.

Sutton-Smith, B. A structural grammar of games and sport. Paper presented to the International Society for the Sociology of Sport, Heidelberg, October, 1975.

Sutton-Smith, B., Abrams, D., Botvin, G., Caring, M., Gildesgame, D., and Stevens, T. The importance of the storytaker: an investigation of imaginative life. Urban Review, 1975, *8* 82-95.

Sutton-Smith, B., Botvin, G., & Mahony, D. Developmental structures in fantasy narratives. *Human Development,* in press.

Werner, H. The concept of development from a comparative and organismic point of view. In Harris, *The concept of development.* Minn: U of Minn Press, 1957.

The Society and Geography of the Story World[1]

Daniel H. Mahony, Teachers College, Columbia University

The systematic study of children's extemporaneous stories from the viewpoint of developmental psychology has not until recently extended beyond those told by five year olds. Pitcher (1963) and Ames (1966) wrote down the stories told in a nursery (360 from 123 children and one each from 270 children respectively), and analyzed the stories by first recording the frequency of occurrence of various kinds of story characters and actions and then offering what might be called 'psychoanalytic' interpretive models thereof. The recent study of Sutton-Smith (1975) is based upon a wider sample and differs from the earlier studies in both size and method of data gathering. The sample's measurements are: 800 stories from 250 children aged 5 to 11 in a public elementary school, 400 from 22 nursery school children in an ongoing longitudinal project, and 250 stories from adolescents and adults gathered by graduate students. The interpretive models range from a bare structural analysis of character and action manipulation to an in-depth analysis of a particular kind of story character, and though the work of coordinating what has been gathered has only begun, there is hope that some of the models may be applicable to other expressive areas (Sutton-Smith et al, 1976).

The existing models interpret what might be called the 'surface' of the stories. Those from the anthropologists Propp (1928), Dundes (1964), Maranda (1971) and the recent developmental models of Sutton-Smith (1976), Botvin (1976) and Abrams (1976) look either to kinds of story actions, kinds of plot outcome or at a particular kind of story character. Other models such as those of Pitcher and Prelinger (1963), Ames (1966) and Gardner (1973) also interpret the surface but further imply that the surface is an effect, the cause of which is the intersection of certain underlying ego processes. These models do not however, deal with the problem of how characters or actions or plot outcomes are made possible at all (transmitted to the surface) even given the underlying processes. Where the existing models have focused on classes of action (e.g., attack, defense, fight, flight), classes of fate reversal (villany-villany nullified, lack-lack liquidated), or classes of plot outcome (success-failure), a model is needed that describes the role of classification itself, as well as the roles of other cognitive systems in the construction of the story surface.

The present paper offers a first step toward a structural model that might interpret the 'subsurface' by examining the organization of the surface manipulation of story characters *regardless of the kinds of characters they are.* In so doing we might view the influence of various underlying cognitive systems more clearly.

I. *Interaction Patterns*

We begin by adapting Moreno's sociograms to view the development of the complexity of character interactions with each character represented by a small circle and an arrow that indicates the direction of the interaction.

> the dog went on the puppet...the puppet went on the house...the house went on the pigeon (Girl, 2)

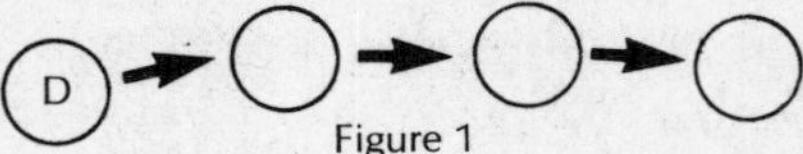

Figure 1

In the first example, we see a chain effect where one character acts upon another, that character upon another, etc. There is no established central character.

> Robin...a monster came and Robin got scared...people...they crashed...they swallowed and pushed him up...down on the floor they got...roar there was a tiger coming (Boy, 2)

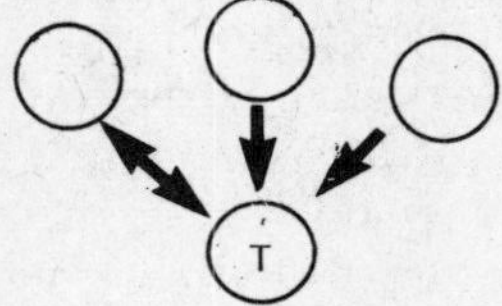

Figure 2

In the second example we find a *central character* (Robin) involved in action or interaction with other characters more than any of the other characters are and is the center of interaction. These two characteristics serve for the time being to provide loose operational definition of 'central character' though there are problems with this. One can imagine a story where there is a character that fulfills both criteria (center of interaction and most interactive) and yet not be judged as the main character. Who is the main character of *Moby Dick?* This indicates that the 'main' character and the central character are not necessarily the same. Pitcher and Prelinger (1963) and Maranda (1971) employ a 'most frequently mentioned' criterion for a central character, but exceptions to this are possible. Yet there is considerably good agreement among observers as to which character is the main character. A good case in point is the next story where the robber is mentioned as frequently as the little girl, and, is 'introduced.'

> once there was a robber...and then a girl was lost...and the robber came and put her in jail...and then the police came and got her out of jail...and then the police put the robber in jail (Girl, 4)

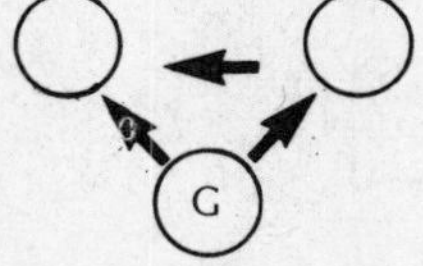

Figure 3

In the preceding and next examples we find the *coordination of others.* Here, each of the 'other' characters not only relates to the central character but to the other as well.

> tiger catched the cat...then the cat ran away...he don't like tiger...then the tiger just ran away to the cows...then the cows ran and ate the cat up (Boy, 4)

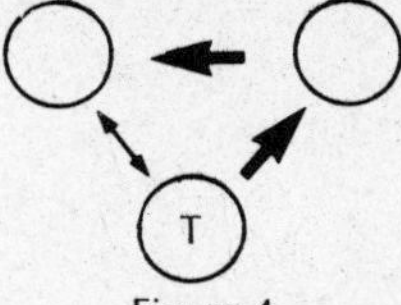

Figure 4

In the last example we find a much more complicated social situation.

> Chapter 1.
> Once upon a time a boy named Brian was walking about 110 Bedford Street and talking to Gil and then Dave came up and said, "Let's go to Gil's house at 23-B." And Brian said, "No, let's go to my house at 40 Bleeker Street and invite the girls over for lunch." And then Gil said, "Who shall we invite?" "Sara and Tsara." And then Brian asked, "We're going to have lots of fun." And Gil said, "Tisk, tisk."
> Chapter 2.
> The girls came over and when they walked in, out of nowhere came and leaped on top of the girls. And all of a sudden Brian came out and took off the girls' clothes. And Gil said, "I have a bone." And finally Brian finished them off with his lips.
>
> Chapter 3.
> When the girls' mother found out about the sexual assault to their daughters, they steamed over to Brian and Gil and Dave and said, "GOOD WORK." And Brian, Gil and Dave lived happily ever after with the girls parents. The end (Boy, 10)

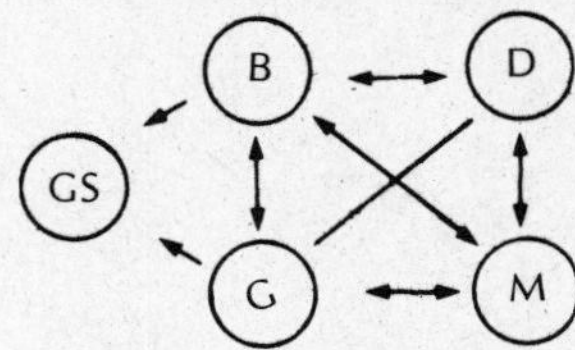

Figure 5

Here is a four-way interaction system that is similar to the type found in the Little Red Riding Hood tale where Little Red, the hunter, Grandmother, and the wolf all interact with each other. (The mother is less interactive and fits the situation of the girls in the sample story.)

We note here that playground games can also be represented with the sociograms. For example, early tag when viewed through a sociogram reveals the egocentric coordination of 'It' as the central character (fig. 2). All the others coordinate to the 'It' and do not coordinate to each other while later games of tag require the cooperation (coordination) of others (fig. 3) such as in prisoners' base, and games like basketball have patterns similar to the last (Stevens, 1976).

II. *Groups*

Next we examine the development of the coordination of *groups* of characters. A group of characters is operationally defined as a collection of characters mentioned by the author usually with some sort of plural noun. In this first example we see the "children" as a group that is coordinated 'as one,' and there are no interactions amongst the group's member children. The symbol for this type of group is indicated by the circle figure and consists of two small inner circles that stand for members of the group, an outer circle that stands for the boundary of the group, and an inner boundary line that in this case indicates that there are no interactions between its members.

> the man stayed home...the children went out...then a cookie monster came...then the cookie monster went away...and the mommy was angry...and then the father was angry...and then the children went out again...then the father went out...then the mother went out...they went to the park...then they went home...and then the father was doing work...and then it was getting late...the children went to sleep...and the mommy and the father went to sleep. (Girl, 2)

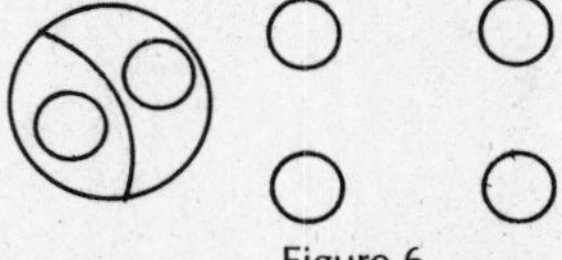

Figure 6

The symbol is said then to refer to a *nonpermeable* group, that is, the individual members do not interact with other characters that are outside of the group. The following contain further examples of the nonpermeable group.

> monkeys...they went up sky...cookie monster...he flew down in the sky...fall down in the sky (Boy, 2)

Figure 7

> frogs...they went in a house...they went in a park...they pushed on the people...they people got hurt...they got mad at the frogs (Boy, 2)

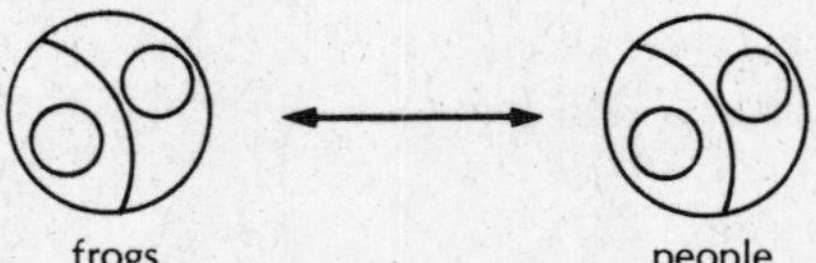

Figure 8

> once lived three little pigs...and a wolf came along...and said "knock...knock on my chinny chin chin"...and the wolf blowed the house down...and they ran to another house...and the wolf chases them there...and said "knock...knock on my chinny chin chin...and the wolf went to another house made out of bricks...then the wolf went on the chimney...and he went in it and fell in the fire...that's it (Girl, 3)

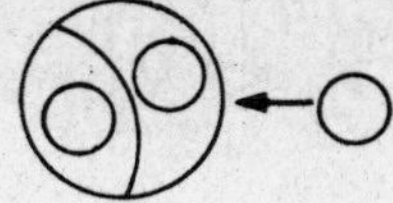

Figure 9

Once there was two bears. And they went to the country and they got a country house and they went swimming. Once they went swimming and they got lost. And there was a nice whale that picked them up and brought them back to their house. Then he said, "Goodbye," and asked them next time if they got lost to come with him to his house. And they went to his house next time they got lost and lived happily ever after. And they got rid of their country house and went to live in the whale's house. The end. (Girl, 6)

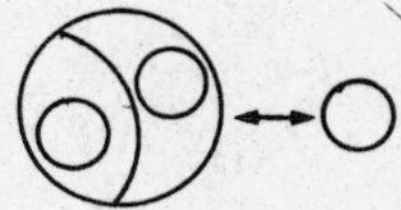

Figure 10

With the stories of six-year-olds we begin to find *permeable* groups of characters. The operational definition of this type of group is that the characters are introduced and manipulated 'as one,' but soon particular members of the group have some sort of interaction with other characters.

There was a father that had a little girl that's name was Sally. They had a duck pond. Once the little girl went out to the duck pond to see the ducks and she saw one little duck that was lost. And she took it home and she lived happily ever after. (Girl, 5)

The symbol for this situation is constructed with the dotted outer boundary line that indicates that the group is permeable and the solid inner boundary line that indicates that the members do not interact with each other.

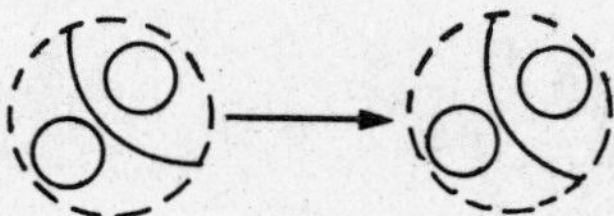

Figure 11

(The number of inner circles need not correspond to the actual number of members in the group.) In the above example the ducks are introduced 'as one,' but one of the ducks is selected for rescue, and the girl has interactions with characters outside of her alliance with her father.

By nine years of age in our sample, permeable subgroups emerge. That is, a larger group of characters is introduced as one and then a smaller group made up of members of the larger group is separated, so to speak, and has its own interaction with other members of the totality of story characters.

Once upon a time there was a bomb that blew up the world. And then Jupiter they started building a new world. But the people went crazy because they weren't Earthlings. They were Jupitrons and suddenly Mars blew up and they were trying to fix up Mars too. But they only had two million people, but a quarter million died because they were on Earth too long. And another half million more died because they were trying to fix up Mars. Then Venus blew up and then another quarter million other people died because they were trying to fix up Mars. So they only have a million more people. Then Uranus and Neptune blew up and they sent space ships over to Neptune and Uranus. But the space ships saw a red beam of light and it kept trying to blow them up, but it kept missing. And they found out that it was going to blow up the universe. Just at that moment it blew up Pluto and Mercury and then they knew that they had to move to another solar system. And then they moved and Saturn came along too and the two planets mated and got some more planets, seven more planets. And they lived happily ever after in the new solar system. (Boy, 10)

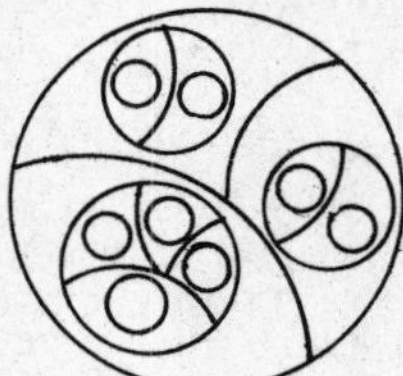

Figure 12

The symbol for this is represented by the above diagram, using the same criteria as before. The subgroup itself can be permeable or nonpermeable, with the nonpermeable type found much earlier. It is interesting to note that at this point the children do not seem to go through a shift from nonpermeable to permeable sub-groups indicating that the repertoire might be cumulative, that is, all of the preceding types of character manipulation may immediately be made available upon a reorganization such as is permeability. Another story with permeable subgroups is found at the end of section IV.

III. *Valence*

In some cases the groups are formed after each member of the group is introduced separately. In the first example we see a group formed after King Kong and the two helpers (Frankenstein and Godzilla) are separately introduced.

Once upon a time there was a ferocious monster King Kong...and he had two helpers and the helpers were named Frankenstein and Godzilla...and then they all went out and scared the people...and when the people got out of the houses..and then they tore them up after they learned how to make camps...and then the monsters made a fire and then they ate the people...and then they got so fat that they popped...the end (Boy 4, 9)

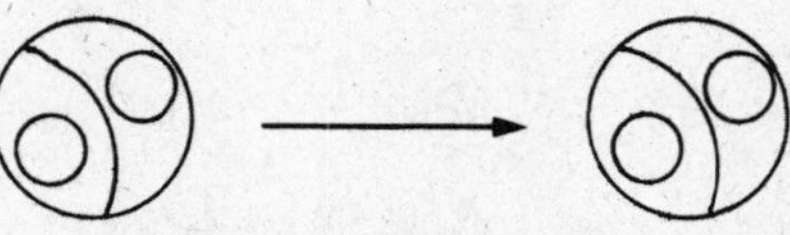

Figure 13

We adopt the term *valence* from physics that refers to a bonding activity and for the purpose of the present study provides a useful way of viewing those stories wherein the *formation* of nonpermeable groups can be viewed.

The group that consists of the evil types and the second group "the people" are both nonpermeable groups. Thus, the valence is only a + valence in our terminology because we can see only the formation of the group. Had the group become permeable the valence would have been positive *and* negative with the term 'negative valence' referring to the dissolution of the bond. After the group is formed and treated 'as one' by the authors, each individual member is free to interact with other characters or groups of characters. The next story serves to illustrate this second type of valence, *reversible valence*.

> Robby and Robee went to, um, Rock Mountain, and they started to climb it. (Here comes the funny part) And they ran into a looney and the looney hit Robby. And Robby swinged around and hit him and made him hit Robee. And then Robee hit him and made...(Story continues) (Boy, 6)

Figure 14

The following story illustrates a systematic dissolution of the alliance.

> Once there was a girl named Rita. She lived on an old block in the hundreds up on the East Side. Her mother was a cleaning lady and that was the way she supported her family. She always made Rita work, help with the work. One day her friend Rosa came up and asked her if she'd like to go for a walk down the block. So, she told her mother that she'd do her work later. So, they both went down the stairs and out on the block. They were walking down the block that nobody ever went on when Rita felt a knife in her back. She turned around and she saw that it was only her little brother with his fake knife. So then he said, "Mom said she wants you home so she can go out for a while and you can walk with Rosa later." So they all walked back to Rita's house and Rita said goodbye to Rose and walked upstairs with her brother. That's the end. (Girl, 9)

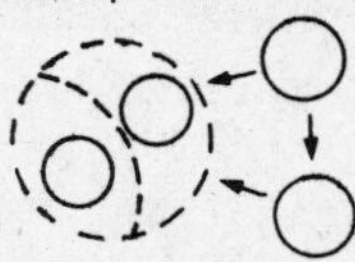

Figure 15

The earliest reversible valences appeared in the stories of the six and near-six-year-olds. The ducks story (fig. 11) thus contains both types of permeable groups, i.e., those introduced 'as one' (the ducks) and those whose formation (+V) can be viewed (father/daughter alliance).

IV. *Reverse Polarity Groups*

The *reverse polarity* groups are usually of the polarity or morality type, good guys/bad guys, *et al.* We wish here only to propose that polarity is 'superimposed', if you will, on the types of character manipulation we have just seen. In the earlier example of the frogs and people (fig. 8) we saw two nonpermeable groups in opposition, and the following stories contain examples of reverse polarity groups that are the nonpermeable, permeable, and subgroup type. Our point is that polarity seems to be a separate consideration that perhaps is the result of a different organizational system than the character manipulation system, since it may simply be a matter of superimposition 'on' or a placing of polarity 'within' other systems of character manipulation.

The following three examples illustrate reverse polarity applied to nonpermeable, permeable, and groups with permeable subgroups.

(nonpermeable)

About a Martian. There were two Martians. They lived on a planet X. There was another planet with which they were having a battle. The other people were named the 0 men. These were the X men. I like the X men better. They had a war. They shot off a lot of rockets. And the X men win. Then they all played tic tac toe. And the X men won again. (Boy, 6)

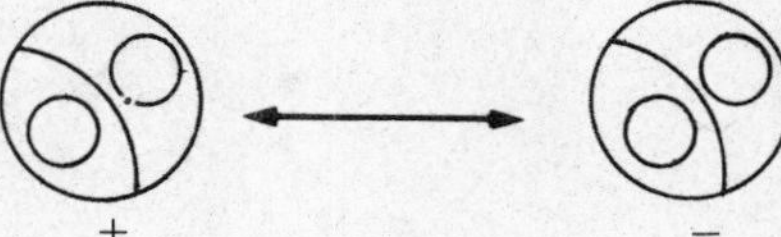

Figure 16

(permeable)

The Super pirate pumpkins had a big crash on a big pumpkin boat rock. Then the good guys went on an island. And the bad guys threw a big pumpkin rock. Then the pirate boat sinked. Then they all went into the life boats. Then when they got in the boats, they were rubber and they sinked again. Then they went in a metal boat and the bad guys got away from the good guys. Then pumpkin Superman crashed into their boat and beat them off. Then pumpkins Superman drove off in the boat with all the money and then went to the pumpkin bank and put the money back in. And then the pumpkin robbers got locked up in jail because they stole the boat and the boat had money in it. (Boy, 5)

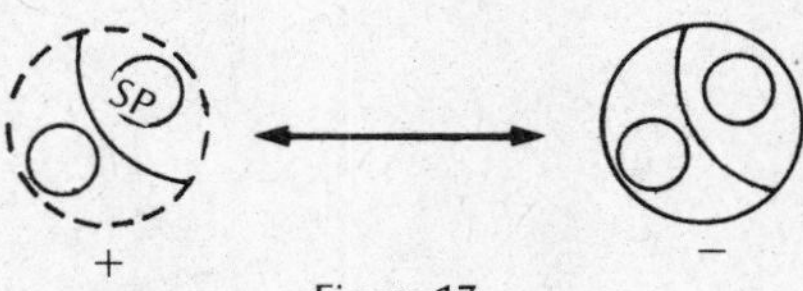

Figure 17

(permeable subgroups)

It's about a German squadron of planes flying over the hills and the French base came out of the ground. Guns came out of the hills and radar. They shot down one of the planes and then the two guys parachuted down in a double parachute. Then they saw a big bomber. (Aside to story taker: I wonder if it should drop a bomb? I want the French to win.) Then we shot with one of our artillery guns and got one of the engines. Perfect shot. And then we pushed a button and the missile popped out of the hill. (I won't know if we need to fire it.) And then the bomber dropped one bomb. And it landed on a big platform full of machine guns. It blew up. Then we got mad at the bomber and we pushed a button and the anti-bomber gun came out. It shot out lots and lots of little tin missiles and they landed all over it. And then there was no more bomber. And then three of the planes left and there was only one left. (Five to begin with, one shot down). And then the pilot of the other plane looked around and said, "Where did everybody go?" (With a German accent.) So he got scared of being all alone over a French base and he went home too. And so then there were no more German planes. We won. The end. (Boy, 10)

Figure 18

V. *The Story Space*

A few of the earliest stories take place in a *simple single space* or a chain of simple single spaces. We determine this type of story space from the verbs 'came' and 'went'. In the following story, the action seems to take place in a single central space.

The mother went out...then the father went out...then the mother went out again...and then the father went out...then the children went out...then policeman came...the mother came back from the meeting...then the father came back from the meeting... then a cookie monster came...and the policeman came again...then the cookie monster went away (Girl, 2)

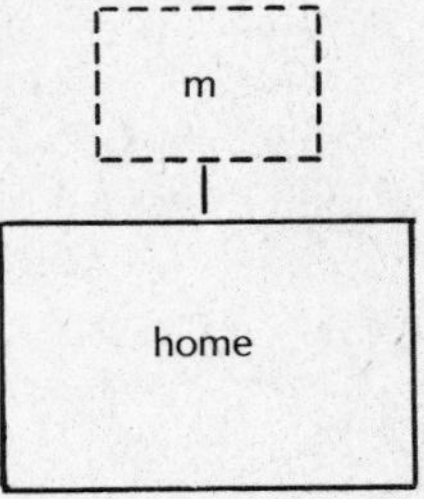

Figure 19

In the earlier example (fig. 8) of the frogs, "...they went in a house" implies a transversal from an undisclosed space. When the storyteller continues with "...they went in a park," he has shifted the action to a new place where, presumably, the rest of the story occurs. The point is, though, that the spaces are not coordinated into a larger space where two locations are connected by the reverse transversals of any character.

I'll tell you a story. He's going to be a pumpkin man. Once upon a time, there was a pumpkin man. And he lived in a little pumpkin house close by the city. And he wanted to go to the city, so he went to the pumpkin-mobile and he went faster than the speed bullet, more powerful than a locomotor. He could go down the highest hill in a single bound. And he went so fast that he past-ted the store than we wanted to go to. Then when he got back home, he went to bed. (Boy, 5)

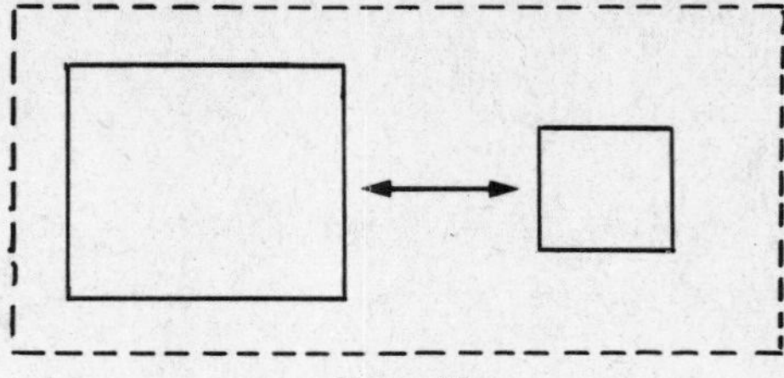

Figure 20

In the above we find two separate locations connected by his transversals from 'home' and 'away' and back 'home' again. The odyssey is not reported in a 'came/went' fashion, indicating that the author sees the two spaces from a third viewpoint. Thus, this storyteller has coordinated a larger space that is the result of two separate, smaller spaces. Another example of this is the earlier Rita and Rosa story (fig. 15), where the characters traverse a path to another space, "an old street..." and then back again. In general, we have found that the central action reversals occur in the 'other' space as in pumpkin man passing the store that he wanted to go to and Rita's crisis (knife at her back) on an old block. (Cf. Sutton-Smith, et al., 1976).

Even later we find the 'complex multispace' encompassing another location that is noncontinuous with an initial location, and has the added feature that a parallel duration in time is attributed to both spaces. This we call *parallel action* and is indicated in the stores by markers such as 'while' or 'meanwhile' and marks the coordination of space and time.

> Once upon a ghostly afternoon Mary and Little Eva Hotchkins were sitting in the living room of the Hotchkins' manor. They got a disturbing phone call saying that Mr. H., an airforce pilot was killed in flight. The telephone call said to come to the war office. They both ran downstairs and outside to the chauffeur. Mrs. H. put her head on his shoulder and started to weep. He tried to comfort her and he asked her what was the matter. She said in a cry, "He is dead." The chauffeur named Roy asked 'Who is dead?" "Mr. H.," she cried. They jumped into their Rolls Royce and zoomed to the war office.
>
> Meanwhile in the war office some crooks were taking it over. They tied up all the executives and staff of the way office and hid them in the basement. They changed their clothes with the executives and went to work. (Story continues) (Boy, 11)

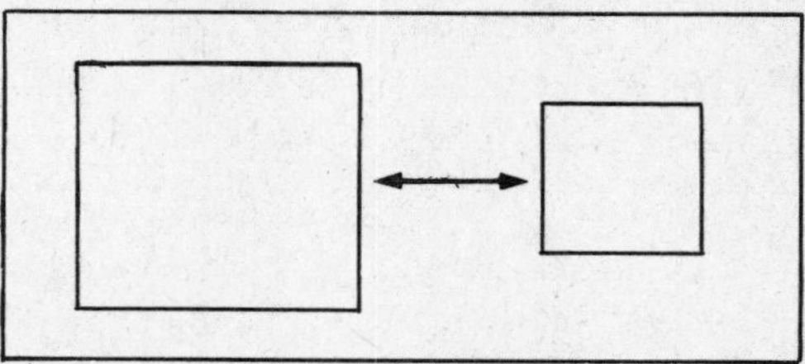

Figure 21

VI. *Discussion*

What might we say about the various lines developed here? We have seen:

a) a developmental shift from nonpermeable to permeable groups of characters and a later shift to permeable subgroups;
b) a shift from nonreversible to reversible valence;
c) the application of reverse polarity to groups;
d) the contemporaneous nature of the above shifts;
e) a steady increase in the complexity of the story sociograms;
f) a parallel order of shifts in the spatial organization of the story world with all of the above.

Immediately noticed are evidences of *reversibility*. By the age of six the authors can produce stories with reverse relationships between characters (good guy/bad guy), reverse spatiotemporal transversals (pumpkin man's reversible odyssey, fig. 20), and reversals in the fate of characters (Rita's survival, fig. 15). Reversibility seems further evident in the story sociograms which illustrate the directional reversals inherent in any interaction, in reciprocal actions (the police and the girl, fig. 3) and reciprocal viewpoints ascribed to characters ("they saw each other"), and in the coordination of inversion and negation in a single story character (reversals in Rita's path and fate). Even further there is reversible valence (the unbonding of Robby and Robee, fig. 14). And, as if exploring the role of reversibility in the construction of the surface weren't enough, there arises the question of the role of *classification* in character manipulations (groups and subgroups), in classes of actions and plots, and in the reverse polarity groups. And we have only begun the exploration of the 'subsurface' for we have yet to look at the contributions of other cognitive systems such as seriation, conservation, mental imagery (static and kinetic), space and time, to name a few.

Some more general issues might arise here as well. Firstly, there is the problem of the nature of fantasy structures and their relation to the non-fantasy activities of the child. Is the organization of the story world isomorphic to the organization of the child's experience? Relevant is the idea that space *is* the coordination of objects and not a container that surrounds them (which goes back at least to Leibniz and Kant). Consequently the view that the *spatial and social* organizations found in the story world are inextricably intertwined due to the nature of the processes that construct them seems not unharmonious. Piaget (1956, 1966) and others (Laurendeau and Pinard, 1970) have investigated the same intertwining of spatial and social organization. Similarities can be seen in the necessary (though not sufficient) operations that are required to coordinate the various views of an object (coordination of viewpoints), and in the coordination of the viewpoints of others in social interaction.

Secondly, the experimental methods for investigating the child's view of the world require the child to perform specific tasks, mostly the solution of problems. We offer here the notion that the extemporaneous stories of children might provide another method for determining the stage of cognitive development based upon a structural analysis of the stories. In addition, it might be possible to say that where existing research has focused on the child's *maintenance* of equilibrium, the present research investigates the child's *manipulation* of equilibrium.

Thirdly, a developmental social psychology of early childhood might be possible if it can be established that the child's understanding (coordination) of story characters mirrors his real world, social understanding. The level of social understanding would be viewed in the classroom, the playground, the story, and all three compared using the sociograms.

Lastly, it is possible that children organize the story world in exactly the same way as their 'real' experience and, fantasizing further, it is logically possible at least that reality is an externalization of fantasy and not vice versa! We might even find some cognitive processes occurring in fantasy activity that are not to be found elsewhere.

NOTE

[1]This study was funded in part by the National Institute for Education, project #3-4015, Grant #NEG. 00.5.0133.

REFERENCES

Abrams, D.M., Sutton-Smith, B. The development of the trickster in children's narratives. *Journal of American Folklore,* 1977, #354.

Ames, L.B. Children's stories. *Genetic Psychology Monographs,* 1966, *73,* 337-396.

Botvin, G. A Proppian-structural analysis of children's fantasy narratives. Paper delivered to The Association for the Anthropological Study of Play, Atlanta, 1976.

Dundes, A. *The morphology of North American Indian folktales.* Helsinki, Finland, F F Communications, #195, 1964.

Gardner, H. *The Arts and Human Development.* New York: Wiley, 1973.

Laurendeau, M. and Pinard, A. *The Development of the Concept of Space in the Child.* New York: International Universities Press, 1970.

Maranda, E.K. and Maranda, P. *Structural Models in Folklore and Transformational Essays.* The Hague: Mouton, 1971.

Moreno, J. L. *Who Shall Survive?* New York: Beacon House, Rev. Ed., 1953.

Piaget, J. and Inhelder, B. *The Child's Conception of Space.* London: Routledge and Kegan Paul, 1956.

Piaget, J. (and seven collaborators) *The Moral Judgment of the Child.* New York: Free Press, 1966.

Pitcher, E.G. and Prelinger, E. *Children Tell Stories.* New York: International Universities Press, 1963.

Propp, V. The Morphology of the Folktale. *International Journal of American Linguistics,* 1958, *24,* #4.

Stevens, T. Cognitive Structures in Sports Tactics. Paper delivered to The Association for the Anthropological Study of Play, Atlanta, 1976.

Sutton-Smith, B. (and five collaborators) The importance of the storytaker: an investigation of the imaginative life. *Urban Review,* 1975, *8,* 82-95.

Sutton-Smith, B., Botvin, G. and Mahony, D. Developmental structures in fantasy narratives. *Human Development,* 1976, *19,* 1-13.

A Developmental Analysis of the Trickster from Folklore

David M. Abrams, Teachers College, Columbia University

The common plot of the trickster tale in world folklore is of a lower-order evolutionary creature, such as a spider, frog, raven, rabbit, or fox, who counters the physical aggression of more powerful figures with cunning wit and trickery. The early view was that the trickster was the expression of a lower level of cultural development. The evidence for this position was 1) many cultures with rich traditions of trickster stories did not also have heroic legends, which would suggest a higher level of cultural aspiration, and 2) the actions of tricksters are usually infantile, impulsive, and obscene. Boas (1898) and Lowie (1909) suggested that with the evolution of culture, mythology and folklore may have followed a pattern of a first stage, where there are only stories of unsuccessful, childlike tricksters; a second stage, where the trickster successfully defeats his opponents and inadvertently provides boons for man, so that in that sense there is a trickster and culture hero combined in the same figure; and a third stage, where there are two distinct traditions, one being of trickster tales and the other, stories of heroes who improve the world for others, as in the Viking legends of the Scandinavians or the myths of the ancient Greeks. This position has persisted in the field largely due to the continued popularity of Radin's (1956) collection of the Winnebago Indians' tale cycle of Wakdjunkago, whose many episodes include his right arm fighting with his left; telling his anus to watch over roasting ducks as he sleeps; awakening with a penile erection holding up his blanket and mistaking it for the chief's banner; scattering villagers by breaking wind; and wading through his own excrement.

Contemporary interpretations, however, have called attention to the cross-cultural differences. Feldmann (1963) notes that the African trickster tends to be mercenary and greedy, and Abrahams (196) points out that the Afro-American trickster is generally much more clever and successful than the self-defeating and promiscuous trickster of the American Indians. Levi-Strauss (1955) theorizes that the trickster is created out of a desire to mediate opposites, such as life and death, God and the Devil, human culture and the natural environment. The implication is that the trickster is the outcome of a more logically sophisticated level of culture, for in order to create such tales, the mythic mind must be able to understand the reversible logic of mutually exclusive classes.

This paper examines these two conflicting hypotheses regarding the origin of the trickster, but from the standpoint of child development. We begin with an investigation of children's interest in the major trickster figure in American childhood traditions, namely the *Bugs Bunny* cartoon, moving

then to a comparison of the stories of children from five to eleven years of age. A predominance of trickster elements in the stories of the five-to-seven year-old children would support the notion that the trickster is characteristic of a lower level of socialization. On the other hand, if Levi-Strauss is correct that the ability to tell a trickster tale depends upon the prior development of a reversible logic, which Piaget (1966) claims the child does not begin to acquire until seven-to-nine years of age, then we would tend to find more trickster elements in the narratives of the older group of children.
year-old children would support the notion that the trickster is characteristic of a lower level of socialization. On the other hand, if Levi-Strauss is correct that the ability to tell a trickster tale depends upon the prior development of a reversible logic, which Piaget (1966) claims the child does not begin to acquire until seven-to-nine years of age, then we would tend to find more trickster elements in the narratives of the older group of children.

56 children participated in the study, with 14 females and 14 males in the 5-7 year-old group and 14 females and 14 males in the 8-11 year-old group. Each child was asked to name his or her three favorite television programs and to make up a story.

Bugs Bunny Cartoons

Bugs Bunny was the most frequently mentioned program by the younger children. 78% of this group reported watching it as compared to only 3% of the 8-11 year-olds, which is a highly significant different by chi-square analysis ($X^2 = 12.2$, p .001). The older children were more interested in shows like *The Brady Bunch, All in the Family, Star Trek,* and TV movies. *Bugs Bunny* cartoons were randomly sampled by tape recording the morning *Bugs Bunny* program in New York City every third weekday for a two-month period. 31 cartoons were recorded, which were then analyzed according to the scheme of Maranda and Maranda (1970). Scoring the outcome for the central character, which is defined as the character most frequently mentioned, the Marandas assign a plot to one of four levels: No response to conflict or threat (level 1); the protagonist attempts to mediate the conflict, but fails (level 2); the protagonist successfully nullifies the threat (level 3); and the initial situation is permanently transformed with a resulting personal gain or status elevation (level 4). Narratives without any clear expression of a conflict are scored level 0.

In 9 out of the total 31 plots, Bugs is egotistical and manipulative, and ends up being exposed to public disgrace. In "Winner by a Hare," Bugs is racing a turtle, who slowly cruises along. Bugs teases him, tries to scare him, and puts a rocket on his back, trying in vain to get the turtle to win the race, since he had bet on him. But the turtle puts the rockets on Bugs's back, so Bugs wins, and the turtle rushes in to collect his winnings, as he had bet on him to win. In "Bugs Bunny and Friends," he lectures his nephew Clyde on the central role of rabbits in American history in order to help Clyde with a forthcoming test in school. Clyde fails the test due to this misinformation. "Rhapsody Rabbit" has him giving a piano recital in a large concert hall. A little mouse pops out of the piano, Bugs chases him around, and the mouse finally finishes the piece Bugs was playing. These tales would be classified as Maranda level 2, since Bugs' trickery and braggadocio ultimately backfire.

In the more prevalent type of tale (22 of the total 31), Bugs successfully defeats the villain usually by humiliating him. In "Stage Door Cartoon," Elmer Fudd chases Bugs with a rifle, but Bugs tricks him and runs away. It ends with Fudd on stage before an audience with his pants down. In "Bugs Versus the Crusher," he challenges a huge wrestler, who simply throws him around. After repeatedly falling on his face, he decides to put on a disguise, tricks the Crusher into walking into a metal door, and finally sends him up in the air by exploding a bomb that was meant for himself. These tales would be classed as Maranda level 3, since the villains are temporarily put out of commission rather than permanently vanquished.

A content analysis of the cartoons showed that the high frequency elements tended to be found in the predominant Maranda level 3 cartoon: trickery (1.00), humor (.97), violating taboo (.93), pretense (.93), reverse behavior (.93), superpowers (.90), individualism (.90), bodily changes (.90), oral behavior (.90), clumsiness (.87), impulsivity (.83), fearless daring (.83), humiliation of the villain (.71), and good deeds (.69).

Children's Stories

1) The stories of the 56 children followed a pattern of all four Maranda levels, corroborating the findings of Sutton-Smith *et al.* (1975) that these levels represent the stages in the child's development of the hero tale: 4-5 year-olds' stories have the protagonist overwhelmed with fear before a threatening monster; 6-7 year-olds have the protagonist try to run away or throw something at the monster; 8-9 year-old stories confront the monster and temporarily incapacitate it by kicking it out the window or by some other action; and 10-11 year-olds' protagonists permanently overcome the threat and end up stronger than at the beginning of the story. Contrasting the two lower levels with the two higher ones shows a significant age difference ($X^2 = 4.6$, p .05). This suggests that 5-7 year-olds, for whom *Bugs Bunny* is the most popular television show, tell stories that are predominantly of levels 1 and 2, while the majority of the cartoons are a level 3 Maranda type tale.

2) The content analysis of the stories supports this. Comparing the order of frequencies of trickster elements in the cartoons (see above) with the frequency order for a similar scoring of the younger children's stories results in a correlation coefficient of only .12, which is nonsignificant by the Spearman rank order correlation test (Runyon and

Haber, 1971). But the rank order correlation between the cartoons and the older children's stories yields a coefficient of .91, which is significant beyond the .01 level. In other words, the high frequency trickster elements in the cartoons tend to be found in the older children's narratives much more so than in those of the younger children.

3) The rank order correlation between the stories of the two age groups is not significant, although chi-square tests show highly significant differences for some of the elements considered separately. The younger group's stories have more oral behavior, narcissism, and clumsiness, with the greater frequency of clumsiness found to be statistically significant ($X^2 = 5.3$, $p \; .02$). The narratives of the older group, on the other hand, have more of the elements of trickery, violating taboo, and pretense ($X^2 = 5.04$, $p \; .02$).

Stages of the Trickster Tale

Combining the results of the Maranda scoring and the content analysis enabled us to identify four stages in the child's development of the trickster tale, which roughly parallel the first three Maranda levels. At five years of age, there is a Maranda level 1 tale type that could be called the *stage of physical clumsiness.* Here is a story by a 5 year-old girl:

> One day there was a big Rollarman and then, "I hate animals, because they're too sweet!" And then—there are a lot of jokes coming up here. And I'm going to do a Rollarman. And then I throw myself in the garbage and then he fell in the garbage. And then he took off. And then I bumped myself for real, too. And then I killed myself for good—bang, bang. And then you said, "I hate kitties. They stink!" And then my ear flew open into the far away sky. The end.

The many instances of physical clumsiness are climaxed by the dramatic image of the disembodied ear in the last line, which seems to accentuate the feeling of little physical self-control.

The 6-7 year-olds relate a slightly more advanced slapstick clown story, which we call the *stage of moronic self-defeat.* There is still much clumsiness, but the protagonist now attempts to do something about his situation. But everything he tries fails. A 6 year-old boy told this:

> Once there was a man and he went swimming. But when he came out of the pool to go home—he always made a fire when he got home—he made a fire. But the match kept going out, because his bathing suit dripped. Now he's really mad at himself for dripping on the match, and so he didn't like that. So he started to undress himself and do it the right way. But after he did it the right way, he forgot how to dive, and so he learned how to dive. And then he forgot how to undress himself. And then he learned how to undress himself and forgot how to dive. And then he remembered how to dive, but forgot how to undress himself again. And on and on...The end.

Concern over intellectual failure is here added to the physical clumsiness of the first stage. The protagonist tries to do things, but fails and forgets what he has just learned. The trickster stories at these first two stages appear to deal with the young child's concerns over physical and intellectual self-management that may well be intensified at the beginning years of elementary school.

At around 7-8 years, there emerges a *stage of the unsuccessful trickster,* where the use of trickery by the protagonist makes its appearance. There is still ultimate failure, however, as we see in this story by a 7 year-old boy:

> There was a dog named Smokie, and he teared up the house. And do you know what he sounded like when he was chained up—roo, roo, roo, roo. And then he said in a very squeaky voice, "I want a cigarette!" Nope, my mom says no. My brothers says, "Give him the peace pipe." Then he broke out of his chain and he went to the cigarette box and he took all the cigarettes and smoked them all at the same time. And then he took the money and bought cigarettes. And he took all the cigarettes and put 'em in his hair and his hair used to pop out every time he would have a cigarette.
>
> And he went to India to get a peace pipe. He met the Indian Chief, who said, "How!" And Smokie said, "Ruff! Me want to smoke peace pipe." But the Indian Chief said, "You can't smoke the peace pipe unless you make peace." And the Smokie was upset. He barked, "Roo, roo, roo, ruff!" And then he jumped on the Indian Chief and made peace with him. He took him into the teepee and locked him up. He said, "Me smoke 'em peace pipe now." So he took this peace pipe and put it in his hair and his hair popped out. And he said, "How many times does my hair have to pop out?" And this peace pipe got fire in his hair and he went, "Roo, roo, roo, roo." And then he said, "That peace pipe is not so peace, when you have it in your hair!" The end.

In this story, there is a great deal of violating taboo—tearing up the house, taking cigarettes and money, fighting with the Chief—and this behavior seems to be punished in the end with his hair popping out.

The *stage of successful trickery* seems to occur between 9 and 11 years of age, but may occur earlier, as in this story by an 8 year-old boy:

> Once upon a time there were two babies. They loved, they hated spinach. So once their mother gave them a big pot of spinach, each with one fried egg on it. And they hated it so much, they threw it at their mother. She gave them another pot of spinach with two eggs on it this time and they were even madder and they threw it at their father this time. Then their mother gave them two pots of spinach with six eggs on it. They threw it at their sister. Then, when Nixon heard of this, he called them "The Fried Egg Family". But baby was angry at Nixon. So when Nixon came to their house, they did nothing to him. But as he was walking out the door, the baby saw him and then they stuck out their weenies and then they put their weenies to work. And when Nixon saw these things, he flipped. But then, they pulled in their weeners and put two buns on top of them and put some catsup and spinach and then Nixon got right back up and started to bite. All of a sudden, the babies went pissing and shot their X-Y-Z. And Nixon was so upset he almost, his heart almost cracked. But then they had more strategy.
>
> So when he was walking over the mountain, they made flying hamburgers and then Nixon screamed, "We're being invaded by flying hamburgers!" And then the babies made flying hamburgers shoot out missile hotdogs. And then Nixon had a very good idea! And he ate it—the hotdogs. But Nixon was so dumb, those hotdogs were solid metal and when he bit on them, they cracked his teeth and he was so upset. And then a lady came and said, "Will you help me cross the street?" And Nixon said, "Whaaaaaaah?" "You are wierd, man," the lady said. And then the babies had little

> bit more strategy. They started shooting spinach with fried eggs on top. And then New York called Nixon "The Fried Egg President". That's all.

In this story, told during the Watergate scandal, the babies humiliate the villain Nixon with their tricks and make him the fool—the Fried Egg President. The clowning babies, therefore, effect a power reversal in the best tradition of the Maranda level 3 *Bugs Bunny* tales. The mocking of authority figures may be a way for the child to assert his independence from parental control.

Rather than finding a level 4 trickster tale, where the power reversal between protagonist and villain would have to be permanent, the oldest children in our sample seemed to tell a more peer-oriented trickster-like tale that was still a Maranda level 3, as in this story by a 10 year-old boy:

> Once upon a time there was a boy named Jimmy. Jimmy had a sister named Heidi. Jimmy and Heidi were in love. They slept in the same bed together. They had a lot of babies. But Jimmy didn't like Heidi, so he found a new girlfriend. His girlfriend's name was Dorothy. Dorothy was just right. Jimmy and Dorothy were madly in love with each other. So they finally got married. They had 10,000 babies. Jimmy was not satisfied, so they had 10,000 more. Well Dorothy wasn't right, so he gave up Dorothy. Jimmy married a new girl named Jessica. Well Jimmy knew Jessica wasn't right, so he gave her up and met a new girl. The new girl was named Julie. Julie and Jimmy were so happy together so they got married and had 10 million babies. But that wasn't enough for Jimmy, so they had 10 million more.
>
> ...My name is Jimmy. Let me explain how you have babies. You lie in bed with all your clothes off with another person of the opposite sex. You come close to each other and, whoops, my mother's coming, we have to continue the story.
>
> Anyway, to get back to the story, Jimmy and Julie were madly in love. This reminded Jimmy of his school days when he and another girl were kissing in the bathroom, the boys' bathroom, of course,, and while they were kissing, their braces got caught together. While their lips were touching each other, the principal walked in. Jimmy didn't mind, but he got out of the braces mess and started kissing the principal, who was female. That girl got so mad at Jimmy that she slapped him on the ponderosa (the rear end) and walked out. Well back to the story. Jimmy and Julie were having a good time together, a real good time, and they both lived happily ever after. The end. P.S.*Very* happily ever after.

This would be a successful trickster tale, for the elements of clumsiness (the braces sticking together), violation of taboo (incest between siblings, repeated sexual intercourse, kissing principals), superpowers (the million-plus procreations), and individualism (the picaresque wandering from female to female) combine with a successful ending for the hero. Storytelling has become more of a group experience, as in the above story, where the storyteller addresses the surrounding audience and weaves the names of his classmates into the narrative in a ribald, titillating manner, and the content seems to have shifted towards using the trickster genre to explore forbidden sexual interests in one's peers.

Contrasting the two lower trickster stages with the two higher ones shows a significant age difference ($X^2 = 6.63$, p .02). No sex differences were found.

The Trickster as Agent of Socialization

Given the ubiquitous presence of trickster figures in world folklore, the stages in the child's ability to generate such characters in his own story-telling that we have identified suggests that the child is acquiring competence in a part of human culture. Moreover, it would appear that this socialization process is related to the important changes in social and cognitive development that are also taking place at this time. The period from 5-7 years is the time when the child begins to shift from dependency upon parental authority to increasingly autonomous interaction with peers (Fromm, 1941) and from the egocentric, magical thinking of pre-operations to the reversible logic of the stage of concrete operations (Piaget, 1966). The trickster represents the extreme of this development of psychosocial independence, for he not only lives and acts alone, which forces him to remain autonomous. His repertoire of tricks characteristically employ the logical operations of reversibility, class inclusion, and seriation, which are the main operations acquired in middle childhood (Inhelder and Piaget, 1964). In an African Kru tale, the trickster uses the reversible logic of countering a king's command to weave a mat of rice grains by asking for an old mat of the same kind to use as a pattern, thus escaping the king's impossible command by posing an equally impossible condition (Feldmann, 1963). The Ibo of Nigeria have a tale where a frog wins a race with a deer by posting his relatives at regular intervals along the racecourse so that the deer thinks the frog is always ahead (Basden, 1921). This strategy is based on the operation of classification, for it turns on the logical confusion of a member with its class. Spider in a Hausa tale uses the logic of an ordered series in the trick of taking a loan from a series of animals who habitually prey on each other and arranging his payment so that each animal that comes to collect is devoured by a stronger creditor (Tremearne, 1917).

The young child's fascination with watching *Bugs Bunny*, then, may be due to its ability to help socialize the 5-7 year-old child to his next stage of social and cognitive development. Our results showed that the predominant plot level and the high frequency elements in *Bugs Bunny* cartoons are a stage ahead of the young child's own narratives. It is not until late in middle childhood (ages 8-11 years) that the child is able to create characters with the ribald independence and logical cleverness of folk tricksters. The appearance of characters that mock authority figures and that employ logical trickery is no doubt related to the child's development of social independence and reversible operations at this stage of development.

The Trickster as Symbolic Inversion

One might certainly question whether the regressive, obscene, and deceitful elements in trickster tales have any socialization value. Victor Turner's (1968) answer to this is his notion that symbolic inversions of social values helps the community from disintegrating in reality. Telling tales of tricksters who violate the taboos of society allows individuals to misbehave in the realm of the imagination so that they need not misbehave in reality. But it also has a regenerating effect, for in mocking the social order, making fools into kings and kings into fools, it restores everyone to the level of their common humanity (Turner, 1969). For the child, however, perhaps the best suggestion regarding the socialization value of such reality reversals comes from Chukovsky's (1925) study of the word play of 2-5 year-olds, written over fifty years ago. He noticed that when little children are learning the idea of logical proportion, they may joke about "the cow that sat on a birch tree and nibbled on a pea." Or they may recite such rhymes as:

Sam, Sam, the Soft Soap Man,
Washed his face in a frying pan,
Combed his hair with a wagon wheel
And died with a toothache in his heel.
(Withers, 1970, pg. 39)

Submitting one's conceptions of reality to wild distortions, Chukovsky argued, is one way that the child clarifies the conceptions of himself. Through his nonsense, the child acquires a stronger mastery of the sense from which it derives. By creating trickster figures that possess social independence and logical strategies in exaggerated proportions, then, may be said to be one way that the older child acquires these developmental skills, while the exaggerated clumsiness and moronic self-defeat in the younger child's trickster stories may be a way that he frees himself from such maladaptive behavior.

Adaptive Potentiation

The great danger of interpreting these chronological developments in trickster storytelling and cartoon watching as exclusively due to socialization, however, is that such an interpretation might be more due to our desire to justify the phenomena than to give a complete account. Like other forms of play, the real value of creating trickster stories may be that they allow the child to engage in a voluntary activity for its own sake. Reality can be turned upside down and social rules broken with such freedom, perhaps because there may be no explicit adaptive intent. Nonsense can simply be nonsense. The creative license that play provides gives the individual the opportunity to explore alternative forms of behavior that are difficult to explore in the rest of one's social existence. Hence, play engaged in for the sake of play helps the individual become more flexible and creative. This theory of play has been formulated by Sutton-Smith (1975), where play is seen as *adaptive potentiation.* In his view, nonsense is not merely the anti-structure of sense, as Turner (1974) suggests, it is also proto-structure for potential futures (Sutton-Smith, 1972). The implication is that creating trickster tales and being exposed to them in *Bugs Bunny* cartoons allow children opportunities to explore a variety of behavior patterns, some of which may have creative, adaptive value, and some of which may simply be ridiculous.

Conclusion

In sum, our results shed some light on the question of the origin of the trickster tale that has intrigued anthropologists for several generations. From the standpoint of child development, the major shift in trickster narrative is from the clumsy, slapstick clown figures of 5-7 year-olds to the more successful and logically clever tricksters of 8-11 year-olds. This, therefore, lends some support to the views of Boas (1898) and Lowie (1909) that regressive trickster tales precede more successful ones in the evolution of human culture, and it also lends some support to the position of Levi-Strauss that the ability to create trickster tales depends upon the development of a reversible logic. Our developmental analysis suggests that the differences noted anthropologically may be due to differences in the level of complexity with which the trickster is presented in different cultures.

Trickster tales appear to have the function of helping to socialize the young child to his next stage of social and cognitive development, helping him acquire the personal autonomy and logical operations so critical to middle childhood. But in addition, the nonsense and trickery of these tales also tends to heighten the child's flexibility about social roles. The trickster tale enables the storyteller to violate taboo in the innocent guise of humor, thus widening the latitude for the exploration of alternative forms of behavior. As a guide to this freedom of self-expression, the trickster more than any other character seems to embody the true spirit of creative playfulness.

REFERENCES

Abrahams, R.D. Trickster, the outrageous hero. In T. Coffin, III, (Ed.), *American Folklore.* Washington, D.C.: U.S. Information Agency, 1968, pp. 193-201.

Basden, G.T. *Among the Ibos of Nigeria.* London: Seeley Service and Co., 1921.

Boas, F. Introduction. In J. Teit, Traditions of the Thompson River Indians of British Columbia, *Memoirs of the American Folklore Society,* 1898, 66, pp. 1-18.

Chukovsky, K. *From Two to Five.* Berkeley: University of California Press, 1971 (Originally published in 1925).

Feldmann, S. *African Myths and Tales.* New York: Dell Pub. Co., 1963.

Fromm, E. *Escape From Freedom.* New York: Farrar and Rinehart, 1941.

Inhelder, B. and Piaget, J. *The Early Growth of Logic in the Child: Classification and Seriation.* New York: W.W. Norton, 1964.

Levi-Strauss, C. The Structural Study of Myth. *Journal of American Folklore,* 1955, 28, 428-444.

Lowie, R.H. The hero-trickster discussion. *Journal of American Folklore,* 1909, 22, 431-433.

Maranda, P. and E.K. *Structural Models in Folklore and Transformational Essays.* The Hague: Mouton, 1970.

Piaget, J. *The Psychology of Intelligence.* Totowa, N.J.: Littlefield, Adams and Co., 1966.

Radin, P. *The Trickster: A Study in American Indian Mythology.* New York: Schocken Books, 1956.

Runyon, R.P. and Haber, A. *Fundamentals of Behavioral Statistics.* 2nd rev. ed., Reading, Mass.: Addison-Wesley, 1971.

Sutton-Smith, B. Games of order and disorder. Paper presented to Symposium on Symbolic Inversion, American Anthropological Association, Toronto, 1972.

—— Play as adaptive potentiation. *Sportswissenschaft,* 1975, 5, 103-118.

Sutton-Smith, B., Abrams, D.M., Botvin, G., Caring, M., Gildesgame, D., and Stevens, T.R. The importance of the storytaker: An investigation of the imaginative life. *Urban Review,* 1975, 8, 82-95.

Tremearne, A.J.N. *Hausa Superstitions and Customs.* London: Staples Printers, 1917.

Turner, V. Myth and symbol. In *International Encyclopedia of the Social Sciences.* New York: Macmillan, 1968.

—— *The Ritual Process: Structure and Anti-Structure.* Chicago: Aldine Pub., 1969.

—— Liminal to liminoid in play, flow, and ritual: an essay in comparative symbology. *Rice University Studies,* 1974, 60, 53-92.

Withers, C. *Counting-Out Rhymes.* New York: Dover, 1970 (Originally published 1946).

Structural Parallels in Dreams and Narratives: Developmental/Sex Differences in Dreams and Stories of Girls and Boys

M'Lou Caring, Teachers College, Columbia University

Introduction

This study proposes to investigate the developmental nature of stories, dreams and their relationship. It is also interested in how these phenomena reflect psychosocial and cognitive development. Secondly, it proposes to investigate sex differences in psychosocial and cognitive levels. The data for this study are the stories and dreams of 5-7 and 8-11 year old girls and boys. The measure of psychosocial development is Elkan's Eriksonian checklist. Elkan (1969) culled Erikson's works for references to his eight stages of psychosocial development and produced a list of 144 items. (Appendix I) The measure of cognitive level is the Mahony Story Stages. Mahony (1976) looked at the relationships between and among the characters, objects and actions in children's stories and found a developmental sequence in cognitive organization. (Appendix III).

Review of the Literature

Since Freud, dreams have been seen as significant and reflective of intrapsychic life. Dream research, however, has been handicapped by a lack of explicit theory and methodology, and by the rejection of manifest content as valid data. Further, the focus of earlier studies tended to be on the nature of the children's dreams as a whole rather than on developmental differences between age groupings.

Freud's theory posits development as a process of fixed sequence where earlier forms may reappear later as well. Thus differences may be significant while there are similarities. Since Freud's stages are completed by age six, a developmental analysis of reported dreams would be difficult.

Erikson's theory added psychosocial modes of growth to Freud's psychosexual ones. Erikson's redefinition and extension of Freud's developmental theory to include the entire life span make such a developmental study possible.

Erikson's theory lends itself to a comparison of sex differences in psychosocial development, by placing importance on the context of a particular social order and the effect on development of society's response to the individual's struggle to adapt. His model lent itself to the methodology of the checklist by specifying, at each level of development, the nature of the social encounter and the nature and implications of the successes and failures as the individual struggles to adapt to the world around him. (Elkan 1974:7)

The Elkan checklist was developed for use on the manifest content of dreams. Two studies (Reis 1951; Sheppard and Karon 1964) designed to test the hypothesis that results based on manifest content alone correlate well with results based on manifest plus latent content showed clearly positive results. Developmental differences in the manifest content of boys' dreams have been documented by Elkan (1969), L. Mack (1974) and R. Mack (1974). In 1969, B. Elkan conducted a study to define developmental aspects of dream life using the manifest content of children's reported dreams. Using a checklist she constructed from Erikson's works, she systematically studied children's dreams and confirmed the hypothesis that a relationship exists between manifest dream content and developmental level.

Foulkes' studies of normal boys are relevant here for comparison with Elkan's and as a link between children's stories and dreams. Foulkes (1967, 1969) collected dreams in a dream lab from 4-6 year olds and 6-12 year olds. He describes the dream as realistic, related to everyday life and without disturbing affect or impulse.

Domhoff and Kamiya (1964) have shown laboratory dreams to be more mundane and realistic than recalled dreams. This suggests that children may selectively recall the most vivid and intense dreams although this is not the content of most dreams. L. Mack (1974) reviews Foulkes' findings and suggests that they are consonant with Elkan's.

Both Elkan and Foulkes have a common analytic theoretical ego bias which may also account for the agreement of their findings. Foulkes states the most coherent interpretive framework for him is the dream as an ego process continuous with waking ego functioning. Erikson's theory also posits the concerns of waking and dream life as arising from the struggle to cope with and integrate one's personal, social and environmental demands.

L. Mack suggests that Elkan's more structured method of analysis results in clearer delineation of developmental differences between age groups than does Foulkes' more global and quantitative method (1974:10).

R. Mack (1974) found developmental psychosocial differences between the dreams of American and Tunisian males. He suggested how these differences reflect the differing cultural emphases. The play research of Sutton-Smith (1968) and Sutton-Smith and Savasta (1972) suggests that differing cultural emphases affects the play behavior of American boys and girls. In the first study he shows that boys and girls are familiar with different (sex preference) toys and come up with more novel (non-standard) uses with these sex preference toys.

Sutton-Smith & Savasta (1972) summarized sex differences in game playing of 5-12 year olds and studied the play of three year olds and found similar sex differences. Boys preferred games where success is achieved "through active interference in the others' players' activities" and "for games permitting personal initiative" (1972, p. 2). Girls prefer games where competition is indirect and where rules dictate every move, games of internal elaboration and accomodation to another person. The study of three year olds shows that the sex differences described above are present even earlier. Although there were no sex differences in types of play (exploration, testing, imitation) there were clear sex differences in categories of play. Girls used "inclusion-exclusion" while boys used "attack" (1972, p. 5). In view of these sex differences in play and games documented from ages 3 to 12, we might expect to find similar sex differences in other expressive forms: dreams and stories. Erikson's emphasis on the social context of development suggests that his theory, as operationalized in Elkan's checklist, could measure such differences.

Erikson's Psychosocial Theory of Development

Erikson's theory can be understood as an elaboration of Freud's childhood psychosexual theory of development: the aspects of personality and psychosexual development that result from the interactions between the child's psychosexual development and the restrictions and demands of the child's particular socio-cultural milieu. The psychosocial crises are part of the model in which the child progresses sequentially through a fixed "ground plan" of developmental tasks and crisis, with each task or crisis having its appropriate period of ascendancy. (Erikson, 1954, p. 52) According to Erikson, before this time the individual cannot fully be aware of or experience the critical alternatives relevant to the tasks or their resolution. During each critical period, the *focus* is on the relevant psychosocial "concerns", although both earlier and later concerns may be present. The experiences and strengths gained (or not) during earlier stages determine, to a great extent, the effective resolution of each new developmental crisis.

Erikson (1963, pp. 247-269) presents eight stages of psychosocial development spanning birth to old age.

Stage I: Basic Trust vs. Mistrust. The fundamental task of this stage is the establishment of basic trust, learning to rely on the constancy of the outside world provided by the nurturing figure. This stage corresponds to Freud's psychosexual oral stage. The infant's primary mode of relating to his environment is through his mouth: sucking, biting, being fed, and as such involve the development of the capacity to get and receive what is given. An Elkan checklist example is number 76. Is the dreamer provided for by others, do others attempt to provide for him?

Stage II: Autonomy vs. Shame and Doubt. This stage corresponds to Freud's anal stage. The fundamental task of this stage is the gradual development of internalized controls over holding on and letting go made possible by muscular maturation. The achievement of these controls leads to the development of autonomy and a capacity for choice. An Elkan checklist example is number 54. Do any characters in the dream unleash or release hostile powers? For example, does anyone shoot a gun, throw a weapon or release a ferocious beast?

Stage III: Initiative vs. Guilt (Erikson, 1963: 255-56). This stage corresponds to Freud's phallic stage and the beginnings of Oedipal conflict, occurring at about 4-5 years and is characterized by the intrusive mode of relating to the environment. "Initiative adds to autonomy the quality of undertaking, planning and 'attacking' a task for the sake of being active and on the move..." (Erikson 1963, p. 255). The conscience begins during this period and internalized observation, guidance and punishment. An Elkan checklist example is number 29. Is the dreamer in danger of bodily injury?

Stage IV.: Industry vs. Inferiority. This stage corresponds to latency when sexual drives are temporarily subdued. The child's sphere of activity moves from the home and family to the school and neighborhood. Peers become important as the child begins to develop a sense of cooperation and belonging, having a place in the social and work structures in his environment. An Elkan checklist example is number 42. Does the activity of the dream take place in school, above the level of nursery school?

Stage V: Identity vs. Role Diffusion. This stage coincides with puberty and adolescence. It is a time of inner turmoil and confusion about emerging sexuality, and concern about social and occupational goals. An Elkan checklist example is number 98. Is the dream concerned with the issue of proper recognition for function and status in society?

Stage VI: Intimacy vs. Isolation. The task of this stage of young adulthood is the risking of an individual's identity in sexually and emotionally intimate relationships with others and in commitment to one's work and beliefs. An Elkan checklist example is number 58. Does the dreamer prefer to be alone?

Stage VII: Generativity vs. Stagnation. This stage focuses on creativity directed towards "caring for", parenting, educating and leading the next generation. An Elkan checklist example is number 48. Does the dreamer need to be needed?

Stage VIII: Ego Integrity vs. Despair. This stage corresponds to the later years of life. The individual who has achieved ego-integrity has a respect and love for humanity, an acceptance of the necessity of his own beliefs and style of life as well as others'. With this acceptance of what his life has been and is comes an acceptance of death. An Elkan checklist example is number 17. Does the dreamer convey a sense of solidarity with all human beings?

Although Erikson's stages approximate chronological stages, he is adamant that each stage may appear in some form throughout life. The outcome of the struggles at each level are final in determining what the individual brings to the next stage, and in an important sense, the outcomes of the struggles are never final. Each conflict may reoccur as the present situation revives "prior" conflicts of growth and problems of adaptation.

Cognitive Developmental Theory: Mahony Story Stages

Cognitive developmental theory, of which Piaget's is the best known model, posits first physical then mental operations; manipulations first of objects, then of their representations, symbols, and finally, operations on the operations themselves. Mahony in turn looks at the operations performed within the story between and among the characters (objects) and actions.

The Mahony Story Stages is a cognitive structural model for examining the cognitive organization of children's spontaneous stories. The model was constructed by analyzing the relationship between the characters, objects and actions in the stories of children 2-11 years old. (See Appendix II)

A preliminary attempt to examine dreams in terms of the Mahony story stages has revealed difficulty in distinguishing between the organization of the dream itself and the organization of the reporting of the dreams. This distinction has special import for a theory which holds the distinction between the form and the content as superimposition of a particular theoretical framework on an organization which is the dream or story. Thus there may be two different levels of organizations in a reported dream: one proper to the dream itself and one the organization of the recollection.

Proposal and General Hypotheses

Dreams may be seen as a form of fantasy; a recent study by Elkan (1969) established that the manifest content of dreams of normal male children reflect age appropriate developmental concerns according to Erikson's theory of psychosocial development. The studies of L. Mack (1974), R. Mack (1974) and Foulkes (1967, 1969) lend support to these findings. They suggest that for the most part dream content is congruent with waking life in manifest content (Foulkes) and developmental concerns (Elkan). Thus these same concerns may be expected to manifest themselves across fantasy modes. This study proposes to further investigate the pervasiveness of psychosocial developmental concerns as well as cognitive levels in child's fantasy both waking and sleeping, conscious and unconscious, through an analysis of children's spontaneous stories and dreams.

The first hypothesis of this study is that dreams and stories will reflect the same stage of psychosocial development; there will be no differences in the highest Eriksonian stage scored.

The second hypothesis is that there will be significant sex differences in psychosocial stage with boys at Stage IV and girls at Stage III. Erikson's theory would predict 6-11 year olds involvement with the concerns of Stage IV, Industry vs. Inferiority, and that earlier concerns will be found as well for all groups (sex and age) and conditions (stories and dreams). In *Childhood and Society,* (1963), Erikson describes how different cultures emphasize different aspects of the stages to create a person and personality consonant with the culture. This idea is also supported by the findings of R. Mack's (1974) study of developmental differences of Tunisian and American males dreams. Sutton-Smith & Savasta's (1972) play and game research suggest such different emphases might exist between the sexes in this culture.

The third hypothesis is that there will be significant age differences and no sex differences in cognitive organization of stories. This hypothesis follows from the findings of Piaget and Mahony. Piaget would posit the 5-7 year olds at the preoperational period of his theory of cognitive development and the 8-11 year olds at the concrete operational period. Mahony would expect the 5-8 year olds to be at Stage 3a: single plane reversals, and the 9-11 year olds to be at Stage 3b: double plane reversals.

Since the theoretical approach of the scale makes the scoring of dreams unfeasible at this time, I will venture no hypotheses regarding cognitive levels of dreams.

Dreams and Procedure

Subjects: The subjects in this study were 56 children attending an "open classroom" public school. Their parents were mostly artists and professionals; in terms of socio-economic status, middle to upper middle class. The subjects were 28 girls and 28 boys divided into two age groups: 5-7 year olds and 8-11 year olds; each group contained 14 children.

Experiments: The collectors were all psychology graduate students at Teachers College who were spending at least one day each week at the school participating in a federally supported study of children's expressive development. They were all known to the children.

Procedure: Stories were elicited from children with the simple, unstructured request. "Tell me a story", the dreams by "Do you ever dream?", and if yes, "Would you tell me one?" Once a subject had begun, interventions were limited to encouragement when appropriate, such as "and then what happened?" Dreams were usually elicited after a child had told a story.

Sampling: Subjects included in this study were systematically selected when they had given both a dream and a story on the same day. All stories and dreams were typed, one on a page and drawn randomly for scoring.

Scoring: The randomly drawn stories and dreams were scored for psychosocial level according to an Eriksonian checklist devised by B. Elkan (1969). (Appendix I) The stories were scored by a cognitive structural story scale devised by Mahony (1976). (See Appendix II) The judges were unaware of the expressive mode of the item being scored and the sex and age of the author.

Scoring using the Elkan checklist was done by this experimenter and a master's-level graduate student unfamiliar with Erikson's theory.

There were five training trials during which each judge scored and then discussed from 5 to 10 stories and dreams from Elkan's sample and the aforementioned study of children's expressive development. The training stopped when 70% agreement was reached without discussion. No item was accepted unless scored positively by both judges.

Cognitive scoring, using Mahony Story Stages, was done by Dan Mahony and his assistant. They achieved 85% agreement.

Measures: The Elkan Checklist

The Elkan checklist was used as the measure of Erikson's psychosocial developmental stages. A chart showing the references in Erikson's works corresponding to each checklist item can be found in Elkan (1969). The complete checklist can be found in Appendix I.

Each dream and story was read, then each question and item of the checklist was asked and all items scored positively were noted. Thus each dream may have more than one item scored as well as a score of the highest stage.

The following dream is from an eight year-old boy:

> It happened in the school. It had Bob, Jeff and Richie in it. I went up some unknown stairs, I didn't know. There was a straw house, part of the school. I leaned against it and it fell in. It was real dark. They kept on running after me, trying to beat me up ("Who?") Bob and a few other kids I didn't know. I got out and I went down a few steps and I was out again. Then there was 2 girls standing outside the place, I thought they were guarding the place. They ran after me on the street—somehow I got out on the street. They got me with a rope but I pushed it off. This really fast running guy with a really flat hat, he kept running after me. I was on a hill and it was snowing. I kept on running and falling and hiding. And after a lot of that happened it stopped. ("No more to the dream?") No, just the same a little longer and then it stopped.

The following are examples of Elkan checklist items, how they reflect Erikson's stages and relevant quote(s) from the above dream scored for the item.

"Is the dreamer in danger of bodily injury?" is item number 29. It reflects a concern with Erikson's Stage III: Initiative vs. Guilt, in which the fear of finding the genitals, and the body in general, harmed is intensified. "They kept running after me, trying to beat me up..." "They ran after me on the street...They got me with a rope..." These are two instances of a positive scoring of item 29.

Stage IV: Industry vs. Inferiority, is concerned with changing the focus from home to neighborhood and school and thinking of oneself playing and learning without supervision. The following items reflect this concern: Item 42: Does the dream take place in a local neighborhood, as opposed to home, *but not under the guidance of older children or elders?* Item 44: Does the activity of the dream take place in school, above the level of nursery school? The same dream from an eight year-old boy begins: "It happened in the school. It has (he names classmates) in it." To answer question 42, we need to look at the whole dream to see that the action does not take place under the guidance of the older people.

The highest stage of development at which a child scored was considered to be the child's developmental level, even though earlier crises were present or even predominant in the dream. The rationale behind this is rooted in the nature of Erikson's theory of psychosocial development. Erikson sees development as a process in which the organism evolves through successive stages of growth, each characterized by its own central crises. The child's developmental stage is defined by the latest level of achievement attained; aspects of earlier stages may be present to some extent, either as unresolved conflicts or ongoing concerns, but conflicts relevant to later stages of development will rarely be noted. Thus, in any given dream several stages of development may be represented in the manifest content; the highest level scored is considered to reflect the child's level of development. (L. Mack 1974: 36-7).

The Mahony Story Stages

The Mahony stages are a measure of cognitive organization, looking for "manifestation of conservation and reversibility whether in character or actions" (Sutton-Smith, Botvin, and Mahony 1976). A description of his analysis can be found by reading the paper cited above and Mahony (1976). The description of the stages found in Appendix II is taken from the former.

This example includes excerpts from the story of a 9 year-old girl and the Mahony scoring:

> Once upon a time there existed a little troll. He lived in the forest. One day he was taking a walk around the forest. He found a monkey. So then he said, "What's that brown thing in the tree over there?" So he went out of the forest to a town and he went to a store and in the store he bought a book about things he could find in a forest. So he went back with his new book and went back to the forest and went back to that tree... So he took the monkey down from the tree, because he was a little monkey and couldn't get down by himself.
>
> So then he went back to town and went to the little school that would teach his monkey and the monkey learned how to talk right away. And the little man took the monkey back to his home and they lived happily ever after.

The story was scored 3a because its elements are organized into a whole. There is a reversible string of actions, seen in the troll's return in space from forest to town back to forest. "Coda" markers, "Once upon a time" and "happily ever after" are related to conversation in showing the child's need to account for continuity in the story.

Results

The dreams and stories of the 5-7 year-old girls and boys and the 8-11 year-old girls and boys were scored as described in the last section and the Fisher exact test was employed to determine whether the differences in psychosocial and/or cognitive developmental level by sex, age and/or mode (dream/story) were significant. The distribution of highest scores was determined and then the Stages were collapsed into two groups I-III, IV-VIII. It was necessary to collapse the scores this way for a 2x2 contingency table for the Fisher exact test and to maintain the critical stages of III & IV in separate cells.

All significant levels were derived from tables of Fisher exact tests in *Non-Parametric Statistics* (Seigel, 1956).

These tests are recommended especially when expected cell frequencies may be less than five which renders a chi square test inappropriate.

Restatement & Test of Hypotheses: Results of this Study

1. The hypothesis that psychosocial development levels reflected in the manifest content of children's stories and dreams would not differ for sex or age by mode was supported. Dreams and stories reflect the same psychosocial developmental concerns; they were scored for the same highest Eriksonian Stage. (See Table 1 & 2)
2. The hypothesis that psychosocial level would differ by sex, especially for the older group with girls at Stage III and boys at Stage IV was supported at the .025 level of significance for 8-11 year olds. (See Table 2)
3. The hypothesis that cognitive levels reflected in the manifest content of stories would differ by age with older children at a higher level and no sex differences was supported. (See Table 4)

Table 1

Comparison of the Frequency of Psychosocial Development Levels (Highest Stage Scored) of Children Stories and Dreams by Age and Sex

Mode		Age	Sex	Level:	1	2	3	4	5	6	7	8
A	S	5-7	M			1	6	4	2			1
	D						9	3	1	1		
B	S	5-7	F		1		8	3	1			1
	D				2	1	7	3	1			
C	S	8-11	M		1		4	4	1	2	1	1
	D					1	4	5	3	1		
D	S	8-11	F		1		9	1	1		2	
	D					1	10	2				
TOTALS					5	4	57	25	10	4	3	3

Table 1 shows the highest Eriksonian stages scored for each story and dream by sex and age. Rows A, B, C, D, arrange the frequencies of highest stage scored for the comparison between stories and dreams for each age and sex. As can easily be seen they are very much the same.

Table 2

2x2 Contingency Tables for the comparison of Highest Eriksonian Psychosocial Development Stage scored for boys and girls by age and mode.

5-7 yr. old stories

	Girls	Boys
III or lower	9	7
IV or higher	5	7

5-7 yr. old dreams

	Girls	Boys
III	10	9
IV	4	5

8-11 yr. old stories	Girls	Boys
III or lower	10	5
IV or higher	4	9

8-11 yr. old dreams*	Girls	Boys
III or lower	11	5
IV or higher	2	9

*significant at .025

Table 2 shows the comparison of frequency of highest stage scored between groups for age and sex. These are the contingency tables with stages I-III & IV-VIII of Table 1 collapsed for use of the Fisher exact test. Looking at these tables, only in the comparisons between the 8-11 year-olds are there differences, with the boys more at Stage IV and the girls more at Stage III. According to Erikson's Theory this difference should not be significant. By the Fisher exact test only the dreams of 8-11 year old girls and boys are significantly different at .025, with the stories showing the same trend.

Table 3

Comparison of Frequency of Cognitive Levels in Stories of 5-7 year old and 8-11 year old girls and boys.

		Mahony Story Stages 2b	3a	3b
5 - 7	Girls	5	8	1
	Boys	1	11	2
8 - 11	Girls		1	12
	Boys		1	11
TOTALS	5 - 7	6	19	3
	8 - 11		2	23

	Mahony Story Stages 3a	3b
5 - 7	25	3
8 - 11	2	23

Table 3 shows the comparison of boys and girls at each age level at each Mahony stage. There is very little sex difference here; age is the variable differentiating between stages.

Discussion

The hypothesis that stories and dreams would reflect the same level of psychosocial concerns was supported for both sexes and age groups. Stories and dreams can be seen as two expressive modes of fantasy, forms of play. These children, boys and girls, at each age, reflect the same psychosocial developmental concerns in their stories as in their dreams.

It has been suggested that in the delay in reporting a dream, from the unconscious to the conscious, some aspect is lost. L. Mack (1974) has shown in her comparison of dreams reported upon awakening in a dream lab, mostly about everyday occurrences (Foulkes, 1967 & 1969), and dreams reported later (Elkan, 1969), that both kinds of dreams show concerns with the same psychosocial issues. These findings, coupled with those of the present study, suggest that the psychosocial concerns of children are manifested similarly in their unconscious (dreams) and conscious (stories) expressive productions. This similarity is not manifested in the cognitive organization of these phenomena.

The Mahony scale, developed for analyzing cognitive organization in stories, could not be used effectively for dreams which we attempted to analyze sometimes appeared to be at a lower level, and sometimes at a higher level, but the organization could not be adequately mapped by the scale. These findings suggest that stories and dreams differ in their cognitive organization while showing a similarity in psychosocial developmental concerns.

The hypothesis that the cognitive levels of stories would show significant age differences and no sex differences was supported.

The hypothesis that the girls would show prolonged concern with Stage III, Initiative vs. Guilt, was supported for 8 - 11 year old girls' dreams, with a parallel trend for the stories. The 8 - 11 year old girls and boys were scored for many of the same items indicating that the aspects of their concerns and the sequence of ascendency are similar. It is rather the lack of Stage IV responses from the older girls which accounts for the difference and suggests an over involvement with Stage III, Initiative vs. Guilt.

According to Erikson's Theory, Stage III concerns pleasure in attack and conquest and feeling competent, which may be seen as balancing the loss of an exclusive attachment to the mother and the guilt, fear and resentment over the competition and conflict with the same sex parent for the opposite sex parent. Girls in this culture are not encouraged, as boys are, to be aggressive or to take the initiative. Perhaps the initial negative feelings toward the self (guilt) and toward the same sex parent are being displaced by the boys and discharged in their vigorous activity: "attacking" a task, being "on the move". This type of activity is generally unacceptable for girls, especially preadolescents, as are the 8 - 11 year olds in this sample. It may also be that girls, constrained socially from taking initiative actively, become more involved with the guilt (as well as fear & resentment) over the competition and conflict (Oedipal) of this stage. Since prior to this stage, both girls and boys are attached to the mother, it is perhaps more difficult for the girls to be suddenly in competition with the mother on whom she is still dependent.

In both a summary of sex differences in game playing of 5 - 12 year olds and a study of play of 3 year olds (Sutton-Smith & Savasta, 1972), sex differences are found which; 1) support the notion of differential cultural emphases being placed (taught) to girls and boys, and 2) suggest how these differences relate to sex roles. Games preferred by boys 5 - 12 years old include those where success is achieved "through active interference in the other players' activities" and "for games permitting personal initiative" while girls prefer games where competition is indirect and where rules dictate every move. (Sutton-Smith & Savasta, 1972, p. 2)

These authors studied the play behavior of 3 year old girls and boys from professional or semi-professional families to see if these differences were present earlier. Although there were no sex differences in types of play (exploration, testing, imitation), there were clear sex differences in categories of play. Girls used "inclusion-exclusion"; "controlling others by threatening exclusion," offering inclusion: "physically through smiling, giving gifts, verbally through requests or by asking for a turn, and strategically through appeals to status, distraction to others as targets and reasoning" (1972, p. 5). Boys used "attacks": physical, verbal and strategic, i.e.; "portraying to another child a fantasy of what will happen to him if he doesn't comply (1972, p. 5)." There were no differences in authority, supplication, or child-adult power usages or in physical, verbal or strategic modes. Rather there was a distribution across all three modes in the boys' use of attack and the girls' games of inclusion and exclusion.

From a societal perspective, these authors suggest that boys are playing games of those who expect to be powerful or at least compete for power while the girls play games of internal elaboration and accomodation to the other person. The important consideration of boys is the battle for power and for girls socialibility and inclusiveness. The authors suggest that these characteristics are probably essential to powerlessness, rather than to femininity as such. (1972, p. 3) These findings show clear sex differences in play which are congruent with the sex differences described in Stage III of Erikson's theory.

The strength and continuity of these differences in attack and vigorous strength and Erikson's emphasis on initiative as a "necessary part of every act" (1963, p. 255) suggest both the existence of these differences in play stories and dreams and the difficulty girls may have in resolving the conflicts and tasks of Stage III, Initiative vs. Guilt.

The sex difference suggests a cultural/social effect as well as that documented (L. Mack, 1974) of socio-economic status on the rate of development through the stages of Erikson's theory. R. Mack (1974) in his cross cultural developmental study of American and Tunisian males' dreams, confirmed the sequence of development according to Erikson's theory, but not the chronological ascendence, and attributes the "developmental" differences to cultural/social factors. The findings of this study corroborate his. Although boys and girls are growing up in the same culture, social factors affect sex differences in psychosocial "development."

The results of this study for boys basically corroborate Elkan's (1969) findings and Erikson's theory. There is a trend toward developmental shift from 5 - 6 to 8 - 9 although they are not significantly different as Elkan's were.

Almost all instances of items at Stages II & III were present for girls and boys suggesting they are both on the same Eriksonian developmental continuum, with girls behind boys.

Socio-economic status was measured by father's occupation. The subjects of this study were upper middle and middle class, while Elkan's were all upper-middle. Considering L. Mack's findings that her subjects of lower socio-economic status were at least one level below Elkan's and therefore below Erikson's chronologically age-appropriate stage, the findings of this study could be anticipated to fall between them as they do. These findings support the notion that Erikson's theory was developed, in terms of chronological/stage relationships, on upper-middle class boys and any deviation by sex or socio-economic status will result in a divergence from Erikson's expectations.

Conclusion

The findings of this study confirm Erikson's sequence of developmental stages while questioning the chronological age/stage relationship he suggests. The Elkan checklist was found to be a useful, valid measure of Erikson's developmental stages.

Of particular interest and most important for this study, the findings confirm these hypotheses: 1) Dreams and stories are parallel reflectors of psychosocial concerns of children. 2) There are statistically significant differences between the psychosocial stages of 8 - 11 year old boys and girls dreams: The girls' concerns are at a lower level than boys' showing an extended involvement with initiative, guilt, and aggression and suggesting a lag in resolving the conflicts related to these issues. 3) There are statistically significant differences in the cognitive organization of stories by age and not by sex. The differences in cognitive organization between dreams and stories are such that the dreams could not be analyzed with the story measure.

The similarities in psychosocial concerns in these dreams and stories, and the differences in cognitive organization, suggest an important and interesting focus for further research. This study demonstrates the need for more serious exploration of girls development in particular, and psychosocial development sex differences in general. This study also suggests the value of fantasy phenomena and play and game research as resources for this endeavor.

BIBLIOGRAPHY

Domhoff, G., & Kamiya, J. 1964. Problems in dream content study with objective indicators: A comparison of home and laboratory dream reports. *Archives of General Psychiatry,* 11, 519-524.

Elkan, B. 1969. Developmental differences in the manifest content of children's reported dreams. Unpublished doctoral dissertation, Columbia University.

Erikson, E. H. 1969. Identity and the life cycle. *Psychological Issues,* 1, 18-171.

Erikson, E. H. 1963. *Childhood and Society.* (2nd ed.) New York: Norton,

Foulkes, D., Larson, J., Swanson, E. M., & Rardin, M. 1969. Two studies of childhood dreaming. *American Journal of Orthopsychiatry,* 39(4), 627-643.

Foulkes, D., Pivik, T., Steadman, H., Spear, T., & Symond, J. 1967. Dreams of the male child: An EEG study. *Journal of Abnormal Psychology,* 72, 457-467.

Mack, L. 1974. Developmental differences in the manifest content of dreams of normal and disturbed children. Unpublished doctoral dissertation, Columbia University.

Mack, R. D. 1974. *A Cross-Cultural Comparison of the Developmental Levels in the Manifest Content of the Dreams of American and Tunisian Males.* Unpublished doctoral dissertation, Columbia University.

Mahony, D. 1976. A Piagetian analysis of children's narrative. Paper presented at the annual meeting of the Association for the Anthropological Study of Play, Atlanta.

Reiss, W. J. 1951. *Comparison of Personality Variables Derived from Dream Series with and without Free Association.* Unpublished doctoral dissertation, Western Reserve University.

Seigel, N., 1956. *Nonparametic Statistics for the Behavioral Sciences.* McGraw-Hill, 1956.

Sheppard, E. and Karon, B. 1964. Systematic Studies of dreams: relation between manifest dreams and associations to the dream elements. *Comprehensive Psychiatry,* 5, 335-343.

APPENDIX I
Elkan Checklist with Scoring Key

Item	Crisis Level
1. Are there expressions of sibling rage directed at older siblings?	3
2. Is there an expression of rage from an older sibling?	3
3. Does the dreamer associate with his peers?	3
4. Does someone in the dream deliberately expose his buttocks? To score this item there must be a clear emphasis on the exposed buttocks rather than general nudity.	2
5. Are there expressions of rage directed at younger sibs?	2
6. Does someone in the dream become invisible in order to confound observers but not as a defense against attack?	2
7. Does someone in the dream try to become a part of, or express the desire to be a part of, a selective (peer) group?	5
8. Does someone in the dream hide or wish to hide, not from attack, but from observing eyes?	2
9. Does the activity take place in the nursery school, local neighborhood, street corner, barnyard, etc. as opposed to home *but under the guidance of older children or elders?*	3
10. Does the dreamer give up certain advantages in order to save an initmate relationship or commitment of affiliation?	6
11. Does the dreamer try to get others to provide what he needs?	1
12. Does the dreamer watch others exercising technological skills and craftsmanship?	4

13. Are policemen, firemen, teachers, etc. recognizable by their uniforms and do they function as heroes in the dream? 3
14. Is the dreamer engaged in competitive activity with his peers in the areas of occupational apprenticeships? 5
15. Is there concern in the dream regarding regulations, e.g. law and order? 2
16. Is the dream concerned with status as reflected by dress, address, or family connection? 5
17. Doe the dream convey a sense of solidarity with all human beings? 8
18. Is the dream concerned with religious ideologies or rituals? 5
19. Do any characters in the dream compare themselves to others in relation to sexual characteristics? 3
20. Is the dream concerned with the issue of exploitation of someone by an authority figure? 2
21. Is the dreamer afraid of bodily injury? 3
22. Does the dreamer accept his parents, recognizing their faults but wishing for no other or demanding no change? 8
23. Is the dreamer developing special talents, talents special to himself rather learning socially required tasks? 5
24. Does the dreamer feel depressed by the idea that time is short, it is too late for alternative plans or that he is doomed as a "has been"? 8
25. Is the dreamer in a state of boredom? 7
26. Does the dreamer feel very small? 2
27. Does the dreamer experience a sense of duty associated with loyalty? 5
28. Is the dream concerned with the acting out of rituals? 5
29. Is the dreamer in danger of bodily injury? 3
30. Is the dream about a threatening ferocious animal, monster, stange creature, or ghost? 3
31. Does the dreamer suffer from injury to remedial appliances such as braces, glasses, or hearing aids? 3
32. Is the dreamer a part of a group of companions as in the sense of a clique or gang? This item does not refer to a group of friends engaged in a common task unless there is some reference which indicates that the group identifies as a social unit. 5
33. Does the dreamer shift with ease from the role of follower to that of leader or vice versa? 8
34. Is a theme in the dream concern about whether or not a job is finished? 4
35. Is the dreamer taught how to do something? 4
36. Is the dreamer cautious about making a commitment? 6
37. Do any characters in the dream argue? 3
38. Doe the dreamer try to stick by his ideals and his long term commitment to others in the face of difficulty? 6
39. Is retaliation for transgression a theme of the dream? 3
40. Is the dreamer concerned with throwing an object? 2

41. Does the dreamer defiantly protray himself as having evil traits? 5
42. Does the activity of the dream take place in a local neighborhood as opposed to home, *but not under the guidance of older children or elders?* 4
43. Does the dreamer feel comfortable with his own body? 5
44. Does the activity of the dream take place in school, above the level of nursery school? 4
45. Does the dreamer as a subordinate, *not* as a teacher, help someone else do a job? To score this item the dreamer must be portrayed as an assistant or "helper." 4
46. Is the dreamer afraid he has not gotten adequate instructions? 2
47. Is the dreamer racing around, keeping active at all times, not in response to danger, but because continual activity is a good thing? 3
48. Does the dreamer need to be needed? Is he pleased to be needed? 7
49. Does the dreamer feel that he must respond to an arbitrary or irrational authority? Is he concerned that he is expected to respond to such an authority? 2
50. Do expressions of rage come from a younger sib? 2
51. Does the dreamer struggle with the concept of the inevitability of his life's role? 8
52. Is a theme of the dream concern with whether or not a job is well done? 4
53. Does the dreamer function as a parent in a house hold? 7
54. Do any characters in the dream unleash or release hostile powers? For example, does anyone shoot a gun, throw a weapon, or release a ferocious beast? 2
55. Is there a sentiment of moral indignation in the dream? 3
56. Does the dreamer experience retaliation for transgression? 3
57. Is the action between a competitor and the dreamer? 3
58. Does the dreamer prefer to be alone? 6
59. Is the dreamer preoccupied with death from natual causes? 8
60. Is the dreamer concerned about defending his territory of action? 2
61. Does the dreamer "sink" into the ground in order to avoid embarrassment, or response to embarrassment? 2
62. Is the dreamer concerned about the discrepancy of how he feels to himself and how he appears to others? 5
63. Is the dreamer experimenting with various social and occupational roles? To score this item the dreamer should not be represented play-acting a role. For example, if the dreamer is playing house and he is the daddy this item should not be scored. If the dreamer dreams that he is seated at the table in his father's usual place and he functions or feels as if he were the daddy, then this item should be scored. 5
64. Does the dreamer try to become the favorite, the "chosen one"? 3
65. Is the dream concerned with a political ritual? 5
66. Is someone in the dream a scapegoat? 2

67. Is the dreamer curious about what is happening? 3
68. Does something unpleasant happen to an older sibling? 3
69. Does an older sibling escape from something unpleasant? 3
70. Is the dreamer pleased with his bad behavior? Is he triumphant when he gets away with misdeeds? 2
71. Does the dreamer give up certain beliefs in order to save an intimate relationship or a commitment of affiliation? 6
72. Does the dreamer try to seduce someone? 3
73. Is the defense of status an issue in the dream? 2
74. Does the dreamer cover himself or want to cover himself to alleviate his sense of exposure? 2
75. Does the dreamer insist that without any fight or effort on his part, but as his prerogative, he takes precedence above all others? 1
76. Is the dreamer provided for by others? Do others attempt to provide for him? 1
77. Is the dream concerned with political ideologies and issues? 5
78. Does the dreamer do a job without having any interest in it at all? 4
79. Is the repetition of a pattern an element in the dream? 2
80. Is the dreamer insistent on having a choice? 2
81. Is the dreamer afraid of being "closed up," "fenced in," left with no outlet? 2
82. Does the dreamer feel that he is a scapegoat? 2
83. In the dream does something unpleasant happen to the parent of the same sex? 3
84. Is gambling a theme of the dream? 3
85. Do any characters swear? 2
86. Does the dreamer feel ill at ease with his own body? 5
87. Does a nurturing figure leave in the face of the dreamer's demands? 1
88. Does the dreamer have an erotic exchange with the parent of the opposite sex? Does the dream present an erotic image of the parent of the opposite sex? 3
89. Does the dreamer play house? 3
90. Is control of physical functions a theme of the dream? 1
91. Does the dreamer compare himself to others in relation to skills? 3
92. Does the dreamer defend his body? 2
93. Does the dreamer accept the possibility of his own death without panic? 8
94. Is the dream concerned with the issue of intolerance of any kind of deviation? 5
95. Does the dreamer deny his fear in a dangerous situation? Does he express fear and then retract it? Within the dream are fearful images transformed into more benign images? 3
96. Does the dream indicated a sense of cultural continuity with past generations? 8
97. Is hoarding a theme of the dream? 2

98. Is the dream concerned with the issue of proper recognition for function and status in society? 5
99. Does the dreamer carefully nurture his own needs, looking after himself as if he were an only child? 7
100. Does the dreamer act or want to act in concert with his peers or as a member of a team to accomplish a task? 4
101. Does the dreamer wish to destroy those looking at himself just because they are looking at him? 2
102. Is the modality of some of the action in the dream "receiving" or "holding on to"? 1
103. Does some unpleasantness happen to a younger sibling? 2
104. Is the dreamer aware of his helplessness and the need for others to rescue him? 1
105. Does the dreamer release an object or a person? 2
106. Does the dreamer express an abhorrence of competitive activity? 5
107. Does the dream express the belief that a curse or catastrophe will befall those who break vows? 5
108. Does the dreamer continue to struggle with a difficult situation? 1
109. Is punctuality an issue in the dream? 2
110. Does the dreamer assume an assigned task in a cooperative enterprise? 4
111. Does the dreamer feel guilty for crimes committed or thoughts of aggression or hostility? 3
112. Is petting a theme of the dream? 6
113. Does the dreamer deny his anger in a situation wherein he is provoked? Does he express his anger and then withdraw it without any change in the nature of the provocation? 3
114. Is the dreamer afraid of poisonous or noxious substances which may reside in his body, his home or his room? 2
115. Is this a dream of impotence or paralysis, of wanting to do something and being unable to move? 3
116. Does religion as an institute of faith figure in these dreams? 1
117. Is addiction to inhaling, smoking, imbibing, munching, swallowing a theme of the dream? 1
118. Does the dreamer feel ashamed of being looked at in the sense of being caught too soon and/or unprepared? 2
119. Does the dreamer withdraw or want to withdraw from a difficulty without trying to cope? 1
120. Does the dreamer believe that he can depend on others to provide what he needs? 1
121. Is the dreamer threatened with bodily injury? 3
122. Does the dreamer take an arbitrarily suicidal risk? 1
123. Is the dreamer trying to master tools and/or technology in order to make something? 4

124. Does the dreamer demand independence and freedom above all other conditions? 2

125. Does the dreamer feel "cut of from paradise," abandoned by all, or empty of all resources? 1

126. Is the dreamer a show off in the sense that he sticks his neck out in a dangerous situation? 3

127. Is the dream concerned with the problem of satisfactory sexual mating? 6

128. Does the dreamer take on a nurturing role? To score this item the dreamer must take on the nurturing role in fact, not in play. He must perform the nurturing act himself and not function as one who directs or brings a second person into the care of the nurturing person. 7

129. Do individuals in the dream compare themselves in relation to size? 3

130. Does the dreamer dream of being a ferocious animal, monster, or creature? 3

131. Is the dreamer concerned with or in the act of guiding or teaching the next generation? 7

132. Is deprivation of sustenance a theme of the dream? 1

133. Is the dreamer worried about what goes on behind his back, literally or figuratively? 2

134. Is cleanliness a theme in the dream? 2

135. Does the dreamer demand to appropriate something? 2

136. Does the dreamer give up certain possessions in order to save an intimate relationship or a commitment of affiliation? 6

137. Is the dreamer determinedly literal even when it makes no sense or leads to an unjustified, rigid form of behavior? 2

138. Is exploration of new territory a theme in the dream? 3

139. Is inadequacy of equipment a theme of the dream? 4

140. Is orderliness, counting, or saving a theme of the dream? 2

141. Is enjoyment of competition a theme of the dream? 3

142. Does the dreamer clutch an object or a person? 2

143. Does the dreamer destroy or eliminate those looking at himself? 2

144. Does the dreamer feel deprived of stimulation? 1

APPENDIX II
The Mahondy Story Stages

The following has been taken from the Sutton-Smith, Botvin and Mahony 1976 article, pages 9 - 11:

"Stage I: free association (under 2 years). The earliest tales of children are fragmentary and without central themes or sequential organization. Characters and actions are not systematically related. There are sentences, but they do not seem to us to be connected. Of course in the child they might be. However, no story is conveyed and so we leave it at that.

Stage II: central character, nonreversible string (2 years). Stage IIa: now there is the same character from the beginning to end, but he is the only character in the story. There is no one else. The story is entirely egocentric perhaps, but at least the central character is found throughout:

> The airplane flew up in the sky. And after he flew up, he flew down in the park. This goes up in the airport. It had a little accident and it had to fix it. The airplane fell down (2 years old.)

Stage IIb: Then other characters appear, but they have no reality apart from their relationships to the main character (egocentrism). The actions of the characters are simply strung together in a nonreversible string.

> The doggie: The doggie jumped over the fence. The doggie went on the swing. He swinged on a swing. And he was in a park. The doggie jumped over the bike. The doggie jumped over the bear. The doggie jumped over a truck. The fence wiggled away (2 years old(.

Stage IIc: enduring others (3 years). At stage II there are others in the story but the main character is egocentric, the others act upon or are acted upon by the main character but there is no interaction between the other characters themselves. As in spatial development, the child initially coordinates all things to himself and only later coordinates the objects to each other. At this level (IIc), however, we begin to get the conserved other. The other character is mentioned several times; he appears and reappears. Here is an example from a 3 year old girl.

> The monster and spider man: The girl cried. He named Hook. He hurts girls. He go away. The end.

Stage IId: coordinated others (4 years). At this stage, interactions develop amongst the other characters also. The others are coordinated together as well as to the main characters. Thus, a 4 year old says:

> Once there was a robber and then a girl was lost. And the robber came and put her in jail. And then the police came and got her out of jail. And then the police put the robber in jail.

Stage IIIa: single reversible string (5 years). AT age 5 - 6 years the major new event is the emergence of plot conversation. The child is concerned with combining the string of actions of the story in some organized way. As in classic conservation experiments, there tends to be an initial state (ball of clay), the middle transitional state (rolled to a sausage) and the return to the first state (ball again). The initial state is usually in the home or some safe place. Then there is action and danger elsewhere. Finally, there is a return to the original situation. We have apparently, in this way at least, a reversibility of events in narrative just as we have them in physical conservation. There now more regularly appear markers (..happily ever after..) indicating that the child feels compelled to account for the continuing state of things. Introductory direction markets also indicate the need to select a point in a continuing past existence to start the story (..once upon a time..). According to Applebee (1973), 50% of all children use these markers by 5 years of age. Thus, a string of operations becomes reversible in that the operations at the end serve to return the main character to the state at the beginning of the string.

> I'll tell you a story. He's going to be a pumpkin man. Once upon a time there was a pumpkin man. And he lived in a little house close by the city. And he wanted to go to the city. So he went to the pumpkin mobile and he went faster than the speed of a bullet, more powerful than a locomotor. He could go down the highest hill in a singly bound. And he went so fast that he past the store that he want to go to. Then when he got home he went to bed. And that's the end. (5 years old.)

Stage IIIb: double reversible strings - parallel action and subplots. Towards 8 and 9 years, the simple and reversible plot sequence is modified by the addition of parallel of a subordinate order. Words like while and meanwhile appear (meanwhile back at the ranch). The child can now hold one plot in mind while developing a subplot, and then return to the first plot. On the Piagetian time scale he is into parallel durations. There is further organization into chapters which are initially simple chains but soon they acquire the reversible structure."

Cognitive Structure in Sport Tactics: A Preliminary Investigation

Thomas Ray Stevens
Teachers College, Columbia University

To participate successfully and enjoyably in sports, one must be able to function physically, socially, and intellectually. While both the physical and social aspects of sports have been studied from medical, psychological, sociological, and anthropological points of view, it has only been fairly recently that cognitive abilities in games and sports have begun to be observed and analyzed. The focus of this paper is to begin looking at the logical and structural complexities of the strategies and tactics involved in team sports, focussing on the game of basketball. To obtain a full understanding of the logic and structure and not simply a surface or end-state view, the problem was approached developmentally. We therefore will be able to see the logical components of the strategies and how they combine or coordinate; we therefore will be able to see the underlying structures of formal sports tactics.

The study was done with an adolescent population for several reasons, perhaps the most important being that adolescents are the group most actively involved with sports. During adolescence, sport, as a social and socializing experience, has great importance (Loy and Ingham 1973) and there is the opportunity for daily and organized participation. Also it is during the adolescent period that the child can move from a concrete and egocentric understanding of what is happening on the field or court to a more abstract and formal comprehension of the ideas and strategies involved in the team, goal-oriented play-of sports.

Most of the previous research in cognition has been done on younger or older populations. Most of the previous research on play and games has been done on younger populations while most research on sports has been done on adults. The study of adolescence, to a great extent, has been the excluded middle. In the area of adolescent cognition, Inhelder and Piaget (1958) have contributed the most complete model. They describe the adolescent's ability to use sixteen binary operations of propositional logic and their ability to use a lattice to structure their thinking. Less formally, the idea of the development of formal thought involves a decresance of egocentrism and the increasing ability to perform functions on abstract ideas, rather than on concrete objects or ideas. Van den Daele (1975b) has described ego and cognitive development in graph theoretical or group terms, showing an increasing number of points and connectors, showing the ability to deal with increasing numbers of concepts and functions. Both theories suggest that it is through the adolescent years that the child develops his cognitive abilities far enough to deal abstractly with the types of concepts involved in sport strategies — the coordination of individuals on a team to reach a goal while a team of others is attempting to block that goal.

In the realm of cognition and play and games, a great deal has been said about the development of schemes that may be utilized and necessary in later life and in a non-ludic realm. Erikson states that "child's play is the infantile form of the human ability to deal with experience by creating model situations and to master reality by experiment and planning." (1963:222) The Russian psychologist, Vygotsky, suggests (1967) play as an abstraction, a condensation of past experience into a summary representation, as well as a prototype of future behavior. For Piaget (1962), play is at the forefront of assimilation, the area of behavior where the child is most advanced in his thinking and at a level which other areas will only later approach. Sutton-Smith, citing evidence from research on play and creativity, from ethological work on play and from anthropological studies of culture and play, suggests, "play's biological and cultural function as one of adaptive potentiation. In those situations where innovative play is required, play potentiates novel responses..., then they are ready for later uses." (1975a:7)

Other work on play and cognition has dealt with symbolism (Piaget 1962, El'Konin 1966, Vygotsky 1967), divergent thinking (Lieberman, 1965), and many other areas including cognitive structures necessary for particular interactions at different levels of play (Piaget 1962, Sutton-Smith 1975b).

This last area of research, which has been the foundation for much of my own work, has been done by Sutton-Smith and his students (Sutton-Smith 1972, 1975b, Sutton-Smith et al. 1976). Mahony's work on cognitive structure and children's narrative is the most obvious example (Mahony 1976). In the 1975 paper, Sutton-Smith has developed a structure of games which uses the types of interactions as the basis of the structure: primary interactions of reversals, secondary interactions involving reversals and coordinations, and tertiary interactions involving reversals, coordination, and sub-group differentiations. With these types of ideas as a catalyst and a foundation, the most formal level of play, sport, became an area to view the development of the logic and cognitive structures of adolescence.

Seventy-two boys and girls from grades seven through twelve at a private school in New York City were interviewed for the study. The subjects were chosen randomly and represented a full scope of sports involvement — from the total non-participant to the completely involved, "three letter" athlete. In the interview the subjects were asked to diagram and simultaneously describe "plays" from three sports. For the purposes of this study I have limited the analysis to the diagrams of basketball plays. From the diagram and descriptions, a full diagram was drawn (since, in many cases, options of movements were described but not drawn) and then the play was translated into a functional, logical calculus.

An example of a play diagram and the logical translation are given (Figure 1). Since neither the diagram nor the logical sentence are obvious or self-explanatory, a description of the play is necessary. In the diagram, solid lines represent passes or shots of the ball and broken lines represent the pattern of the players' movement, the numbered lines show time sequence and/or simultaneity. The players' positions at critical times are note by the player number and a subortinate number for the place in the time sequence, i.e. player 2 starts at the space marked 2_1. The play is as follows: Player 1 throws the ball to player 2 at space 2_1. Player 5 then runs a pattern around players 3 and 4, who afford a "pick" or stationary block to free player 5 from his defender. If player 5 is free, player 2 passes him the ball at space 5_2 and player 5 shoots at the basket, Z. If player 5 is not free he continues running to space 5_3 and player 3 runs around player 4's "pick" (or stationary block) and player 2 passes him the ball at space 3_2. Player 3 then shoots.

Figure 1

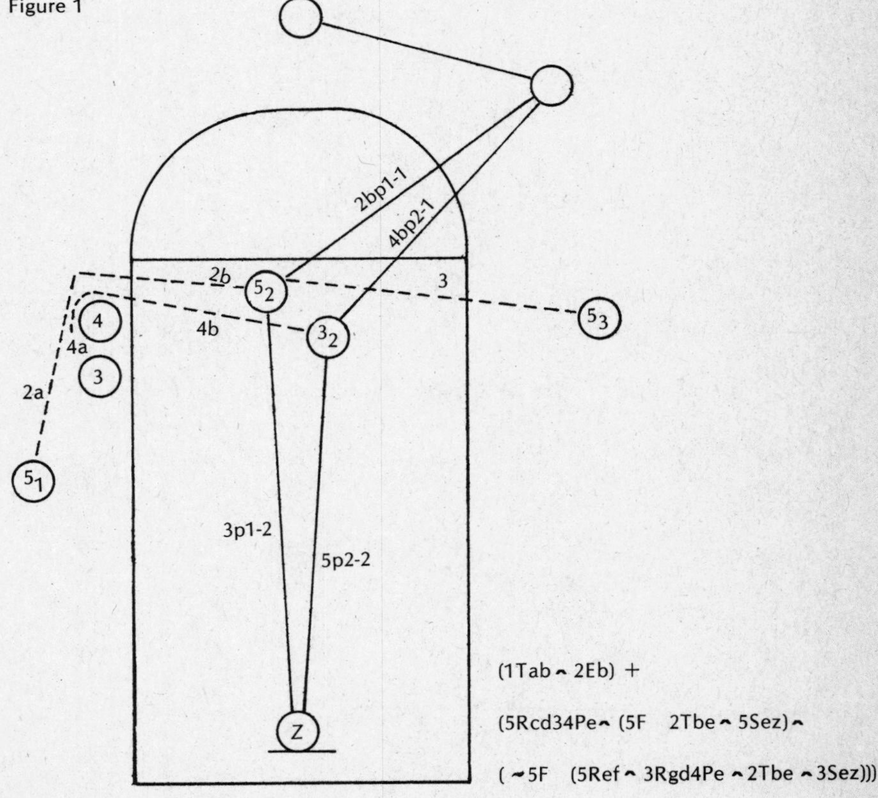

(1Tab ⌢ 2Eb) +

(5Rcd34Pe ⌢ (5F 2Tbe ⌢ 5Sez) ⌢

(~5F (5Ref ⌢ 3Rgd4Pe ⌢ 2Tbe ⌢ 3Sez)))

The logical sentence describes the same play but an explanation of the notation is called for: Numbers represent players (as in the diagram), capital letters are functions or actions, such as T is throwing or passing, R is running, S is shooting, E is being at a point to receive a pass, a F is the state of being free to attempt a shot. Lower case letters represent point on the court. The rest of the symbols are basically those from standard logic: the arrow signifies an implication, the caret is an "and" statement, the inverted caret an "or" statement and the "squiggle" shows negation. The only other symbol is the plus sign, "+", which is an "and" statement with the additional idea of sequence, "and then".

Figure 2

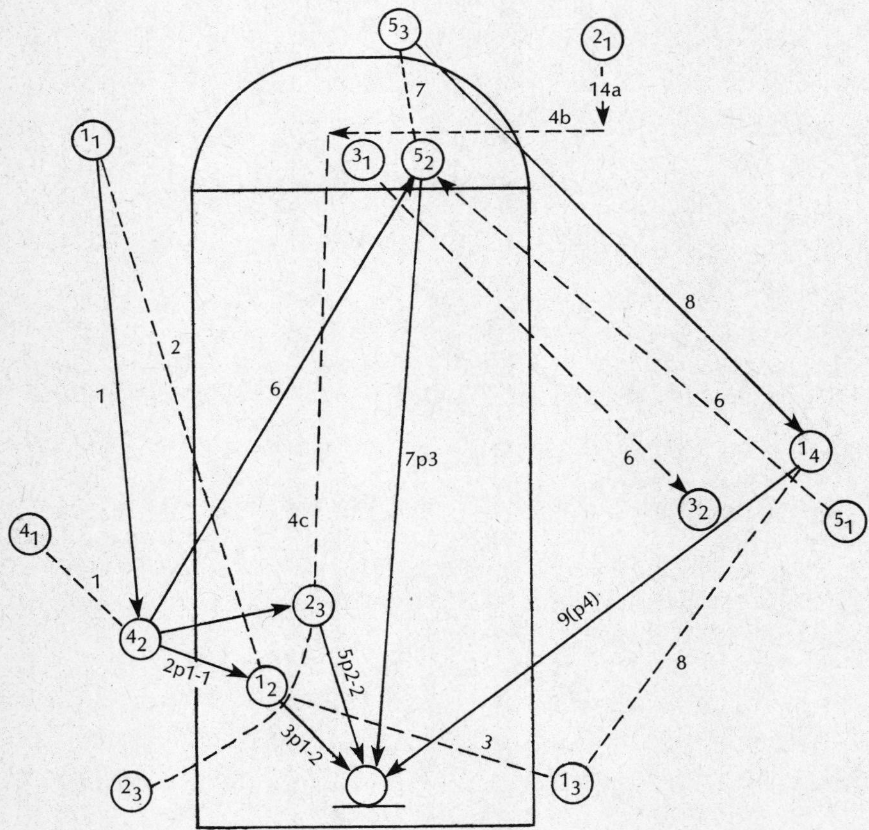

Figure 3

(1Tab ∧ 4Rcb) +

(1Rad ∧ (1F 4Tbd ∧ 1Sdz) ∨

(~1F ➤ 1Rde ∧ 2Rfgh3Pi (2F 4Tbi ∧ 2Siz) ∨

((~2F ➤ 2Rij ∧ 3Rk5Pl ∧ 5R13Pk 4Tbk) +

((5F ➤ 5Skz) ∨

(~5F ➤ 5Rkm ∧ 5Tmn ∧ 1Re3Pn ∧ 1Snz)))))

An example of a complex play, diagrammed by a sixteen year old boy who was very involved in sports, is also given to show the extent of the complexity that some of the plays demonstrate. (Figures 2 and 3) Player 1 throws the ball to player 4 as player 4 reaches space 4_2. Player 1 proceeds to run toward the basket, and if he is free, player 4 returns the pass and player 1 shoots. If player 1 is not free, he continues to the spacd 1_3 and player 2 runs a pattern toward the basket, around player 3 who is setting a "pick" to free player 2 from his defensive man. If player 2 is free, player 4 will throw him the ball and player 2 will shoot. If player 2 is not free, he will continue running to space 2_3, player 3 and player 5 will change positions (picking or blocking each other's defensive men), and player 4 will throw the ball to player 5. If player 5 is free, he will shoot. If he is not free, he will go to space 5_3, player 1 will run by player 3's "pick" to space 1_4, and player 5 will throw the ball to player 1. Player 1 will then shoot. The play is then over. As can be clearly seen, the tactics involved in sports can be extremely complex.

Figure 4

Level I

1Tab
1Rab

Figure 5

Level II

1Tab ∧ 2Eb

a. 1Tab ∧ 2Eb ∧ 2Tbc ∧ 3Ec

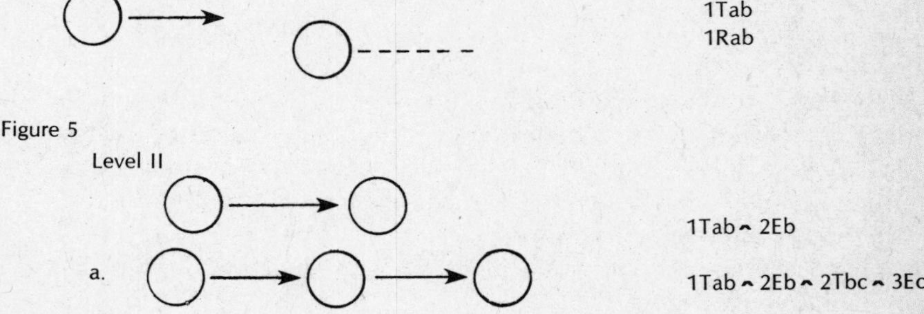

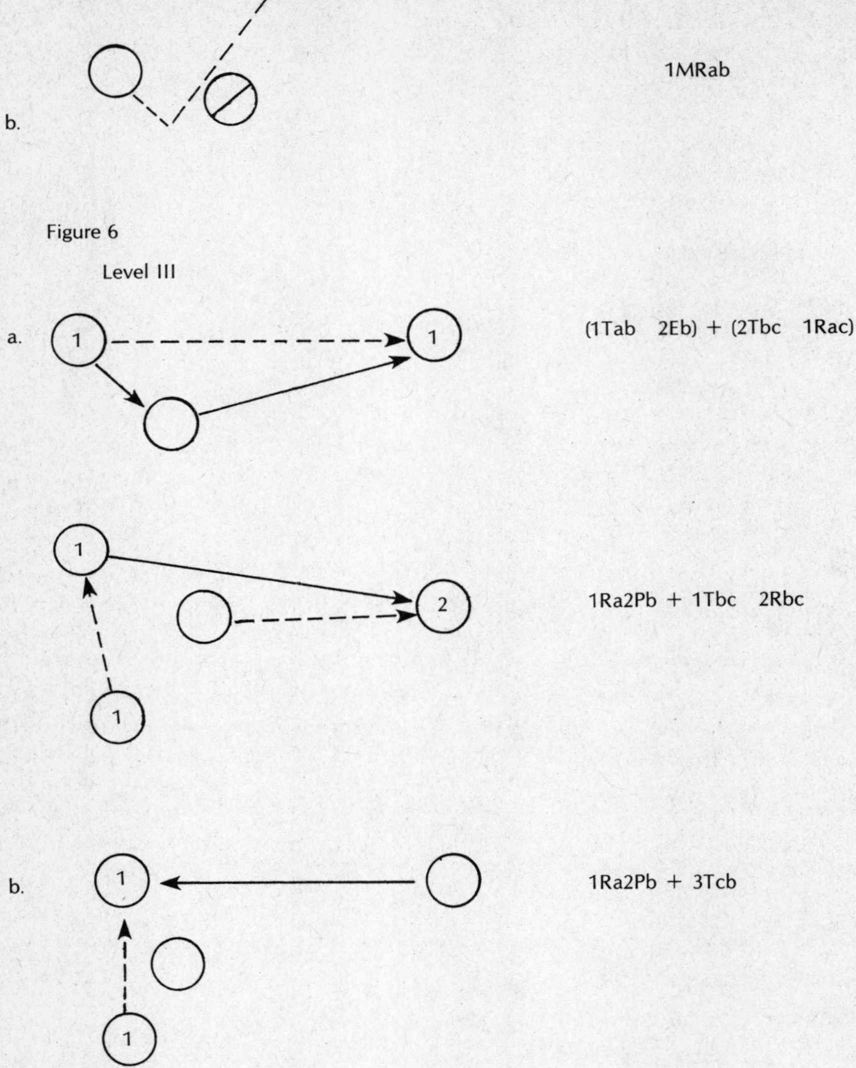

By breaking down the diagrams and looking, cross-sectionally, at the development of their complexity, a structural system of tactics was developed. Earlier structures become integrated and subordinated to later structures. (van den Daele 1974, 1975a). A description of the structures and what they represent is:

Level I: Simple actions by a player. A player shoots the ball, runs, or throws the ball. (Figure 4)

Level IIa: An action involving another player on the same team. One player passing to another. These actions may be strung together but without any coordination other than a simple sequence. One player passes to another, who passes to another, and so on. (Figure 5a)

Level IIb: An action involving a player from the other team. This could be examplified by a simple fake. (Figure 5b)

Level IIIa: An action involving another player and then the first player again. A "give and go" or a "pick and roll" are two examples. In the first case, player 1 passes to player 2 and then runs to receive a return pass. In the second case, player 1 sets a "pick" to stop player 2's defender and the "rolls" or moves away from the play to receive a pass from player 2. (Figure 6a)

Level IIIb: A set of actions coordinating several players, with the actions forming a simple unit. An example of this would be a "double pick" where two players set to block a third player's defender. Another example would be a block set to free a second player to receive a pass from a third player. (It should be noted that at Level III and above, the defense is always taken into account.) (Figure 6b)

Level IV: A coordination of coordinations in which several options for actions are possible. This would be a series of coordinated actions, Level III tactics, in which the actions in the coordination are contingent on previous coordinations. (Figures 1, 2, and 3)

Level V: A coordination of the coordinated coordinations. These may be plays which recycle, so, if no options are open to be taken, the play starts again or a new set of options are started. Another example is a play which sets up, or makes more efficient, a following play. This is much more evident in American football. A final example of Level V tactics would be a coach's "game plan".

As can be seen, each level becomes integrated and subordinated to the next: simple actions become part of acting with another, actions with one other become part of coordinated actions, coordinated actions are then coordinated, until, finally, those are coordinated and become part of a larger plan.

In terms of the logical calculus, we start with simple functions (Level I), move on to simple "and" statements (Level II), on to "and" statements with several functions and actors (Level III), and then to sentences that involve implication, negation, and "or" statements (Level IV). It is at Level IV that we find the first imbedded statements—statements with larger statements. Level V brings the idea of imbedding one step further. The strategy of the whole game is imbedded in one sentence.

We have shown a development of cognitive structures in sport tactics which parallel structures found in other theories of cognitive development.

The structures are very similar to those that Mahony described (1976), can be seen as similar to those that van den Daele describes (1975b), and are even similar to structures found by Isaacs (1956) in his work on relatability. We have seen, not to our surprise, but in some detail, that the logical complexity of the tactics increases with age.

There are several questions and considerations that must be mentioned. Perhaps the largest question, in terms of the validity of the findings, is whether the increases of logical and structural complexity are due to maturation or learning. There is no doubt that learning does play a role; the more experienced athletes did diagram more complex plays, but the parallels with other findings in cognitive growth do suggest strongly that cognitive maturation is an important factor. It is also the fact that even "sport involved" younger adolescents did not attain Level III tactics, where it would appear formal operations would be demanded.

There is also the question: If cognitive development in play is in advance of other areas of cognition, why do these cognitive structures of sport tactics not appear earlier, rather than later, than in other areas? I suggest that the reason is bound up in the structure of sport itself. Sport, as an agent of socialization, subordinates the individual to the group and subordinates his actions to structures of the sport itself (Loy and Ingham 1973). The good player, according to Caillois is "someone who takes into account that he has no right to complain of bad luck, not to grieve about misfortune, the possibility of which he has deliberately accepted if not courted. In a word, a good player is one who possesses sufficient equanimity and does not confuse the domains of play and life." (1959:159) It has been found in other studies, now in progress at Teachers College, Columbia University, that cognitive, affective, and creative levels may be damped by imposing greater structure. Sutton-Smith and others have found evidence of this in ongoing studies of children's filmmaking. The dissertation research of Lee Petersen (1976) which includes the effects of structured stimuli on children's story telling also supports this notion.

On the other hand, one may say that these structures and abilities in sport are actually precursors in a new realm of social interaction and manipulation. In sports, the adolescent has his first opportunity to manipulate and work with his peers, both concretely and abstractly. This is as the peer group has gained significant importance as a social support and reference group, similar or approaching that found in "adult" society.

Another question is whether "higher is better." In a recent college basketball game (March, 1976), Rutgers University used basically Level II and III tactics and soundly defeated the University of Connecticut team, which used Level III and IV tactics. It became obvious that performance was a key factor and that Rutgers was performing more efficiently at Level II and III then their opponents could at Level III or IV. Also, while it is difficult to be certain without interviewing the teams and coaches, one might suspect, that the tactics of Rutgers at Level V were superior.

A final question is: What about the "natural athlete" who performs magnificently, even when the play breaks down? A description of Gale Sayers, a great American football running back, brings the question into sharp focus:

> Formations and plays can be predetermined for Sayers, but he relies more upon the truth of his instincts to break free than upon the meticulous blueprint of a play. A blocking failure does not bind him, but frees him from the rigid rule of the team.
>
> It is at this point that Sayers begins to function fully. With the instincts of an artist and the discipline of an athlete, he pits himself against the defense as a man against environment. He weighs all probabilities, the angle of approaching tacklers, the ratio of his speed to theirs, the distance from each sideline, the number of opponents left, the vectors of his own blockers, and the texture of the field. In an instant, these factors are programmed into motion. His art, like all art, flows from being, not from thinking.
>
> (Oates 1970)

I must disagree with the author. It is obvious that thinking, or at least some cognitive process is definitely and totally involved and functioning. A problem for future research is how one can tap into those processes.

REFERENCES

Caillois, R. 1959 *Man and the Sacred.* Glencoe, Illinois: The Free Press.

El'Konin, D. 1966 Symbolics and its function in play of children. *Soviet Education, 8,* 35-41.

Erikson, E.H. 1963 *Childhood and Society.* New York: W.W. Norton.

Inhelder, B. and Piaget, J. 1958 *The Growth of Logical Thinking.* New York: Basic Books.

Isaacs, K. 1956 *Relatability.* Unpublished dissertation, University of Chicago.

Lieberman, J.N. 1965 Playfulness and divergent thinking: An investigation of their relationship at the kindergarten level. *Journal of Genetic Psychology, 107,* 219-224.

Loy, J. and Ingham, A.G. 1973 Play, games and sports in the psychosocial development of children and youth. In *Physical Activity.* New York: Academic Press.

Mahony, D. 1976 A Piagetian analysis of children's narrative. Paper presented to *The Association for the Anthropological Study of Play,* Atlanta.

Oates, B. (Ed.), 1970 *The First Fifty Years: The Story of the N.F.L.* New York: Simon and Schuster.

Petersen, L. 1976 Constraining the child's storytelling situation: Does it make a Difference? Unpublished dissertation, Teachers College, Columbia University.

Piaget, J. 1962 *Play, Dreams, and Imitation in Childhood.* New York: W.W. Norton.

Sutton-Smith, B. 1975 Current research and theory in play, games and sports. Paper presented to the *American Medical Association,* Annual Meeting, Atlantic City, New Jersey.

Sutton-Smith, B., Botvin, G. and Mahony, D. n.d. Structure in Fantasy narrative. *Human Development,* in press.

van den Daele, L. 1974 Infrastructure and transition in developmental analysis, *Human Development, 18,* 1-18.

1975a Organization and transformation. In K. Riegel and J. Meacham (Eds.), *The Developing Child in a Changing World.* The Hague: Mouton.

1975b Ego development and preferential judgment in life-span perspective. In N. Datan and L. Ginsberg (Eds.), *Life-Span Developmental Psychology: Normative Life Crises:* Vol. IV. New York: Academic Press.

Vygotsky, L.S. 1976 Play and its role in the mental development of the child. *Soviet Psychology, 5* 6-18.

V. Theoretical Considerations in the Study of Play

Editor's Introduction

Constructing, or contributing to the construction of, a comprehensive theory of play is one of the primary aims of The Association for the Anthropological Study of Play, and was a driving force behind the scholarship of its late President, B. Allan Tindall. All the papers in this section focus on theoretical issues, the first three specifically, the last three more generally.

In his efforts to provide new theoretical directions for sport sociology, Allen Sack begins with an effort to establish just what "play" is. Although perhaps he over-generalizes about the cultural universality of a work-play dichotomy, he considers as fundamental to an understanding of the concept the degree of *obligation* involved. From this premise he argues that many — though, contrary to the assertions of Harry Edwards, not all — games and sports more closely approximate work, and that professional sport is not play at all. Sack finds inadequate the typologies of sport, game, and play as offered by various theorists, and constructs his own typology which he offers as a better guide for the sociology of sport.

Finding inadequacies in the treatment of play in the area of developmental psychology, Elizabeth Mouledoux also aims to contribute to the development of theory. Her focus is on establishing a comprehensive terminology (is *all* social science plagued by terminological problems?) by applying the classifications of Piaget and Caillois to data collected from her own investigations of play activity among children, and by comparing the applicability and utility of these two sets of classifications. As does Sack, she defines play on the basis of freedom from obligation. I think it is useful for researchers to note, although Mouledoux mentions it only briefly, that her investigations were designed to include observations of *audience* as well as performers, noting that the "rapt alert observation" of young children "is an integral part of on-going play activity" and "*deserves consideration as a type of play activity in its own right,* and not only as a category of social interaction" (my emphasis).

Studies of fantasy are numerous, but Ernestine Thompson and Tanya Johnson have offered some fresh and very interesting insights into an area of fantasy which has been widely ignored by students of human behavior, but which may well be culturally universal, and is certainly vital in the socialization process where it does occur: the creation of and interaction with an imaginary playmate. They realize that the I.O., an individual creation, and what they call "consensual imaginary figures" — e.g., the Bogey Man and the Tooth Fairy — are related as to the socialization functions they serve, and they explore this latter area as well. Their findings are admittedly tentative, but they are quite interesting, and should stimulate further research into this area.

The text of Brian Sutton-Smith's Keynote Address, "Play, Games, and Sports...Socialization or Innovation?", delivered at the 1976 Annual Meeting, was too long for inclusion in this volume. At his suggestion I have taken instead an earlier paper which he wrote for the Association's *Newsletter;* this is followed by some "footnotes" to his Keynote Address. In these two papers he reviews social science approaches to and theories of play, and suggests some elements which ought to be included if an approach is to be uniquely "anthropological." Following on some of his viewpoints — and assuming an Editor's prerogative — I have concluded this book with a paper of my own, written originally for the *Newsletter* in response to the same paper by Sutton-Smith which is included here. His and mine, I feel, form a complementary pair which ought not to be separated. In my contribution I suggest that before a cultural theory of play can be developed, we must look deeper into the nature of culture itself, into its biological roots; and we must look much deeper than we have into what I argue is the fundamental nature and function of play; specifically, what play does for the organism.

The text of the book is followed by a comprehensive bibliography of studies of play, organized under several topical and areal categories, very kindly submitted by Helen Schwartzman as an Appendix. This bibliography was originally assembled for Dr. Schwartzman's article, "The Anthropological Study of Children's Play," in B. J. Siegel, ed., *Annual Review of Anthropology* (Palo Alto: Annual Reviews, Inc., 1976, pp. 289-328), and is reproduced here, with some modification, by permission of the Editor of the *Annual Review.* It is our hope that *Proceedings* of subsequent years will devote a section to keeping this bibliography current as (we hope) the field expands and generates new studies.

Sport: Play or Work?

Allen L. Sack, University of New Haven

The sociology of sport, while making some progress toward developing precise concepts, has still not adequately staked out the boundaries of its field of investigation. More specifically, a review of the literature reveals considerable disagreement and inconsistency concerning the concepts play, game, and sport. Some writers, like Huizinga and Caillois, treat play and games as virtually synonymous terms.[1] Likewise, Loy, by defining both games and sport as "playful" competitions comes very close to making sport a subcategory of play.[2] Edwards, on the other hand, argues that play and sport have nothing in common and places them at opposite ends of a continuum.[3] It will be argued here that all of the above formulations are inadequate because they fail to make explicit the essential difference between sport as work and sport as play. It is the relationship between sport, work, and play that will constitute the central concern of this paper.

Play and Work

Many contemporary discussions of the play concept find their starting point in Johan Huizinga's classic work *Homo Ludens.* According to Huizinga, play is

> a free activity standing quite consciously outside "ordinary" life as being "not serious," but at the same time absorbing the player intensely and utterly. It is an activity connected with no material interest, and no profit can be gained by it. It proceeds within its own proper boundaries of time and space according to fixed rules and in an orderly manner. It promotes the formation of social groupings which tend to surround themselves with secrecy and to stress their difference from the common world by disguise or other means.[4]

Although in need of considerable refinement, Huizinga's definition does nonetheless point to some of the most important features of play. First, play is a free or voluntary activity. A person plays because he enjoys it, and when he no longer finds the activity gratifying, he is free to stop. According to Huizinga, "play can be deferred or suspended at any time...it is never a task".[5] Neither the ballplayer who attends practice for fear of losing his scholarship nor the child who is forced to participate in little league baseball can truly be said to be playing. The more one is obliged to participate in a given activity (whether one likes it or not) the less that activity resembles play.

The second important characteristic of play is that it stands outside ordinary life and is not "serious". This can be interpreted to mean that play is set apart from the pragmatic concerns associated with making a living. A person engages in play because it is intrinsically rewarding, not because it is a means to some end lying outside of the sphere of play itself. To quote Huizinga, "play interpolates itself as a temporary activity satisying in itself and ending there".[6] Play is never imposed by physical necessity. Thus, it is bracketed off from what one often considers to be "real" life. It should be added, and Huizinga was well aware of this, that play can proceed with the utmost seriousness within its own boundaries.

The sport of mountain climbing serves well to illustrate the separateness of the play sphere. If a man climbs a mountain to establish a weather observatory or to train soldiers in winter survival techniques, his actions more closely resemble work than play. As climbing ceases to be an end in itself and becomes infused with the concerns of the workaday world, the more the play element retreats to the background. On the other hand, if a person endures the pain associated with high altitude climbing, risks serious injury and even death, merely for the sake of climbing to the summit, this represents play in its purest form. With a seriousness readily interpreted as insanity by more "practical" people, the climber carves out his play world from the side of a mountain, a world replete with dangerous crevasses, impossible overhangs, and endless snow fields. Not only does the climber make very little effort to avoid such obstacles, but he may actually seek them out. While such behavior may appear strange from the perspective of the ordinary world, it makes perfectly good sense according to the rules that govern the artificial play world of the climber.

Closely related to this idea that play is separate is Huizinga's insistence that play is connected with no material interest and no profit can be gained by it. It would be more accurate to say, however, that play *is pursued* for no material interest or profit. In this latter form, the statement simply re-emphasizes the point that play, in its purest form is intrinsically rewarding. The more that one pursues an activity for extrinsic rewards, or is subject to pressures and demands emanating from outside the play world, the more the activity becomes work. Of course, it is quite possible that play can lead to a wide variety of rewards which are extrinsic to the play act. For instance, it may improve one's health, help doctors to learn more about the physical effects of life at high altitudes—it might even lead to the acquisition of sums of money, as often occurs at a race track. However, an activity is only play as long as the actor's primary motivation is independent of such extrinsic rewards and the demands on which these rewards are continent.

With regard to Huizinga's assertion that play proceeds within its own proper boundaries of time and space according to fixed rules, a few words are in order. First, inasmuch as all human behavior proceeds within boundaries of time and space, this quality is not particularly helpful in defining play. The question of rules is not so simple. On the one hand, one might argue that *all* social behavior is governed by rules, and that play, being social behavior, is no exception. On the other hand, those who are offended by such an oversocialized view of man would argue that man is also capable of impulsive, unstructured, and creative activity which is freed from social conventions. Adherents to the latter position are apt to assert that play can have both its spontaneous and structured manifestations.[7] It is important to note, however, that whichever interpretation is chosen, the existence of normative regulation *per se* does not preclude an activity from being play. In fact, it is precisely the challenge created by rules, freely accepted, that makes some forms of play so fascinating.

In summary, suffice it to say that play is characterized by its freedom, separateness, and its lack of dependence on material interest or profit. Although most play activity is governed by rules which are freely accepted by participants, some play forms, e.g., lovers frolicking in autumn leaves or children rolling recklessly down a grassy embankment, have little or possibly no normative regulation. Generally speaking, the more an activity is a task or obligation oriented to the pragmatic concerns of making a living and pursued for profit or material interest, the more it approximates work.

It should be noted that this conception of work, and the notion that work and play are opposites might be appropriate only in societies as we have known them to date. In some future society, economic scarcity and repressive forms of work organization could conceivably be eliminated. Under these conditions, work would be transformed into what Marx called unalienated labor.[8] When work is intrinsically rewarding and is not imposed by physical necessity, and when the worker gains control over his own activity, work becomes indistinguishable from play. However, at present, and throughout most of history, the majority of men have experienced play as an escape from, rather than as a vital part of their work. Thus, the distinction between work and play presented in this paper seems entirely justified.

Games, Play, and Work

The concept of game is often confused with play. This is especially obvious in Caillois' influential article, "The Structure and Classification of Games."[9] In that article, Caillois adopts a modified version of Huizinga's definition of play and then goes on to treat play and games as synonymous terms. As a consequence, games staged for mass entertainment by paid professionals, being far more like work than play, would not be covered by Caillois' classification. His classification of games can also be criticized for being too broad. While kite flying, waltzing, and riding merry-go-rounds can easily be subsumed under the heading of play, it would be straining a bit to call them games.

TABLE 1
Caillois' Classification of Games

	AGON Competitions	ALEA Chance	MIMICRY Pretence	ILINI Vertigo
PAIDIA ↓		Comptines	Childish	Children's
Noise	Races not reg-	Heads or	imitation	swings
Agitation	Combats ulated	tails	Masks	Merry-go-
Laughter	Athletics		Costumes	round
Dance				Tetter-
Hoop	Boxing	Betting		totter
Solitaire	Fencing	Roulette	Theatre	Waltz
Games of	Football			Outdoor
patience	Checkers	Lotteries		sports
Crossword	Chess ↑			Skiing
puzzles				Mountain
LUDUS				climbing

If Caillois' work is viewed as a classification of play only, the abovementioned difficulties immediately disappear. In fact, when viewed in this light, Caillois' classification makes significant contributions to the understanding of the play phenomenon. One of Caillois' key contributions is his classification of play forms by the motives of participants. Some types of play are primarily competitive, others depend on chance or fate. Still others are appealing because they give one a chance to indulge in pretense or to achieve a feeling of vertigo. Caillois calls these motives agon, alea, mimicry, and ilini respectively. Caillois' other major contribution is his recognition that play can be relatively spontaneous and unstructured (paidia) or highly regulated and organized (ludus). This classification of play by motive and degree of normative regulation is a significant addition to, and refinement of, Huizinga's formulations.

The problem still remains, however, of finding an adequate definition for the term game. John Loy is somewhat more precise in distinguishing between games and play than is Caillois. According to Loy, a game is "any form of playful competition whose outcome is determined by physical skill, strategy or chance employed singly or in combination."[10] This goes beyond Caillois' rather loose usage of the term game by adding the idea of competition. For Loy, games always involve a struggle to win. Competition may be with individuals, teams, animate and inanimate objects, or with ideal standards. When defined in this way, playful activities like flying kites, riding teeter-totters or dressing up in costumes, would not be treated as games unless these activities were somehow to become competitive.

Loy's definition, while helping to separate the concepts play and game, still fails to deal adequately with professional games. This is because by defining a game as a "playful" competition, he ends up making it a subcategory of play. It is this writer's contention that to define professional sport in terms of various elements of play is to distort its most essential features. Drawing on the discussion of work and play presented at the outset of this paper, it is obvious that the games of professionals fall far toward the work end of the work-play continuum. The professional ballplayer even when he enjoys his work, cannot escape the fact that his sport participation is a task, to which he is obliged to submit. If he misses a game or a practice session he may be fined or in some other way sanctioned. This obviously violates the freedom so critical to play.

It is also clear, contrary to what Loy has argued, that professional games are as productive and utilitarian in motive as any other work activity.[11] The professional ballplayer is well aware that he is laboring to make a living and the pressures of the workaday world are constantly intruding into his games. He can hardly ignore the fact that a series of "blown" plays, bad games, or serious injuries can put an end to his career and threaten the well-being of himself or his family. The product he produces is entertainment and the payment he receives is financial security. Upon hearing the final gun that ends his game, the professional athlete is as likely to express feelings of relief as is any other worker when a whistle ends his working day. Professional games then, inasmuch as they (1) involve activity that participants are obliged to perform (2) are oriented to the pragmatic concerns of ordinary life, and (3) are pursued for profit or material gain, share almost nothing in common with play.

What is necessary to improve Loy's definition of a game, therefore, is the addition of the idea that games can be both play and work. The following definition, expanding Loy's somewhat, allows the introduction of this idea: A game is any form of competition, staged primarily for the enjoyment of either participants or spectators, whose outcome is determined by physical skill, strategy, or chance employed singly or in combination. Such a definition allows for the inclusion of games produced by professionals. When the entertainment needs of spectators are given highest priority, games tend to become work. When the sheer joy of participation is emphasized, the play element reigns supreme.

Sport, Play and Work

Having discussed the concepts of play, work, and games, it remains to examine their relationship to sport. Probably the best way to distinguish between a game and a sport is to treat a game as a unique event and a sport as a pattern.[12] Loy, following this approach, defines sport as "an institutionalized game demanding a demonstration of physical prowess."[13] What this means is that the sport of American football, for instance, consists of the formalized norms which have crystallized over the past 100 years to regulate the behavior or modern-day football players. Sport then, is a more or less stable pattern of culture and social structure. It has a history and will be passed on into the future. A game, on the other hand, is a concrete event. That is, it is an actual acting out or occurrence of a sport.

Although satisfactory in most respects, Loy's definition is in need of some refinement. First, it is obvious that the inadequacies of his definition of the term "game", discussed above, will carry over into his definition of sport. The result is that professional sport is misrepresented as play. The revised definition of games this writer presented above serves to eliminate this problem. Another refinement of Loy's conception of sport would be to distinguish among institutionalized games which demand varying degrees of physical prowess. For instance, it might be useful to separate sports like pool, bowling, or archery from ice hockey, football, and cross country ski racing. The former, while demanding high levels of physical skill, do not demand total physical involvement to the point of bodily exhaustion. It is only participants in the latter activities, because of the sheer physical endurance demanded, that should be referred to as athletes. More will be said on this later.[14]

In summary, it can be said that the basic problem with definitional efforts discussed so far is that they tend to treat all sport as play and are thereby inadequate for dealing with professional sport. This problem is more than mere terminological quibbling. To treat professional sport as a playful activity distorts the very nature of that activity and blinds the researcher to similarities between the sport world and the world of work. Like the average layman, scholars are often taken aback by the intrusion of strikes and collective bargaining into the realm of sport. They will probably even be more bewildered when big-time intercollegiate athletes start demanding salaries. Such naivete is to be expected when even key concepts in the discipline of sport sociology fail to recognize professional athletes as workers rather than players. A classification of sport which treats some forms of sport as work could serve to sensitize social scientists to issues that are routinely ignored when sport is confounded with play.

Play and Sport as Opposites

Having dealt with the problem of confounding sport with play, it is now necessary to discuss an error in the opposite direction. That is, some writers argue that sport has nothing whatsoever in common with play. This argument receives its clearest expression in the work of Harry Edwards.[15] Whereas Loy's conception of sport draws attention away from the study of sport as work, Edwards leaves no room for sport as a play activity. A summary and critique of some of Edwards' arguments should illustrate how his conception of sport in general comes close to this writer's conception of sport as work.

According to Edwards, as one moves from play to sport the following occurs:

1. Activity becomes less subject to individual prerogative, with spontaneity severely diminished.
2. Separation from the rigors and pressures of daily life becomes less prevalent.
3. The relevance of the outcome of the activity and the individual's role in it extends to groups and collectivities that do not participate directly in the act.
4. Goals become diverse, complex, and more related to values emanating from outside of the context of the activity.
5. Formal rules and structural role and position relationships and responsibilities within the activity assume predominance.
6. Individual liability and responsibility for the quality and character of his behavior during the course of the activity is heightened.
7. The activity consumes a greater proportion of the individual's time and attention due to the need for preparation and the degree of seriousness involved in the act.
8. The emphasis upon physical and mental extension beyond the limits of refreshment or interest in the act assumes increasing dominance.

It is this writer's contention that of the eight criteria Edwards uses to distinguish play from sport, the first four actually highlight quite effectively the key differences between play and professional sport. What Edwards is saying is that sport, like work, imposes severe limitations on an individual's freedom, is immersed in the pressures and concerns of ordinary life, and is always pursued for rewards which lie outside of the sphere of play itself. It is obvious that for Edwards, sport and professional sport are virtually synonymous terms and have little, if anything, in common with play. The last four criteria, it can be argued, are of no value whatever for distinguishing between the concepts play and sport because they focus on qualities that vary considerably within play itself.[16] The major problem with Edwards' definitional effort, however, is that it makes playful sport logically impossible.

In Edwards' scheme, racketball between friends, if entered freely, kept separate from the pressures of the workaday world, and pursued for no material gain or profit cannot constitute a sport. This is true regardless of the fact that the rules of racketball are rigidly codified and institutionalized, its participants often push themselves unmercifully, and players get tremendous self satisfaction from improving the quality of their games. Likewise, mountain climbing pursued voluntarily and solely for the instrinsic rewards one gains from a competitive struggle against nature, would not be a sport by Edwards' definition. The climber may train on his own to develop his climbing skills, he may ultimately push himself to the limits of human endurance and expose himself to conditions few would endure for any price. Yet, because he enters this activity freely, has no desire for rewards other than those derived from climbing itself, and accomplishes his end without being driven by authoritarian coaches and screaming hoards of spectators, this climber cannot, according to Edwards, call his efforts sport.

It would appear that Edwards, like so many other people in the world of sport, assumes that physical competition is only taken seriously when pursued by skilled professionals in rationalized and commercialized settings. The assumption is that those who play at their games are not concerned with the quality and outcome of their performances. Admittedly, play may at times be little more than "fun and games". However, playful competition can also be undertaken with an intensity that is unsurpassed in even the most highly organized professional contests. To assume that human beings will strive for bodily excellence only when under compulsion or when seeking financial gain is to underestimate the potential of playful or truly amateur sport.

An Attempt at Synthesis

At this point, an attempt to construct a typology of sport utilizing elements from each of the formulations criticized above is in order. Along with Edwards, I feel that play and sport must at times be treated as polar opposites, but only when play is contrasted with professional sport. Edwards errs by ignoring those forms of sport activity that should properly be regarded as play. Like Loy and Caillois, I would argue that some forms of sport can best be defined as a subcategory of play. The weakness of their formulations, however, is that they tend to misrepresent sport activity that should properly be regarded as work. To eliminate some of these shortcomings, a typology of sport is needed that is broad enough to treat sport as both work and play.

Another distinction which should be made within sport itself is between athletic and nonathletic sport. All sport, by definition, is dependent on physical prowess. However, as Weiss, Edwards, and others have argued, only if one makes a concerted physical effort, involving exertion to the limits of fatigue and endurance, can one be an athlete participating in a game.[17] By dividing the realm of sport along a dimension of work and play as well as along a dimension of nonathletic and athletic sport, the following typology emerges.

TABLE 2
A Typology of Sport

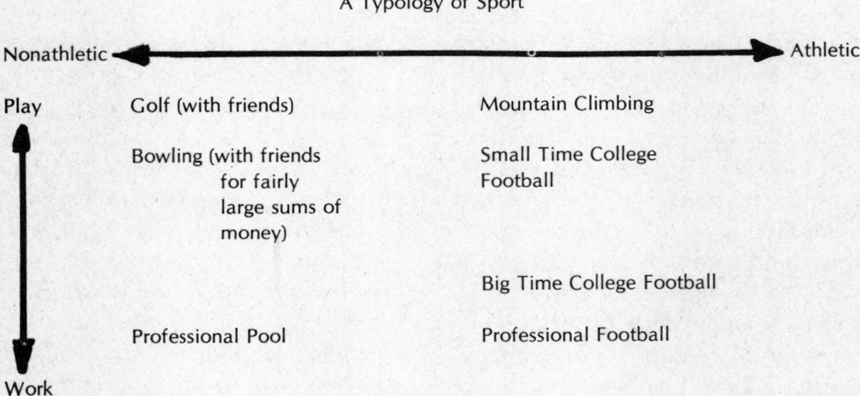

In the above typology, sport is defined as an institutionalized game, dependent on physical prowess. A game is defined as any form of competition, staged for the enjoyment or either participants or spectators, whose outcome is determined by physical skill, strategy, or chance employed singly or in combination. Play and work represent ideal types, i.e., mental constructs composed of the most characteristic or essential elements of each phenomenon. All game occurrences of sport fall along a continuum from play to work. It should also be noted that some types of sport fall somewhere between the athletic and nonathletic. Golf, shuffle board, bowling, and curling, are examples which come to mind. Thus, the area between athletic and nonathletic sport must also be viewed as a continuum linking two ideal types.

According to this typology, the boundaries of sport sociology reach beyond the world of play while at the same time excluding certain forms of play from consideration. A study of those who pursue careers in professional hockey, for instance, would constitute a study in the sociology of both work and sport. The tasks performed by professional athletes can hardly be called leisure or play. The same can be said of college athletes at the "big time" level. Some forms of play that would fall outside the sociology of sport would be dancing, riding a bicycle, sexual intercourse, riding a merry-go-round, taking a walk, and camping, provided these activities are neither competitive nor institutionalized.

In conclusion, it can be said that the sociology of sport is concerned with the activities encompassed by the above typology. It also studies the organizations and institutional frameworks that govern behavior related to sport. As Loy has pointed out, the sport order includes "such organizations as sporting goods manufacturers, sport clubs, athletic teams, national governing bodies for amateur and professional sports, publishers of sport magazines, etc."[18] At a higher level, sport sociology studies the relations between the sport order and the broader institutions of society and culture. The sport order, it should be noted, is itself part of the more encompassing institution of recreation and leisure. The main advantage of the typology of sport developed in this paper is that it builds on earlier formulations but at the same time makes explicit that fact that sport can occur as both work and play.

NOTES

[1]See Johan Huizinga, *Homo Ludens* (Boston: Beacon Press, 1959), pp. 1-27. Roger Caillois, "The Structure and Classification of Games," and *Sport, Culture, and Society,* eds. John W. Loy and Gerald S. Kenyon (London: The Macmillan Company, 1969), pp. 44-45.

[2]John W. Loy, "The Nature of Sport," *Sport, Culture and Society,* eds. John W. Loy and Gerald S. Kenyon (London: The MacMillan Company, 1969), pp. 43-61.

[3]Harry Edwards, *Sociology of Sport* (Homewood, Illinois: The Dorsey Press, 1973), pp. 43-61.

[4]Op. cit., p. 13.

[5]Op. cit., p. 8.

[6]Op. cit., p. 9.

[7]Roger Caillois, for instance, argues that there is a free and impulsive element at the origin of even the most complex and rigidly organized forms of play. Caillois calls this element paidia and distinguishes it from ludus which he feels gives play its structure and discipline. See Caillois, op. cit., p. 50.

The Development of Play in Childhood: An Application of the Classifications of Piaget and Caillois in Developmental Research

Elizabeth D. Mouledoux, Concordia University

There is very little in the literature on children's play which would meet the criteria of developmental study as advanced recently by Joachim Wohlwill (1973), or earlier by Heinz Werner (1957; Werner and Kaplan 1964). Rather, most studies are either differential, comparing behavior at two or more age levels, or experimental, studying the effects of experimental manipulations on behaviours at two or more age levels. Neither of these approaches, Wohlwill argues, is developmental, which involves studying (1) how developmental changes occur with age, that is, over time (thus requiring some type of longitudinal focus), and (2) how change occurs in systems which are developing simultaneously with other developing systems (thus requiring an interdisciplinary approach). This view is consistent with Werner's assumptions of (1) *holism,* that "any activity is dependent upon the context, field, or whole of which it is a constitutive part"; (2) *directiveness,* that "activities...function in the realization of ends imminent in the activity of the organism as a whole"—and includes "the tendency of the organisms to develop towards a relatively mature state"; and (3) *continuity* and *discontinuity,* that "developmental changes necessarily entail both continuity (progressive gradual differentiation) and discontinuity (emergence of new hierarchal structures)." (Werner and Kaplan, 1964: 3-7).

While Piaget's theory of cognitive development—and its associated theory of play (1962)—is widely acknowledged as a developmental theory of play, most research allegedly based upon Piaget's work fails either to use Piaget's own classificatory scheme or to maintain a developmental approach. To take one example, in a recent study Rubin (1974) states as his purpose, "to carefully examine the relationship between Piaget's (1962) play categories, as elaborated by Smilansky (1968), and the child's ability to role-take and to classify" (p. 171). However, the play classification used by Rubin included only four categories: functional play, constructive play, dramatic play, and games with rules. It may be questioned whether these few static categories can be taken to represent Piaget's own classificatory scheme, which includes, besides the formal types themselves, terms reflecting levels of complexity within types and terms designating combinations of formal types.

In addition to the simplification of Piaget's terminology, there is the failure of research to maintain a developmental approach. This seems to be due in part to the demands of research methods which cannot accomodate a developmental approach. For example, Rubin's research noted above, from which he draws conclusions about developmental stages, is cross-sectional research using one-minute time samples in a single setting (nursery school playroom). Similarly, Eifermann's (1971) large-scale computerized playground research, while including vast numbers of subjects over the school years, is of limited applicability to developmental questions because of the methodologically imposed restriction to a single setting (school playgrounds) and the potentially inhibiting time restriction (10 minute recess periods).

While Piaget's theory and classification of play is developmental in nature and more complex than research based upon it would indicate, there is nevertheless reason to think that if properly researched, Piaget's theory would still be found lacking in its presentation of play over the formative years. Even casual observation raises doubts about the completeness of Piaget's classification at school-age, and the literature quickly suggests numerous gaps: Games of vertigo and of chance (Caillois 1961); cooperative children's games (Eifermann 1971); neglect of the complexity of traditional children's games (see, for example, the Opies, 1969); the subordination of play to cognitive development (Sutton-Smith 1966); the neglect of affect (Singer 1973), and, we might add, neglect of content and the social component.

In a previous paper (Mouledoux 1976) I had occasion to note that the work of Roger Caillois (1961) not only offered a comprehensive general theory of play, but also had the rare quality of presenting a clearly defined terminology well adapted to research, although little use has been made of it. Caillois' focus begins where Piaget's leaves off, that is, with play as it approaches a mature state in the school-age child; however, Caillois also includes an implicit principle of development and terminology applicable to earlier forms of play. Caillois' concepts have a dual character, referring to the structures of games, which structures at the same time allow for the expression of basic human impulses and tendencies. And while play is an avenue of personal expression, it is always seen in a social context and as a part of culture. (Games are played by individuals, but they are also cultural products). For such reasons, Caillois' theory seemed an excellent choice to supplement Piaget's more highly articulated developmental study of the young child.

There is no doubt that the study of play suffers from lack of a terminology which can be applied over the range of the developmental period and which is compatible with the nature of play in its mature state. Our purpose and plan, reported here, is to contribute toward developing a suitable terminology by applying the classifications of Piaget and Caillois to the same data. The data will be derived both from naturalistic observations of children aged two to twelve, and interviews, in a wide variety of play settings. Noting in advance what appear to be common lacks in both classifications, other special classifications and exploratory dimensions are included.

Procedure

Developmental psychology students were given verbal instruction in the methods of observational research and interview and in theories and classifications of play. Preliminary instructions to observers included two key methodological concepts, the *play setting* and the *play episode*. The *play setting*, similar to Wright's (1956) behaviour setting, was our point of departure in deploying observers, who were instructed to observe children anywhere they chose, where on rational grounds play was the most likely type of activity to be expected; on the other hand, we also alerted observers to the possibility of observing instances of play in unexpected (non-play) settings and asked them to record these whenever possible. Our concern with this approach was, first, to maintain an openness in observers with regard to what is play and where it takes place, and secondly, to assure a wide sampling of play settings within the area of greater Metropolitan Montreal to which we were restricted for this research.

The second key methodological concept was the *play episode* which was our unit of analysis. A play episode was defined as a self-contained unit of play, of variable duration in time, but consistent as regards structural type, level of complexity, content and social dimension. Observers were alerted to expect that within observational periods, the number of play episodes recorded might vary considerably in relation to age and other subject characteristics, situational influences and the type of play itself. Pragmatically the end of one play episode and the change to another could be recognized when in classifying data from the narrative recording, there arose a need for a different classificatory term on any one of the main components in the appropriate classification and analysis chart. (These charts are included in the summary of instructions for observers which may be found in the Appendix).

The observations took place in three phases, as follows: (1) *Direct Observation of Children, aged two to six years.* Observers were instructed to choose a play setting to observe either a single child playing alone, or a group (in the latter case they were to focus on one child and follow it if the group broke up). In this phase we used ten observers, who recorded activities of a total of 74 children, 51 males and 23 females, ranging from 20 months to six years. The settings included nursery schools, playrooms in homes, bedrooms, backyards, playgrounds, apartment block courtyards. Among non-play settings, observations were made in a hotel lobby, a supermarket, and a shopping centre arcade. (2) *Direct Observation of Children, aged six to twelve years.* The same instructions were given with regard to play settings and the choice of subjects. In this phase records were obtained by 40 observers, on a total of 277 children, 176 males and 101 females, ranging from 6½ to 12 years. Approximately one quarter of the children were observed playing in mixed sex groups, and 19 children were observed playing alone. There were in addition 14 three-to-six-year-olds who were part of older play groups, and there were three instances reported in which one or more adult men were part of a boys' play group. Outdoor play settings chosen by observers included playgrounds, skating rinks, backyards, streets, sidewalks, empty lots, and open fields in suburbs. Among the indoor settings were school gyms, home playrooms, living rooms, bedrooms, and basements. The non-play settings included a restaurant, a church, a kitchen, and a music practice room. (3) *Interview of Children over six years.* Interviewers were instructed to try to find out what the children did "when they could do whatever they wanted" and to avoid using only the terms "play" or "games", which might serve to restrict children in reporting their freely chosen activities. In this phase, 18 researchers interviewed 36 children, 20 male and 16 female between the ages of 6½ and 12 years.

Classification and Analysis

Data, which were recorded in sequential narrative form, were later classified independently by each observer and myself, using the classifications summarized in Table 1. As shown in the Instructions (see Appendix), each observer summarized his or her observations and classifications in appropriate charts for each phase. The writer prepared master charts by age and sex for each of the three phases of the investigation. From inspection of these charts, qualitative comparison was made of the uses and limitations of the various classifications at different age levels. For the present report, analysis of the data was entirely by inspection, as the research question at this point was: When the classifications of Piaget and Caillois are applied to the same data, how do they compare in terms used, and in adequacy of terminology to the data at different age levels?

Table 1. Outline of Classifications and Dimensions
Used in Analysis of Data on Children's Play and Games

Piaget

I. Practice or exercise play (can be either *sensory-motor* or *mental*)
   1) Mere practice - repetition of a skill out of a useful context
   2) Fortuitous combinations - chance patterning of acquired activities
   3) Intentional combinations - planned patterning
   4) Practice play becoming *Construction*
   5) Practice play combined with *Symbolism*
   6) Practice play becoming socialized and developing rules (verges on Game with Rules)

II. Symbolic play
   1) Simple pretending and imitative play - brief isolated episodes
   2) Symbolic combinations (combinations of pretending and imitative episodes into whole scenes)

Table 1. continued

3) Ordered symbolic combinations (like symbolic combinations but with a greater degree of coherence, realism and shared symbolism)
4) Symbolic constructions (like ordered symbolic combinations but with construction or making of things as part of or preparation for the dramatic play)

III. Games with rules - games of competition with
1) either *sensory-motor* combinations *or intellectual* combinations
2) Source: either *traditional,* handed down from one generation to another *or* regulated by spontaneous temporary agreement among players.

Caillois

I. Classification of play and games: includes:

A. Basic types and combined types
1) Agon (Competition)
2) Alea (Chance)
3) Mimicry
4) Ilini (vertigo)
5) Agon (Competition) and alea (chance)
6) Mimicry and vertigo
7) Alea (chance) and vertigo
8) Agon (competition) and mimicry

B. Playful activities which are not games of a basic or combined type may be classified as either:
1) Paidia - undifferentiated, spontaneous, unstructured, exuberant
2) Ludus - mastery of skills, for the sake of the mastery (e.g.: crossword puzzles, yo-yo) or as preparatory to the use of skills in structured games of the basic types

II. Rating for Degree of Discipline (Mastery, Challenge, Control, Enrichment)
Rate structured play and games on a five point scale between the two extremes of Paidia and Ludus

Paidia /________/________/________/________/ Ludus

Social Classifications

I. **Partens** (1929) classification of social play of pre-school children:
1) unoccupied behaviour
2) solitary play
3) onlooker behaviour
4) parallel play
5) associative play
6) cooperative play

II. Games with rules may be classified as follows:
Competitive ____________ Cooperative ____________ Intermediate ____________
Individual__________Team__________One per side__________Central Person__________

III. Social or Collective Symbolism (Describe use of language, rules, roles, gestures, songs, music, chants, rhymes, morals, customs, heroes, fictional characters, etc. as such appear in play)

IV. Corruptions of the play spirit (Caillois) Describe violations of the characteristics of play.

Affective Dimension - Describe in narrative form observed instances of: Aggression, Nurturance, Joyfulness, Inventiveness, Involvement.

Manifest Content - Describe in narrative form, in ordinary language, the theme of the play activity (may be most applicable for games involving mimicry, including both "symbolic play" and traditional games of childhood. (See e.g., Opie, 1969)

Results

In Table 2, we have arranged across from each other in two columns, the terms from Piaget's and from Caillois' classificatory schemes which appeared as counterparts to each other when the classifications were applied to the same data records. As the subscripts show we indicated the classificatory terms which were available in one scheme without a counterpart in the other, and terms in either scheme which were not required by the data, or found to be not useful.

Table 2. A comparison of the classifications of Piaget and Caillois when applied to the same observational data

PIAGET	CAILLOIS
Practice Play	**Paidia to Ludus**
Mere practice play	Paidia
†Fortuitous combinations	
Intentional combinations	Ludus or *Ludus plus vertigo
Practice becoming Construction	Ludus, higher degree
Practice, with Symbolism	Ludus, with Mimicry
Practice, verging on Rules	Ludus, with early forms of Competition and/or Chance
	*Ludus, with Vertigo
	Paidia to Wan
Symbolic Play	**Mimicry**
Simple pretending and Imitative Play	Ludus, early form of Mimicry
†*Five subtypes of above	
Symbolic combinations (dramatic play)	Mimicry (Ludus implicit)
†*Four subtypes of above	
Ordered symbolic combinations	Mimicry (Ludus implicit, higher degree)
Symbolic constructions, verging on art, or work	Mimicry, and Ludus (higher degree than preceding)
Games with Rules	**Ruled Games**
Competitive, with Chance elements	Competition
	*Chance
	Competition and Chance
	*Competition and Mimicry
	Games of Improvisation
Symbolic play: Symbolic combinations or Symbolic Constructions	Mimicry
	*Vertigo
	*Mimicry and Vertigo
	†*Chance and Vertigo

*Available in one of the two classifications only, no counterpart in the other.
†Classification not needed for our data
**This dimension, not available in Piaget's classification, may be comparable to Parten's term *onlooker behavior* and combined with Mimicry, to C. Buhler's Passive Play (e.g., looking at pictures, listening to stories).

Inspection of Table 2 shows that, as different as these two theories are in their approach and method of study, there is considerable overlap in the application of their classifications. It may be seen, however, that Caillois' scheme provided terminology of several types which was required by our data and for which there was no counterpart in Piaget's classification. Among Caillois' terms the only category which had no occasion to use was the combined category of Games of Chance and Vertigo. It may be either that this category was defined too subjectively to be detected by observation, or that in fact this type is not applicable to the kinds of Chance games which school-aged children play; Caillois' empirical reference for this type is to the gambling games of adults. With regard to Piagetian terms which were not used for our data, it must be noted that these terms represented a fineness of distinction not suitable for our methodology; they might, however, prove feasible for intensive longitudinal study of young children.

Similarities between Piaget and Caillois

Before commenting on differences between the two classifications, we should point out that there exist considerable areas of agreement, as indicated in part by Table 2. We found that both classifications included four kinds of concepts or principles: (1) Both have formal concepts defining types of play from a structural standpoint, and there is, moreover, some agreement on the major types which both include, although Piaget lacks some basic types given by Caillois; (2) Both classifications include terms which provide a way, different though they may be, of describing levels of increasing complexity within the same structural type; (3) Both classifications include *combinations* of formal types and a notion of types merging into and changing to other types as a play episode progresses over time; and (4) both provide a way to recognize the tendency of play to combine with or change into other "non-play" forms, such as art or work. This agreement between two otherwise very different theories supports the contention that play study requires a complex and varied terminology. In other words, a few static concepts are not sufficient for the developmental study of play.

For the remainder of the paper, we shall present and discuss some of the differences between the two classifications disclosed by our research, as it bears upon the question of terminology for developmental study. Numerous points of theoretical interest will have to be bypassed for lack of space to consider them.

Practice Play — Piadia and Ludus, Vertigo

Sensori-motor practice play is the only type of play found in infancy, but practice play, both motor and mental, may be seen throughout life whenever a new skill is acquired. Moreover, the developmental sequence, from mere to fortuitous to intentional combinations, is not confined to infancy, but recurs at any age with new skills (Piaget, 1962:117). The repetition of actions, with their inner developmental sequence, "merely for functional pleasure, or for the pleasure obtained from awareness of new powers" (p. 117) is paralleled by Caillois' concept of *paidia and ludus*[1], described as follows: "Such a primary power of improvisation and joy, which I call *paidia,* is allied to the taste for gratuitous difficulty which I propose to call *"ludus."* (Caillois, 1961: 27). This dimension, from spontaneity to inventing such implements as will enrich the activity, we found applicable to data classified as a category of *practice play* by Piaget. However, Caillois' dimension can be used in two ways, one, as a type of playful activity in itself, or two, as an aspect of games of the four basic types, so that specific games of vertigo, mimicry, chance or competition, will reflect varying degrees along the dimension from spontaneity to difficulty and complexity.

Another advantage of Caillois' dimension, *Paidia to Ludus,* is its ability to cope with construction, which, when it is a part of playful activity may be seen as one of the many ways in which persons pursue the tendency to invent and master difficulty. Building, sewing, drawing, making rhymes, improvising dialogue, devising substitutes for real sports equipment, inventing rule variations, collecting information, and so on, are all different ways of enriching play activities. When not a part of play, any of these might become something else, that is, some variety of art, craft, knowledge, or work.

Although the parallels between the two classifications are considerable, one category which we found necessary and which Piaget does not recognize is that of *Vertigo.* While Piaget recognizes practice play becoming construction, combining with symbolism, or verging on rules, he has no category for vertiginous play.

Caillois' terms do present problems. The words themselves, *paidia* and *ludus,* are awkward to handle, but more important, the concept seems to be multi-dimensional and requires further distinctions and clarification.

"Paidia to Wan" — Onlooker Behaviour

The category of "onlooker behaviour" from Parten's (1929) social classification was needed for most preschool recordings and used in several recordings of children over seven. This rapt, alert observation is an integral part of on-going play activity in young children, directed not only toward persons, but toward all kinds of sights and sounds. It deserves consideration as a type of play activity in its own right, and not only as a category of social interaction.

Although not originally included in our outline of classifications, in the process of classifying data we discovered the potential use of Caillois' *Paidia to wan* dimension as a counterpart to Partens' *onlooker behaviour,* but with more theoretical content. Caillois proposes "wan"[2] as a different path than "ludus" for the "metamorphosis of paidia" and identifies it with a civilization like classical China which "unlike western civilization was less directed toward purposive innovation." He compares *wan* to "indefinitely caressing a piece of jade while polishing it, in order to savour its smoothness or as an accompaniment to reverie..." (p. 33). He gives short shrift to a consideration of Western civilization, which does have an ancient tradition of contemplation and still maintains a contemplative ideal however obscured by the modern preoccupation with domination, mastery, and control (e.g., see Dupre, 1976). We suggest that the possibility of alternative paths of development, between invention and mastery, on the one hand, and contemplativeness and appreciation, on the other, is a provocative insight, not without relevance to existing literature in child development (e.g., Kagan's (1966) impulsivity *vs.* reflectiveness, and White's (1976) discovery of the significance of "steady staring" in the development of intelligence), and in the study of leisure (e.g., Pieper's 1952 discussion of leisure in terms of the contemplative attitude).

Symbolism and Rules

It was at the school-age level (7 to 12 years) that the superiority of Caillois' classification was recognized. And this was due not only to Caillois' inclusion of a wider range of basic types — both Vertigo and Chance were necessary categories at this age level — but because of a crucial theoretical difference between the two. Caillois recognizes the persistence of games of mimicry, along with *ruled games,* throughout the 7 to 12 age period, and into maturity, while Piaget represents *symbolic play* as "declining after the age of four" (1962: 145) and being replaced either by games with rules, or by work and "adaptation to reality," as it combines with construction (1962: 145-6). As a result, with Caillois terminology, one can classify Mimicry alone and in combination with games of Competition and Vertigo, and one can acknowledge the frequently accompanying *construction* elements as *ludus;* but, in Piaget's classification, combining a *symbolic play* category with *games with rules* is *theoretically inconsistent.* The fact that in classification we were often forced by the data to make the inadmissable combination of symbolic play and rule games, argues for the inadequacy of Piaget's theory and classification, with regard to symbolism, symbolic play, and rules.

Symbolism, Stages, and Definition of Play

Piaget's understanding of the symbol as egocentric, immature, and replaceable by rational thought and rules, and his tying of "symbolic play" to this understanding of the symbol, has resulted in confusion in terminology and theory, which has influenced many who do not knowingly accept Piaget's approach. Piaget stands among those rationalists described by Dupre (1972) who understand that "rational thought at a certain stage of reflection must take over and substitute for the symbol" (p. 157). And Eliade

(1969) might have been criticizing Piaget when he objected that, "Symbolic thinking is not the exclusive privilege of the child, of the poet, or of the unbalanced mind..." (p. 12).

Further light may be thrown on this problem by examining Werner's (1957) conception of play in the context of symbol formation. Werner writes:

> Make believe play, that is, an essential attitude of playfulness, entails an intention towards representation of something external to the play activity. The older the child becomes, the more this intention comes to the fore, in other words, the more the sphere of playful representation becomes an autonomous domain separated from the sphere of "serious action." (p. 94).

and further on he refers to a study which indicates that

> ...there is a noticeable increase in make-believe behaviours observable in children between the ages of 2 and 4½. (p. 96).

From the above we can see that the emergence of the symbolic function is prior to the emergence of the make-believe attitude, and, the make-believe attitude, correlated with the *intention* of representation, and the separation of the playful representation from the "serious," is essential to *playfulness.* From this, we might suggest that (1) all play assumes the symbolic function and involves a make-believe attitude. The terms "symbolic play" and "make-believe" play are therefore misleading as applied to one type of play alone; and (2) the early forms of play-like activities which precede the emergence of a make-believe attitude, *are not true play;* these forms would include the functional exercise or practice of infancy, and, at a transitional stage, the "simple symbolic and imitation episodes" which emerge in the second year of life. With the onset of a capacity for make-believe, true play begins. This view is in keeping with approaches in the study of language and art, where it is regularly acknowledged that there are presymbolic stages (e.g., vocalization and scribbling) and transitional stages (e.g., the symbolic schema in art; Read, 1943), which precede the beginning of true language and drawing.

Play as a make-believe attitude is in keeping with Huizinga's meaning, for to take play too seriously (as if it were real and serious) or not seriously enough (like the spoilsport) violates the play spirit, and reveals the failure of the make-believe attitude. Caillois, although he seems in the details of his work to be in keeping with this approach, supports the confusion in terminology by distinguishing, in his criteria of play, between "governed by rules" (which included Competition and Chance) and "make believe" (Mimicry and Vertigo). However, he describes the former as "under conventions that suspend ordinary laws," and the latter as "awareness of a second reality" (p. 10), and both of these imply awareness of the not-ordinary and not-real, that is, a make-believe attitude.

Concluding Remarks

Our research reported here has been directed toward a terminology for developmental study which is consistent with a developmental approach and with the manifestations of play over the range of development and in its mature forms. Noting the demands made by developmental study and by the complex nature of play, we chose Piaget's and Caillois' as theories which met these demands in some measure and provide well-developed classification schemes adaptable to research. We compared these two classifications and theories by applying them both to the same data, gathered by a method intended to respect the nature of play and the demands of developmental study. In comparing the outcomes of our classification process, we found significant areas of agreement between the two schemes, particularly with regard to the varied number and kinds of concepts which both have included. Structurally, both classifications provided rough counterparts for the same basic types of play, but their terminologies have different theoretical bases, and Caillois provides a wider variety of terms. Caillois recognizes the play of vertigo and provides a possible approach to analyzing the prevalent "onlooker-behaviour." After school age and the emergence of a capacity for rules, the superiority of the Caillois classification becomes more apparent.

Failures of Piaget's theory to account for the nature of play, particularly evident after the onset of rational thought, can be related to his rationalist conception of the symbol. Revisions in thinking about the symbol and its relationship to play and to the capacity for make-believe, partly in the light of Werner's developmental study of symbol formation, would lead, in our opinion, to reassessment of the "stages" of play—to include early "pre-play" and transitional symbolic forms—and of the definition of play.

Finally, as is obvious, we have had to be selective in what we included and some of our findings could not be presented. The important area of the *content* of play, always neglected by structuralists, including Piaget, requires further exploration and is neglected here for reasons of space. Also unreported are findings concerned with how children's play relates to adult activities and how this relationship varies with age. While we are unable now to pursue many suggestions raised by our research, we believe that our comparison of Piaget and Caillois has raised some questions and has pointed to some directions for further study.

NOTES

[1]Caillois explains that he has chosen the term *paidia* because its root is the word for child (in Greek) and he wishes thereby to convey the undifferentiated, spontaneous, exuberant manifestations of the play instinct (1961: 27-28). On the other hand, *ludus* (from Latin) may be translated as game, sport or school, thus implying discipline, enrichment, training, skill and mastery (1961: 29). While *paidia* is undifferentiated, one may speak of *ludus* "as soon as conventions, techniques and utensils emerge" (p. 29). At this point also, the early forms of competition, chance, mimicry and

vertigo begin to differentiate from the spontaneous, undifferentiated activity denoted by *paidia*. It may be added that in this conception Caillois reveals an implicit assumption of childhood development as progressive differentiation.

[2]Caillois describes in some detail the derivation of the Chinese term *wan* (1961: 27 and 33-35), and its relation to other Chinese terms denoting structured games comparable to the four basic types (i.e., chance, competition, mimicry and vertigo). Caillois concludes (p. 35) that "the channeling of the free energy in *paidia* toward invention (*ludus*) or contemplation (*wan*) manifests an implicit but fundamental and most significant choice (for a culture)."

REFERENCES

Caillois, Roger 1961 *Man, Play and Games*. New York: Free Press. (Translation by M. Barash of Les Jeux et Les Hommes. Paris: Gallimard, 1958).

Dupre, Louis 1972 The Other Dimension. New York: Doubleday & Co.

1976 The Religious Crisis of our Culture: The Yale Reveiw 65 (204-217).

Eifermann, R. 1971 Social Play in Childhood. In *Child's Play*. R. Herron and B. Sutton-Smith, Eds. New York: J. Wiley, pp. 270-297.

Eliade, Mircea 1969 *Images and Symbols*. New York: Sheed and Ward. (Translated by P. Mairet, from the French. Paris: Gallimard, 1952).

Kagan, J. 1966 Generality and dynamics of conceptual tempo. *Journal of Abnormal Psychology* 71: 17-24.

Mouledoux, Elizabeth 1975 The Observational Study of Play; A Guide for Developmental Psychology Students. Unpublished.

1976 Theoretical Considerations and a Method for the Study of Play. *In* The Anthropological Study of Play: Problems and Prospects, (Proceedings of the First Annual Meeting of the Association for the Anthropological Study of Play). D. F. Lancy and B. A. Tindall, Eds., Cornwall, N.Y.: Leisure Press.

Opie, Iona, and Peter Opie 1969 *Children's Games in Street and Playground*. Oxford: Clarendon Press.

Parten, M.B. 1929 *An Analysis of Social Participation, Leadership, and Other Factors in Pre-School Play Groups*. Unpublished Ph.D. Thesis, University of Minnesota.

Piaget, Jean 1962 *Play, Dreams and Imitation in Childhood*. New York: W. W. Norton (Translation of La Formation du Symbole chez l'Enfant, 1945).

Pieper, Josef 1963 *Leisure: The Basis of Culture*. New York: New American Library. (Translated by Alexander Dru, from the German, 1952).

Read, Sir Herbert 1967 The Art of Children. In *The World of the Child*. Toby Talbot, Ed. New York: Doubleday (First published in Education through Art, 1943).

Rubin, K. H. and R. L. Maioni 1975 Play Preference and its Relationship to Egocentricism: Popularity and Classification Skills in Preschoolers. *Merrill-Palmer Quarterly* 21: 171-179.

Singer, J. L. 1973 *The Child's World of Make-Believe: Experimental Studies of Imaginative Play*. New York: Academic Press.

Sutton-Smith, Brian 1966 Piaget on Play: A Critique. *Psychological Review* 73: 104-110.

Werner, Heinz 1957 *Comparative Psychology of Mental Development*. New York: International Universities Press.

Werner, Heinz and Bernard Kaplan 1963 *Symbol Formation*. New York: J. Wiley and Sons.

White, Burton 1976 Bright Kids Exposed to Stimulus. *Montreal Star*, February 25.

Wohlwill, Joachim 1973 *The Study of Behavioral Development*. New York: Academic Press.

Wright, H. G. 1956 Psychological development in Midwest. *Child Development* 27: 265-286.

APPENDIX
INSTRUCTIONS FOR OBSERVATIONS AND INTERVIEWS

1. Direct Observation of Children aged 2 - 6 years in Play Settings

Observations:

(a) Remember to record the necessary background information (time, place, setting and subject characteristics)

(b) Record a minimum of three separate observation periods, of at least 15 minutes each; do narrative recording (what you actually see and hear, with any inferences bracketed, written in ordinary descriptive language)

(c) Remember to make frequent notations of time in the margin, and to try to mark the time of change from one *play episode* to another.

Classification and Analysis of Observational Data:

(a) Transcribe raw data (typed or clearly written) marking off each play episode with red pencil.

(b) Analysis and classification of data should then be summarized into a chart, as below:

No. of Episode	Time	Sex and age of each player	Roles/ Imitations/ Actions	Objects used	Classifications			Affective Dimension
					Piaget	Callois	Partens	

(c) Comments, as needed, to clarify and elaborate issues of note or problems in data collection or analysis.

2. Direct Observation of Children aged 7 - 12 years in Play Settings

Observations:

(a) Record background information

(b) Record a minimum of three separate observation period, of at least 15 minutes each; use narrative recording

(c) Record time at beginning, when there is a change from one play episode to another, if this occurs, and at the end of the observation period. Note if play episode is ongoing and if it continues before and after your observation period.

Classification and Analysis of Observational Data:

(a) Transcribe raw data

(b) Summarize your data and analysis in a chart, as follows:

Background Information			Activity		Classifications			
Age(s) and Sex(es)	Language(s)	Place	(Name or describe briefly)	Manifest Content	Piaget	Caillois Type(s)	Social Degree of Discipline	Affective

APPENDIX continued

(c) Comments, as needed

3. Interview of Children over 6 years concerning "Free Time" and Play Activities

Interviews:

(a) Interview two children, preferably a boy and a girl.

(b) Interview in an informal, conversational, casual manner. DO NOT probe or insist if child is reticent. Tell the child and, if applicable, the child's parent(s) what you are doing. Remember you are trying to find out what children do when they do whatever they like; what they play when alone and with other children, at school and at home, indoors and out, in summer and winter, and so forth. Try to get the child to describe in detail unfamiliar games and activities, variations on standard games, self-invented games, chants and songs accompanying games, etc. Do not prolong interview beyond the period of the child's interest; you may, if possible, continue on more than one occasion.

(c) Record relevant background information

Classification and Analysis:

(a) Summarize and classify the "free-time" activities of each child on a chart as follows: (Under "Other" comment on "non-play" activities).

Activity (Name or describe briefly)	Manifest Content	Classifications			
		Piaget	Caillois	Social	

(b) Comments: (1) Choose at least three of the more unusual or unfamiliar games or activities listed in the chart and describe in detail. (2) Comment as needed to elucidate any matters of interest or note in the interview.

The Imaginary Playmate and Other Imaginary Figures of Childhood

Ernestine H. Thompson and Tanya F. Johnson, Augusta College

Just because we have terms for it doesn't make the humanization process any easier—to understand or bring about. What we are really trying to explain is how the infant develops into a human being able to perform as a functioning member of his society. Society has its agents—tangible and intangible. All the child has to do is construct his social reality, a world he can live in because he understands its meanings; and, of course, at the same time construct and, hopefully, internalize his own self identity, and become a distinct personality, aware of and able to relate to self and others.

One medium at the child's disposal is make-believe or symbolic play. This capacity for transcending and thereby being able to attach meaning to and shape empirical reality which is recognized in language development is also a vital ingredient in ludic symbolism. The ability to pretend, imagine and create are essential and often overlooked parts in the process that makes us human. Play is a complex and large tapestry. There are many strands and threads woven together into a pattern that is not easily separated. One vivid thread that appears quite frequently in make-believe play is the phenomenon of the "imaginary other"—an entity, either human, animal or object, existing only in the mind of the individual, with whom that individual has sustained interaction, and over whom the individual exercises control.

Approximately one in four Americans has had an Imaginary Other (I.O.) at some time in his life.[1] Although a relatively common performance, this occurrence has received backpage and mixed reviews from educators, physicians, psychologists, psychiatrists, anthropologists and sociologists. Most research has been done by psychologists and psychiatrists using the case study approach. Only eight scientific, systematic studies have been published.[2] Recognizing the limited efforts in relating the nature and use of this phenomenon to the socialization process, this research attempts to explore these areas. The second part of this exploration will compare the imaginary playmate with consensual imaginary figures perpetuated by American society as a means of controlling the child in some way (Santa Claus, Tooth Fairy, Bogey Man, Easter Bunny and Sandman).

I. THE IMAGINARY PLAYMATE

An interesting consequence of a review of the eight systematic studies is that in spite of their differing orientations, time of research, techniques, size and composition of samples, their conclusions (six of the eight used control groups) found the construction occurring in approximately one in four cases. They all agreed that I.O. creators tend to be brighter than average, that more females than males have or report having I.O.'s, that most I.O. creators are not only children, and that most have real companions available for play. In summary, most writers agree that I.O. subjects are not lonely, create I.O.'s for reasons unknown to them but later assign warm, affiliative roles to their I.O.'s, and that such constructions may have some bearing on later life behavior of I.O. subjects. Recent research that we have done in this area would support all of these conclusions. In fact, our research based on demographic questionnaires, distributed to Augusta College and Paine College students, and detailed, in-depth interviews with post-I.O. subjects and their parents lends at least tentative support to our general hypotheses that (1) Togetherness, rather than loneliness, is the cause of I.O. construction. (2) The imaginary other does play discrete roles. (3) There is an ongoing consistency in the level of "talkativeness" of imaginary other subjects as a response to problem solving and interpersonal associations in later life. Therefore, interaction with the Imaginary Other is a kind of anticipatory socialization.

The I.O. phenomena cannot be understood outside of the interactional milieu in which it exists. Svendsen (1934), for example, says, "...it is essential that the phenomenon be interpreted always against the background of the specific social situation, particularly the child's social relationships." This has directed our theoretical approach, methodology and techniques.

The Theoretical Perspective

The socio-psychological characteristics of the imaginary other require a rigorous and comprehensive theory that will be able to articulate the mental process which permits the creation of an unseen other existing only in the mind's eye, be able to establish the mechanism through which this phenomenon is turned outward into the interactional sphere and is incorporated into the socialization process, be able to demonstrate how the I.O. operates as a separate entity, discern how this association with the I.O. serves to integrate the individual into real experiences and also effectively handle the unique, unpredictable aspects of the I.O. construction. No other theory seems to manage all of these criteria better than symbolic interactionalism.

The dimensions of the theory which help to explain imaginary constructions and their relationship to the individual and society are the reflexive process, role-taking, objects, "me" and "I" respectively. In briefly defining and using these terms we have used an eclectic approach.

Reflexive Process — The central variable in symbolic interactionism is the *self*. It is both a subject and an object. Becoming an object to ourself is called the reflexive process. As a consequence of this process we can make indications to ourselves—hold conversations in the mind. According to representatives of symbolic interactionism, the construction of an unseen other can be viewed as a part of a larger process wherein we talk to ourselves in order to know who we are and where we are in relation to the external world.

Role-taking — The socialization process may be briefly defined as the development of the self. The crucial mechanism for behavioral transitions toward this end is what Mead (1962) calls role-taking—being able to internalize the attitudes of the organized community by putting yourself in the place of others. Both Cooley (1922) and Mead agree that the I.O. provides a representation of the social group. It is, however, a unique representation because the individual writes the script. They also agree that this is a universal occurrence and its chief function is the building of the self into role-taker. Because of the insulation and isolation from real encounters we can more accurately characterize this relationship as a kind of anticipatory socialization.

Object — The interesting question posed by the I.O. construction is how, when the I.O. exists in the child's mind, it can become a separate entity. Mead's understanding of object is useful here. According to Mead, objects are human constructs. Once the individual has created an I.O., it acquires the status of an object capable of functioning as an other. Because of the unique aspect of its creation and resultant possibilities for manipulation of roles we are more informed about what the individual desires in and from this special relationship and just how the interaction is arranged to achieve these ends.

The "Me" — Once the I.O. becomes a separate entity it is a viable source of role performance. Therefore, in some ways and to some degree, it represents the "me" — the objective, meaningful, predictable aspect of the self which comes into the consciousness of the individual by means of enculturation. Internalizing the "me" is the foundation of self-consciousness. In referring to the source and composition of the "me" symbolic interactionists use such terms as *generalized other* and *significant other.* In keeping with the jargon employed by some symbolic interactionists, we have divided roles of the "other" into *Generalized Other* (GO) (sanctions of the group demanding compliance, but not requiring a social relationship), *Role Specific Other* (RSO) (evaluation by others which the individual actively seeks, but again requires no real social relationship to be manifested in the execution of the role), and *Orientational Others* (OO) (close personal affiliation where sanctions and evaluations are subordinated to a dynamic, open, relatively unpredictable interaction between the subject and the object.)[3]. In other words we have classified GO as rule giver roles, RSO as audience roles, and OO as companionate roles. These designations provide empirical criteria for determining exactly what roles imaginary others play.

The "I" — The "I" has been defined as the indeterminant part of the self that responds to the "me"; but, itself, is spontaneous and unpredictable. This dimension of self facilitates unique reactions to the generalized and particular others. It is a recognition and acknowledgement of the "I" of the self that enables us to approach and understand the unpredictable emergence, the changing and multiple roles played and the departure of the I.O. in the subject-I.O. relationship.

Methodology

Objectives and Hypotheses

The objective of this research is two-fold—to determine to what degree the imaginary other, through the child's play, serves to help the child with social-cultural-psychological reality; and to determine how this type of imaginary construction compares with the nature and use of specific consensual imaginary figures (C.I.F.)—Santa Claus, Bogey Man, Sandman, Easter Bunny, and the Tooth Fairy—that are used primarily in family interaction relationships. Within this framework there are several specific objectives which have guided this investigation: (1) to collect information about the origin, first occurrence and child's actual play involvement with the I.O.; (2) to ascertain the roles children assign to their I.O. and the implications of these designations in the child's socialization process; (3) to determine the degree to which the child actually defines the I.O. as real; (4) to determine the circumstances that surround the departure of the I.O. and the child's and parents' involvement and attitude toward this leaving; (5) to examine retrospectively the subject's attitude toward the I.O. construction and relationship; and (6) to determine the degree of belief that exists in, the roles assigned to, and the parental use of consensual imaginary figures that are well-known to American children. These objectives have generated four specific hypotheses which will be tested in this study.

Hypothesis 1 — Although the socio-cultural system provides the child with meaning and examples of imaginary figures, the creation, image and control of the imaginary playmate are determined and uniquely defined by the child.

Hypothesis 2 — Children with the I.O.s tend to assign concrete roles to them and provide them with characteristics which will allow the I.O. to function as real entities that play a role in anticipatory socialization. They become significant others.

Hypothesis 3 — Although they serve real purposes I.O.s nevertheless are constructed as play (pretend) objects; the duration and intensity of involvement as well as departure are under the control of the child. For this reason we would expect indifference or no sense of loss at the departure of the I.O.

Hypothesis 4 — C.I.F.s, unlike the I.O., represent collective norms, values and ideology and are used basically within the context of the family to teach and perpetuate these (a form of social control.) Therefore, they become generalized others.

In-Depth Interviews

In order to learn everything we could about the I.O. phenomenon and the social environment in which it occurs, a non-probability, purposive sample was selected. It included 59 individuals who have had I.O.s at one time in their lives but are no longer engaged in the relationship, and their parents. Our interviewees were located through personal contact and media advertising in the Augusta, Georgia area. They range in age from 6 to 67; 47 are female and 12 male. At the time of the I.O. construction they lived in various sections of the U.S. and abroad. It should be emphasized that the persons interviewed were those who initially volunteered or willingly agreed to be interviewed. Therefore, they should be expected to reflect a positive bias toward the I.O. phenomenon and quite possibly toward that period of their childhood. We also felt it was important to get information and recollections from both the subject and his parents in order to get a more comprehensive input. Interview schedules containing 213 questions for subjects and parents (in most cases this proved to be the mother) respectively were administered over two interview sessions. Each interview took approximately one and a half hours per respondent. Therefore interviewers spent about six hours with each family.

Imaginative Figures and Play Questionnaire

One hundred and eighty Augusta College and Paine College students responded to an Imaginative Figures and Play Activities Questionnaire. These questionnaires elicited information in four general areas: (1) degree of familiarity, importance, parental acceptance and source of information about generally imaginary figures—King Arthur, Paul Bunyan, angels, etc.; (2) degree of belief in, perceived function and parental use of the five C.I.F.s that we have designated as essentially family-interactional imaginary-creatures, (3) questions about imaginative play and behavior and (4) general demographic information.

Findings

Information about the Origin, Source and First Occurrence of the I.O.

In response to the direct question, "How did N. become your playmate?", twenty-one subjects said the I.O., "Just came" or "was there one day." ("She came during a tea party.") Twenty-two said they thought it up or consciously created it. ("I needed a husband to play house." "I made her up to have a friend.") Sixteen subjects could not recall how the I.O. came into being. In discussing the introduction of the I.O. to the family, 11 parents and children could not recall the circumstances and 10 subjects reported that they did not tell anyone about their I.O. until some time after its departure. Of the 49 parents who knew about the I.O., 27 found out by observing the child's behavior while 22 knew because the child told them about it. Generally, neither the parents nor the subjects were very clear about the exact occasion on which the family first met the I.O., but a few have vivid recollections. One father discovered the I.O. just before he almost sat on him. One family was informed during a car trip that Teeny Ghost was flying along outside so her litter (imaginary babies) could rest in the back seat. All the information we have gathered from the subjects and parents about the origin, source and first appearance of the I.O. supports the hypothesis that the I.O., while conceivable because of general cultural conditions, seems to come in a rather unique way from the mind of the child and that no specific cultural or social causes can be pinpointed to account for its occurrence. The I.O. source might well be explained in terms of the "I" aspect of the self—the unpredictable, spontaneous element that can only know what has occurred after the occurrence.

Characteristics of I.O.s and Concrete Roles They Play

Before we specify the nature of the roles attributed to I.O.s and how they meet certain needs, it might be well to describe the actual characteristics imputed to I.O.s that enable them to function as real entities (objects) allowing the child to anticipate real life roles and role relationships. We found that most frequently the I.O. was a human being (52 human, 4 animals and 3 others—ghost, talking star and fuzzy ball). Twenty-five I.O.s were female; 21 male; and 9 were neuter or mixed. Thirty-one I.O.s were the same age as the child; 15 were older; 6 younger; 3 varied in age; 1 had no age; and 8 subjects did not recall the age of their I.O. In general they tended to be very similar in likes, dislikes and abilities. Although a few subjects reported their I.O.s were always with them, we found that I.O.s lived in a variety of places including other houses in the neighborhood, outside, in the child's room, under the bed, in a shoe box, in the washroom and in the wall. One I.O. hung out in the school yard for recess activities and one played outside but came in the house occasionally to break things. The life span of the I.O. ranged from 6 months to over 4 years (average—slightly over 2 years).

When subjects were asked if their imaginary other played a specific role or roles, 57 of the 59 answered affirmatively. Seventy percent of the former assigned more than one role to the I.O. Figure 1 presents hierarchical arrangements of reported roles played by the I.O. First, each role was classified in terms of social relationships divided into Generalized Other (GO) — rule giver; Role Specific Other (RSO) — audience; or Orientational Other (OO) — companion. Therefore role classifications move from the impersonal to the most personal associations. Then within these categories, sub-roles were placed in a hierarchical order from the most general performance to the most specific. Our objective was not to determine how many I.O.s reflect the GO, RSO and OO, but, rather, the degree to which the several transactions between the I.O. and the subject represent the varieties of role performances outlined in Figure 1. When we examine this frequency of role interaction, the data show a number of interesting results. Eighty-seven percent of the roles fell within the Significant Other (RSO, OO) categories. Fifty-nine percent represented the OO exclusively. Therefore, we can say that most subjects saw the I.O. as a close, warm and loving companion who made few demands. Conversely, only 13% of the roles specified represented the GO. We must assume then that I.O.s do not act primarily as cultural mediators whose obligations are to make the subject a good working member of the society.

Actual Play Involvement with I.O., and Its Departure

What did the child and the I.O. actually do together? Thirteen subjects reported that talking was the only activity ("things that bothered me"; "what would be fun to do"). Twenty-three said play was the only activity (games, tea parties, chase, explore); 14 said they both talked and played with their I.O.s and 9 reported engaging in other activities such as—just being together, eating, traveling, riding. In all the subjects treated their I.O.s as "real" objects with whom they could engage in real interaction unique only in the aspect that the child was in control of the situation. Furthermore, all of the subjects labelled the relationship as happy and satisfying. Yet our data yields an interesting reaction to the departure of the I.O. With the exception of 4 subjects who were somewhat sad and 5 parents who were very relieved, the departure of the I.O. met with rather overwhelming indifference from the remainder of parents and subjects. For any number of reasons ("lost interest", "we moved") and in a variety of ways ("just disappeared or was gone one day", "faded away", "flushed down the john and never returned.") The I.O. disappeared leaving behind pleasant memories but no profound regrets. We would suggest that the feeling of indifference that seemed to accompany the I.O.s' leaving can best be explained in terms of the unique nature of this phenomenon. The I.O. is created by the child. He gives it shape and meaning and determines the nature and intensity of the relationship. There comes a time—perhaps the

Figure 1. Roles Played by the Imaginary Other

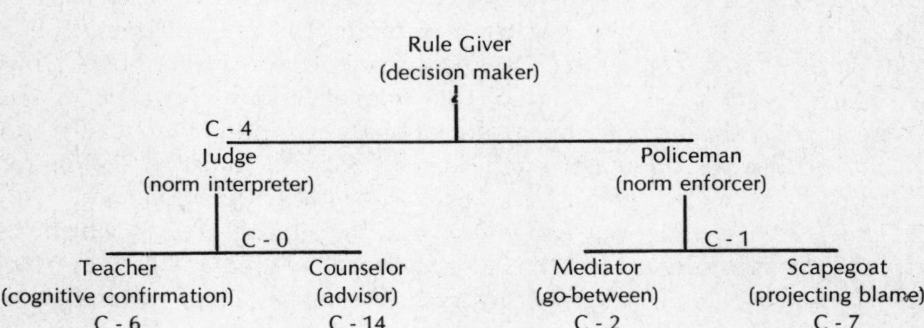

II. Role Specific Other C - 76 (28%)

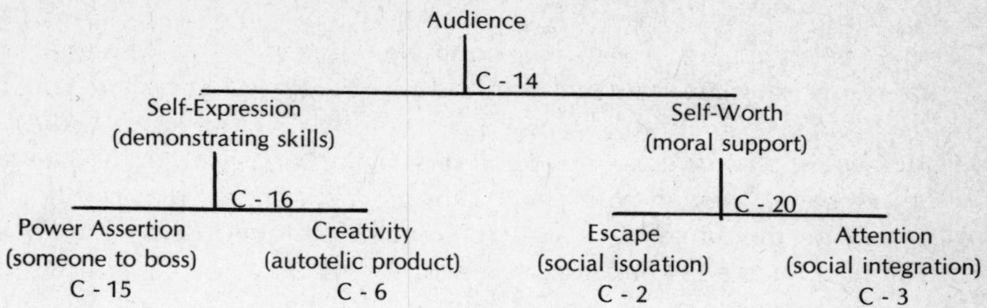

III. Orientational Other C - 159 (59%)

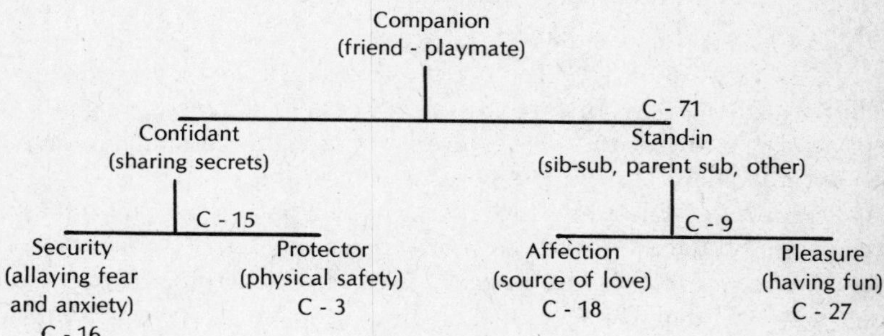

*This refers to the frequency with which children report the I.O. plays this specific role in each of the three sections. Within each section there is a breakdown of this total into one of the seven roles to which the role more clearly applies.

**This figure represents the percentage of roles within each of the sections.

result of social and parental sanctions against too much pretense, new activities and friends or just maturity—when the child no longer needs to be so in control of his relationships or when new experiences dominate his attention. The I.O. goes—often unnoticed by the child—when he is ready for it to depart. It has served its purpose; it was never real and the real world takes precedence. It would seem, furthermore, that the little feeling evoked by the departure of the I.O. would support the hypothesis that the creation, intensity of the relationship and purposes served as well as the departure of the I.O. are under the control of the child.

II. CONSENSUAL IMAGINARY FIGURES IN AMERICAN CULTURE

Probably all societies have created, borrowed and used imaginary figures that become associated with the family unit and are used by parents to provide solidarity, teach norms and values and also as a means of social control. The C.I.F.s we have selected to examine are Santa Claus, the Easter Bunny, the Sandman, Tooth Fairy and the Bogey Man. Although these figures range in origin from ancient European lullabies and general folklore (Bogey Man, Sandman) to a religious renewal symbol (the Easter Bunny) to distinctive American versions of traditional figures and lore (Santa Claus and the tooth Fairy), they all have several things in common. They have for the most part become a part of family interaction customs (ritual, ceremonies, and stories), they are well-known to most American children; and they are perceived and used as sources of rewards and punishment, pleasure and fear. They give as well as take and with the exception of the Bogey Man (a fearful taker) are all associated with rewards—gifts, eggs, sand for pleasant sleep and dreams, and money for teeth.

Findings Source of Information

We asked the 180 respondents to the Imaginary Creatures Questionnaire to tell us where they first heard about certain imaginary figures. Their responses in terms of the figures used in this research and in comparison with the imaginary playmate were rather revealing.

The figures in Table 1 reveal that C.I.F.s are a part of our cultural heritage passed on through the family—the primary source of information. It is interesting to note that the Bogey Man is learned through peer contact essentially and that the Sandman is the most unfamiliar of the imaginary figures. This may be an indication of the reported decline in story-telling and other customary parent bed-time customs. The fact that all but 6% of our subjects reported that they had heard of the I.O. outside the family and 83% have no idea where they first heard of such a phenomenon would again lend support to the suggestion that this kind of construction is created spontaneously by the child as a response to the socialization process.

Table 1. Source of Information about Imaginary Figures

	Parents	Siblings	Friends	School	Church	Books	T.V.	Movies	Other	Never Heard Of	Don't Recall
I.O.*	3**	3	15	4	-1	3	3	10	9	21	83
Santa Claus	78	9	4	1	-1	0	0	0	1	-1	2
Bogey Man	35	23	25	1	1	-1	0	0	1	3	8
Easter Bunny	72	8	6	2	1	3	0	0	2	1	5
Sand Man	42	5	10	5	0	3	5	0	0	13	15
Tooth Fairy	81	7	7	1	2	-1	1	0	-1	1	3

*Twenty-eight percent of the questionnaire respondents reported they had I.O.s as children. As a group they differed in no other aspects from the other respondents.
**Numbers represent *percentage* of respondents who indicated the listed sources as providing them with first information about the figures. The totals for each figure will be more than 100% since several respondents listed more than one source.

The Reality of Imaginary Figures

Table II. provides some preliminary evidence for the degree of control the five family interactional cultural imaginary figures have over the child as compared with the I.O. Whereas the subjects believed that the *imaginary other* was, in fact, imaginary (data that can be supported by our other research with I.O. subjects) and therefore incapable of exercising actual control over the child; in the majority of cases, the C.I.F.s were believed to be real or at least half real rather than imaginary. Since we find that parents and siblings are primarily responsible for the introduction of the C.I.F. to the child and that subsequently the child finds them credible figures, we must assume that through them the family can exert a good deal of sociocultural control.

Table II. Perceived Realness of Imaginary Figures

	I.O.	Santa	Bogey Man	Sandman	Easter Bunny	Tooth Fairy
Real	34%	90%	37%	27%	74%	67%
Half Real	8%	9%	48%	46%	17%	24%
Imaginary	58%	1%	15%	27%	9%	9%

The Functions of Imaginary Figures

Subjects were asked about the roles they understood the I.O. and the C.I.F.s played or the functions they served. We have already noted the overwhelming representation of significant other roles which appeared in the performance of the I.O. vis-a-vis the child. Table III. shows that the subjects believed that C.I.F.s function in the same way. The exception to this is, of course, the Bogey Man whose apparent penchant for evil and wronggoing would automatically rule out manifestation of significant other behavior.

Table III. Subjects' Interpretation of Functions Performed by Imaginary Figures

	I.O.	Santa	Bogey Man	Sandman	Easter Bunny	Tooth Fairy
GO	13%	16%	72%	21%	6%	7%
RSO	28%	4%	28%	75%	13%	7%
OO	59%	80%	0%	4%	81%	86%

In sum, both the I.O. and the C.I.F. function as significant other and primarily as orientational other. Whether parents and other cultural agents perpetuate these forms as a way of binding themselves more closely to their children, to compensate for gaps in the parent-child relationship, or as a pleasant way to ease the child through the potential traumas of socialization, is not clear. These issues should provide interesting and valuable avenues for further research.

Parental Usage of Cultural Imaginary Figures

Besides considering the functions served by imaginary figures, we wanted to know how subjects felt their parents used these figures—to teach some lesson (GO perspective); to give the child a sense of self-worth or attention (RSO); or to provide the child with an affectionate friend (00). In Table IV., we find a different breakdown from Table III. Whereas the Bogey Man and Santa had opposing functions in Table III., when they are viewed in terms of parental usage, both are seen as representations of the generalized other (figures outside of the child's control—in the case of the Bogey Man a punishment and Santa a reward). The remaining three categories of Sandman, Easter Bunny and Tooth Fairy are distributed rather uniformly among the three areas. Clearly, the Tooth Fairy becomes an audience (a source of attention) when she brings the child money for his tooth. Therefore, it is logical for subjects to believe that their parents used these figures as RSO.

Although we cannot confirm the hypothesis that C.I.F.s operate as generalized other, we can say they are seen by children as devices whereby parents can maintain a considerable degree of control over the child, and, for the most part, fill categorical roles that are not unlike those of the I.O.

Table IV. Subjects' Interpretation of Parental Usage of Cultural Figures

	I.O.	Santa	Bogey Man	Sandman	Easter Bunny	Tooth Fairy
GO	N.A.*	52%	80%	26%	30%	26%
RSO	"	33%	3%	38%	41%	51%
OO	"	15%	17%	36%	29%	23%

*Not applicable - Studies we have done with I.O. subjects reveal that children do not feel that their parents use the I.O. in any manner. Actually most parents have no or very limited involvement with their childs' I.O.

Discussion

This research has raised a number of questions and no definite answers. Further work might well consider the following questions: (1) Is the I.O. phenomenon a universal occurrence as Cooley and George Herbert Mead suggest; or are Margaret Mead and Bettleheim correct in their assessment of it as a culture-bound event? (2) With what frequency does this construction take place in other cultures, how is it viewed, to what degree is it accepted and integrated into the socialization process, and does it play a part in family interactional relationships? (3) Does the appearance of the I.O. depend on subject's age or does it manifest itself throughout the life cycle? (4) What are the significant C.I.F.s employed in other sociocultural systems? and, (5) Is there are correlation between C.I.F.s and the I.O. in those cultures which demonstrate both events? The research possibilities seem limitless and for this reason we must say—in the end is our beginning.

NOTES

[1]Most child development texts cite statistics from one fourth to one third. The systematic literature shows that at least one fourth of their sample had imaginary companions. Our own preliminary research with college students and nursery school children not reported here show that at least one in four members of the cluster samples had imaginary companions at some time in their lives. Therefore, we feel relatively safe extrapolating this figure and inferring that such a numerical presentation would be found in the society at large. (These data only refer to studies done in the United States.)

[2]These studies, listed alphabetically, include: Ames and Learned (1949); Hurlock and Burstein (1932); Jersild, Markey and Jersild (1933); Manosevitz, Prentice and Wilson (1973); Svendson (1934); Vostrovsky (1895); and Wingfield (1947).

[3]For a distinction between Role Specific Other and Orientational Other see Denzin (1972); for a delineation of the dimensions of the orientational other and a characterization of it in contrast to the reference group see Kuhn (1964).

BIBLIOGRAPHY, INCLUDING REFERENCES USED BUT NOT CITED

Ames, Louise Bates and Janey Learned 1946. "Imaginary Companions and Related Phenomena." *The Journal of Genetic Psychology,* 69, 147-167.

Bender, Lauretta and Frank B. Vogel 1941. "Imaginary Companions of Children." *American Journal of Orthopsychiatry,* 11, 55-66.

Blumer, Herbert 1969. "Sociological Implications of the Thought of George Herbert Mead." *Sociological Theory.* Ed. Walter Wallace. Chicago: Aldine.

Burlingham, Dorothy T. 1945. "The Fantasy of Having a Twin." *The Psychoanalytic Study of the Child,* 1, 205-210.

Cooley, Charles Horton. *Human Nature and the Social Order* 1922. New York: Charles Scribner's Sons.

Denzin, Norman K. 1972. "The Significant Others of a College Population." *Symbolic Interaction, A Reader in Social Psychology.* Eds. J.G. Manis and B.N. Meltzer. Boston: Allyn and Bacon.

Fraiberg, Selma 1959. *The Magic Year.* New York: Scribners.

Goffman, Erving 1963. *Behavior in Public Places.* New York: Free Press.

Harriman, Philip 1937. "Some Imaginary Companions of Older Subjects." *American Journal of Orthopsychiatry,* 7, 368-370.

Hurlock, E.B. and M. Burstein 1932. "The Imaginary Playmate: A Questionnaire Study." *Journal of Genetic Psychology,* 41, 380-392.

James, William 1961. *Psychology, A Briefer Course.* New York: Harper Torchbook.

Jersild, Arthur T. 1968. *Child Psychology.* Englewood Cliffs: Prentice-Hall.

Jersild, A.T. and F.V. Markey and C.L. Jersild 1933. "Children's Fears, Dreams, Wishes, Daydreams, Likes, Dislikes, Pleasant and Unpleasant Memories." *Child Development Monograph,* no. 12. New York: Teachers College, Columbia University.

Kuhn, Manford H. 1964. "The Reference Group Reconsidered." *Sociological Quarterly,* 5, 5-24.

Manosevitz, Martin and Norman Prentice and Frances Wilson 1973. "Individual and Family

Correlates of Imaginary Companions in Pre-School Children." *Developmental Psychology,* 8, 72-79.
Mead, George Herbert 1962. *Mind, Self and Society.* Chicago: Chicago Press.
Nagara, Humberto 1969. "The Imaginary Companion: Its Significance for Ego Development and Conflict Solution." *The Psychoanalytic Study of the Child,* 24, 165-196.
Schaeffer, Charles 1969. "Imaginary Companions and Creative Adolescents." *Developmental Psychology,* 1, 747-749.
Standard Dictionary of Folklore, Mythology and Legend. Vol. I and II. New York: Funk and Wagnalls Co. (1950).
Stone, L. Joseph and Joseph Church 1968. *Childhood and Adolescence.* New York: Random House.
Sutherland, Margaret 1971. *Everyday Imagining in Education.* London: Routledge and Kegan, Paul.
Svendsen, Margaret. "Children's Imaginary Companions." *Archives of Neurology and Psychiatry,* 33 (1934), 985-999.
Vostrovsky, Clara 1845. "A Study of Imaginary Companions." *Education,* 15, 393-398.
Wolf, Eric R. 1964. "Santa Claus: Notes on a Collective Representation." *Process and Pattern in Culture.* ed. Robert A. Manners. Chicago: Aldine Publishing Company.

Towards an Anthropology of Play

Brian Sutton-Smith, Teachers College, Columbia University

At the 1972 meeting of the American Anthropological Association, in a symposium on play, Margaret Mead presented the opinion that from any worthwhile scientific point of view, anthropologists had never really studied the subject. There were a few records here and there of high quality, there were the many accounts in the Human Relations Area Files, but in general, these records did not tell you how this play was functioning in the lives of the players. It was too cursory to allow any very clear interpretations in most cases.

Unfortunately, although there has been more activity on this subject in psychology, the interpretation might well be the same. For both cases, I think there are at least two reasons. First, there has been the general neglect in social science of the expressive and non serious subject-matters, a neglect there is now some signs will be remedied. Secondly, there is the inherent difficulty in studying these subject matters. They tend to be ephemeral. They tend more easily to freeze under observation. Thirdly, they are related to the rest of life in ways we are not easily able to understand. Because of our work oriented way of life which makes us see the world in characteristic ways, it seems particularly difficult for us to generate a theoretical framework which is appropriate to play. In the face of play we are like anthropologists in a strange place, with a strange group and in a state of culture shock.

In our book, *The Study of Games* (Wiley, 1971) Eliot Avedon and I reviewed the major work of the early anthropologists, in particular the work of Tylor and Culin who used games largely as a part of their larger arguments over cultural diffusion versus the independent invention of cultural traits. In the same book we demonstrated that early folklorists also used games in a similar tendentious way believing that through games scientists could reconstruct the character of early history. The names of the American scholar, William Newall, and the British folklorists, Gomme, Betts, and Spence are remembered in this light. Even the more recent British folklorists Peter and Iona Opie give us a version of the same notion, when they say that although games may not be used to reconstruct the past, they can at least be used to show the continuity with the past. They say, "From this point of view the study of games remains important, not for the purpose of reconstructing history, but for the purpose of illustrating the continuity of human nature." (Avedon and Sutton-Smith, 1971, p. 161). Let me say of the Opies that their interest in what they term "Child Life and Literature" to which they devote almost every day of both their lives is a totally admirable preoccupation. Their home in England is a most impressive library of everything associated with children in the history of recent centuries. More than any one else I know they seem to realize that the changing treatment of children is a focal point for understanding the history of civilization.

But, my point here, is that like Tylor and Gomme, they perpetuate the notion that there is one *language of play and games,* and that we can understand what that language is simply by putting those plays and games on record. If we could actually achieve such a goal, then Margaret Mead's skeptical review of the facts would be out of order. But, of course, she is right. All these esteemed scholars were not really concerned with play and games, they were concerned with other more important and serious subject-matters, such as diffusion. They were neglecting play at the very moment it was being studied. While this is a less fair charge to bring against the Opies, it still holds true. Although their focus is more completely on play and games, their functional assumptions lead to the same result. Because they take their human nature for granted, they in effect always *study text without also studying context.* So we never really do know how or what these plays mean to those that use them. We have the record of play and games they provide, but little insight into what they mean to the players, which is Mead's point about the anthropological literature on the subject.

It is not my business here to deal with the psychology of play, but in the book *Child's Play* (with R. E. Herron, Wiley, 1971), I came to very similar conclusions. The collections of children's play and games in the early part of this century were meant to be illustrations of the necessary stages through which children must go. They were meant to indicate facts about human evolution. In the thirties most of the study of play had to do with the management of the kindergarten. Who plays with blocks; who plays with sand? Do children fight more or less when they have play apparatus? In the psychoanalytic studies of play, which constitute the largest body (if we take doll play therapy and diagnosis into account) of play studies in any subject-matter, play is conceived of as a *projection* of those other more important human subjects: aggression, eroticism, dependency, anality and the like. Here we have *context without text.* The play is studied to tell us once again only about human nature that is not play. This time not about diffusion, evolution, nor management, but about human conflict. Actually there is probably more information about the way play functions in human nature in this body of material than there is anywhere else. But the problem is one can not always tell with those who write about play diagnosis and therapy which of their intuitions are brilliant insights and which are simply their own projections. When the theory of play as projection is confused with the projections of the theorist as player, the rest of us must necessarily be a little uncertain about the conclusions that are offered. In the more recent studies of play as a cognitive or a voluntary behavior, there continues, I have argued, to be a reduction of play to cognitive structures on the one hand or exploratory behaviors on the other, such as care in *Child's Play,* Wiley, 1971, Section 8. Once again we are not able to focus on play without using it as an illustration of some thing else that is more important, although I would hasten to point out that I think the increasing intensity of this circumjacent activity is having a cumulative effect of our knowledge. When you look at those who give us only text, like the Opies and the folklorists, and those who give us only context, like most psychologists, some glimmering of the relations between both begins to merge.

In *The Study of Games* Avedon and I suggested that the new studies of Roberts and others, that is the cross-cultural studies of games, represented a new start in the anthropology of play. Yet while this was certainly true on an empirical level because much new information was added, one has to question whether any real breakthrough was accomplished on a theoretical level; or whether Roberts, myself and others, did not simply serve once more to reduce games to some other more important functions, and in doing so have the subject-matter elude us once more. Let me briefly review what we did achieve in our studies.[2]

The Roberts - Sutton-Smith Studies.

These studies show:

1. That in cross-cultural studies there are hundreds of statistically significant associations between the presence of games and other cultural variables.
2. Different types of games (strategy, chance, physical skill and central person) have different patterns of association. There are also patterns associated with the absence of games and with the presence of more types of games.
3. The cultural variables with which associations have been made include

child training variables, economic, technological, political and sociological variables.

These are in brief the major cross cultural findings. The *interpretations* from the more simple to the more complex are as follows:

1. That games are in some way functionally related to structure. They are not trivial or unessential or random.
2. That more complex cultures have more complex games and more types of games and that these various associations are merely an index of general complexity (cultures with no competitive games are very simple; cultures with all types are the most complex). This argument has been amplified by Don Ball of the University of British Columbia, Vancouver, Canada.
3. That there are meaningful structural relationships between each type of game and its patterns of association. Thus strategy is linked with obedience, training and social system complexity; chance is linked with responsibility, divination, nomadic habits and economic uncertainty; physical skill is linked with the tropics and hunting; central person games are linked with independence, training and marriage.
4. That the way to explain the linkages both with child training variables and cultural variables is in terms of the *conflict-enculturation hypothesis,* which says that conflict engendered by child training procedures (one is both rewarded and punished for interest in certain behaviors) leads to a readiness to be aroused by symbolic systems (games) which configure the conflict (in their role reversals). Involvement over time in these rewarding game patterns leads to mastery of behaviors which have functional value or transfer to culturally useful behavior.
5. That the way to prove this pattern of hypothesis is to show that the same patterns hold within our own culture as were to be found cross-culturally in the original studies (sub-system replication). Studies of adult preferences for games, of children's preferences, and of children's play appear to provide support for the original patterns of relationships. See, in particular, the studies of Tick Tack Toe in *The Folkgames of Children.*
6. That the way the enculturation aspect of this thesis occurs is through the games acting as models of cultural power relationships, that is those involving strategy, chance, force or arbitrary status. Studies of the character of power in games when compared with the exercise of power in the family suggest that there is no simple parallel between the two spheres, although factor analytic studies of such family power do yield some factors that are interpretable as strategy, force and chance.[3]

Now let me return to my original point about most of the work in anthropology and psychology—that it is a study of context without much reference to text. These studies of mine with Roberts are susceptible to the same criticism. What is textual here are the determinants of outcome (strategy, chance, etc.). That is all we have to say about games. What is contextual are the asserted relationships about psychogenic and sociogenic correlates. We are saying, like Durkheim or Malinowski, that games do not exist randomly in the structural fabric, they are there for a cultural purpose. As models of power, they replicate the larger systems of power of which they are a part and serve their purpose within these as "buffered training systems," to use our phrase. To say this is to subordinate the game to the larger system. Granted we make it more than the sort of ephemera that the word "projection" implies. Our acquaintance with the vigor of play in the cross cultural materials saves us from that. We put more life into play as the notions of miniature power systems and buffered models suggest, and we do imply that they are larger systems for learning. Our games are systems for the socialization of conflict, as I have recently argued,[4] and the socialization of power, as we argued earlier.

What has been occurring recently within sociology and anthropology, and has existed for a long time within literature, is the realization that these minor cultural systems such as games, and more obviously novels, do not exist simply to socialize members into the normative systems of the culture of which they are a part. On the contrary, the very nature of many of these systems is to challenge and even to reverse the systems of which they are a part. This thesis was taken up in a two part seminar of the American Anthropological Association in 1973 entitled "Forms of Symbolic Inversion." Here there was a study of the role of the trickster in folklore, of the fool at court; of the role of festivals such as the Mardi Gras; of inversion within ritual in simple cultures; of reversal in the power terminology of marginal groups; of reversals in the alienated groups of hippies, addicts and communes; of reversals in sex groups in all their current variety; and finally; of reversals in leisure, including a study of my own which I have called "games of order and disorder."[5]

Games of Order and Disorder

What all the investigators were concerned with in these papers was to attempt to understand the role of such inversions in culture. By and large, these phenomena were pictured as anti-structure set off in a compensatory or cathartic relationship to the rest of the culture, a point of view originally, but no longer, taken by Victor Turner in his outstanding work on these problems, *The Ritual Process* (Chicago: Aldine, 1969). I took the view that these phenomena could also be considered as *proto structure,* that is as a source of novelty or as a source of new culture. To quote, "The normative structure represents the working equilibrium, the anti-structure represents the latent system of potential alternatives from which novelty will arise when contingencies in the normative system require it. We might more correctly call this second system the proto cultural system because it is the precursor of innovative-normative forms. It is the source of new culture."

Let me briefly summarize my argument. It was that the anomalous class of pastimes, if considered in conflict terms, could be viewed as a set of oppositions between order and disorder, between anarchy and chaos. That these pastimes were in effect games in which the players did not compete with each other, but with the forces of chaos. That children between the ages of three and six years are preoccupied with such games. That there are four stages in their development: (1) games in which all act in concert and then collapse (Ring-a-Ring-a-Roses, Hand Holding, and Winding Up and Out amongst the Trobrianders);[6] (2) One or more players has a central role in bringing about the collapse (Poor Pussy, Jack-a-Balan) usually by causing them to laugh by absurd mimicry, etc.; (3) There is a coordinated series of actions leading to a climax of chaos (Consequences, My Aunt Went to Paris); (4) Actions are coordinated toward the downfall of a central figure (King of the Golden Sword, Queen of Sheba). This series of (1) to (4) covers the age levels in order from about four years to fourteen. There are many examples in the Human Relations Area Files from all culture areas, but insufficient to use in any statistical sense. The games have been, by and large, just too ephemeral for anthropologists and others to note seriously. They are, however, just one part of a more general concern with chaos, tumult, and vertigo in mankind's leisure which was first focussed for us, I believe, by Roger Caillois in his book *Man, Play and Games* (Glencoe, Illinois: The Free Press, 1961) and are exampled by all the arts of clowning acrobatics, fun fair vertigo, danger, hazard, and dizziness with which we are familiar in the worlds of play and entertainments.

In my analysis of these and other games I suggested various ways in which role inversions could occur and thus provide the player with a novel experience (rather than simply with a replication of cultural experience). *First,* each player gets a turn at roles he may not get usually. Most cultural relationships are asymmetrical. Most game relationships are symmetrical. They model equality of turn taking, where life does not. There is more reversibility of roles in games than is to be found in the normative structure. Dominant persons tend to hold on to their dominance in every day affairs. What is usually inverted, therefore, is not the cultural dimensions (success of failure) but access to the roles within it. At least that is true for competitive games which both model power relationships as we said, but give leeway of access to these where that does not always exist elsewhere. *Secondly,* games of order and disorder are a special case, because they model the system only to destroy it. Their ambivalence is much more fundamental. They are both the most fundamental form of games (establishing for the young the roots of cooperation) and the most radical (upsetting the orders of motor, conventional inpulse and social hierarchical control). *Thirdly,* all games provide a great deal of leeway within any given role for tactical variations and innovation. There are always new ways to be more strategic, to deceive or to cheat. These may be miniscule in the larger scale of the game, but they are indeed often reversals of the usual procedures for life and not unsuggestive of the way things might be done differently.

So in sum, we have in games behavior in which conventional roles are mocked (the games of order and disorder); we have in games an unconventional access to roles; and we have in games access to novelty within role. All of which I would contend could be seeds of potential novelty for the larger society, which is a thesis in the interpretation of play to which I will return shortly.

The Six Cultures Studies[7]

It was always my hope that the extensive work of John and Beatrice Whiting would ultimately provide us with sufficiently convincing evidence on children's play that we might finally begin to get some idea of how we might resolve the various issues of cultural replication and reversal in children's play. It does not look as if it will do this, although there are some important relationships to be found there. The work on the Nyansongo of Kenya, for example, shows that in cultures where the children are an important cog in a fragile economic machine, there is little scope for them to play. The major job for these children is herding the cattle. It is reported that "fantasy play is almost non-existent among these children." (B. B. Whiting, 1963, p. 173) All that was observed was some fairly desultory physical play such as blocking streams and swimming, climbing trees, shooting birds with slings, fighting with each other, tussling, chasing and exchanging blows, watching cars on the roads. This is consistent with the studies of Dina Feitelson who reports that in the carpet weaving cultures of the Middle East where children are an economic asset, they also begin early in direct imitation of adult activity and do not indulge greatly in what you or I might call play.[8] The studies of Sarah Smilansky of hierarchical cultural groups in Israel are of similar importance.[9] This does not mean that all relatively simple cultures do not play, because the records of play amongst Australian aboriginal groups are very extensive. What seems to be critical is whether or not the adults have a direct economic need to train the children in highly normalized means of survival. In such cultures the "work ethic" makes real sense. The adults know what must be done to survive and they cannot afford the wasted time of child play. Children are an important cog in the machine. The same position prevailed in England in the early half of the nineteenth century when pauperism was widespread and young children were exploited in mines and factories as a necessary way of helping each family to survive. The Australian aborigines, as Michael Salter's collection shows so clearly, have an open ended environment for their children. There is much they can teach, but much also the child must learn through self reliance, including the fact that he must deal with novel circumstances. Play seems to be most relevant in such "open" societies and much less relevant in "closed" ones. It has more value for foragers than for tillers.

Even within complex societies when there is more leeway for the children to roam about and choose their own companions, there seems to be more play activity. In the Whitings' study when the Taira of Okinawa are compared with the even more culturally complex Rajputs of India whose children are restricted to sibling play in back yards, the former show much more activity. The Taira have tag, marbles, rope jumping, races, team chasing, houses, robbers and peddlers, kick the can, hopscotch, ball bouncing, tip cat, wrestling and prisoner's base; whereas the Rajputs have much less: the imitation of parent cooking or farming, dolls, small toy models, bows and arrows, hoops, wagon grinders and scales, plus some chasing and seesaw.

Nevertheless, as a society gets to be more complex, there are more problems, more novel contingencies which must be managed; so not surprisingly, the more complex cultural groups in the Whiting study (USA, India, Okinawa) exhibit more types of play than the less complex groups (Mexico, Philippine and African). One can manage this in the simplistic terms of arousal theory and say that novelty prompts exploratory activity; and then add the recent findings that more exploratory activity is usually followed by more play. Or we can break it down as we did in the cross cultural studies, showing what sorts of games go with what sorts of complexity. Or we can suggest, as I have more recently, that there are certain varieties of play which are relevant to certain types of cultural problems. Thus, there is exploratory play, imitative play, testing play and constructive play, and there are the social forms of sociodrama, contesting and make-believe.[10] It is possible to look at, for example, the aborigines and see that most of their play involves exploration and testing; whereas, in a symbolic and achievement oriented culture like ours, most play involves make-believe and contesting. It is my opinion that future research in the anthropology of play will go further along these lines into the careful specification of types of play and the type or subset of the cultural system to which it is related either directly or indirectly.

There are some other possible differences between the society with the most observed play in the Whiting study, the Taira of Okinawa, and the society with the least observed play, the Nyansongo of Kenya, and these are worth mentioning as leads to future research. The family unit in Taira is nuclear, there are private courtyards so privacy is possible. Children can wander in an open and friendly society of other children; they meet more children who are not their kin. There is a school and there are competitive games at the school. There is more interaction with the father. There are more outsiders in the playgroups. Children under five are seldom given chores; they do not have to look after younger children to any extent. There are various specialized buildings such as shops. Children are self assertive. In the Nyansongo, by contrast, where subsistence agriculture prevails, the children must help with the work; they must help with the care of the younger children. Under the mother's control they help with many chores, getting fuel, cooking. They are members of an extended family and they are discouraged from leaving their immediate home environment. There is no school and no organized play; however, there is some dirt throwing and rough-housing by boys. There is little interaction with the father. The children are very much under the mother's control and dominance. These are all interesting contrasts. It is simply not possible yet for us to know which of these variables is intrinsic to the difference in play and which merely is an accidental associate. Intuition suggests the complexity, the play groups, the privacy, the father stimulation, and the lack of chores might all be important contributors.

A Theory of Play

As well as a clearer specification of types of play and types of relationship to cultural system, clearly we need a more useful theoretical account of play. We need an account which focuses on all the issues of both text and context. I have elsewhere set out what I think are some of the requirements of an adequately research oriented description of what this play theory should be.[11] It must pay attention to the antecedents of play, the structure of play, the consequences of play, and the relationship of all of these within larger ideological frames of reference. Within this approach it needs to focus separately on cognitive, motivational and affective variables as these have entered into different research programs. The antecedents and consequents and the involvement with ideology have to do with the context of play, the sort of thing that psychologists and anthropologists usually care about. The structure has to do with the text which has traditionally been the concern of folklorists and recreationists.

Let me deal first and most briefly with *text.* Here I have found it useful to think of playing cognitively as a form of *abstraction.* By this I mean a novel formulative process by which the child creates meaning and organization out of his prior experience, following here Vygotsky's interpretation of play rather than Piaget's. Conatively, I believe it is best thought of as a form of *power reversal.* Affectively, as a form of *vivification* of experience.

The *antecedent context* can emphasize the relationship prior to exploratory activity, as does Piaget, to antecedent power relationships or to antecedent signal activity, following Bateson. It can stress the nature of stimulus, motivational and affective quiesence as necessary for play. Or it can emphasize the paradoxical carry over of long-term enduring motives and conflicts into the play itself. My own preference is for finding parallels first between dreams and play, and, secondly, between play, games and sports and other forms of human expressive activity, such as narrative myth. Whether or not and how these systems emerge depends pretty much on the sort of cultural context, work-oriented or open-oriented, that I have been describing above.

The *postcedent context* includes the novelty to which play as abstractions give rise (now confirmed by a developing body of research), the flexibility which is an outcome of the power reversals, and the sense of revival which comes from the special quality of vivifying affective experience in play.

The transfer of these outcomes depends on the prevailing ideology. In a closed work ethic society there is no scope for the novelty and facetiousness to which play gives rise. In an open society this novelty is a source of potential adaptation, albeit an overproductive source being no guarantee of preparation, as Groos thought, but at least of the promise of being ready.

In this interpretation as seen in the analysis of games above, the play, games and sports both mirror and provide potential novelty about the larger society. In this interpretation also, social scientists, including anthropologists, have been mainly concerned with what I would like to consider the *integrative* functions of play in society. They have been concerned, as were Roberts and I, with normative socializing. The more static the society the more relevant that type of play theorizing is. What an increasingly open society like ours needs, however, is to consider the *innovative* functions of playing and try to account for the ways in which novelties introduced into the text ultimately transfer back to the society at large. What are the laws by which text is re-introduced to context? These should be able to be handled in probabilistic terms at least.

Any anthropology of play is in danger of succumbing to integrative theories because anthropology has tended to deal with relatively static societies. Perhaps in a complex culture such as our own we might be in danger of paying too much attention to novelty, although this is hardly to be feared as yet. The normative view of culture is still too strong with us.

In this paper what I hope to have indicated, if not always spelled out, are some of the areas into which research must probe as well as some of the theoretical problems with which play students must cope if we are, indeed, to overcome the relative ineffectiveness to date of research in the anthropology of play.

NOTES AND REFERENCES

[1]This paper results, in part, from a project, "Enculturation of the Imagination in Early Childhood," supported by grant # NEG-00-3-0133 from the National Institute of Education. It was originally prepared for the Symposium on Recreation at the State University of New York College at Brockport, August 1974. This version is derived from one which appeared in The Association for the Anthropological Study of Play *Newsletter,* 1, 2, Fall 1974. A fuller treatment of this subject will be provided in my forthcoming *Dialectics of Play* (Schorndorf, West Germany: Verlag Karl Hoffman, in press).

[2]The best single source for these studies is my book, *The Folkgames of Children* (Austin: University of Texas Press, 1973).

[3]These studies are described in Sutton-Smith and Rosenberg, *The Sibling* (New York: Holt, Rinehart and Winston, 1971, Chapter 4).

[4]In Gruppe, O., ed., *Sport in the Modern World: Chances and Problems.* Berlin: Springer-Verlag, 1974, pp. 70-75.

[5]To appear as "Games of Order and Disorder" in a volume to be published by the University of Texas Press, under the editorship of Barbara Babcock Abrahams.

[6]Trobriand references from Malinowski, B., *The Sexual Life of Savages,* 1969. Other references in B. Sutton-Smith, *The Games of New Zealand Children* (Berkeley: University of California Press, 1959; republished in *The Folkgames of Children,* op. cit.).

[7]B. B. Whiting, ed., *Six Cultures: Studies of Child Rearing* (New York: Wiley, 1963).

[8]These references and a more extensive discussion are to be found in B. Sutton-Smith, "Play as Adaptive Potentiation," *Sportswissenschaft* 5 (1975), 103-118.

[9]B. Sutton-Smith, "The Games of Two Cultures," in *Folkgames of Children,* op. cit.

[10]B. Sutton-Smith, "Children at Play," *Natural History* 80 (1971), 54-59.

[11]B. Sutton-Smith, "Play, Games and Sports in Industrial Society," paper presented at the meeting of the International Sociology Association, Toronto, August 1974.

Play as Adaptive Potentiation

Brian Sutton-Smith

Much of the material contained in my Keynote Address delivered to the 1976 annual meeting of The Association for the Anthropological Study of Play has now been published in various forms in a number of places (Sutton-Smith 1974, 1975a, 1975b, 1975c, n.d.), and so it does not really matter that the full text of that address cannot be included in this volume. However, as so often happens, by the time one arrives at the podium the address prepared beforehand is no longer the address in one's head. And so I would like to add the following as a footnote to the original text.

I have always felt some ambivalence about the "classic" theories of play (Gilmore, 1971) but have managed to avoid much mention of them in almost thirty years in the field, a host of articles on the subject and several books. I'm not sure as to the source of my ambivalence, whether it was the trauma of my own first undergraduate essay on the subject, or the hundreds of student essays I have pretended to mark ever since. Suffice it to say, that in this present address I have for the first time overcome my antipathy to "surplus energy," "recapitulation" and the like, and wish to make an arbitrary foray into this marshland once more.

Prophylactic Theories

It appears to me that the "classic" theories may be considered to fall into two categories, the *prophylactic* and the *preparatory*. The first which includes the "surplus energy," "recapitulation," "relaxation," "recreation," "compensation" and "projection" theories, implies that play is a subsidiary form of adaptation in human life. While this view was at first a counteraction to the early nineteenth century work ethic within which play has little value, it is not in line with current preparatory theories and with the fact, for example, that approximately a third of the gross national budget in modern times is devoted to some form of play (sports, television, theatre, etc.). What I like about the prophylactic group, however, is that wittingly or not it allows for irrational elements in human behavior, whether these be expressed in cathartic, atavistic, excessive or compensatory terms. Although in these theories the major aim is to provide some palliative for man's condition (hence prophylaxis), there is here also some admission of the player's penchant for madness of which most current preparatory theories take little account. Take, for example, the following story told to us by one of the seven year old boys in our narrative project.* This story is a form of fantasy play at least, and perhaps an embryonic art form as well, because it is systematically structured for the listener with a beginning and an ending and is replete with fantasy characters. This is the sort of phenomena with which any adequate theory of play must deal but which is usually paid little attention as a normative occurrence in most modern thought on the matter.

ABC Wee-Oh

A baby was walking down the street making trouble and when the baby saw a man passing her, she said, "You suck your buggers, 2 times, yeh, yeh," Then they went to a music studio and they heard, "Keep coming in ABC, ABC, ABC, 1, 2, 3." And then the baby said, "I can do the whole alphabet. ABCDEFGHIJKLMNOPQRS and TUV, W and XYZ. That's how!" And then the baby said, "I think I'm so smart just because I have one tooth out." Then the baby said, "I am superman, you can't hurt superman." Then the man said, "You're messing up the whole music studio. Kick the baby out." Then another baby said, "I never saw a baby with a moustache," while putting his fingers on his nose. Then he said, "Me Chinese, me tell joke, me go peepee in your coke." And then the baby that was getting kicked out said, "You're not Chinese, you're American."

Then they saw three ladies kicking their legs up and saying, "Legs, legs, legs are here!" Then the girl said, "I shave my eyelashes everyday." And then the baby said, "I think I'm so great because my teeth don't need to be fixed." Then the baby walked into an A & P Wee-O Store and everyone was saying, "Wee-O!"

Then the baby said, "It passed my bed-time, I better find my way home." Then he accidentally walked into a museum while the guard was asleep, and he climbed up a plastic tree and there was a rope hanging on it and he said, "Me Tarzan!" Then the baby swinged out the window and about a mile and landed through the chimney into his house and said "Me Santa Claus." And then he climbed into bed and went to sleep. That's the end.

**Editor's Note:* Professor Sutton-Smith is referring to the project conducted by himself and his students at Teachers College. See Section IV of this volume.

Preparatory Theories

Beginning with Groos' theory as espoused in the *Play of Animals* (1898) and *The Play of Man* (1916), the theory of animal or children's play as a preparation and practice for adult life became an important part of the tradition of play theorizing. Most works on animal play still view it in these terms. In a recent work on *Play Fighting* (1975), for example, Owen Aldis presents the view that those animals play more that must spend more of their adult energy in skillful attempts to overcome their prey. He contends that the exercise of muscle and the co-ordination of skill in the play period is correlated directly with requirements of adult adaptation. In 1944, a Dutch historian, Huizinga, presented the even more radical thesis that culture itself begins as play. Culture is first "played" before it settles down into the institutional forms that we know as language, war, law and art. While his speculative thesis was at first greeted with some skepticism, in the years since 1944 there has been increasing evidence that would tend to support his view that play is a creative centre for subsequent growth. In anthropology we have discovered that in those tribes where children play most, in subsequent years they have the greatest requirements for complex and flexible responses. In psychology we have discovered that those who play most are also the most creative. All of these developments, therefore, strongly suggest that play is preparatory for subsequent life. Despite their emphasis however, no one has been able to tie such play behaviors directly into adult adjustment. There appears to be some sort of *indirect* connection but not a direct one. The characteristics of expressiveness, of light heartedness, of relaxedness and of bubbling energy which were noted by the earlier non preparatory theories are still there. Play may be some sort of a preparation but it is also some sort of a relaxed, irreverent and inconsequential phenomena.

Socialization

The burden of this presentation is devoted to showing that most researchers in play, games or sports have simply assumed that these phenomena prepare for adult roles without actually testing for the relationship. Typically the researcher has been content to show a correlation between a play, game or sports form and a cultural form and then has gone onto assume that a socialization function was, therefore established. In this way play has been associated with such things as peer socialization, sex role socialization and adult modelling; games have been associated with cultural customs, child rearing and cultural complexity and sports have been related to social status, achievement and group collectivization, usually without the investigator specifically demonstrating any transfer from one activity to the other. The implicit assumption that these phenomena were socializing has simply precluded the need to prove the connection.

Now I am not arguing that play may not be socializing, only that the relationship itself has to be proven. There are lots of things about play, such as the investigation of materials, territories and other persons, the establishment of play hierarchies, and of meta-communications which seem to be undoubtedly socializing, but they are after all, not play itself. They are simply circumjacent to play.

The problem with the constant assumption that play socializes is that we fail to look at the other things that are also occurring in play which do not obviously model adult process in the world in which the child lives. Helen Schwartzmann (1976) in her paper, for example, mentioned that much of the play which is said to facilitate sex role socialization is often in reality also a satire on it. In that light I can recall that girls who play "Mother May I" spend as much time in cheating and disparaging the mother as they do in playing out her role of arbitrary authority. Children who play schools, play at nonsense as much as they play at school. Disorder is as relevant to play imitation as is order. And most socialization theories do not account for that as well as they should. Roberts and I, in our theory of games as Models of Power*, for example, assumed that games had to exist because adults would not teach the arts of trickery and deception elsewhere. A further disadvantage of assuming that play prepares for adult roles is that we do not look at the parallels carefully enough. If we did we might make our hypotheses more specific and actually learn much more about socialization. In A. W. Miracle's paper on the play of Aymara, he shows how the adults attempt to push the children into the necessary economic work roles, and will not accept a child as an adult until he can give up play. The children for their part have to be furtive in their practice of play, which Miracle explains as necessary nevertheless for their socialization. What strikes one as interesting, however, is that the particular dialectic between parent and child itself may be a form of socializing. If Aymara parents are people who must be able to maintain a sober face to their conquerors while at the same time keeping access to alternative and well developed thought systems for their own survival then they would have been well serviced by the imitation of that very system in the parent-child relationships. The continued existence of the Aymara for two thousand years despite various conquerors, Inca and Spanish, certainly suggests some such socialization secret.

To this point, however, I have been discussing that type of play socialization which is assumed to *integrate* the individual into society in some way. The more interesting recent socialization theories are those implied by Huizinga's which change society in new directions. I have reviewed this material in other papers and discuss this as socialization through *innovation*.

The notion, however, that play can sometimes integrate an individual into society, and other times give him useful innovative competences for society, means that play is quite variable in itself. Sometimes play participation is highly imitative of adult society, at other times it contains the variability hinted at in the innovative theories.

While we know little about the continuum that leads from the one to the other, it does seem that the more constant, and stable the play conditions the more probable it is that the more repetitive imitative types of play will give way to the more variable and playful types. Which means that it should be possible to identify those cultural conditions which facilitate rather routine, stereotyped modelling in play and those cultural conditions which facilitate playful variability.

**Editor's Note:* See Roberts, J. M. and B. Sutton-Smith (1962), Child Training and Game Involvement, *Ethnology* 2, 166-185; Sutton-Smith and Roberts (1972), Studies in an Elementary Game of Strategy, in B. Sutton-Smith, ed., *The Folkgames of Children,* Austin: University of Texas Press; and Sutton-Smith and Roberts (1972), The Cross-Cultural and Psychological Study of Games, in B. Sutton-Smith, ed., *The Folkgames of Children.*

Adaptive Potentiation

Let me return now to the classic theories to see if I can find a formulation that allows play to contain the socialization that prepares (integration or innovation) and the play which is prophylactic because it makes nonsense out of normative behavior.

One way to resolve these contradictions, which are inherent in these two trends in play theory, is to say that play does not directly prepare but only that it is preadaptive. That is, play gets responses ready, but does not decree that they shall ever be used beyond the play itself. Or to put it another way, play potentiates responses, rather than prepares them. This has been called play as *adaptive potentiation* (Sutton-Smith, 1975a). As an essential part of this theory it can be pointed out that the player cannot experiment with his potential future unless he feels completely free to do whatever he wishes to do. He must feel unconstrained by everyday requirements. He must have the freedom to be ridiculous or inventive. Unless one feels such personal freedom it is difficult to try out all the response combinations and response permutations that real experimentation requires. It is in this sense that play has to feel intrinsically non serious or it cannot feel free. Its triviality is in part a burden of work ethic history but in part also an essential precondition for freedom to be variable in play.

But the notion of prophylaxis is even more fundamental than has been suggested. It is not just that the freedom to be irrational gives one the greatest possible freedom to be oneself (exploring all personal permutations), the freedom to indulge the opposite, as one can in play (Mother May I) or in rites of reversal, is itself a cognitive activity, which liberates thought. If the most primitive of all forms of thinking means discovering opposites as some have contended then play indeed and these cultural customs provide an adaptive system that makes thought possible. The exhilaration of inverting usual behavior is a pantomime of the capacity to think in terms of reversals. As we know from Piaget, without such capacity for reversals, logical operations cannot emerge.

It is this way then that I would bring the older notions of prophylaxis to the fore. They are approximations to the description of play as an acted out process of reversibility testing. This acting out which is both liberating and intrinsically motivating because it puts the player in control, then makes possible the exploration both of routine modelled responses (integrative potential) and variable responses (innovative potential). Whether these potentiated responses subsequently result in other forms of cultural adaptation depends on the condition in the surrounding culture; whether the responses are encouraged or whether there is cultural conflict permitting the emergence of such new forms out of play and fantasy into "serious" cultural discourse.

The point of this footnote is I hope to help in sharpening our observation of the different forms (routine and variable) within play itself as well of as the typical inversions of behavior that occur, but also to attract our attention to the necessity of showing which of the potentiated responses enter into other spheres of adaptation, and to the probability they have of such emergence.

NOTE

This material appeared first as "Footnotes to the TAASP Keynote Address in Atlanta, 1976" in The Association for the Anthropological Study of Play *Newsletter,* 3, 2, Summer 1976.

REFERENCES

Gilmore, J. B. 1971. Play: A Special Behavior. In R. E. Herron and B. Sutton-Smith, eds., *Child's Play.* New York: Wiley.

Miracle, A. W. 1976. Functional Analysis of Aymara Games and Play. Paper presented at TAASP Annual Meeting, Atlanta.

Schwartzman, H. B. 1976. Research on Children's Play: Suggestions and Predictions. Paper presented at TAASP Annual Meetings, Atlanta.

Sutton-Smith, B. 1974. Play as Novelty Training. In J. D. Andrews, ed., *One Child Indivisible.* NAEYC Conference Proceedings, pp. 227-258.

—1975a. Play as adaptive Potentiation. *Sportswissenschaft* 5, 103-118.

—1975b. Play, the Useless Made Useful. *School Review* 83, 197-214.

—1975c. Forschung und Theoriebildung im Bereich von Spiel und Sport. *Zeitschrift fur Padagogik* 21, 325-334.

—n.d. *Dialectics of Play.* Schorndorf: Verlag Karl Hoffman (in press).

Laying the Groundwork for an Anthropology of Play

Phillips Stevens, Jr., State University of New York, Buffalo

Prefatory note: It is my hope that this essay can be regarded as a *precursor* to Brian Sutton-Smith's insightful paper, "Towards an Anthropology of Play". I have tried to avoid undue repetition of his observations and suggestions, and will instead refer the reader to them, and to his several other writings. It is my aim here to direct attention to aspects of what seem to me the most fundamental basis—and, therein, justifications—for our field of study. I will also offer some reflections upon the present state of our investigations. This paper is adapted from a lecture delivered to the Department of Sociology, State University of New York College, Fredonia, March 17, 1976, and further from a version which appeared in the TAASP *Newsletter,* 3, 2, 1976.

Responses to the revelation that I am President of the Association for the Anthropological Study of Play range from the politely incredulous ("the anthropological study of *what?*") to the downright cynical ("Yeah. I see. Well, when you can't make it in an established business, you can always set up your own company."). In any case, the existence of our Association is held by some as further evidence of the absurd lengths to which anthropologists will go in their interpretation of The Study of Man. And I must confess, my office in our Association is an achievement I do not widely boast about.

Why? Play is an integral aspect of human social behavior. Play, moreover, is a phenomenon at least as old as the emergence of the phylogenetic Class, Mammalia, from which the genus *Homo* is a very recent offshoot. Why have we come so late to its serious study? The answers, I suppose, lie at least partly in the evolution of our present system of social values, and partly in a (perhaps resultant) narrow view of the subject. We can quickly dismiss the first. Then, I hope, we can broaden our perspectives on this universal phenomenon, and consider some of the ways anthropology might contribute to our understanding of it.

The avoidance of play as a subject meriting serious scientific study probably has its roots deep in the Western, particularly the Christian, social and philosophical heritage. The value placed on work was elevated almost to the level of the sacred by our Puritan forebears, and became institutionalized in the Protestant Ethic. Work was a Christian virtue. Anything else received an opposite connotation; it was the enemy of work, hence the enemy of Christ. Play was permitted only to children, and then with severe restrictions. It constituted self-indulgence, hence, a slipping from virtue. These sentiments persisted through the Victorian period and, indeed, persist, even in much of the scientific community, today.

Biologists, zoologists, (e.g. Groos 1898) and more recently primatologists (e.g. Suomi and Harlow 1971; cf. also Loizos 1967) and anthropologists (e.g. Bateson 1952) have long studied play among animals, but research funds usually have been made available for the study of similar activities among human groups only when the phenomenon is given a more respectable label, such as "recreation" or "leisure," and then it is studied principally in relation to its counterpart, work. [It is only fair to recognize, however, the important work of Bruner, Jolly, and Sylva (1976), whose publication on the role of play in development and evolution appeared after the initial writing of this paper, and some aspects of which lead in the direction of some of the comments I offer below.]

But many of the world's peoples do not place such a value on work for work's sake; indeed, many lack the work-play dichotomy in their social perceptions. And there exists a more fundamental fact with which anthropologists must reckon: both animals *and* people play from birth to death. Moreover, there is solid evidence that play is not only an integral aspect of the mammalian way of life, but that it is necessary and vital to "normal" development of both the organism itself, and of its maturation as a social being. We social scientists, particularly we anthropologists, have come very late to the serious recognition of what is a vitally important behavioral phenomenon.

Approaches to the Study of Play

But before returning to what should be our starting-point, we must address a question to which we as yet have no satisfactory answer: what *is* play? As Edward O. Wilson has recently (1975:164) observed, "No behavioral concept has proved more ill-defined, elusive, even unfashionable." Our Association is entering its fourth year of existence without having satisfactorily delineated the parameters of what it is we are talking about.

There is the respectable study of *sport,* most often conducted within departments of Physical Education. Some innovative sociology departments offer courses in the sociology of sport in their curricula, recognizing, I suppose, that sport is social behavior, and that a team of players both constitutes a society, and reflects the values and social behavior of the larger society. But I am not going to talk here about sport, mainly so that I will not be forced to elaborate on my sentiment that it does not belong under the heading of "play".

The study of *games* has received wider anthropological attention; indeed, insights into the nature, origins, functions, and types of games are about all anthropology is credited with having contributed to the study of play and it is probably this focus that comes to mind when the name of our Association is mentioned. Anthropological investigations of games date back at least to E. B. Tylor's and Stewart Culin's arguments over the origins of the Aztec lot game, *patolli* (see Erasmus 1950 for a critical synthesis of these early studies). It should be noted, however, that Tylor and Culin, and subsequent researchers such as Boas, Kroeber, and Murdock, were concerned less with the content and context of games, than with the resolution of the then-current anthropological problem of diffusion vs. localized evolution and modification. Investigations of games are certainly a good deal earlier than these, however, and our reference to them depends on where we place the origins of "anthropology". The Greeks and Persians, for example, set down treatises on ball-game strategies as early as the First Millenium B.C. The most widely cited modern anthropological study is the cross-cultural investigation of Roberts, Arth, and Bush (1959), who found certain correlations between games of strategy, chance, and skill, and aspects of social values and cosmological perceptions over 50 societies. But the contributions of Roberts *et. al.* are generally seen more as refinements in cross-cultural methodology, than as cultural contextual analyses of games *per se.* Recently (1971) Csikszentmihalyi and Bennet have sought to construct "an exploratory model of play", again relying largely on cross-cultural studies of games. The study of gaming behaviors, strategy, ground-rule manipulation, etc., deriving originally from principles of actual games, has found applications in other fields, e.g., "game theory" in mathematics, and its application in "experimental gaming" in psychology (cf. Pruitt and Kimmel 1977).

Most sociological approaches to play, too, have taken off from sport and games. Many have begun with—and, I think, have misunderstood—Roger Caillois' (1961) views that play, as opposed to sports and games, is free, separate, uncertain, unproductive, and governed by *both* make-believe *and rules.* One recent study which seems to me superior in its breadth and sophistication is that of Harry Edwards (1973). Edwards, too, begins with Caillois, and painstakingly examines each of his components of play. But in his literal interpretation of these elements, he falls into a bind similar to that which constricted his predecessors. For example, he takes off from Caillois to argue that an activity is play *only* when it is *separate, unserious,* and *unproductive.* Thus, he would not allow for recognition of a play element in religion and art (1973:47), "for, like daily life, these have as part of their meaning an aim to achieve some result with respect to reality." (We could discourge at length on the components and "meaning" of "daily life" and, especially, "reality", but let us continue...) Further, Edwards, like several others, is irked by the assertions of Caillois, amplified by Weiss (1969:139), that play is governed by rules. In his flat declaration that these two scholars are wrong, he echoes the shortcomings of the general sociological approach to play: "If rules were in fact a necessary element in play activity, the elements of voluntary commencement and termination of play, that of nonutilitarian engagement, and the element of separation from seriousness would all be negated" (1973:48).

I am not certain that Caillois had in mind what I am going to suggest, but I think his inclusion of "rules" as a component of play is correct, *if* we will allow ourselves to recognize that there are at least two dimensions, or "levels", of "rules". The fact is, and this fundamental fact has been overlooked by the great majority of writers on the subject, *play is at once a biological and a cultural phenomenon.* Both biologically- and culturally-based behavior phenomena are governed by rules. Still, play constrained by rules? We'll return to this apparent paradox shortly.

In any case, in finally reaching a definition Edwards does recognize that play is bounded, even if the boundaries are "arbitrary":

> Play is a voluntary and distinct activity carried out within arbitrary boundaries in space and time, separate from daily roles, concerns, and influences and having no seriousness, purpose, meaining, or goals for the actor beyond those emerging within the boundaries and context of the play act itself (1973:49).

I have dwelt upon Edwards' analysis because I think he has very well synthesized the disparate views of many of his colleagues, and has gone them several steps further. Helpful, for example, is his having placed play, recreation, contest or match, and sport or athletics along a continuum, listing components as present or absent on a sort of Guttman Scale (1973:58-9). This is a useful beginning. But, although they are too many to list here, I think his 15 components of "play" leave some important omissions.

Most psychological, sociological, and anthropological discussions of play (*a la* Piaget 1951, Sutton-Smith, Caillois, Roberts *et. al.,* and Edwards) eventually illustrate their arguments by reference to the games, or the play behavior, or both, of *children.* Indeed, unless we allow for a broader perspective, the focus of our Association may be in danger of becoming the Anthropological Study of Children's Games.

So let us leave sports and games, and consider "play" as a much broader phenomenon. The real starting-point for both sociological and anthropological approaches to play has been Huizinga (1950). Considering his working definition, let us note how he reconciled both the problems of boundaries and of "rules". We might also compare the rest of his phraseology to Edwards'. The quotes are his own.

> Summing up the formal characteristics of play we might call it a free activity standing quite consciously outside "ordinary" life as being "not serious", but at the same time absorbing the player intensely and utterly. It is an activity connected with no material interest, and no profit can be gained by it. It proceeds within its own proper boundaries of time and space according to fixed rules and in an orderly manner...(1950:13).

Huizinga's treatise is truly a monumental work. It should be read and carefully re-read by any student of play. Yet, although it has been widely cited, and has been highly praised by mythologists, historians, philosophers, even theologians, it has received only passing anthropological attention.

Credit for re-directing our attention to Huizinga should go to Edward Norbeck (1976b); indeed, through his several recent writings on the subject (1968, 1971, 1974a, 1974b, 1976a) he should probably be acknowledged as having laid the foundations for an anthropological study of play. In his 1971 article he sets down a definition which contains some now-familiar elements:

> For all forms of life, play may be defined as voluntary, pleasurable behavior that is separated in time from other activities and that has a quality of make-believe. Play thus transcends "ordinary" behavior.

(I have put "ordinary" in quotes. Norbeck does not.) But he does on:

> Human play differs uniquely from that of other species, however, because it is molded by *culture,* consciously and unconsciously. That is, human play is conditioned by *learned attitudes and values* that have *no counterpart among nonhuman species.* (1971: 48; my emphases)

Norbeck rightly stresses the *cultural* component, the basic conditioning factor that distinguishes the anthropological from the sociological focus. Indeed, it is the vital necessity of recognizing the cultural element in play, games, and sports which the founders of our Association—several of them, significantly, physical educators—saw as the primary message to be received from an "anthropological" study of play. But in adhering too closely to the sentiments in Norbeck's final sentence, it seems to me, we are back in the '30s and '40s, the era preceding the study of free-ranging lower primates, the era preceding the serious consideration of the biological bases of human behavior, and the era in which Kroeber's concept of the "superorganic" came to dominate anthropological thinking about culture. Today we are, perhaps reluctantly, coming to recognize that there is a deeper dimension to culture, one which our view of humankind as a special group whose behavior patterns "have no counterpart among nonhuman species" has not allowed us to acknowledge. And so, too, in our study of play we must recognize a deeper dimension. Otherwise, we really will not have advanced much beyond Tom Sawyer's reflection, "Work consists of whatever a body is obliged to do...Play consists of whatever a body is not obliged to do."

Toward a Biological Perspective

Play is a cultural universal. It is possibly also universal within the class Mammalia. The fact of its universality among human groups, alone, merits its serious anthropological study. But there may be another implication in the discovery that a particular behavior complex is found among all human groups. In a pioneering paper, begun in 1951 but not published until 1958, the anthropologist Earl Count offered a suggestion, the import of which is only just coming to be recognized. Taken slightly out of context—he is speaking specifically of the incest taboo—he observes that the universality of certain patterns of cultural behavior

> suggests that they are *not* culturally determined but involve subcultural, innate, psychobiological processes such as psychoanalysis is trying to discover. (1958:1079-80; my emphasis)

Play is everything Huizinga, Norbeck, and Tom Sawyer say it is, but it is more: *Play is first and foremost a biological event.* Let us consider the following.

—Man is a vertebrate, and like many vertebrates he is a social being. Further:

—like all social animals, man's sociality and his biology are functionally and causally interrelated.

—We know that, in the development of the organism, certain hormonal and other mechanisms must be triggered, and they must be triggered at the right time; otherwise the organism may remain permanently stunted, either physiologically, or socially, or both. We do not fully understand the nature of these mechanisms, nor just how they are activated; we do know what can happen to the organism if they are *not* triggered by appropriate stimuli, or if such stimuli are received too late.

—We suspect that the "mothering" complex, consisting in lactation, suckling, parent-contact, and perhaps even certain auditory stimuli as well (e.g., a heart-beat), may be vital to the activation of certain neurophysiological mechanisms. The nature of the mother's post-partum biology indicates that she, too, may suffer if she does not "mother". Babies who share in this mother-infant "trophallaxis" (Count 1958:1062) seem to develop more quickly than those who receive similar nutrition but are denied "mothering". Moreover, experiments in hospital wards for premature babies, in the U.S. with motor-driven rocking incubators, and in Japan with piped-in heart-beat sounds, suggest that such stimuli are vital to the fetus *in utero*. (It has been suggested that play, too, may begin with the "cavorting" of the fetus in the womb.) The individual's social life begins in its relationship with its mother.

—But, after weaning—indeed, we suspect, throughout life—physiological mechanisms still need periodic stimulation, now through participation in social relationships, some of which still involve physical contact, most of which are non-contact role-playing situations.

—*Play,* I submit, is the next vital stage following the mothering complex. Not to say that the mother does not "play" with her baby, nor that such play does not provide vital stimulation to the infant. But now, following separation from the close psycho-physical bond with the mother, the individual's participation in free, social play provides the stimuli necessary to his healthy, systemic development as a social being. Here, again, we do not know precisely what goes on. We know of the effects of play *deprivation* among monkeys. Suomi and Harlow (1971:74) summarize the findings of their research on social behavior of Rhesus monkeys *(Macaca mulatta)*:

> All work and no play makes for a dull child. No play makes for a very socially disturbed monkey. When wire-cage reared animals reach physiological maturity they are incompetent in virtually every aspect of monkey social activity. They prefer to sit in a corner, rather than engage in social grooming, a prerequisite of monkey etiquette. Their aggressive behavior is both ill-advised and ill-directed. Wire-cage reared adults will viciously attack a helpless neonate or they may suicidally attack a dominate male—an act few socially sophisticated animals are stupid enough to attempt. In the absence of social events, wire-cage reared monkeys will attack themselves, often rending skin and muscle to the bone in a flurry of self-aggression.
>
> Monkeys denied the chance to play at sex are seldom proficient at sexual play. Although their hearts may be in the right place, more important things are not... When such females become mothers, another adverse consequence of lack of early play interaction becomes obvious. Motherless mothers, as we call them, are not good mothers...
>
> A monkey does not need playmates to perform adequately in intellectual endeavor, but it sorely needs them to become a functioning member of a social unit. A similar observation regarding human behavior might not be far from the truth...

Suomi and Harlow's observations are supported by the recent research of Oakley and Reynolds (1976) and, as the former suggest above, similar stunting—*permanent* physiological, emotional, and social damage—can result from play deprivation among human children. We lack, and because of our ethical considerations, can never intentionally acquire, such data on human subjects. But this lack is probably due also to our basic failure to recognize this as a vitally important area for research. The bio-social functions of children's play probably constitutes the most seriously deficient area of our field of study.

There exists sufficient justification for such study. Earl Count observed recently (1973:86) that "group play among juveniles is the embryogenesis of socialization, in which the members of the group mutually stimulate their maturing neuro-psychic processes." Earlier, Caroline Loizos (1967) reviewed the more significant studies of play among higher primates, and concluded that

> Far from being a "spare-time", superfluous activity in either human or subhuman primate, it may be that *play at certain crucial early stages is necessary* for the occurrence and success of *all* later social activity within one's own species. (1967:275; my emphase)

And the above sentiments form the basis for the working hypothesis of Laughlin and McManus (n.d.), who are presently engaged in a comprehensive study which argues that "play is a fundamental attribute of the ontogenesis of all higher social animals", and which aims to go further, into cultural institutionalization of play as games, to suggest that "gaming is an evolutionary refinement of play" (p. 1).

—Finally, I have said above that we need to examine more closely the bio-social functions of children's play. But, as Loizos (1967:238) has noted, "to regard play as practice for adult function does not account for the fact that adults as well as infants play in most mammalian societies in which play occurs at all." Our investigations should not stop with the organism's attainment of puberty. How does play function in the later development of the organism, through its role as parent and agent of socialization, even into the period of declining sexual activity in later life? One of the most traumatic "rites of passage" the human being raised in a Western culture may experience is *retirement,* when he is shuttled off by society to a position of isolated non-productivity. Gerontologists know full well the therapeutic effects of play among the aging. But we still do not know just what is going on.

The field is vital, and wide open, but our approaches to it have been sporadic, at best. We must resolve at least two basic problems. First, the ethics of our research demand data to prove a theory, but research among members of our own species is constrained by ethics of another sort. We may be able to attach electrodes to the bodies of individuals engaged in play, and those who are not, in order to "measure" aspects of the complex physiology of play. But clearly, suspecting what we do, we cannot separate groups of individuals at crucial stages in their life cycles into those allowed to play, and those deprived of play. We have sufficient precedents in the comparative study of play among primates; what we need in order to reach what we suspect will be similar conclusions among human groups—unless we will be content to assume such conclusions—is a refined and ethical methodology.

The second problem is far more fundamental, and concerns just what it is we think we have been talking about. Part of the problem, as Robert M. Fagen (1974) has pointed out, is that there have been two quite distinct approaches to the study of play, but their distinctions have not generally been recognized. He calls them the *structuralist* and the *functionalist*. The structuralist approach is concerned with the form, appearance, spatial-temporal orientation, and kinesiology of play. Those psychological, sociological, and anthropological definitions we have cited earlier derive from structuralist approaches. The functionalists, on the other hand, "define play as any behavior that involves probing, manipulation, experimentation, learning, and the control of one's own body as well as the behavior of others, and that also, esssentially, serves the function of developing and perfecting future adaptive responses to the physical and social environment" (in Wilson 1975:164).

The learning-of-adult-roles function of play has been criticized by Loizos; she also criticizes the adaptation-to-environment function:

> Again, it is simply not necessary to play in order to learn about the environment. The animal could explore as, in fact, some mammals that do not appear to play certainly do; for example, the rat. Of course, it is inevitable that during play, or during any activity, an animal will be gaining additional knowledge about what or who it is playing with; but if this is the major function of play, one must wonder why the animal does not use a more economical way of getting hold of this information (1967:238).

The problem with any functional explanation, of course, is that function does not necessarily indicate cause for being. But refinements to this, and to the structuralist approach, should be suggested elsewhere; for the purposes of this paper we can agree with Fagen, there have been these two approaches, and they have not been clearly demarcated. Wilson is right, too: play is clearly adaptive behavior, and it serves, among other functions, to develop selective advantages in the organism. This is the area that anthropology is uniquely equipped to elucidate, but with which we have been hesitant to grapple. Perhaps we can look forward to a fruitful blending of the two approaches in Laughlin and D'Aquili's (1974) concept of "biogenetic structuralism", and in the application of this concept to the linking of the biological bases of play with its cultural manifestations, as Laughlin and McManus (n.d.) are currently trying to do.

I now find myself on very thin ice, and I shall gingerly back off. I am a cultural anthropologist, having read only in and around the materials I have cited above. But it is clear to me that "culture" is far more than "learned attitudes and values that have no counterpart among nonhuman species", and that any approach to culture must *first* consider its phylogenetic foundations. So, too, we cannot meaningfully discuss cultural manifestations of play, such as games, contests, and sports, without first considering its neuro-physiological correlates, its evolutionarily selective aspects, and what it does, fundamentally, for the organism itself. In other words, whether we are studying manifestations of the phenomenon in lower mammals, monkeys or apes, or among human infants, children, teenagers, or aging adults, we should address ourselves to the question, "What is *really* going on here?" This is the point of my paper; it is here that "the groundwork for an anthropology of play" should be laid.

On the "Rules" of Play; and Some Final Considerations

Before concluding, I would like to return briefly to the seemingly paradoxical question of "rules" of play, and then offer some observations regarding our present research directions.

I said earlier that play is at once a biological and a cultural phenomenon, and I observed that both biologically- and culturally-based phenomena are governed by rules. Caillois and Huizinga had both included governance by rules in their definitions of play. But, following the structuralists' approaches, we will have difficulty acknowledging the presence of "rules", unless we can allow for the operation of at least two "levels" of rules. What I shall, for the purpose of this paper, call "overt" rules govern the conduct of games, contests, and sports, and it is certainly this level to which Edwards (1973:48) was referring when he denied their existence in play. But there is a more basic, perhaps far more important level of "rules", which I shall here call the "covert". This level can be seen to have two dimensions, which might be labelled as the "pre-cultural" and the "cultural". But on the basis of the discussion in the preceding section of this paper, I will subsume them under our now broadened concept of what is "cultural". Animal play can be seen to be governed by "rules" of territoriality, of social relationships, especially of dominance and dependence, of physio-sexual cycles, and by a host of as yet vaguely understood perceptual messages. So, too, is "cultural" play.

Culture is, perhaps most fundamentally, a set of rules for behavior. It includes perceptions of the rules by which the world is governed, as well as semantic, semiotic, kinesic, proxemic, and other sub-consciously communicated rules of human interactive behavior. It is an understanding of the operation of rules on this level which explains how urban Zulu play soccer (Scotch 1961), how Utes play basketball (Tindall 1973, 1974, 1975b), how Dani play "flip the stick" (Heider 1975), and how Bachama joke with each other (Stevens 1973, 1974). The "covert" level of rules corresponds to what B. Allan Tindall (1975a) and his former colleagues at the Center for Studies of Cultural Transmission at the State University of New York at Buffalo have called "the hidden curriculum". It was in reference to this covert dimension of "rules" that prompted Tindall (1975c) to tell the UNESCO sponsors of the recent (April 1976) International Conference of Ministers and Senior Officials Responsible for Physical Education and Sport for Youth, that the issues to which they were to address themselves "have no cross-cultural validity".

As I hinted above, culture depends upon communication. Communication is a complex system, consisting at once of the interaction of several subsystems, and of a hierarchy of levels, or paradigms; and it involves not only the verbal-auditory, but *all* the other perceptual systems as well. Gregory Bateson (1955, 1956) has pointed out problems in levels of meaning in communication, and paradoxes we can get into when, for example, the message, "This is play," is itself a playful message. Bateson is looking at the content of communication, the message itself. Again, I suggest we go deeper. As well as investigating *what* is being communicated, we should ask *how* it is being communicated; we should look into the nature of the communication process. This is especially important for the study of play. If we can understand the nature and dynamics of communication systems, then we can ask, for example, what is going on when the messages, "This is now play," "This is play," and "This is no longer play," are being communicated; and we can ask how does the system, when it communicates, or receives, these sorts of messages, differ from when it communicates, or receives, other sorts of messages?

Needless to say, elucidation of the "covert" level of rules governing play behavior requires a careful, rigorous methodology. But this level exists, and failure to recognize it may seriously affect the conclusions of research into play and play-forms.

We should broaden our perspectives on play, to include those dimensions I have discussed in this paper, as well as to include, as Norbeck (1971) has urged us to, such other cultural manifestations as dancing, singing, wit and humor; histrionics and other forms of play-acting and mimicry; art, music, and other esthetic endeavors (cf. Klopfer 1970); and induced states of psychological transcendence. We should also be willing to look at such disparate behavior complexes as religion and ritual, and sexual behavior, in terms of play. We should consider play-forms as they correlate with stages in the life-cycle. And we should include within our scope such forms of apparently non-social play as fantasy and day-dreaming.

If we do not thus broaden our perspectives, I submit, we may become guilty of academicism, by which I mean the testing and re-testing, proving and re-proving, of already well-established theories. Unless we can offer fresh insights, or new methodologies for their study, we should avoid attempting to "prove" such "givens" as the following:

—Play is reflective of, and expressive of, cultural values.

—Play is instructive of social roles.
—Play facilitates the development of motor control.
—Play is a release mechanism.

Let us look further and deeper, into the fundamental *vitality* of play, and set as our first priority the discovery of answers to the question, "What is *really* going on?"

REFERENCES CITED

Bateson, Gregory 1952 *The Nature of Play — Part I: River Otters.* 16 mm. film.

1955 A Theory of Play and Fantasy: a Report on Theoretical Aspects of the Project for Study of the Role of Paradoxes of Abstraction in Communication. In *Approaches to the Study of Human Personality.* American Psychiatric Association, Psychiatric Research Reports No. 2, pp. 39-51. Republished as A Theory of Play and Fantasy, in G. Bateson, *Steps to an Ecology of Mind.* New York: Chandler, 1972.

1956 The Message "This is Play." In B. Schaffner, ed., *Group Processes: Transactions of the Second Conference.* New York: Josiah Macy, Jr. Foundation.

Bruner, Jerome S., Alison Jolly, and Kathy Sylva, eds. 1976 *Play: Its Role in Development and Evolution.* New York: Basic Books.

Caillois, Roger 1961 *Man, Play and Games.* New York: Free Press.

Count, Earl W. 1958 The Biological Basis of Human Sociality. *American Anthropologist* 60, 1049-1085.

1973 *Being and Becoming Human: Essays on the Biogram.* New York: Van Nostrand, Reinhold.

Csikszentmihalyi, Mihaly, and Stith Bennett 1971 An Exploratory Model of Play. *American Anthropologist* 73, 45-58.

Edwards, Harry 1973 *Sociology of Sport.* Homewood, Ill.: Dorsey Press.

Erasmus, Charles 1950 Patolli, Pachisi, and the Limitation of Possibilities. *Southwestern Journal of Anthropology* 6, 369-387.

Fagen, R. M. 1974 Selective and Evolutionary Aspects of Animal Play. *American Naturalist* 108 (964), 850-858.

Groos, Karl 1898 *The Play of Animals.* New York: Appleton.

Heider, Karl 1975 From Javanese to Dani: The Transformation of a Game. Paper presented at the 74th Annual Meetings of the American Anthropological Association, San Francisco, December.

Huizinga, Johan 1950 *Homo Ludens: A Study of the Play Element in Culture.* Boston: Beacon Press.

Klopfer, Peter 1970 Sensory Physiology and Esthetics. *American Scientist* 58(4), 399-403.

Laughlin, Charles, and Eugene d'Aquili 1974 *Biogenetic Structuralism.* New York: Columbia University Press.

—, and John McManus. n.d. The Biopsychological Determinants of Play and Games. Unpublished ms.

Loizos, Caroline 1967 Play Behavior in Higher Primates: A Review. *In* Desmond Morris, ed., *Primate Ethology.* Chicago: Aldine. (Garden City, N.Y.: Doubleday & Co., Anchor Books, 1969).

Norbeck, Edward 1968 Human Play and its Cultural Expression. *Humanitas* 5(1), 43-55.

1971 Man at Play. *Natural History,* Special Supplement, December, 48-53.

1974a The Anthropological Study of Human Play. In E. Norbeck, ed., *The Anthropological Study of Human Play.* Rice University Studies 60(3), Summer, 1-8. Houston: Rice University.

1974b Anthropological Views of Play. *American Zoologist* 14, 267-273.

1976a Religion and Human Play. In A. Bharati, ed., *The Realm of the Extra-Human.* World Anthropology Series. The Hague: Mouton.

1976b The Study of Play — Johan Huizinga and Modern Anthropology. In David F. Lancy and B. Allan Tindall, eds., *The Anthropological Study of Play: Problems and Prospects.* Cornwall, N.Y.: The Leisure Press, pp. 1-10.

Oakley, Fredericka B., and Peter C. Reynolds 1976 Differing Responses to Social Play Deprivation in Two Species of Macaque. In David F. Lancy and B. Allan Tindall, eds., *The Anthropological Study of Play: Problems and Prospects.* Cornwall, N.Y.: The Leisure Press, pp. 179-188.

Piaget, Jean 1951 *Play, Dreams, and Imitation in Childhood.* Heinemann. (New York: W. W. Norton, 1962).

Pruitt, Dean G., and Melvin J. Kimmel 1977 Twenty Years of Experimental Gaming: Critique, Synthesis, and Suggestions for the Future. In Marc R. Rosenzweig and Lyman W. Porter, eds., *Annual Review of Psychology.* Vol. 28. Palo Alto: Annual Reviews, Inc., pp. 363-92.

Roberts, John M., M. J. Arth, and R. R. Bush 1959 Games in Culture. *American Anthropologist* 61, 597-605.

Scotch, Norman A. 1961 Magic, Sorcery, and Football among Urban Zulu: A Case of Reinterpretation under Acculturation. *Journal of Conflict Resolution* 5(1), March, 70-74.

Stevens, Phillips, Jr. 1973 *The Bachama and their Neighbors: Non-Kin Joking Relationships in Adamawa, Northeastern Nigeria.* Ph.D. dissertation, Northwestern University. Ann Arbor: Xerox-University Microfilms. Cat. no. 74-7828.

1974 The "Rules" of Social Joking Behavior: A West African Illustration and its Implications for the Anthropological Study of Play. Paper presented at the Inaugural Meetings of The Association for the Anthropological Study of Play, London, Ontario, April.

Suomi, Stephen J., and Harry F. Harlow 1971 Monkeys at Play. *Natural History,* Special Supplement, December, 72-75.

Tindall, B. Allan 1973 *The Psycho-cultural Orientations of Anglo and Ute Boys in an Integrated High School.* Unpublished Ph.D. dissertation, University of California, Berkeley.

1974 The Cognitively Shared Dimensions of Basketball: An Example from Ute Culture. Paper presented at the Inaugural Meetings of The Association for the Anthropological Study of Play, London, Ontario, April.

1975a Ethnography and the Hidden Curriculum in Sport. *Behavioral and Social Science Teacher* 2(2), 5-28.

1975b The Perceptual and Cultural Meaning of Basketball. Paper presented at the 74th Annual Meetings of the American Anthropological Association, San Francisco, December.

1975c Questions about Physical Education, Skill, and Life-time Leisure Sports Participation. Position paper solicited by UNESCO, for the First International Conference of Ministers and Senior Officials Responsible for Physical Education and Sport for Youth, April, 1976.

Weiss, Paul 1969 *Sport, A Philosophical Inquiry.* Carbondale and Edwardsville: Southern Illinois University Press.

Wilson, Edward O. 1975 *Sociobiology: The New Synthesis.* Cambridge, Mass.: Harvard University Press.

APPENDIX

Works On Play: A Bibliography

Helen B. Schwartzman
Institute for Juvenile Research, Chicago

EVOLUTIONARY & DEVELOPMENTAL STUDIES

Appleton, L.E. 1910. *A Comparative Study of the Play Activities of Adult Savages and Civilized Children*. Chicago: Univ. of Chicago Press.

Bruner, Jerome S.; Jolly, Alison, Sylva, Kathy; ed. 1976. *Play: its Role in Development and Evolution*. New York: Basic Books.

Buhler, K. 1930. *The Mental Development of Children*. New York: Harcourt.

Chamberlain, A.F. 1910. *The Child: A Study in the Evolution of Man*. London: Charles Scribner.

Gesell, A. 1946. *The Child From Five to Ten*. New York: Harper.

Hall, G.S. 1904. *Adolescence,* Vol. I. New York: D. Appleton.

Lowenfeld, M. 1967. *Play in Childhood*. New York: John Wiley.

Piaget, J. 1948. *The Moral Judgment of the Child*. New York: Free Press. 1962. *Play, Dreams and Imitation in Childhood*. New York: W.W. Norton. 1971. Response to Brian Sutton-Smith. In *Child's Play,* eds., R.E. Herron; B. Sutton-Smith, pp. 337-339. New York: John Wiley & Sons.

Reany, M.J. 1916. *The Psychology of the Organized Group Game*. Cambridge: Cambridge Univ. Press.

Sutton-Smith, b. 1975. Developmental structures in fantasy narrative. Presented at Ann. Meet. Am. Psycholog. Assoc., Chicago.

Babcock, W.H. 1888. Games of Washington children. *Am. Anthropol., 1:243-284.*

Brewster, P.G. 1952. Children's games and rhymes. *The Frank C. Brown Collection of North Carolina Folklore*. Durham, N.C.: Univ. Press, 1:32-219. 1953. *American Non-singing Games*. Norman, Oklahoma: Univ. of Okla. Press. 1971. The importance of collecting and study of games. In *The Study of Games*. E. Avedon & B. Sutton-Smith (Eds.), New York: John Wiley, pp. 9-17.

Culin, S. 1891. Street games of boys in Brooklyn. *J. Am. Folklore,* 4:221-237. 1895. *Korean Games, with Notes on the Corresponding Games of China and Japan*. Philadelphia: Univ. Pennsylvania Press. 1907. *Games of North American Indians*. 24th Ann. Report Bur. Am. Ethnol.

Douglas, N. 1931. *London Street Games*. London: Chatto & Windus

Gomme, A.B. 1894. *The Traditional Games of England, Scotland and Ireland,* Vol. 1. London: David Nutt. 1898. *The Traditional Games of England, Scotland and Ireland,* Vol. 2. London: David Nutt.

Howard, Dorothy. 1958. Australian 'hoppy' hopscotch. *West. Folklore,* 17:163-175. 1959. Ball bouncing customs and rhymes in Australia. *Midwest Folklore,* 9 (2):77-87. 1960. The 'toodlembuck'—Australian children's gambling device and game. *J. Am. Folklore,* 73:53-54. 1971. Marble games of Australian Children. In *The Study of Games,* E. Avedon & B. Sutton-Smith (Eds.), New York: John Wiley, pp. 179-193.

Newell, W.W. 1883. *Games and Songs of American Children.* New York: Harper & Row.

Opie, I.; Opie, P. 1959. *The Lore and Language of School Children.* New York: Oxford Univ. Press. P. 1969. *Children's Games in Street and Playground.* Oxford: Clarendon Press.

Stearns, R.E.C. 1890. On the Nishinam game of 'Ha' and the Boston game of 'Props.' *Am. Anthropol.,* 3(4):353-358.

Sutton-Smith, B. 1952. The fate of English traditional games in New Zealand. *West. Folklore Quart.,* 11:250-253. 1959. *The Games of New Zealand Children.* Berkeley: Univ. of Calif. Press. 1972. The meeting of Maori and European cultures and its effect upon the unorganized games of Maori children. In *The Folkgames of Children,* ed., B. Sutton-Smith, pp. 317-330. Austin: Univ. of Texas Press.

Sutton-Smith, B.; Rosenberg, B.G. 1972. Sixty years of historical change in the game preferences of American children. In *The Folkgames of Children.* ed., B. Sutton-Smith, pp. 258-294. Austin: Univ. of Texas Press.

Tylor, E.B. 1879. On the game of Patolli in ancient Mexico, and its probable Asiatic origin. *J. Anthropol. Inst. Great Britain & Ireland,* 8:116-129. Remarks on the geographical distribution of games. *J. Anthropol. Inst. Great Britain & Ireland,* 9:23-30. 1971. On American lot-games as evidence of Asiatic intercourse before the time of Columbus. In *The Study of Games.* E. Avedon & B. Sutton-Smith, (Eds.), New York: John Wiley, pp. 77-93

SOCIALIZATION/ENCULTURATION STUDIES

Eifermann, R. 1970. Cooperation and egalitarianism in Kibbutz children's games. *Hum. Rel.,* 23:579-587. 1971. *Determinants of children's game styles.* Jerusalem: Israel Acad. Sci. and Humanities. 1971. Social play in childhood. In *Child's Play,* eds. R.E. Herron, B. Sutton-Smith, pp. 270-297. New York: John Wiley & Sons

Fischer, J.; Fischer, A. 1963. The New Englanders of Orchard Town, U.S.A. In *Six Cultures: Studies of Child Rearing,* ed. B.B. Whiting, pp. 869-1010. New York: John Wiley.

Fortes, M. 1970. Social and psychological aspects of education in Taleland. In *From Child to Adult,* ed. J. Middleton, pp. 14-74. New York: Natural History Press.

Goldberg, S.; Lewis, M. 1969. Play behavior in the year-old infant; early sex differences. *Child Dev.,* 40:21-31

Gump, P.V.; Sutton-Smith, B. 1972. The 'It' role in children's games. In *The Folkgames of Children,* ed. B. Sutton-Smith, pp. 433-441. Austin: Univ. of Texas Press.

Lancy, D.F. 1974. *Work, play, and learning in a Kpelle town.* PhD. thesis, Univ. of Pittsburgh. 1975. *The Role of Games in the Enculturation of Children*. Presented at 74th Ann. Meet. Am. Anthropol. Assoc., San Diego. 1976. The play behavior of Kpelle children during rapid cultural change. In *The Anthropological Study of Play: Problems and Prospects,* eds. D. Lancy, B. Allan Tindall. Cornwall, N.Y.: Leisure Press.

Lever, J. 1974. *Games children play: sex differences and the development of role skills.* Ph.D. thesis, Yale Univ., New Haven. 1975. *Sex-Role Socialization and Social Structure: The Place of Complexity in Children's Games.* Presented at Ann. Meet. Pacific Sociolog. Assoc., Victoria, B.c.

Maccoby, E.E. 1959. Role-taking in childhood and its consequences for social learning. *Child Dev.,* 30:239-252.

Maccoby, M.; Modiano, N.; Lander, P. 1964. Games and social character in a Mexican village. *Psychiatry,* 27:150-162.

Maretzki, T.; Maretzki, H. 1963. Taira: an Okinawan village. In *Six Cultures: Studies of Child Rearing,* ed., B.B. Whiting, pp. 363-539. New York: John Wiley.

Mead, G.H. 1934. *Mind, Self, and Society.* Chicago: Univ. of Chicago Press.

Mead, M. 1928. *Coming of Age in Samoa.* New York: Morrow. 1930. *Growing Up in New Guinea.* New York: Morrow.

Minturn, L.; Hitchcock, J. 1963. The Rajputs of Khalapur, India. In *Six Cultures: Studies of Child Rearing,* ed., B.B. Whiting, pp. 203-361. New York: John Wiley.

Nyedegger, W.; Nydegger, C. 1963. Tarong: an Ilocos barrio in the Philippines. In *Six Cultures: Studies of Child Rearing,* ed., B.B. Whiting, pp. 693-687. New York: John Wiley.

Roberts, J.M.; Arth, M.J.; Bush, R.R. 1959. Games in culture. *Am. Anthropol.,* 61:597-605.

Roberts, J.M.; Sutton-Smith, B. 1962. Child training and game involvement. *Ethnology,* 2:166-185.

Roberts, J.M.; Sutton-Smith, B.; Kendon, A. 1967. Strategy in games and folktales. *J. of Soc. Psych.,* 61:185-189.

Romney, K.; Romney, R. 1963. The Mixtecans of Juxtlahuaca, Mexico. In *Six Cultures: Studies of Child Rearing,* ed., B.B. Whiting, pp. 541-691 New york: John Wiley.

Seagoe, M.V. 1970. An instrument for the analysis of children's play as an index of degree of socialization. *J. Sch. Psych.,* 8:139-144. 1971. A comparison of children's play in six modern cultures. *J. Sch. Psych.,* 9:61-72. 1971. Children's play in three American subcultures. *J. Sch. Psych.,* 9:167-172.

Seagoe, M.V.; Murakami, K.A. 1961. A comparative study of children's play in America and Japan. *Calif. J. Ed. Res.,* 11:124-130.

Smilansky, S. 1968. *The Effects of Sociodramatic Play on Disadvantaged Preschool Children.* New York: John Wiley.

Sutton-Smith, B. 1972. Games of order and disorder. Presented at Am. Anthropol. Assoc., Toronto. 1972. Role replication and reversal in play. In *The Folkgames of Children,* ed., B. Sutton-Smith, pp. 416-432. Austin: Univ. of Texas Press. 1972. The tow cultures of games. In *The Folkgames of Children,* ed., B. Sutton-Smith, pp. 295-311. Austin: Univ. of Texas Press. 1974. Toward an anthropology of play. *The Assoc. Anthropol. Study of Play Newsletter,* 1:8-15.

Sutton-Smith, B.; Roberts, J.M. 1972. Studies in an elementary game of strategy. In *The Folkgames of Children,* ed., B. Sutton-Smith, pp. 359-400. Austin: Univ. of Texas Press. 1972. The cross-cultural and psychological study of games. In *The Folkgames of Children,* ed., B. Sutton-Smith, pp. 331-340. Austin: Univ. of Texas Press.

Sutton-Smith, B.; Roberts, J.M.; Rosenberg, B.G. 1964. Sibling associations and role involvement. *Merrill-Palmer Quart.*, 10:25-38.

Sutton-Smith, B.; Rosenberg, B.G.; Morgan, E.F., Jr. 1972. Development of sex differences in play choices during preadolescence. In *The Folkgames of Children,* ed., B. Sutton-Smith, pp. 405-415. Austin: Univ. of Texas Press.

Whiting, B.B., Ed. 1963. *Six Cultures: Studies of Child Rearing.* New York: John Wiley.

Whiting, J.M. 1941. *Becoming a Kwoma*. New Haven: Yale Univ. Press.

Whiting, J.M.; Child, I.L. 1953. *Child Training and Personality: A Cross-Cultural Study.* New Haven: Yale Univ. Press.

PSYCHOANALYTIC STUDIES

Alexander, F. 1958. A contribution to the theory of play. *Psychoanalytic Quart.*, 27:175-193.

Axline, V.M. 1969. *Play Therapy*. New York: Ballantine.

Erikson, E.H. 1940. Studies in the interpretation of play: part I: clinical observations of play disruption in young children. *Genetic Psychol. Monog.*, 22:557-671. 1941. Further exploration in play construction: three spatial variable and their relation to sex and anxiety. *Psycholog. Bull.*, 38:748. 1951. Sex differences in the play configurations of American pre-adolescents. *Am. J. of Orthopsychiatry,* 21:667-692. 1963. *Childhood and Society*. New York: Norton.

Freud, A. 1964. *The Psychoanalytical Treatment of Children*. New York: Schocken.

Freud, S. 1955. *The Cases of 'Little Hans' and the 'Rat Man.'* Complete Works, Vol. 12. London: Hogarth Press. 1959. *Beyond the Pleasure Principle*. New York: Bantam. 1963. *Jokes and Their Relation to the Unconscious*. New York: Norton.

Gould, R. 1972. *Child Studies Through Fantasy*. New York: Quadrangle

Henry, J.; Henry, Z. 1974. *Doll Play of Pilaga Indian Children*. New York: Vintage Books.

Issacs, S. 1930. *Intellectual Growth in Young Children*. London: Routledge & Kegan Paul. 1933. *Social Development in Young Children*. London: Routledge & Kegan Paul.

Klein, M. 1955. The psychoanalytic play technique. *Am. J. Orthopsychiatry,* 25:223-237.

Landy, D. 1965. *Tropical Childhood: Cultural Transmission and Learning in a Rural Puerto Rican Village*. New York: Harper & Row.

Leven, H.; Wardwell, E. 1971. The research uses of doll play. In *Child's Play,* eds., R.E. Herron & B. Sutton-Smith, pp. 145-184. New York: John Wiley & Sons.

Peller, L.E. 1971. Models of children's play. In R.E. Herron & B. Sutton-Smith, Eds. *Child's Play*. New York: John Wiley & Sons, pp. 110-125.

Roheim, G. 1943. Children's games and rhymes in Duau (Normanby Island). *Am. Anthropol.*, 45:99-119.

Waelder, R. 1933. The psychoanalytic theory of play. *Psychoanal. Quart.*, 2:108-224.

Winnicott, D.W. 1971. *Playing and Reality*. New York: Basic Books

COMMUNICATION STUDIES

Bateson, G. 1971. The message 'this is play.' In *Child's Play,* eds., R.E. Herron, B. Sutton-Smith, pp. 261-266. New York: John Wiley & Sons. 1972. A theory of play and fantasy. In *Steps To An Ecology of Mind,* ed., G. Bateson, pp. 177-193. New York: Ballantine.

Garvey, C.; Berndt, R. 1975. *The organization of pretend play.* Presented at Ann. Meet. Am. Psychol. Assoc., Chicago.

Miller, S. 1973. Ends, means, and galumphing: some leitmotifs of play. *Am. Anthropol.,* 75:87-89.

Schwartzman, H.B. 1973. *'Real pretending': an ethnography of symbolic play communication.* Ph.D. thesis, Northwestern Univ., Evanston (Helen E. Beale). 1976. Children's play: a sideways glance at make-believe. In *Anthropology of Play: Problems and Prospects,* ed., D. Lancy, B. Allan Tindall. Cornwall, New York: Leisure Press.

Sutton-Smith, B. 1971. Boundaries. In *Child's Play,* eds., R.E. Herron, B. Sutton-Smith, pp. 103-106. New York: John Wiley & Sons.

STRUCTURAL STUDIES

Avedon, E.M. 1971. The structural elements of games. In *The Study of Games,* eds., E.M. Avedon & B. Sutton-Smith, pp. 419-426. New York: John Wiley.

Dundes, A. 1964. On game morphology: a study of the structure of nonverbal folklore. *N.Y. Folklore Quart.,* 20:276-288.

Georges, R.A. 1969. The relevance of models for analyses of traditional play activities. *So. Folklore Quart.,* 33:1-23.

Parrott, S. 1972. Games children play: ethnography of a second grade recess. In *The Cultural Experience,* eds. J. Spradley, D. McCurdy, pp. 207-219. Chicago: Science Research Associates.

Redl, F. 1959. The impact of game ingredients on children's play behavior. *Transactions of the Fourth Conference on Group Processes.* New York: Josiah Macy, Jr. Foundation, pp. 31-81.

Redl, F.; Gump, P.; Sutton-Smith, B. 1971. The dimensions of games. In *The Study of Games,* eds. E. Avedon, B. Sutton-Smith, pp. 408-418. New York: John Wiley.

Sutton-Smith, B. 1972. A formal analysis of game meaning. In *The Folkgames of Children,* ed., B. Sutton-Smith, pp. 491-505. Austin: Univ. of Texas Press.

von Glascoe, C. 1976. The patterning of game preferences in the Yucatan. In *The Anthropology of Play: Problems and Prospects,* eds., D. Lancy, B. Allan Tindall, New York: Leisure Press.

CHILDREN'S VERBAL PLAY

Chukovsky, K. 1968. *From Two to Five.* Berkeley: univ. of Calif. Press.

Dundes, A.; Leach, J.; Ozkok, B. 1970. Strategy of Turkish boys' verbal dueling rhymes. *J. Am. Folklore,* 83:325-349.

Gowlett, D.F. 1968. Some secret languages of children in South Africa. *African Studies,* 27:135-139

Haas, Mary. 1964. Thai word games, In *Language in Culture and Society: A Reader in Linguistics and Anthropology,* ed. D. Hymes, pp. 301-303.

Hymes, D. 1964. Children's games and speech play: a topical bibliography. *Language in Culture and Society: A Reader in Linguistics and Anthropology,* ed., D. Hymes, pp. 303-304.

Opie, I.; Opie, P. 1959. *The Lore and Language of School Children.* New York: Oxford Univ. Press. 1969. *Children's Games in Street and Playground.* Oxford: Clarendon Press.

ECOLOGICAL & ETHOLOGICAL STUDIES

Barker, R.; Wright, H.F. 1966. *One Boy's Day.* Archon.

Blurton-Jones, N. 1969. An ethological study of some aspects of social behavior of children in nursery school. In *Primate Ethology,* ed. D. Morris, pp. 437-463. New York: Doubleday.

Blurton-Jones, N., Ed. 1972. *Ethological Studies of Child Behavior.* Cambridge: Cambridge Univ. Press.

Doyle, P.H. 1975. The differential effects of multiple and single niche play activities on interpersonal relations among preschoolers. In *The Anthropological Study of Play: Problems and Prospects,* eds. D. Lancy, B. Allan Tindall. Cornwall, N.Y.: Leisure Press.

Gump, P.V.; Schoggen, P.; Redl, F. 1963. The behavior of the same child in different milieus. *The Stream of Behavior,* ed. R. Barker, pp. 169-202. New York: Appleton-Century-Crofts.

Gump, P.; Sutton-Smith, B. 1971. Activity-setting and social interaction. In *Child's Play,* eds. R.E. Herron, B. Sutton-Smith, pp. 96-102. New York: John Wiley & Sons.

Hutt, C. 1971. Exploration and play in children. In *Child's Play,* eds. R.E. Herron, B. Sutton-Smith, pp. 231-251. New York: John Wiley & Sons.

Johnson, M.W. 1935. The effect on behavior of variations in the amount of play equipment. *Child Dev.,* 6:56-68.

Loizos, C. 1969. Play behavior in higher primates: a review. *Primate Ethology,* ed. D. Morris, pp. 226-285. Garden City, New York: Doubleday.

Parten, M. 1971. Social play among preschool children. In *Child's Play,* eds. R.E. Herron, B. Sutton-Smith, pp. 83-95. New York: John Wiley & Sons.

Schlosberg, H. 1971. The concept of play. In *Child's Play,* eds. R.E. Herron, B. Sutton-Smith, pp. 212-215. New York: John Wiley & Sons.

Shure, M. 1963. Psychological ecology of a nursery school. *Child Dev.,* 34:979-992.

Smith, P.K.; Connolly, K. 1972. Patterns of play and social interaction in pre-school children. In *Primate Ethology,* ed. D. Morris, pp. 65-95. New York: Doubleday.

Updegraff, R.; Herbst, E.K. 1933. An experimental study of the social behavior stimulated in young children by certain play materials. *J. of Genetic Psych.,* 42:372-391.

Van Alstyne, D. 1932. *Play Behavior and Choice of Play Materials of Pre-School Children.* Chicago: Univ. of Chicago Press.

COGNITIVE STUDIES

Almy, M., Ed. 1968. *Early Childhood Play: Selected Readings Related to Cognition and Motivation*. New York: Simon & Schuster.

Bruner, J.S. 1972. Nature and uses of immaturity. *Am. Psychol.*, 27:687-708. 1975. Play is serious business. *Psychol. Today,* pp. 81-83.

El'Konin, D. Symbolics and its functions in the play of children. In *Child's Play,* eds., R. Herron & B. Sutton-Smith, pp. 221-230. New York: John Wiley & Sons.

Issacs, S. 1930. *Intellectual Growth in Young Children*. London: Routledge & Kegan Paul. 1933. *Social Development in Young Children.* London: Routledge & Kegan Paul.

Leacock, E. 1971. At play in African villages. *Natural History,* December, special supplement on play, pp. 60-65.

Piaget, J. 1962. *Play, Dreams and Imitation in Childhood.* New York: W.W. Norton. 1971. Response to Brian Sutton-Smith. *In Child's Play,* eds., R.E. Herron; B. Sutton-Smith, pp. 337-339. New York: John Wiley & Sons.

Sutton-Smith, B. 1971. A reply to Piaget: a play theory of copy. In *Child's Play,* eds., R. Herron & B. Sutton-Smith, pp. 340-342. New York: John Wiley & Sons. 1971. Piaget on play: a critique. In *Child's Play,* eds., R.E. Herron & B. Sutton-Smith, pp. 326-336. New York: John Wiley & Sons. 1971. The playful modes of knowing, *Play: The Child Strives Toward Self Realization*. Wash., D.C.: Nat'l Assoc. Ed. of Young Children, pp. 13-25. 1971. The role of play in cognitive development. In *Child's Play,* eds., R.E. Herron & B. Sutton-Smith, pp. 252-260. New York: John Wiley & Sons.

Vygotsky, L.S. 1967. Play and its role in the mental development of the child. *Soviet Psychol.*, 5:6-18.

EXPERIMENTAL STUDIES

Ammons, R.B. 1950. Reactions in a projective doll-play interview of white males two to six years of age to differences in skin color and facial features. *J. Genet. Psychol.*, 76:323-341

Ammons, R.B.; Ammons, H.S. 1949. Parent preferences in young children's doll-play interviews. *J. abnorm. Soc. Psychol.*, 44:490-505.

Bach, G.R. 1946. Father fantasies and father typing in father-separated children. *Child Dev.*, 17:63-80.

Britt, S.H.; Janus, S.Q. 1941. Toward a social psychology of human play. *Soc. Psychol.*, 13:351-384.

Fein, G.; Apfel, N. 1975. *Elaboration of Pretend Play During the Second Year of Life.* Presented at Ann. Meet. Am. Psychol. Assoc., Chicago.

Gewirtz, J.L. 1950. An investigation of aggressive behavior in the doll play of young Sac and Fox Indian children, and a comparison to the aggression of midwestern white preschool children. *Am. Psychol.*, 5:294-295.

Gilmore, J. 1971. Play: a special behavior. In *Child's Play,* eds., R.E. Herron; B. Sutton-Smith, pp. 311-325. New York: John Wiley & Sons.

Hurlock, E. 1971. Experimental investigations of childhood play. In *Child's Play*, eds., R.E. Herron; B. Sutton-Smith, pp. 51-70. New York: John Wiley & Sons.

Leven, H.; Wardell, E. 1971. The research uses of doll play. In *Child's Play,* eds., R.E. Herron, B. Sutton-Smith, pp. 145-184. New York: John Wiley & Sons.

Sears, R.R.; Pintler, M.; Sears, P.S. 1946. Effect of father separation on pre-school children's doll play aggression. *Child Dev.*, 17:119-243.

Singer, J.L. 1973. *The Child's World of Make-Believe: Experimental Studies of Imaginative Play*. New York: Academic Press.

Singer, J.L.; Singer, D.G. 1976. Imaginative play and pretending in early childhood: some experimental approaches. *Child Personality & Psychopathology,* ed. A. David, Vol. 3. New York: Wiley.

GENERAL REFERENCES

Aries, P. 1962. A modest contribution to the history of games and pastimes. *Centuries of Childhood,* 62-99. New York: Vintage.

Avedon, E.; Sutton-Smith, B. 1971. *The Study of Games*. New York: John Wiley.

Bruner, Jerome S.; Jolly, Alison; Sylva, Kathy; eds. 1976. *Play: its Role in Development and Evolution*. New York: Basic Books.

Caillois, R. 1961. *Man, Play, and Games*. New York: The Free Press.

Daiken, H. 1950. Children's games: a bibliography. *Folklore,* 61:218-222.

Ehrmann, J. 1968. Homo Ludens revisited. *Yale French Studies,* 41-31-57.

Geertz, G. 1972. Deep play: Notes on the Balinese cockfight. *Daedalus,* 1-37.

Goffman, E. 1961. *Encounters*. Indianapolis: Bobbs-Merrill.

Goodman, M.E. 1971. Play, games and humor. *The Culture of Childhood*. New York: Teachers College Press.

Groos, K. 1898. *The Play of Animals*. London: Chapman & Hall. 1901. *The Play of Man*. New York: Appleton.

Herron, R.E.; Haines, S.; Olsen, G.; Hughes, J. 1967. *Children's Play: A Research Bibliography*. Champaign, Ill.; Univ. of Ill. Motor Performance Lab., Children's Research Center.

Herron, R.E.; Sutton-Smith, B., Eds. 1971. *Child's Play*. New York: John Wiley & Sons.

Huizinga, J. 1955. *Homo Ludens: A Study of the Play Element in Culture*. Boston: Beacon.

Hymes, D. 1964. Children's games and speech play: a topical bibliography. *Language in Culture and Society: A Reader in Linguistics and Anthropology,* ed. D. Hymes, pp. 303-304.

Klinger, E. 1971. *Structure and Functions of Fantasy*. New York: Wiley.

Miller, S. 1973. Ends, means, and galumphing: some leitmotifs of play. *Am. Anthropol.*, 75:87-89.

Norbeck, Edward. 1971. Man at play. *Natural History,* December, special supplement on play, pp. 48-53.

Schiller, F. 1875. *Essays, Aesthetical and Philosophical*. London: George Bell.

Spencer, H. 1873. *The Principles of Psychology*. New York: D. Appleton & Co.

Stone, G.P. 1971. The play of little children. In R.E. Herron & B. Sutton-Smith, Eds., *Child's Play*. New York: John Wiley & Sons, pp. 4-14.

Sutton-Smith, B. 1972. *The Folkgames of Children*. Austin: Univ. of Texas Press.

Sutton-Smith, B. 1975. *Current Research and Theory on Play, Games and Sports*. Presented to the 1st Nat'l. Conf. on Mental Health Aspects of Sports, Exercise and Recreation (Am. Med. Assoc.), Atlantic City.

GEOGRAPHIC AREA REFERENCES

AFRICA

General

Leacock, E. 1971. At play in African villages. *Natural History,* December. spec. suppl. on play: 60-65.

Schwartzman, H.B., Barbera, L. 1976. Children's play in Africa and South America: a review of the enthographic literature. *Problems and Prospects in the Study of Play,* ed. D. Lancy, B.A. Tindall. New York: Leisure Press.

West Africa

Bascom, W. 1969. *The Yoruba of Southwest Nigeria*. New York: Holt, Rinehart & Winston.

Beart, C. 1955. *Jeux et jouets de L'ouest africain,* II. Dakar: IFAN.

Bohannan, P., Bohannan, L. 1958. A source notebook on the Tiv life cycle. *Three Source Notebooks in Tiv Ethnography*. New Haven: HRAF.

Fortes, M. 1970. Social and psychological aspects of education in Taleland. *From Child to Adult,* ed. J. Middleton, 14-74. New York: Natural History Press.

Grindal, B. 1972. *Growing Up in Two Worlds*. New York: Holt, Rinehart & Winston.

Lancy, D.F. 1974. *Work, play, and learning in a Kpelle town*. Ph.D. thesis. Univ. Pittsburgh, Pa. 1975. *The Role of Games in the Enculturation of Children*. Presented at 74th Ann. Meet. Am. Anthropol. Assoc., San Francisco. 1976. The play behavior of Kpelle children during rapid cultural change. In *The Anthropological Study of Play: Problems and Prospects,* ed., D. Lancy, & B.A. Tindall. Cornwall, N.Y.: Leisure Press.

Leis, P. *Enculturation and Socialization in an Ijaw Village*. New York: Holt, Rinehart & Winston.

Central and South Africa

Brewster, P.G. 1944. Two games from Africa. *Am. Anthropol.*, 46:239-241.

Centner, T. 1962. *L'Enfant africain et ses jeux*. Elisabethville: CEPSI.

Gowlett, D.F. 1968. Some secret languages of children in South Africa. *Afr. Stud.* 27:135-39.

Kidd, D. 1906. *Savage Childhood: A Study of Kafir Children*. London: Black.

Leacock, E. 1971. At play in African villages. *Natural History,* December, spec. suppl. on play: 60-65.

Read, M. 1968. *Children of Their Fathers: Growing Up Among the Ngoni of Malawi*. New York: Holt, Rinehart & Winston.

Sanderson, M.G. 1913. Native games of Central Africa. *J.R. Anthropol. Inst.* 43:726-36.

Turnbull, C. 1961. *The Forest People*. New York: Simon & Schuster.

Van Zyl, H.J. 1939. Some of the commonest games played by the Sotho people of Northern Transvaal. *Bantu Stud.* 13:293-305.

East Africa:

Castle, E.B. 1966. *Growing Up in East Africa*. London: Oxford Univ. Press.

Harrison, H.S. 1947. A bolas-and-hoop game in East Africa. *Man* 47:153-55.

Lambert, H.E. 1959. *A note on children's pastimes*. Swahili 30:74-78.

Leakey, L.S.B. 1938. A children's game: West Australia and Kenya. *Man* 38:176.

Raum, O. 1940. *Chaga Childhood*. London: Oxford Univ. Press.

CENTRAL AND SOUTH AMERICA

Central America

Edmonson, M.S. 1967. Play: games, gossip and humor. *Handbook of Middle American Indians,* ed. R. Wauchope, 191-206. Austin: Univ. Texas Press.

Garcia, L.I. 1929. Children's games. *Mex. Folkways,* 5:79-85.

Garcia, L.I. 1932. Children's games. *Mex. Folkways,* 7:63-74.

Maccoby, M., Modiano, N., Lander, P. 1964. Games and social character in a Mexican village. *Psychiatry* 27:150-62.

Modiano, N. 1973. *Indian Education in the Chiapos Highlands*. New York: Holt, Rinehart & Winston.

Nerlove, S.B., Roberts, J.M., Klein, R.E., Yarbrough, C., Habicht, J.P. 1974. Natural indicators of cognitive development: an observational study of rural Guatemalen children. *Ethos* 2:265-95.

Romney, K., Romney, R. 1963. The Mixtecans of Juxtlahuaca, Mexico. In *Six Cultures: Studies of Child Rearing,* ed. B.B. Whiting. New York: Wiley. pp. 541-691.

Scheffler, L. 1976. The study of traditional games in Mexico: bibliographical analysis and current research. In *The Anthropological Study of Play: Problems and Prospects,* ed., D. Lancy, B.A. Tindall. Cornwall, N.Y.: Leisure Press.

von Glascoe, C. 1976. The patterning of game preferences in the Yucatan. In *The Anthropological Study of Play: Problems and Prospects,* ed. D. Lancy, B.A. Tindall. Cornwall, N.Y.: Leisure Press.

Carribean:

Beckwith, M.W. 1922. Folk-games of Jamaica. *Publ. Folklore Founda.*, Vassar College, No. 1.

Elder, J.S. 1965. Song games from Trinidad and Tobago. *Publ. Am. Folklore Soc* 16.

Landy, D. 1965. *Topical Childhood: Cultural Transmission and Learning in a Rural Puerto Rican Village*. New York: Harper & Row.

Parsons, E.C. 1930. Ring games and jingles in Barbados. *J. Am. Folklore* 43:326-29.

South America

Cooper, J.M. 1949. A cross-cultural survey of South American Indian tribes: games and gambling. *Bur. Am. Ethnol. Bull.*, 143:503-24.

Henry, J., Henry, Z. 1974. *Doll Play of Pilaga Indian Children*. New York: Vintage.

Hilger, I.M. 1957. *Araucanian Child Life and Its Cultural Background*. Washington DC: Smithsonian Misc. Collect. 133.

Jackson, E. 1964. Native toys of the Guarayu Indians. *Am. Anthropol.* 66:1153-55.

Schwartzman, H.B., Barbera, L. 1976. Children's play in Africa and South America: a review of the ethnographic literature. *The Anthropological Study of Play: Problems and Prospects*, ed. D. Lancy, B.A. Tindall. Cornwall, N.Y.: Leisure Press.

Shoemaker, N. 1964. Toys of Chama (Eseejja) Indian children. *Am. Anthropol.* 66:1151-53.

NORTH AMERICA

General

Abrahams, R.D., ed. 1969. *Jump-Rope Rhymes: A Dictionary*. Austin: Univ. Texas Press (publ. for Am. Folklore Soc.).

Babcock, W.H. 1888. Games of Washington children. *Am. Anthropol.* 1:243-84.

Barker, R., Wright, H.F. 1966. *One Boy's Day*. Hamden, Conn: Archon.

Brewster, P.G. 1945. Johnny on the pony, a New York State game. *NY Folklore Q.* 1:239-40. 1952. Children's games and rhymes. *The Frank C. Brown Collection of North Carolina Folklore,* 1:32-319. Durham, NC: Univ. Press. 1953. *American Nonsinging Games*. Norman: Univ. Oklahoma Press.

Browne, R.B. 1955. Southern California jump-rope rhymes: a study in variants. *West. Folklore* 14:3-22.

Buckley, B. 1966. Jump-rope rhymes—suggestions for classification and study. *Keystone Folklore Q.* 11:99-111.

Chase, H. 1905. Street games of New York City. *In Child's Play* eds. R. Herron and B. Sutton-Smith, New York: Wiley, 71-72.

Cox, J.H. 1942. Singing games. *South. Folklore.* 6:183-681.

Fischer, J., Fischer, A. 1963. The New Englanders of Orchard Town, U.S.A. In *Six Cultures: Studies of Child Rearing,* ed. B.B. Whiting. New York: Wiley. Pp. 869-1010.

Goldstein, K.S. 1971. Strategy in counting out: an ethnographic folklore field study. In *The Study of Games,* eds. E.M. Avedon, B. Sutton-Smith. New York: Wiley. Pp. 167-78.

Hall, J. 1941. Some party games of the Great Smokey Mountains. *J. Am. Folklore* 54:68-71.

Hostetler, J., Huntington, G. 1971. *Children in Amish Society: Socialization and Community Education*. New York: Holt, Rinehart & Winston.

Monroe, W.S. 1904. Counting out rhymes of children. *Am. Anthropol.* 6:46-50.

Newell, W.W. 1883. *Games and Songs of American Children*. New York: Harper.

Parrott, S. 1972. Games children play: ethnography of a second grade recess. *The Cultural Experience,* ed. J. Spradley, D. McCurdy, 207-19. Chicago: Sci. Res. Assoc.

Schwartzman, H.B. 1973. *'Real pretending': an ethnography of symbolic play communication.* Ph.D. thesis, Northwestern Univ., Evanston, Ill. 1976. Children's play: a sideways glance at make-believe. In *The Anthropological Study of Play: Problems and Prospects,* ed. D. Lancy, B.A. Tindall. Leisure Press.

Stearns, R.E.C. 1890. On the Nishinam game of 'Ha' and the Boston game of 'Props.' *Am. Anthropol.* 3:353-58.

Sutton-Smith, B., Rosenberg, B.G. 1972. Sixty years of historical change in the game preferences of American children. In *The Folkgames of Children,* ed., B. Sutton-Smith, pp. 258-94. Austin: Univ. Texas Press.

Wolford, W.J. 1916. *The Play Party in Indiana.* Indianapolis: Indiana Hist. Comm.

North American Indians

Culin, S. 1907. *Games of North American Indians.* 245h Ann. Rep. Bur. Am. Ethnol.

Southeast

Hassrick, R., Carpenter, E. 1944. Rappahannock games and amusements. *Primitive Man* 17:29-39.

Rowell, M.K. 1943. Pamunky Indian games and amusements. *J. Am. Folklore* 56:203-7.

Speck, F.W. 1944. Catawba games and amusements. *Primitive Man* 17:19-28.

Northcentral and Plains

Daniel, Z.T. 1892. Kansu: a Sioux game. *Am. Anthropol.* 5:215-16.

Dorsey, J.O. 1891. Games of Teton Dakota children. *Am. Anthropol.* 4:329-46.

Erikson, E.H. 1963. *Childhood and Society.* New York: Norton.

Gilmore, M.R. 1926. Some games of Arikara children. *Indian Notes* 3:9-12.

Grinnell, G.B. 1923. *The Cheyenne Indians.* New Haven, Conn: Yale Univ. Press.

Hilger, I.M. 1951. Chippewa child life and its cultural background. *Bur. Am. Ethnol. Bull.* 146.

Lesser, A. 1933. *The Pawnee Ghost Dance Hand Game: A Study of Cultural Change.* Columbia Univ. Contrib. to Anthropol. 16.

Searcy, A. 1965. *Contemporary and Traditional Prairie Potawatomi Child Life.* Lawrence: Univ. Kansas Press.

Walker, J.R. 1906. Sioux games, II. *J. Am. Folklore* 19:29-36.

Southwest

Dennis, W. 1940. *The Hopi Child.* New York: Appleton-Century.

Hodge, F.W. 1890. A Zuni footrace. *Am. Anthropol.* 3:227-31.

Leighton, D., Kluckhohn, C. 1974. *Children of the People.* New York: Farrar, Straus & Giroux.

Mook, M.A. 1935. Walapai ethnography: games. *Mem. Am. Anthropol. Assoc.*, 42:167-73.

Opler, m. 1946. *Childhood and Youth in Jicarilla Apache Society*. Los Angeles: Southwest Mus.

Stevenson, M.C. 1903. Zuni games. *Am. Anthropol.*, 5:468-97.

California

Erikson, E.H. 1943. Observations on the Yurok: childhood and world image. *Univ. Calif. Publ. Am. Archeol. Ethnol.* 35, No. 10.

Stearns, R.E.C. 1890. On the Nishinam game of 'Ha' and the Boston game of 'Props.' *Am. Anthropol.* 3:353-58.

Northwest Coast

Wolcott, H.F. 1967. *A Kwakiutl Village and School*. New York: Holt, Rinehart & Winston.

Alaska

Ager, L.P. 1974. Storyknifing: an Alaskan girls' game. *J. Folklore Inst.* Indiana Univ. Publ. 11. 1976. Cultural values in Eskimo children's games. *The Anthropological Study of Play: Problems and Prospects*, ed. D. Lancy, B.A. Tindall. Cornwall, N.Y.: Leisure Press.

Lantis, M. 1960. *Eskimo Childhood and Interpersonal Relationships*. Seattle: Univ. Washington Press.

Ramson, J.E. 1946. Children's games among the Aluet. *J. Am. Folklore* 59:196-98.

ASIA

Brewster, P.G. 1955. A collection of games from India, with some notes on similar games in other parts of the world.*Z. Ethnol.*, 80:99-102.

Culin, S. 1895. *Korean Games with Notes on the Corresponding Games of China and Japan*. Philadelphia: Univ. Pennsylvania Press.

Haas, M. 1964. Thai word games. In *Language in Culture and Society: A Reader in Linguistics and Anthropology,* ed., D. Hymes, pp. 301-3. New York: Harper & Row.

Minturn, L., Hitchcock, J. 1963. The Rajputs of Khalapur, India. In *Six Cultures: Studies of Child Rearing,* ed., B.B. Whiting, pp. 203-361. New York: Wiley.

Mistry, D.K. 1958. The Indian child and his play. *Sociol. Bull.* (Bombay) 7:137-47. 1959. The Indian child and his play. *Sociol. Bull.* 8:86-96. 1960. The Indian child and his play. *Sociol. Bull.* 9:48-55.

EUROPE

Aries, P. /&=½. A modest contribution to the history of games and pastimes. *Centuries of Childhood,* 62-99. New York: Vintage.

Brewster, P.G. 1951. A string figure series from Greece. *Laographia* 101-25.

Chukovsky, K. 1968. *From Two to Five*. Berkeley: Univ. California Press.

Crombie, J.W. 1886. History of the game of hop-scotch. *J.R. Anthropol. Inst.* 15:403-8.

Douglas, N. 1931. *London Street Games*. London: Chatto & Windus.

Gomme, A.B. 1894. *The Traditional Games of England, Scotland and Ireland,* Vol. 1. London: Nutt. 1898. *The Traditional Games of England, Scotland and Ireland,* Vol. 2. London: Nutt.

Milojkovic-Djuric, j. 1960. The Jugoslav children's game 'Most' and some Scandinavian parallels. *South. Folklore Q.* 24:226-34.

Opie, I., Opie, P. 1959. *The Lore and Language of School Children.* New York: Oxford Univ. Press. 1969. *Children's Games in Street and Playground.* Oxford: Clarendon.

Watson, W. 1953. Play among children in an East Coast mining community. *Folklore* 64:397-410.

NEAR EAST

Brewster, P.G. 1960. A sampling of games from Turkey. *East and West* (Rome) 11:15-20.

Dennis, W. 1957. Uses of common objects as indicators of cultural orientation. *J. Abnorm. Soc. Psychol.* 55:21-28.

Dundes, A., Leach, J., Ozkok, B. 1972. Strategy of Turkish boys' verbal dueling rhymes. *J. Am. Folklore* 83:325-49.

Eifermann, R.R. 1970. Cooperation and egalitarianism in Kibbutz children's games. *Hum. Relat.* 23:579-87. 1971. *Determinants of children's game styles.* Jerusalem: Isr. Acad. Sci. Hum. 1971. Social play in childhood. In *Child's Play,* ed., R.E. Herron, B. Sutton-Smith, pp. 270-97. New York: Wiley.

Granqvist, H. 1975.*Birth and Childhood Among the Arabs.* New York: AMS Press.

Smilansky, S. 1968. *The Effects of Sociodramatic Play on Disadvantaged Preschool Children.* New York: Wiley.

Spiro, M.E. 1965. *Children of the Kibbutz.* New York: Schocken

OCEANIA

Melanesia

Aufenanger, H. 1958. Children's games and entertainments among the Kumngo tribe in Central New Guinea. *Anthropos* 53:474-84. 1961. A children's arrow thrower in the Central Highlands of New Guinea. *Anthropos* 56:633.

Barton, F.R. 1908. Children's games in British New Guinea. *J.R. Anthropol. Inst.* 38:259-79.

Burridge, K.O.L. 1957. A Tangu game. *Man* 57:88-89.

Haddon, A.C. 1908. Notes on children's games in British New Guinea. *J.R. Anthropol. Inst.* 38:289-97.

Hogbin, H.I. 1946. A New Guinea childhood: from weaning till the eighth year in Wogeo. *Oceania* 16:275-96.

Mead, M. 1930. *Growing Up in New Guinea.* New York: Morrow.

Roheim, G. 1943. Children's games and rhymes in Duau (Normanby Island). *Am. Anthropol.* 45:99-119.

Rosenstiel, A. 1976. The role of traditional games in the process of socialization among the Motu of Papua, New Guinea. In *The Anthropological Study of Play: Problems and Prospects,* ed. D. Lancy, B.A. Tindall. Cornwall, N.Y.: Leisure Press.

Watt, W. 1946. Some children's games from Tanna, New Hebrides. *Mankind* 3:261-64.

Micronesia

Maretzki, T., Maretzki, H. 1963. Taira: an Okinawan village. In *Six Cultures: Studies of Child Rearing,* ed., B.B. Whiting, pp. 363-539. New York: Wiley.

Polynesia

Best, E. 1922. Pastimes of Maori Children. *NZJ. Sci. Technol.* 5:254.

Best, E. 1925. Games and pastimes of the Maori. *Dom. Mus. Bull.* Wellington, No. 8.

Bolton, H.C. 1891. Some Hawaiian pastimes. *J. Am. Folklore* 4:21-26.

Culin, S. 1899. Hawaiian games. *Am. Anthropol.* 1:201-47.

Emerson, J.S. 1924. Hawaiian string games. *Publ. Folklore Found.*, Vassar College, No. 5.

Firth, R. 1930. A dart match in Tikopia: a study in the sociology of primitive sport. *Oceania* 1:64-96.

Hocart, A.M. 1909. Two Fijian games. *Man* 9:184-85.

Mead, M. 1928. *Coming of Age in Samoa*. New York: Morrow.

Pukui, M.K. 1943. Games of my Hawaiian childhood. *Calif. Folklore Q.* 2:205-20.

Stumpf, F., Cozens, F.W. 1947. Some aspects of the role of games, sports, and recreation activities in the culture of modern primitive peoples: the New Zealand Maoris. *Res. Q.* 18:198-218. 1949. Some aspects of the role of games, sports, and recreation activities in the culture of modern primitive peoples: the Fijians. *Res. Q.* 20:2-20.

Sutton-Smith, B. 1951. New Zealand and variants of the game Buck-Buck. *Folklore* 63:329-33. 1959. *The Games of New Zealand Children*. Berkeley: Univ. California Press. 1972. Marble are in. In *The Folkgames of Children,* ed. B. Sutton-Smith, pp. 455-64. Austin: Univ. Texas Press. 1972. The meeting of Maori and European cultures and its effect upon the unorganized games of Maori children. In *The Folkgames of Children,* ed., B. Sutton-Smith, pp. 317-30. Austin: Univ. Texas Press.

Australia

Berndt, R.M. 1940. Some Aboriginal children's games. *Mankind* 2:289-93.

Haddon, A.C. 1902. Australian children's games. *Nature* 66:380-81.

Harney, W. 1952. Sport and play amidst the Aborigines of the Northern Territory. *Mankind* 4:377-79.

Howard, D. 1958. Australian 'hoppy' hopscotch. *West. Folklore* 17:163-75. 1959. Ball bouncing customs and rhymes in Australia. *Midwest Folklore* 9:77-87. 1960. The 'toodlembuck'—Australian children's gambling device and game. *J. Am. Folklore.* 73:53-54. 1971. Marble games of Australian children. In *The Study of Games,* eds., E.M. Avedon, B. Sutton-Smith, pp. 179-93. New York: Wiley.

Leakey, L.S.B. 1938. A children's game: West Australia and Kenya. *Man* 38:176.

Roth, W.E. 1902. Games, Sports, and amusements. *North Queensland Ethnogr. Bull. No.* 4:7-24 (Brisbane)

Salter, M.A. 1967. *Games and Pastimes of the Australian Aboriginal.* Edmonton: Univ. Alberta Print. Dep.

Indonesia

Bateson, G., Mead, M. 1942. *Balinese Character: A Photographic Analysis.* New York Acad. Sci.

Beran, J.A. 1973. Characteristics of children's play and games in the Southern Philippines. *Silliman J.* 20:100-13. 1973. Some elements of power in Filipino children's play. *Silliman J.* 194-207.

DuBois, C. 1944. *Peoples of Alor.* Minneapolis: Univ. Minnesota Press.

Jocano, F.L. 1969. *Growing Up in a Philippine Barrio.* New York: Holt, Rinehart & Winston.

Nydegger, W., Nydegger, C. 1963. Tarong: an Ilocos barrio in the Philippines. In *Six Cultures: Studies of Child Rearing,* ed. B.B. Whiting, pp. 693-867. New York: Wiley.

Storey, K.S. 1976. Field study: children's play in Bali. In *The Anthropological Study of Play: Problems and Prospects,* ed. D. Lancy, B.A. Tindall. Leisure Press.

Williams, T.R. 1969. *A Borneo Childhood: Enculturation in Dusun Society.* New York: Holt, Rinehart & Winston.